The Messiah and His Kingdom to Come:
A Biblical Road Map

Robert A. Makar

EnerPower Press
an imprint of Energion Publications
P. O. Box 841
Gonzalez, FL 32560
http://enerpowerpress.com

Cover Design by Jason Neufeld, jasonneufelddesign.com

ISBN-10: 1-893729-54-0
ISBN-13: 978-1-893729-54-4

Library of Congress Control Number: 2009903624

TABLE OF CONTENTS

ABOUT THE AUTHOR

Robert Makar received his MBA degree from California State University in Pennsylvania in 1978. Robert spent only 15 years of a 41 year career in the management field. The remaining years were spent in the exact sciences of engineering and mathematics and related fields, his passion during those times. That passion changed when he found a new direction in life—a rededication of his life to the Lord. With spiritual guidance from his church, Robert began to learn the truths of God's plan, especially as it related to his spiritual life. Hidden beneath the façade of a life that had been dedicated to a career of precision and order, he realized a hidden passion for studying God's word and also that he could use his gifts of organization and writing to bring God's messages to others.

The Lord had created Robert with a compulsive personality (a gift he would come to realize) which worked to his benefit in the creation of this arduous written work that has been in the making for almost ten years. God can take our weakest characteristic and turn it into a blessing as Robert discovered.

With prayer for guidance from the Holy Spirit, Robert put his faith in God that He would lead him to the proper research materials and Scripture understanding. This project became a fruit of the Holy Spirit.

FOREWORD

Bob Makar has no-doubt poured his heart and soul into the writing of this book and I know his prayer is that it will be an accomplishment for the Kingdom of God. His work has filled me with equal amounts of admiration and envy. I admire Bob's dedication and his vision, and I envy the time he has spent with his Lord as he researched and wrote.

Almost everything he has written about Biblical chronology is controversial in some way. What he writes about God's kingdom and the way God's actions in history connect to accomplish God's plan is much less controversial. Bob's dedication to Bible study, to finding the truth, and to presenting what he has learned so that others may benefit should be acclaimed by all.

Let me anticipate some reactions to this book:

First, there will be those who don't believe Biblical chronology is possible. I personally doubt the reliability of any calculations based on the genealogies of Genesis 5 and 11 and associated texts. If that is your view, consider laying aside your skepticism for a moment and look at how things might be reconciled. You may not agree, but I think you will find it interesting to see someone struggle with, and ultimately accommodate some of the very difficult source materials. Bob has worked with such difficult-to-reconcile sources as the Septuagint and the Samaritan Pentateuch as they related to his task.

Second, there will be those who think this is all a waste of time. Why bother with all this chronology? I would urge you to consider the important points of the overview. Follow the lines of the chronological road maps and look at where they lead. When you gather the little pieces together and look at the picture from a distance, there are directional lines leading to Jesus, the Messiah.

Finally, I would mention those who may have been fascinated by this kind of calculation. You probably have a range of ideas of your own. You'll be tempted to call everybody else "wrong" and to point out the "mistakes"–mistakes that are actually simply differences of opinion. Bob has avoided this trap by pointing out alternatives and yet giving you the solution he feels best fits the evidence.

As you track your way through chronological details, co-regencies of Israelite kings, fathers and sons, it may look like a jumble. But Bob's purpose here is expressed in those lines on the charts, pointing first to the Messiah as he headed to the cross, and then to the same Messiah coming in glory.

Bob has a great love for God and for truth, his passion for both are clear. He is a man of great faithfulness and integrity. Any student of Holy Scripture will find his work inspiring and practical.

– Rev. Riley Richardson, Myrtle Grove UMC, Senior Pastor

INTRODUCTION

We start with this prayer, "Thank you God, our Father, for the opportunity to be involved in your Kingdom work. Help us to live our lives through your will, and may your will be done through it. Praise your name for your love and guidance. Give us the inspiration and enthusiasm to continue under all circumstances and conditions. All fruits of the Spirit are good—the Son stands in judgment of our work! Let us continue in our worship of you and the study of Your Word."

Serious Bible reading and study are important parts of a Christian's life, a necessary activity for staying close to our Lord and a result of a changed Christian life (Prov. 1:7, 27-29; 2:3-7; 9:10; Psa. 111:10). We start on our salvation journey by understanding the basic concepts of God's plan. As we read and study further, we come to increasingly understand why God introduced this plan and how it would develop throughout the ages. This quest of knowledge is a natural product of the Christian faith. The Christian who puts his/her trust in Jesus has a passionate desire for an enhanced relationship with Him. This relationship is evidenced in part by our prayers and service toward the Kingdom and our hunger for more spiritual knowledge, especially through the Scriptures. Since God inspired the Word (2 Tim. 3:16) and He cannot lie, we can depend on these writings (2 Tim. 2:13; Titus 1:2; Heb. 6:17-18). I believe God, rather than providing a one page set of instructions, desired that we search and study the Scriptures for a more complete understanding of His will. Some Christians might become easily satisfied and less inclined to study if all the answers come too easily.

One must be careful of his/her motivation for Bible study. An academic approach without God's intervention will lead to only a humanistic understanding of His Word. It is in a spiritual sense that God is able to lead us to His truths. The academic world omits in its history books the real reasons behind most world events, failing to include the hand of God in any of them! All history points at God's plan to provide a way for all mankind to have a spiritual relationship with Him. It is only through faith in the Word of God that we gain true understanding of history. The purpose of my work is to provide a systematic method for the study of the Word, a study that will put most of the pieces of Biblical information together in a condensed history, genealogy, and chronology of God's plan for our redemption.

We must always be on guard against trying too hard to interpret Scripture rather than study it. Interpretation efforts can lead us into a false sense of pride for the accomplishments we make or imagine we make. We have no reason to take pride in our works, for we are not made righteous through them; our righteousness comes from the gift of God's grace (Eph. 2:8-10). I have a strong sense that God did not wish for us to dwell too much on the sequence of events in the last days, only to watch for the signs and be ready and prepared for His coming. My objective for this work is to glorify Jesus by showing the truth of His word and the graciousness of the salvation He offers. To study this work of mine without seeing Jesus along each step would be an injustice to the reader. For this reason I have been careful to include as many scriptural references as is possible so the reader may be inspired by the truth of God's Word. Studies of the last days have been open to debate by honest and God-fearing Christians throughout the church age. I do not profess to have presented any new revelations, only to have chosen those ideas and interpretations that I feel best fit what I have studied, researched, organized, and coordinated for this work. We must be careful to refrain from interpretation of those things that God has not yet revealed. Rather than calling my work interpretation or revelation, I would prefer to treat it as a study.

This study consists of graphic illustrations and maps and a commentary that is meant as a supplementary overview. It is suggested that the reader study the many Scriptural references and endnotes for details.

The Spirit uses many sources to help us in our search for truth: reading of scripture, searching research materials, study groups, worship sermons, communion, prayer, etc. Together, with the Spirit's guidance, we mature as Christians; we come to appreciate the infinite wisdom of God. I chose to intermix my own experiences and feelings into this introduction because of the personal effect my work has had on my life—I wish to pass these effects on to my readers for their enrichment.

The desire to put Biblical events in a chronological order became a tool to help and enhance my studies and verify ideas I had developed in my life. An early attempt in my youth to learn of the evolution of so many churches went largely unfruitful because of my spiritual inexperience. It was not until my later years, after I had rededicated my life to the Lord and found Gonzalez United Methodist Church to which He led me, that I experienced what I believe to be a direct spiritual intervention from above. This turning-point event occurred from the work my wife was doing for our church with her Sunshine Friends ministry in which she and a few other ladies brought a little sunshine into the lives of persons in need. One particular lady came to our house because she had missed my wife's visit and, during the course of conversation, she mentioned what a thrill it was to her, a new Christian, to have recently learned of Christ's genealogy in the Scriptures. With my curiosity provoked, I searched for myself and found the truth of her words plus many other truths that had evaded me. A revelation came to me: I had been reading scripture, not studying it! The more I studied and researched, the more I came to understand that I needed help with choosing the right bible guides, research sources, and personal leaderships. This leadership and guidance came from the Holy Spirit in the form of heavenly guidance and from the teachings and inspiration from my church study groups, educators/teachers Henry Neufeld and his wife Jody, and pastors: Marquis Wingard, Winston Jay, Barbara Ray, Riley Richardson and his wife Angie, Curtis Huffman, and Nathan Elliott. This understanding led me to depend on God to lead me in all my study needs.

Sometimes it is difficult to develop a story from a page-by-page Bible study; supporting verses may only be found in other Biblical pages. Understanding the order of events puts these events in proper perspective and helps us to learn of God's perfect ways. It has been said, "I can prove any theology with bible verses." This statement can only be true if we take isolated verses out-of-context, a dangerous practice. For that reason, when possible, I have tried to identify at least two Scripture verses that give identical or similar accounts of an idea or event and to consider the context in which they were written.

We must keep in mind the possibility of gaps in some accounts of scriptural time frames. These gaps probably occur, if they indeed do, for the convenience of the Biblical writers or because of the writers' desires to simplify a narrative for the sake of continuity and focus. In fact, the existence of gaps would tend to bring science and religion into greater agreement about the age of mankind. Several cases can be made for the existence of gaps in chronology, (1) Luke 3:36 adds Cainan to the chronology suggesting a gap, possibly large, making Salah a distant relative of Arphaxad instead of a son. The use of the words "son" and "daughter" was often used in Hebrew writings to refer to near and distant relatives, e.g., Jesus as the son of David, Zaccheus as son of Abraham, (2) during Peleg's lifetime (Gen. 10:25), the Tower of Babel was built and Genesis 11:19 makes no mention of Peleg's ancestors being alive at this time. This omission gives suspicion of a large gap in chronology, (3) it seems that a large time span would be required after languages were changed to divide all the nations of the world (Gen. 10:32), (4) the sudden decrease in life spans from Eber to Peleg: Araphaxad lived 438 years, Salah 433, Eber 464, Peleg 239, Reu 239, and Serug 230. In a nutshell, life-spans were long in the early generations from Adam to Noah (Gen. 5:3-20--from about 800-970 years); medium length from Shem to Eber (Gen. 11:10-17--from about 430-600 years); and short from Peleg to Terah (Gen. 11:18-32--from about 150-240 years). We might also consider the possibility of a large time span existing during the creation of the heavens and earth in Genesis 1:1-3--from the time of darkness to the time of light. See the "Preface" for details. This idea could explain the differences between theologians and geologists about the age of the earth. We will not dwell too long on speculations that do not add to our spiritual enrichment.

My initial goal was to learn the chronology of Messiah's arrival. It seemed logical to think there were others who were seeking the same goal. How satisfying it seemed to be able to share this work. The idea for a chronological display came from my desire for a handy tool I could use as a quick reference for further Biblical study. From this desire came my idea for a road map to direct my journey.

Once I had my road map completed (I thought), I realized it illustrated two congruent lines: a royal (kingly) ruling blood line from Abraham to Jesus and a blood (genealogical) line from Adam to Abraham and then to his grandson, Jacob, and finally on to Jesus. God chose faithful persons to execute His plan.

It became apparent that a commentary was required to clarify the detailed information from the road map and to present God's plan for the world in a condensed and easy-to-read format, in effect an overview. Only the people and events relative to God's plan were included in the road map although sometimes we went off on a tangent when presenting commentary. As we progress on our journey through the ages, we will stop at these times to address many spiritual and theological questions.

The simplistic presentation of this material, organized according to the order of events as they are given in scripture, should be especially valuable to the inexperienced Scripture student. However, it is suggested that more mature students of the Scriptures study this work accompanied by a serious, in-depth study of Scripture with helpful Biblical aids and also writings by credible authors on specific subjects. This suggestion is especially important when we discuss the spiritual things of God's plan. For more detailed study, the "Reference" section includes the works of many experts whose works were used in the research of this book to validate and verify facts and to compare the interpretations of Scripture by others. If I can distinguish between the work of the Holy Spirit and my own feelings, I believe God's hand has been involved in much of my choices of secular materials used for research in my work. I praise God for this guidance and recognize that God can also lead and inspire our use of research materials even when we have acted in a secular manner. When we seek truth through His teaching, He can lead us irrespective of how our choices of materials are made.

With the help of a study bible, concordance, and bible dictionary, a much more in-depth study can be realized. Bible study groups, lectures, libraries, book stores, videos, the internet, etc. are also worthy sources. An effort should be made to check the sources of information for validity. I have tried to create a unique work that combines all these studies into an organized, condensed form highlighted by clear graphic displays. It has been my desire to present as many sides to controversial issues as possible and to remain impartial on many issues that do not affect God's plan for salvation through Jesus.

Since the Bible is the inspired word of God, and God cannot lie, there can be no errors in its original text. By original text, I mean the original manuscripts that Moses, Paul, David, or any other writer used to record the words of God. None of these original manuscripts exists today. Biblical skeptics make the mistake of citing seemingly obvious errors in scriptural verses to prove the entire Bible is in error and therefore not the inspired word of God. Granted there are some human errors that crept into writings because they were copied, recopied, and copied again many times throughout history by human hands. But these minor errors concern dates, numbers, places, names, misunderstandings, etc., that never affect the intended messages from God. From one source, fifteen major variances from Scripture were found from archeological findings and other ancient writings concerning the rules of Hebrew kings. Most of these errors can be identified by comparison to the oldest extant manuscripts. Then of course, many errors accredited to Scripture are in fact errors in the eyes of those who misinterpret it.

The Bible, as one can easily ascertain, was not written entirely in chronological order. The same can be said about its individual books. Sometimes, if not often, the same information is presented in more than one place in Scripture. Sometimes seemingly conflicting accounts, when taken out of context, take much more research to validate. Then there were the times when faith was the only reason for accepting some of the information handed down to us by God. In these cases I chose to accept that which God gave and search no more, realizing that these facts will be made known by God in His accepted time. We must be aware of the authors' personality, style, location, his intended audience, and when the book was written. I believe God seldom gave word-for-word inspiration to the Biblical writers. Rather, He inspired the writers with messages through dreams, visions, and messengers, and they wrote immediately or some time later from their own experiences and life situations. It also seems likely that some writers used manuscripts from previous writers.

Although some parts of the road map made me uncomfortable, I was so proud of my accomplishment that I was ready to make a final draft. However, I had the conviction that more research was necessary. It was not until I had read through Scripture again that I realized that my doubts about validity were true. Did I rely too much on my own intellect? Pride in the intellect can keep us from God's truths (Prov. 3:6-8) as we can see from the influence of the secular humanism movement that exists today. Did this work need more research and study? There were many conflicts and questions to be answered. I prayed that the Holy Spirit would intervene and point me in the right direction.

During the second research, I began checking on other chronologies from various sources only to find that the points that were giving me second thoughts were universal arguing points among chronologists, no two seemed to agree exactly. "If Scripture is irrefutable," I began to wonder, "Why are there so many chronological disagreements?" Seemingly vague scripture and seemingly conflicting and contradictory verses are fodder for the skeptic, but the problem is not with scripture but in the mind of the skeptic. Difficulties arise in understanding scripture because of: Scripture interpretation (and sometimes misinterpretation), insufficient Scripture search, convenient exclusion of certain Bible verses, taking verses out of context, and conflicts with other sources, e.g., history texts and archaeological conclusions. Most of these sources of confusion are quite understandable and are of a human nature. With sufficient study and investigation, these difficult passages can be understood correctly. We must constantly keep in mind that chronology was not the most important goal of the scripture writers. For example, we present three of these difficulties: (1) the Luke lineage (3:36) adds Cainan, possibly a repeat of another Cainan (or Kenan) as in Genesis 5:9-12, see the road map, (2) the Matthew chronology (1:8, 11) omits six kings, possibly a technique of the writer for clarity and/or organization, and (3) Jehoiachin's age upon ascension to the throne is given as eighteen years in 2 Kings 24:8 and eight years in 2 Chronicles 36:9, possibly because he, at the age of eight, began a 10/11 year co-rule with his father, Jehoiakim, before taking the throne alone according to the 2 Kings account. It is quite possible, however, that there are unknown reasons for these conflicts that only God knows, or the author may have been trying to produce a clearer or condensed picture by eliminating some of the details.

Another source of difficulty occurs when cities, countries, and regions were identified as "sons of" as if they were actually sons of someone. For examples, Genesis 10:6 says the sons of Ham were Cush (Ethiopia), Mizraim (Egypt), Phut, and Canaan. Phut was not a son but a region around the southeast coast of the Mediterranean Sea or possibly the south end of the Red Sea, and Canaan was Ham's oldest son and also a region of Israel and Phoenicia. Genesis 10:15 refers to Sidon as a son of Canaan, but in this case Canaan referred to the region since Sidon was a city of Phoenicia.

These controversies did in no way detract from the basic message of God's Word. He created man to have a personal relationship with Him and when that failed through man's sin, He chose the Hebrew nation to be the vessel through which a Savior would be sent to redeem mankind. This is the message that all Christians and those outside the faith need to focus on when reading and studying the Word, especially the Old Testament.

Now the task was to find the true or most likely answers to the controversies. There was no doubt that Scripture was going to be the primary source of my information and the Holy Spirit my guide. A search of chronological bibles and writings gave me many new insights. I am sure that many other researchers have had a sincere dependence on the Spirit's guidance even though we disagree on some points. Maybe this is God's way of telling us to focus on the important message of Scripture-- salvation through Jesus, rather than dwelling on lesser issues. The Lord said in Titus 3:9, "But avoid foolish questions, and genealogies, and contentions, and striving about the Law; for they are unprofitable and vain" (KJV). Also 1 Timothy 1:4 and 2 Timothy 2:15-16 warn of wasting too much time studying and discussing insignificant ideas such as genealogies and fables instead of God's real messages in the scriptures. I have tried to focus this work on God's plan for our salvation, although it has been necessary to provide history, genealogy, and chronology to this story, for this is a story of God's work in the world and our relationship to him. From this I conclude that there are many equally plausible chronologies in circulation today that depend primarily on Scripture for their facts. To suppose that one particular chronological work is the one and only accurate one is wishful thinking. It isn't all that important!

For my purposes, I would seek to produce as accurate a chronology as I could from the Spirit's leading. Any oversights, omissions, or errors would be attributed to my human shortcomings. My primary goal was for correctness in the chronology of events and secondarily in actual dates and periods of time. Scripture would be my primary source of information with other sources, e.g., histories, dictionaries, concordances, non-canonical literature, etc., being used to confirm or enhance Scripture. Three such sources of non-canonical works were (1) the Samaritan Pentateuch, to be discussed later, (2) apocryphal writings between the Old Testament and into the New Testament, to be discussed in the commentary, and (3) the writings of Flavius Josephus. These research materials were used only to confirm or enhance Scripture when they were in agreement with scripture or to provide missing information that was not provided in Scripture so that a better continuity might be realized.

Although I thought my work was finished at that point, I was being prodded by the Spirit for more—God's plan does not stop at the advent of Christ and His church but goes on to fulfillment with His Second Coming and the final judgment in the end times. The Spirit was telling me that I needed to include more commentary on the spiritual side of God's plan. This addition would require further Scripture study on prophecy and a secular world history. I am thankful to our loving God who inspired me through each phase of this work.

Throughout my work, I have tried to present conflicting or different viewpoints on various subjects and then choose the preferred one for detailed commentary. This method, I found, would be especially useful when I got to the end times where theology would become ever so much more prevalent in my presentations. Information on the end time is obtained from apocalyptic writings such as Daniel, Ezekiel, and Revelation. When confronting Christian theological questions, I have usually tried to keep an open mind and let the reader decide from several opinions.

Much of the bible was written in a poetic style. Therefore, we must be careful to identify which passages are literal and which are symbolic. I have used a literal Scripture interpretation unless the context of the text says otherwise; in this case, a symbolic approach was used. We must be warned of the increased possibility of ambiguity in symbolism; it often leads to many more possibilities for interpretation. It seems when God wanted man to receive His revelations immediately, He provided literal messages, and when He wanted to delay the interpretation of His messages for man's later understanding, He used symbolism. Just as God sometimes uses Old Testament Scripture events to foreshadow New Testament events, He also uses symbolism to keep a message hidden until we are ready to receive it, often after the New Testament event has happened (Deut. 29:29; 30:11; Prov. 20:24; 25:2-3; 1 Cor. 13:12; Col. 1:26-27).

Since little is mentioned in Scripture of events between the Old and New Testaments, we must turn to historical writers, being careful to choose wisely. Sources must be reliable, but even reliable sources can sometimes offer questionable information. The most widely cited historian of this period was Flavius Josephus.

Josephus was a Jewish historian, priest, and Pharisee in the first century A.D., probably a non-Christian at least during his earlier writings, but possibly a Christian later. He studied the Pharisees (becoming one), Sadducees, and Essenes and came from a family of priests (becoming one). Josephus often expressed his views through the eyes of the Pharisees. As governor of Galilee, he was against the Jewish wars with the Romans but finally relented and became commander of Galilee. He was captured and taken to Rome but returned with Titus in 70 A.D. when the temple was destroyed (Wars V, 248-265; 275-283; Life of Flavius Josephus 407-421). He was treated well by the Romans, finally becoming a citizen (Life of Flavius Josephus 422-430). Some Jews considered him a traitor (Wars III, 355-360). He gained favor with the Romans when he predicted that Vespasian and his son Titus would become emperors (Wars III, 401); this came true in 69 A.D. He finally became a Roman citizen and from then wrote of his life and deeds. His writings "Antiquities of the Jews," "The Wars of the Jews," among others were often inaccurate, often favoring Roman rule, but they do provide valuable insights on the society, religion, and politics of his era and Jesus' lifetime. Josephus wrote "Wars" first and then "Antiquities" about eighteen years later, a more accurate narration than Wars. Much of "Antiquities of the Jews" is an approximate parallel paraphrase of the Old Testament and ends with the approach of the Jewish wars in 66 A.D., in the twelfth year of Nero (Antiquities. XX, 252-258). Some of the major differences of Josephus' "Antiquities of the Jews" (after the dash) with scriptural chronology (in parenthesis) are:

(2,288) years from Creation to Isaac's death vs 3,833 years—Antiquities I.

Abram born (352) years after the flood vs 292 years—Antiquities I, 148.

About 100 more years each given when Arphaxad, Salah, Eber, Peleg, Reu, and Serug begat their blood line sons which also contradicts his own period of 292 years between Abram's birth and the flood—Antiquities I, 148-150.

Arphaxad born (2) years after the flood vs 12 years—Antiquities I, 150.

Saul reigned (40) years vs 20 years—Antiquities VI, 378.

(480) years from the exodus to the temple start vs 592 years—Antiquities VIII, 61.

(Solomon) built the temple vs David—Antiquities I, 226.

(910) years from Abram's move to Canaan to the temple start vs 1,020 years—Antiquities VIII, 61.

(1,337) years from the flood to the temple start vs 1,440 years—Antiquities VIII, 61.

(2,993) years from Adam to the temple start vs 3,102 years—Antiquities VIII.

(743) years from the exodus to Israel's exile to Assyria vs 947 years—Antiquities IX, 280.

Solomon reigned (40) years vs 80 years—Antiquities VII, 211.

(703) years from Joshua to the exile to Assyria vs 800 years—Antiquities IX, 280.

First temple (Solomon's) lasted (391) years vs 470.5 years—Antiquities X, 147.

(878) years From the exodus to the temple destruction vs 1,062.5 years—Antiquities X, 147.

(1,735) years from the flood to the temple destruction vs 1,957.5 years—Antiquities X, 147.

(3,391) years from creation to the destruction of the temple vs 3,513.5 years—Antiquities X, 147.

We put our faith in the fact that God only reveals what He wants for His own reasons; we need not know all the answers now. I trust in our omniscient God for that which we do not know or understand. I thank our Lord for leading me through the Scriptures and pointing me to other materials to enhance my understanding and for opening my eyes when I became distracted from and misinformed of His Word.

Since canonical New Testament Scriptures ceased during the second century A.D., we are left with the writings of God's church scholars to provide the later historical data of the church's growth. Then we have "The Prophecies" of Scripture to lead us through to the end times. The road map has been made as self-explanatory as possible. Biblical verses are included for those interested in verifying the facts. The road map consists of (1) a main road, **Chronology Turnpike,** leading from creation through the rules of Kings Saul, David and Solomon to where the road (Kingdom) splits into the northern kings route (a dead-end street) of **Israel Street** and the southern kings route of **Judah Avenue** where Solomon's title/blood lines/genealogy continues through Jehoiakim, (2) a side road,

Genealogy Boulevard, taking us on a blood line route from Jacob (Abraham's grandson) through King David where the genealogy splits between his two sons: Solomon (the **Judah Avenue** route) and Nathan (the **Nathan Avenue** route). Both these lineages continue through the kings' reigns and then converge on Zerubbabel where we encounter another split in the blood line--Zerubbabel's sons Rhesa and Abiud carry the two lineages to Jesus along Luke Road and Matthew Road respectively to where they both go through Joseph and on to Jesus.

Three dating systems will be used: (1) the Gregorian, or Western, calendar that includes B.C. and A.D. years, (2) the Jewish calendar, and (3) my yfc (years from creation) calendar. The creation year is given as zero yfc, this date corresponding to 3977 B.C. in the Gregorian calendar and not applicable to the Jewish calendar which dates creation 216 years later. When converting from the Gregorian calendar to another (or vice versa), consideration must be given to the fact that the

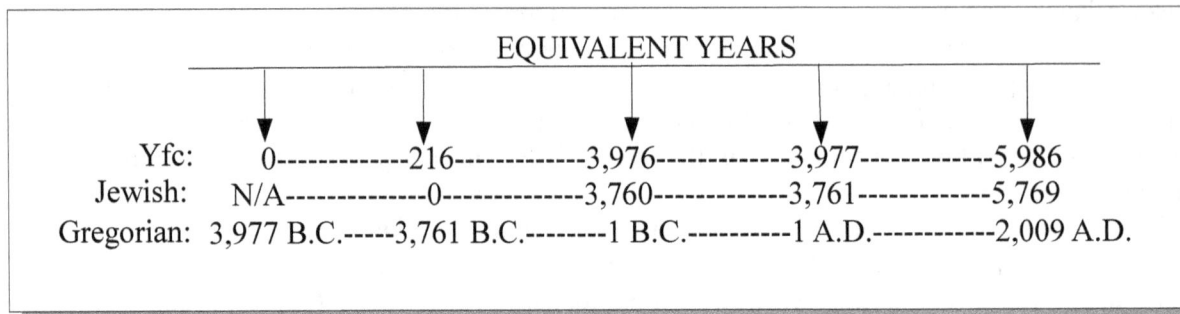

```
                          EQUIVALENT YEARS


Yfc:        0------------216------------3,976------------3,977------------5,986
Jewish:     N/A------------0------------3,760------------3,761------------5,769
Gregorian:  3,977 B.C.-----3,761 B.C.--------1 B.C.----------1 A.D.------------2,009 A.D.
```

Gregorian calendar contains no year zero; time jumps from 1 B.C. to 1 A.D.:

From this display we offer the following two conversion equations:

$$\text{yfc} + \text{B.C.} = 3{,}977 \qquad\qquad \text{yfc} - \text{A.D.} = 3{,}976$$

For simplicity's sake, yfc calendar dates will be used extensively while the Gregorian calendar dates will be inserted as references, more so as we draw closer to New Testament times. The Jewish calendar will only be used sporadically. Instead of mile markers, our maps will contain year markers. Another dating system is often used by scholars: that of replacing the Gregorian B.C. with B.C.E. (before Common Era) and A.D. with C.E. (Common Era). I have chosen not to use this system because it eliminates Christ from our references.

A word of caution is in order when determining the rules of the kings. It was a common practice for a king to have his son be a co-regent with him for all or part of his rule to give him experience and to ensure his rule to follow. Usually, the beginning of the ascension year of a king is counted as year one. Therefore, when a king's reign is given, it will usually be one year less than that given in Scripture. For example, 1 Kings 15:10 says that Asa reigned for 41 years, a span of 40 years (3047-3087 yfc). In other cases the end of the ascension year is counted as year one, e.g., Josiah's 31 year rule (3338-3369 yfc). Sometimes the Hebrew writers counted partial years as whole years, and sometimes they dropped the partial year. A good example of this timing method is the statement in Scripture that Christ would rise (after His crucifixion) in three days. This, according to the Jewish dating pattern, is true: Jesus was crucified on a Friday and rose on a Sunday: Friday, Saturday and Sunday covers three days. But in time span, this is only about 1 ½ days plus possibly some additional hours: part of Friday, all of Saturday, and part of Sunday. It all depends how we accept three days: as all or parts of three different days or a period of three days duration.

The reader (driver) is alerted to watch for stop signs along the way. This sign will alert the reader to a controversy or conflict that is expanded upon in the commentary text. Also, watch for information signs that will provide additional and enhanced information in note form on the road map.

A topical index and a scripture index are available at the back of this book. The scripture index is selective–in many cases, only some of the verses cited are listed. It is therefore suggested that the reader first check the topical index to locate additional verses.

I might suggest to new Christians that it might be helpful to study the "Summary" chapter before beginning from the start of the commentary. Sometimes an overview is beneficial to later study. Also, in all parts of this presentation, always be aware of God's plan even before creation, to provide us with communion with Him. As we shall see, God's plan went through several stages until Jesus Christ came to introduce the final part of this plan: redemption from our sins through God's Messiah. This salvation provides the Christian with a personal relationship with his/her savior. Church affiliation and acceptance of its traditions is not a requirement, only that we recognize our sinful nature, confess our sins, repent, and ask Jesus to come into our lives. God will accept anyone who makes this decision regardless of which Christian church rituals, traditions, and doctrines are practiced provided these practices do not contradict or rewrite Scripture. We must be careful not to substitute these outward practices for the inward spiritual experience we receive by allowing our Lord to be our master. Traditional practices provide, or should provide, only a united way for Christians to worship and not as a means to salvation!

The study of Biblical chronology, genealogy, and history is not a major requirement for our spiritual growth; it is an enhancement. Although interesting and pleasurable, secular study, when taken to extremes, can keep us from spiritual enlightenment. It is only when we undertake these studies with devotional Scripture study that we will be blessed with spiritual understanding. I feel blessed with a deeper appreciation of God's perfect work, a new-found desire for further study, and an ever-growing faith. It has been thrilling to discover how all the pieces of the Bible fit together to tell us of God's plan for us.

God gave us minds to enable us to seek truth. To discover truth requires the intervention of the Holy Spirit. Through prayer we can expect guidance for studying Scripture and finding other sources of inspiration: writings, fellowship, and research. However, we must not expect to rely strictly on prayer—this is the lazy method unless our prayers are exceptional—for we must also act on our desires for revelations. Let us be wary of trying to receive revelations of truths God is not yet ready to reveal—pride of the intellect can lead us along false paths. A blessing will be given to anyone who seeks spiritual growth.

How will these sinful hearts we inherited from Adam and Eve be changed (converted) so we can be made righteous with God? We will discover the answer as we follow God's Plan throughout the ages.

PREFACE

Before creation, only the triune God (the Father, Son, and Holy Spirit) existed as alluded to in Genesis 11:7 where God speaks of "us" in the passage and confirmed by Christ (John 8:58) and the New Testament (Heb. 1:2, 10). God had no beginning and is eternal. The same is true of the Son (Rev. 1:17-18; 13:8) and the Holy Spirit (Gen. 1:2). Time is meaningless to Him, for He lives in the past, present, and future all at once. God is all-knowing and all-powerful, needing nothing for His existence. Before we start our journey of God's plan for mankind, let us look at what existed before creation. Scripture gives only minimal insight on creation.

God created angels (I believe sometime before creation) with free wills to worship and serve Him and to assist Him with His work (Gen. 2:1-2; Neh. 9:6; Job 38:4-7; Psa. 103:20; Heb. 1:7) and for man's protection (Psa. 91:11). The brightest, most rich and powerful, full of wisdom, most beautiful angel created perfect was Satan (Lucifer), an anointed Cherub (Ezek. 28:3-5, 12-16; Jude 9). Because of these attributes, Satan became prideful (Ezek. 28:1-2, 17), wanting to become as God (Isa. 14:13-14; Ezek. 28:2, 6; 2 Thes. 2:3-4), so God cast him out of Heaven (Isa. 14:12, 15; Ezek. 28:6-18; Luke 10:18) along with the fallen angels (demons) who followed him (2 Peter 2:4; Jude 6). Satan is the author of evil (John 8:44; 1 John 3:8), for he initiated sin and would later infect the physical realm of God's creation. Since his banishment out of Heaven and into the earthly realm, Satan has been at work blinding men's eyes from the truth (Job 2:1; Matt. 4:1-9; Luke 4:2-8; 2 Cor. 4:4; 1 Tim. 3:6). However, Satan still has access to God (Job 1:6) and continues to walk the earth (Job 1:7; John 12:31; 1 Peter 5:8) as we see in Satan's descending to earth to tempt Jesus. Satan was and still had power over death until it was taken from him at Calvary (Heb. 2:14) and he continues as the ruler of the universe until he will be defeated by God in the end times.

Much speculation could be made for Satan's part in opposing God's work. We find in Genesis 1:2 that the first stage of creation found the earth dark and without form. Could Satan, now banished from Heaven and roaming the earth, have had any hand in this situation? I believe it is likely that before Satan sinned, he was given dominion over the universe, but when he ascended to Heaven to defy God (Isa. 14:13-14), he was cast out of God's presence and from then on tried to thwart God's work. If this were the case, it could explain the reason for the darkness over creation in Genesis 1:2 and also support a gap theory during the first day of creation (vv. 2-3, see the "Introduction"). Whatever the case may be, Genesis 1:3-4 says God introduced light into His creation and continued His work (Gen. 1:5-28). We offer the following hypothetical illustration; all verses are from Genesis 1:

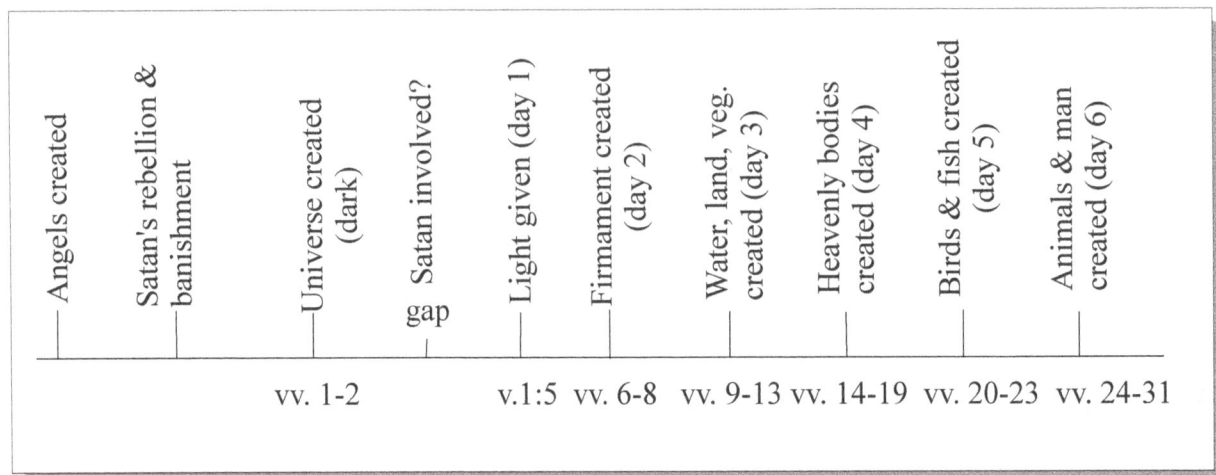

Angels created	Satan's rebellion & banishment	Universe created (dark)	Satan involved? gap	Light given (day 1)	Firmament created (day 2)	Water, land, veg. created (day 3)	Heavenly bodies created (day 4)	Birds & fish created (day 5)	Animals & man created (day 6)
	vv. 1-2			v.1:5	vv. 6-8	vv. 9-13	vv. 14-19	vv. 20-23	vv. 24-31

In anticipation of our study of creation, we must first accept the fact that creation required a creator, namely God. Those who question the existence of God or argue for the "Big Bang" theory of creation cannot answer the question, "Who or what created the original impetus from which all matter originated?" In other words, "How did the first piece of atomic matter come into existence?" Logic tells us that it did not just pop into existence from its own power. Was there a time when nothing existed, including God, and then something (matter) inexplicably appeared? I don't think so! We understand from our experiences and teachings in physics that new matter cannot be created or destroyed; it can only be altered as when we mix chemicals to create a compound or when we burn a log. The only logical answer to these questions is that a higher power caused the origin of the universe, or as some would suppose, intelligent design. This power, God, was so great that matter was created from nothing, by the mere speaking of God (Psa.33:6, 9).

As previously stated, God always existed--He had no beginning. If He had a beginning, someone of a grander nature would have been required to create Him making this new entity a higher god. With this same reasoning taken to its logical conclusion, an endless line of gods would be required and we still would be left without an original creator. This reasoning necessitates that one uncreated god was the originator of all that we know. God in His wisdom gives each of His created beings, unlike all other creatures, a self-awareness of themselves and their environment and also a god-awareness. God is not limited by time and space--He can be everywhere at once. We cannot comprehend, from our limited knowledge, these attributes of God, but they are hinted at in Scripture as we shall see.

We conclude: one god, one creator.

DEDICATION

I dedicate my book to my loving family: my wife, Pat; my children, Robert, Robin, and Roger; my grandchildren, Brook, Joshua, Brandi, Briana, Kristen, Amber, Brenna, and Libby; and great grandchildren, Kyra, Kenneth, and Guage, and with special consideration to my grandson, Quentin, who left us much too early—we miss you so.

May my book be my legacy to you all and a blessing of God's Holy Spirit through Jesus Christ that you may be comforted through Him and led by Him in faith. May you find understanding of His will in your lives and be drawn to His love and forgiveness. May we all be together in Heaven for all eternity because of the saving grace of Jesus—submitting ourselves to accepting Him as our Lord.

CHRONOLOGICAL MAPS

ORIGIN TO NOAH (map 1)

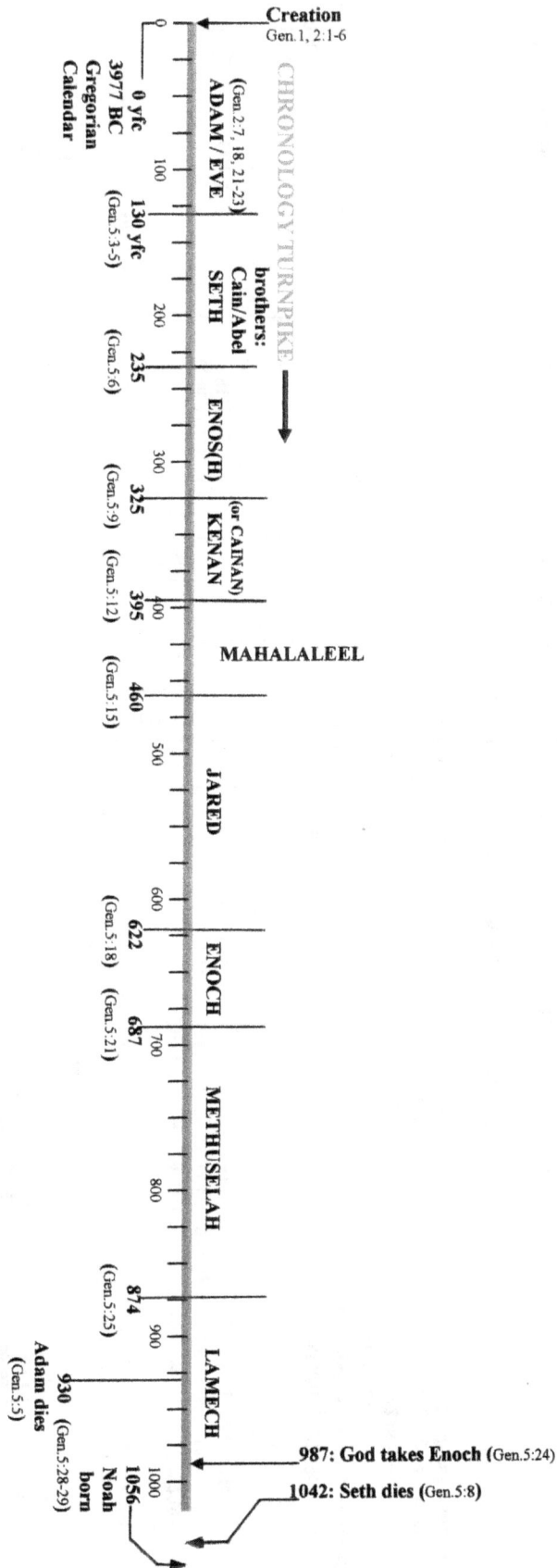

CHRONOLOGY TURNPIKE

Creation
Gen.1, 2:1-6

0

0 yfc
3977 BC
Gregorian
Calendar

(Gen.2:7, 18, 21-23)
ADAM / EVE

100

130 yfc
(Gen.5:3-5)

brothers:
Cain/Abel
SETH

200

235
(Gen.5:6)

ENOS(H)

300

325
(Gen.5:9)

(or CAINAN)
KENAN

395
(Gen.5:12)

400

MAHALALEEL

460
(Gen.5:15)

500

JARED

600

622
(Gen.5:18)

ENOCH

687
(Gen.5:21)

700

METHUSELAH

800

874
(Gen.5:25)

900

LAMECH

930
Adam dies
(Gen.5:5)

987: God takes Enoch (Gen.5:24)

1000

1042: Seth dies (Gen.5:8)

1056
Noah
born
(Gen.5:28-29)

NOAH TO ISRAEL'S MOVE TO EGYPT (map 2)

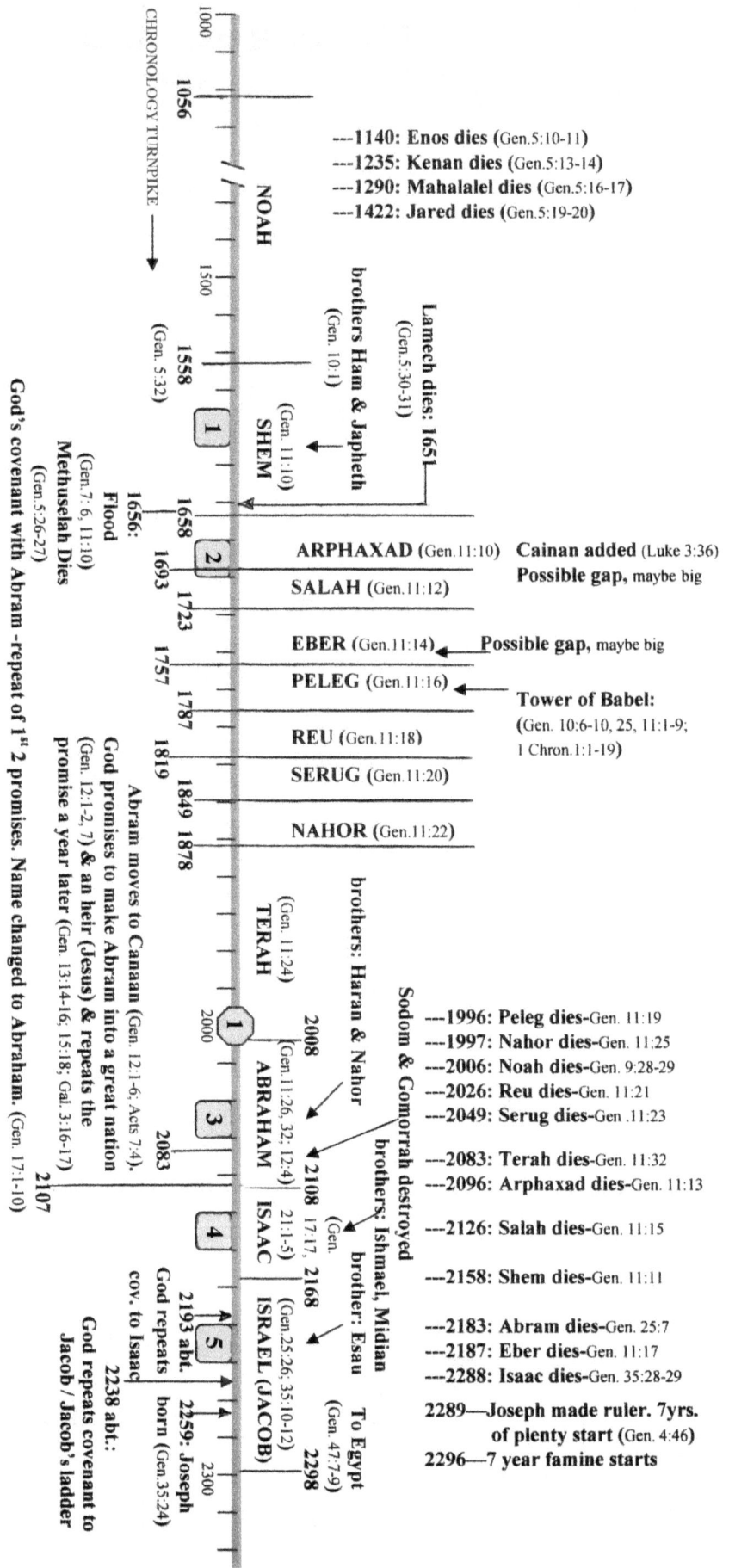

CHRONOLOGY TURNPIKE →

1000
1056
1500

NOAH

---1140: Enos dies (Gen.5:10-11)
---1235: Kenan dies (Gen.5:13-14)
---1290: Mahalalel dies (Gen.5:16-17)
---1422: Jared dies (Gen.5:19-20)

brothers Ham & Japheth (Gen. 10:1)

Lamech dies: 1651 (Gen.5:30-31)

SHEM (Gen. 11:10)
1558 (Gen. 5:32)

1656: Flood (Gen.7:6, 11:10)
Methuselah Dies (Gen.5:26-27)

God's covenant with Abram -repeat of 1st 2 promises. Name changed to Abraham. (Gen. 17:1-10)

[1] **[2]**

ARPHAXAD (Gen.11:10)   Cainan added (Luke 3:36)
1658   Possible gap, maybe big
SALAH (Gen.11:12)
1693
1723
EBER (Gen.11:14) ← Possible gap, maybe big
1757
PELEG (Gen.11:16) ← Tower of Babel:
1787   (Gen. 10:6-10, 25, 11:1-9;
REU (Gen.11:18)   1 Chron.1:1-19)
1819
SERUG (Gen.11:20)
1849
NAHOR (Gen.11:22)
1878

TERAH (Gen. 11:24)
brothers: Haran & Nahor
2008 (Gen.11:26, 32; 12:4)

Abram moves to Canaan (Gen. 12:1-6; Acts 7:4). God promises to make Abram into a great nation (Gen. 12:1-2, 7) & an heir (Jesus) & repeats the promise a year later (Gen. 13:14-16; 15:18; Gal. 3:16-17)

2000
[1]
ABRAHAM
2083
[3]
2083
2107

Sodom & Gomorrah destroyed
brothers: Ishmael, Midian   brother: Esau

---1996: Peleg dies-Gen. 11:19
---1997: Nahor dies-Gen. 11:25
---2006: Noah dies-Gen. 9:28-29
---2026: Reu dies-Gen. 11:21
---2049: Serug dies-Gen .11:23
---2083: Terah dies-Gen. 11:32
---2096: Arphaxad dies-Gen. 11:13
---2126: Salah dies-Gen. 11:15
---2158: Shem dies-Gen. 11:11
---2183: Abram dies-Gen. 25:7
---2187: Eber dies-Gen. 11:17
---2288: Isaac dies-Gen. 35:28-29

[4]
ISAAC 2108 (Gen. 17:17, 21:1-5)
2168 (Gen.25:26, 35:10-12)

[5]
ISRAEL (JACOB)
2298

God repeats cov. to Isaac 2193 abt.
God repeats covenant to Jacob / Jacob's ladder 2238 abt.
2259: Joseph born (Gen. 35:24)
To Egypt (Gen. 47:7-9)

2289—Joseph made ruler. 7yrs. of plenty start (Gen. 4:46)
2296—7 year famine starts
2300

[1] Some descendants of Ham (Gen.9:18, 10:6-20): Perizzites, Hivites, Jebusites, Amorites, Hittites, Philistines, Babylonians, (Gen.), Palestinians, Egyptians, Africans, Descendants of Japheth (Gen.9:26-27, 10:2-5): Caucasian (Gentile) races of Europe & Asia.

[2] Luke's lineage (3:36) adds Cainan between Arpachshad & Shelah, probably a scribal error in repeating Cainan (Kenan). Asshur, son of Shem, brother of Arphaxad, was the father of the Assyrians.

[3] Haran fathered Lot (Gen.11:27) whose descendants: Moabites (Gen.19:37, Deut.2:9), Ammonites (Gen.19:38), Midianites (Gen. 25:1-2) descended from Midian--mingled with and often called Ishmaelites (Gen. 37:25-28, Jud. 8:22-24).

[4] Descendants of Ishmael: Arabians (Muslims), Ishmaelites (Gen.16:9-12, 21:20-21, 25:18).

[5] Descendants of Esau: Edomites (Gen.36:9, Deut.2:4, Jer.49:9-10), Amalekites (Gen.36:12) through grandson Amalek

EGYPT LIFE / EXODUS / JUDGES RULE / SAUL / DAVID / SOLOMON (map 3)

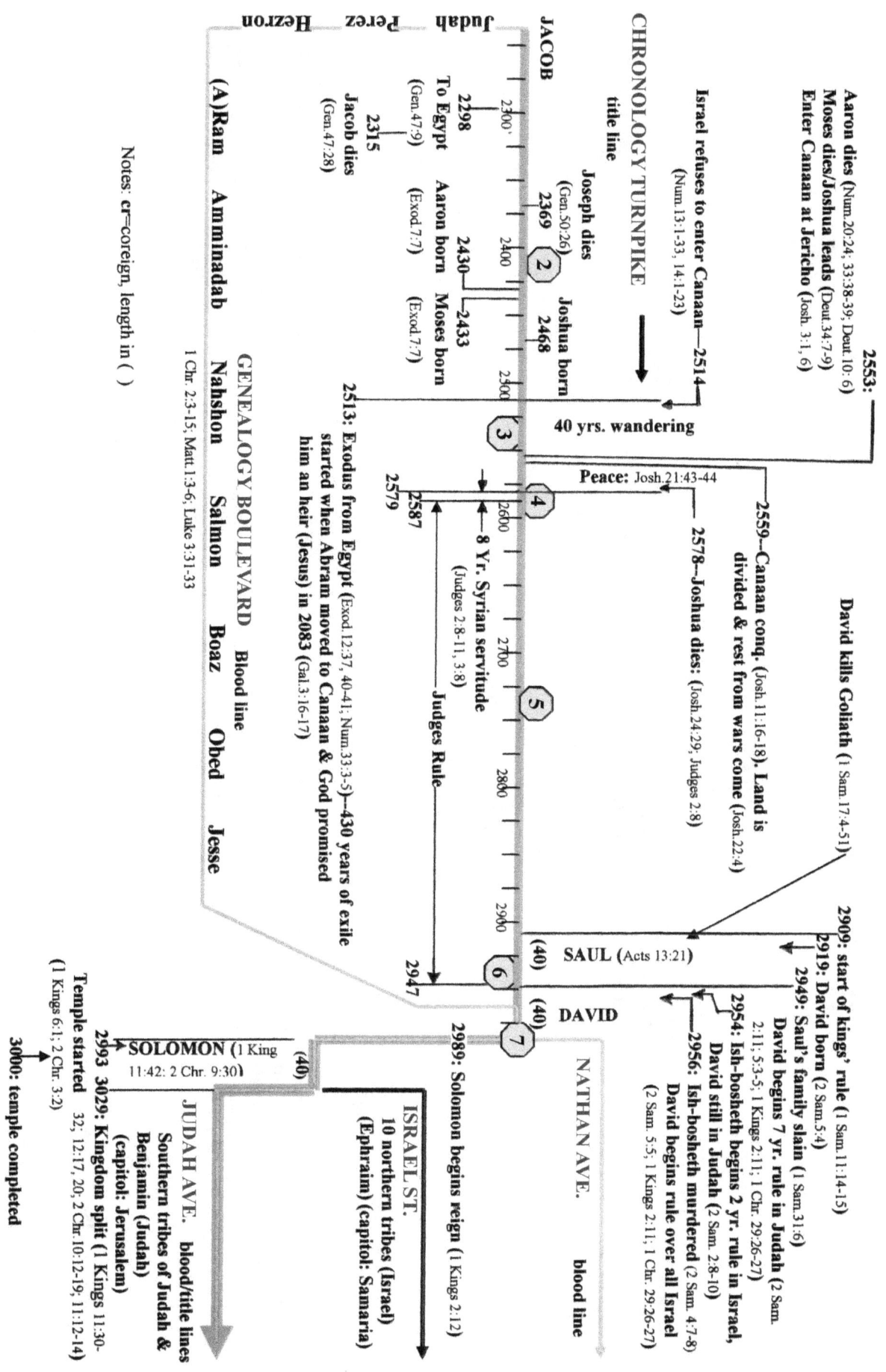

CHRONOLOGY TURNPIKE
title line

CHRONOLOGY TURNPIKE
title line

Aaron dies (Num.20:24; 33:38-39; Deut. 10: 6)
Moses dies/Joshua leads (Deut.34:7-9)
Enter Canaan at Jericho (Josh. 3:1, 6)

2553:

Israel refuses to enter Canaan—2514
(Num.13:1-33, 14:1-23)

David kills Goliath (1 Sam 17:4-51)

JACOB

Judah
Perez
Hezron

2298 — To Egypt (Gen.47:9)

2300

2315 — Jacob dies (Gen.47:28)

Joseph dies (Gen.50:26)

2369

2400

2430 — Aaron born (Exod.7:7)

2433 — Moses born (Exod.7:7)

2468 — Joshua born

2

2500

40 yrs. wandering

3

2513: Exodus from Egypt (Exod.12:37, 40-41; Num.33:3-5)—430 years of exile started when Abram moved to Canaan & God promised him an heir (Jesus) in 2083 (Gal.3:16-17)

2559—Canaan conq. (Josh.11:16-18), Land is divided & rest from wars come (Josh.22:4)

2578–Joshua dies: (Josh.24:29; Judges 2:8)

Peace: Josh.21:43-44

4

2579

2587

2600

8 Yr. Syrian servitude
(Judges 2:8-11, 3:8)

Judges Rule

2700

5

2800

2900

2909: start of kings' rule (1 Sam.11:14-15)
2919: David born (2 Sam.5:4)
2949: Saul's family slain (1 Sam.31:6)

2954: David begins 7 yr. rule in Judah (2 Sam 2:1; 5:3-5; 1 Kings 2:11; 1 Chr. 29:26-27)
Ish-bosheth begins 2 yr. rule in Israel, David still in Judah (2 Sam. 2:8-10)

2956: Ish-bosheth murdered (2 Sam. 4:7-8) David begins rule over all Israel (2 Sam. 5:5; 1 Kings 2:11; 1 Chr. 29:26-27)

2947

6

(40) SAUL (Acts 13:21)

(40) DAVID

7

2989: Solomon begins reign (1 Kings 2:12)

(40)

SOLOMON (1 King 11:42: 2 Chr. 9:30)

NATHAN AVE.
blood line

2993 3029: Kingdom split (1 Kings 11:30- 32; 12:17, 20, 2 Chr.10:12-19, 11:12-14)

Temple started (1 Kings 6:1; 2 Chr. 3:2)

3000: temple completed

ISRAEL ST.
10 northern tribes (Israel) (Ephraim) (capitol: Samaria)

JUDAH AVE. blood/title lines
Southern tribes of Judah & Benjamin (Judah) (capitol: Jerusalem)

GENEALOGY BOULEVARD Blood line

(A)Ram   Amminadab   Nahshon   Salmon   Boaz   Obed   Jesse

1 Chr. 2:3-15; Matt.1:3-6; Luke 3:31-33

Notes: cr=coreign, length in ( )

Chronological Maps - 3

KINGS RULE (map 4)

Matt.1:7-12; 1 Kings 12:1 to 22:53; 2 Kings 1:1 to 25:30; 1 Chr. 9:39 to 29:30; 2 Chr.

Notes: cr=coreign, length in ( )
G=good king, B=bad king

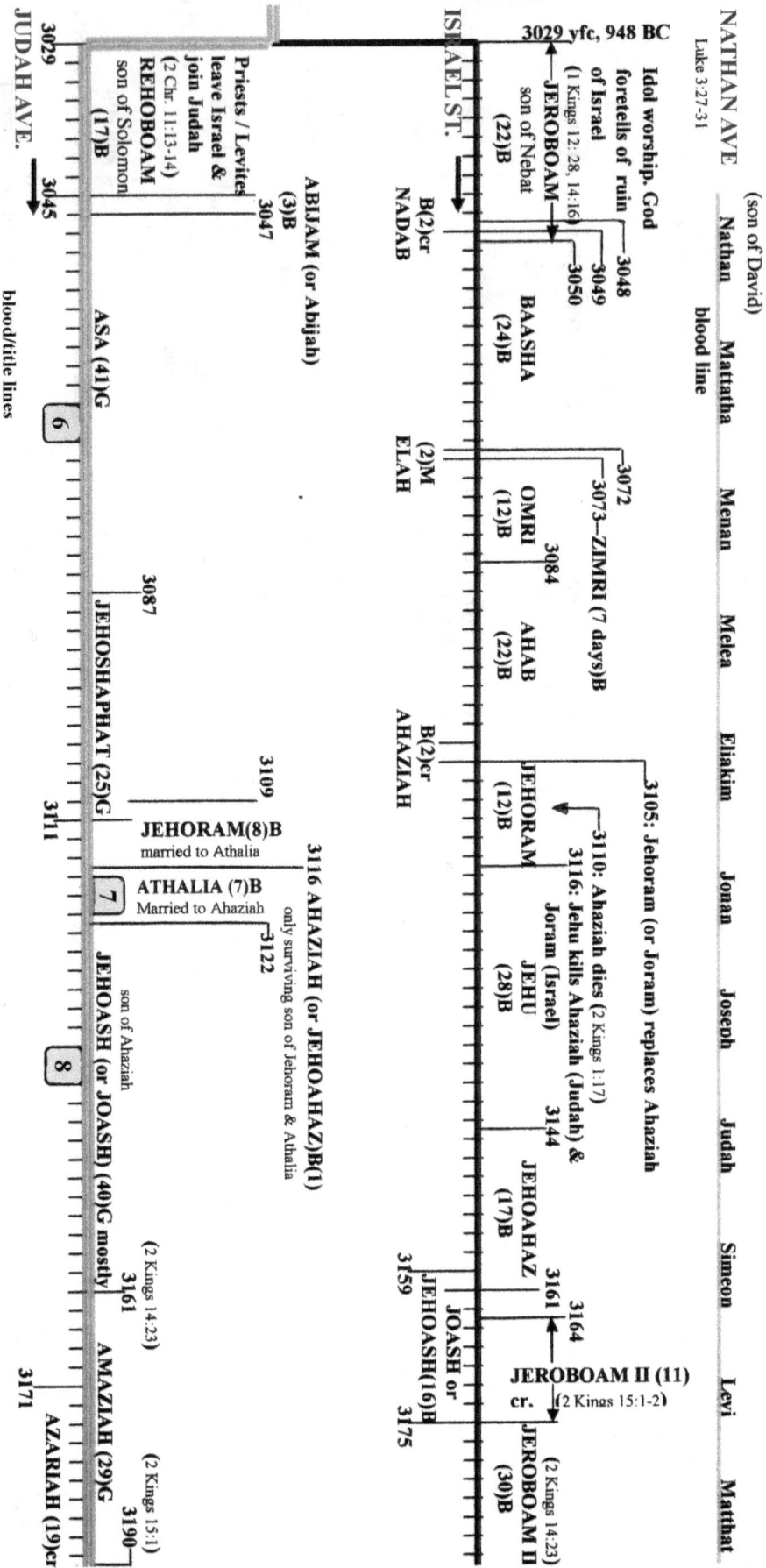

NATHAN AVE

Luke 3:27-31

(son of David)

Nathan   Mattatha   Menan   Melea   Eliakim   Jonan   Joseph   Judah   Simeon   Levi   Matthat

blood line

ISRAEL ST.

3029 yfc, 948 BC

Idol worship. God foretells of ruin of Israel
(1 Kings 12: 28, 14:16)
JEROBOAM
son of Nebat
(22)B

— 3048
— 3049
— 3050

NADAB
B(2)cr

BAASHA
(24)B

— 3072

3073—ZIMRI (7 days)B

ELAH
(2)M

OMRI
(12)B
3084

AHAB
(22)B

AHAZIAH
B(2)cr

3105: Jehoram (or Joram) replaces Ahaziah

JEHORAM
(12)B

3110: Jehoram (Israel) &
3116: Jehu kills Ahaziah (Judah) &
Joram (Israel)
JEHU
(28)B

3144

JEHOAHAZ
(17)B

3161
3164

JOASH or JEHOASH(16)B
cr.

JEROBOAM II (11)
cr. (2 Kings 15:1-2)

(2 Kings 14:23)

JEROBOAM II
(30)B

3159
3175

JUDAH AVE.

3029

3045
3047

blood/title lines

REHOBOAM
son of Solomon
(17)B

Priests / Levites
leave Israel &
join Judah
(2 Chr. 11:13-14)

ABIJAM (or Abijiah)
(3)B

ASA (41)G

JEHOSHAPHAT (25)G

3087

3109
3111

JEHORAM(8)B
married to Athalia

ATHALIA (7)B
Married to Ahaziah

3116 AHAZIAH (or JEHOAHAZ)B(1)
only surviving son of Jehoram & Athalia

3122

JEHOASH (or JOASH) (40)G mostly

(2 Kings 14:23)
3161

AMAZIAH (29)G

(2 Kings 15:1)
3190

AZARIAH (19)cr

3171

POINTS OF REFERENCE:

6 From Asa's ascension (3047):
Nadab ascended in his 2nd year, 2 year reign (3048-3049);
Baasha ascended during his 3d year, 24 year reign (3049-3072);
Elah ascended during his 26th year, 2 year reign (3072-3073);
Omri ascended after his 31st year, 6 year reign (3078-3084) in Jerusalem &
6 years (3073-3078) in Tirzah during a split in Israel
Ahab ascended after his 38th year, 22 year reign (3084-3105)

7 Jehu & Athaliah (of Judah) ascended the same year (3116)

8 From Jehoash's (of Judah) ascension (3122);
Jehoahaz ascended during his 23d year, 17 year reign (3144-3161)
Jehoash (of Israel) ascended in his 37th year, 16 year reign (3159-3175)

ISRAEL EXILE TO ASSYRIA / JUDAH KINGS (map 5)

Notes: **cr**=coreign, length in ( )
G=good king, **B**=bad king

NATHAN AVE.

Jorim   Eliezer   Jose   Er   Elmodam   Cosam   Addi   Melchi   Neri

blood line continued →

ISRAEL ST.

JEROBOAM II (41)B →

3175

Jonah warns Nineveh
(Jonah 1; 2; 3)

Power struggles
(2 Kings 15:8-15)

3205

GAP

SHALLUM (1 mo.)B
3210

3209: ZECHARIAH (6 mos.)B
(or Zachariah)

MENAHEM (10)B

3220

3222

Assyrian invasion bought
off with bribe (2 Kings 15:19-20)

10

PEKAHIAH (2)B →

PEKAH (20)B

3241
tumult

3248
GAP

11

HOSHEA (9)B

End of 10 northern tribes. Probably dispersed worldwide.

3256 yfc:Assyrian invasion & Israel exile (2 Kings 17:6-24; 18:10)
721 BC
3040 Jew

3243

Ahaz hires the Assyrian army to prevent an Israel / Syrian attack. Syria is conquered.
Galilean population taken to Assyria. (2 Kings 15:29; 16:5-9; Isa. 7:1, 20)

3265: God saves Judah from Assyria, killing 185,000
(2 Kings 18:13, 19:32-35, 2 Chr. 32:1, 20-22, Isa. 36:1; 37:33-36)

JUDAH AVE.

JUDAH AVE. →

31/71

cr

3190

9

AZARIAH (or UZZIAH) (52)G/B (2 Kings 15:1-2)

3222

3221

JOTHAM (20)G

3236

3241

AHAZ (16)B

3251

HEZEKIAH (29)G

3280

MANASSEH (55)B

3335

blood / title lines continued →

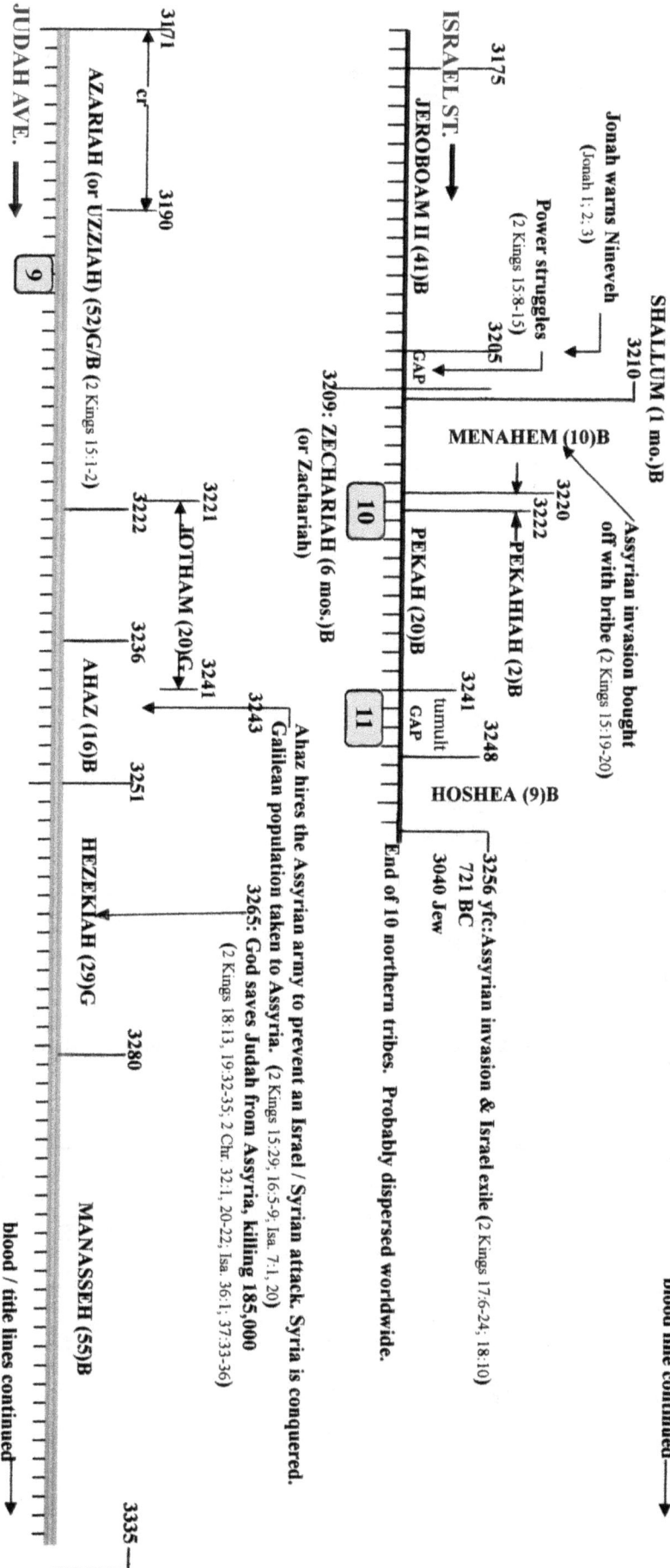

POINTS OF REFERENCE:

9 From Azariah's ascension (3171):
Zechariah ascended in his 38th year, 6 month reign (3209)
Shallum ascended in his 39th year, 1 month reign (3210)
Menahem ascended in his 39th year, 10 year reign (3210)
Pekahiah ascended in his 50th year, 2 year reign (3210-3220)
Pekah began to reign in his 52nd year & reigned 20 years (3222-3241)

10 From Pekah's ascension (3220):
Jotham ascended in his 2nd year, 16 year reign (3221-3236) + 4/5 year coreign
Ahaz ascended in his 17th year, 16 year reign (3236-3251)

11 Hoshea killed Pekah in 3241 but evidently couldn't take control, because of tumult, for 7 more years in the 12th year of Ahaz's reign (2 Kings 17:1-2)

Note: 2 gaps required for literal interpretation of scripture

END OF KINGS RULE / BABYLON EXILE / RETURN TO JERUSALEM (map 6)

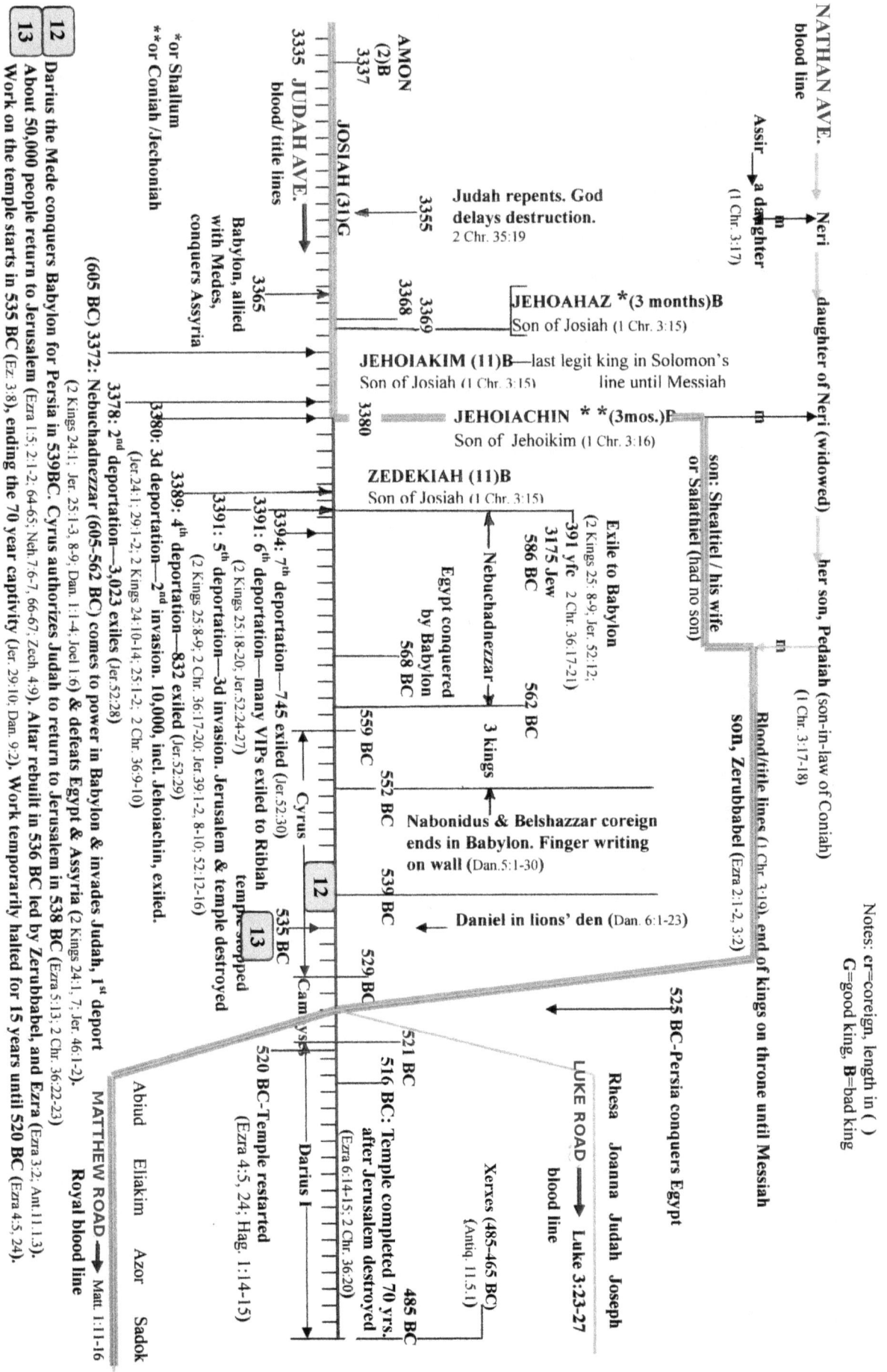

NATHAN AVE.
blood line

Assir ——— a daughter (1 Chr. 3:17)

Neri ——— daughter of Neri (widowed) ——— her son, Pedaiah (son-in-law of Coniah) (1 Chr. 3:17-18)

son: Shealtiel / his wife or Salathiel (had no son)

Blood/title lines (1 Chr. 3:19), end of kings on throne until Messiah

son, Zerubbabel (Ezra 2:1-2, 3:2)

525 BC-Persia conquers Egypt

3335 JUDAH AVE.
blood/ title lines

AMON (2)B
3337

3355 Judah repents. God delays destruction. 2 Chr. 35:19

JOSIAH (31)G
3365

Babylon, allied with Medes, conquers Assyria

3368
3369

JEHOAHAZ *(3 months)B
Son of Josiah (1 Chr. 3:15)

JEHOIAKIM (11)B—last legit king in Solomon's
Son of Josiah (1 Chr. 3:15)   line until Messiah

3380 JEHOIACHIN * *(3mos.)B
Son of Jehoikim (1 Chr. 3:16)

ZEDEKIAH (11)B
Son of Josiah (1 Chr. 3:15)

3375 Jew
586 BC

391 yfc 2 Chr. 36:17-21;

Exile to Babylon (2 Kings 25: 8-9, Jer. 52:12;

Nebuchadnezzar

Egypt conquered by Babylon 568 BC

3 kings

562 BC

559 BC

552 BC

Cyrus

539 BC

12

535 BC

13

529 BC

Cambyses

521 BC

520 BC

Darius I

516 BC

485 BC

Nabonidus & Belshazzar coreign ends in Babylon. Finger writing on wall (Dan.5:1-30)

Daniel in lions' den (Dan. 6:1-23)

520 BC-Temple restarted (Ezra 5:13; 2 Chr. 36:22-23)

516 BC: Temple completed 70 yrs. after Jerusalem destroyed (Ezra 6:14-15; 2 Chr. 36:20)

485 BC

Xerxes (485-465 BC) {Antiq. 11.5.1}

Rhesa   Joanna   Judah   Joseph

LUKE ROAD ——— Luke 3:23-27
blood line

MATTHEW ROAD ——— Matt. 1:11-16
Royal blood line

Abiud   Eliakim   Azor   Sadok

3378: 2nd deportation—3,023 exiles (Jer.52:28)

3380: 3d deportation—2nd invasion. 10,000, incl. Jehoiachin, exiled. (Jer.24:1; 29:1-2; 2 Kings 24:10-14; 25:1-2; 2 Chr. 36:9-10)

3389: 4th deportation—832 exiled (Jer.52:29)
(2 Kings 25:8-9; 2 Chr. 36:17-20; Jer.39:1-2, 8-10; 52:12-16)

3391: 5th deportation—3d invasion. Jerusalem & temple destroyed (2 Kings 25:18-20; Jer.52:24-27)

3391: 6th deportation—many VIP's exiled to Riblah

3394: 7th deportation—745 exiled (Jer.52:30)

(605 BC) 3372: Nebuchadnezzar (605-562 BC) comes to power in Babylon & invades Judah, 1st deport (2 Kings 24:1; Jer. 25:1-3, 8-9, Dan. 1:1-4; Joel 1:6)

temple stopped

temple destroyed

12
Darius the Mede conquers Babylon for Persia in 539BC. Cyrus authorizes Judah to return to Jerusalem in 538 BC (Ezra 5:13; 2 Chr. 36:22-23). Altar rebuilt in 536 BC led by Zerubbabel, and Ezra (Ezra 3:2; Ant.11.1.3). Work temporarily halted for 15 years until 520 BC (Ezra 4:5, 24).

13
Work on the temple starts in 535 BC (Ez. 3:8), ending the 70 year captivity (Jer. 29:10; Dan. 9:2), Work temporarily halted for 15 years until 520 BC (Ezra 4:5, 24).

*or Shallum
**or Coniah /Jechoniah

About 50,000 people return to Jerusalem (Ezra 1:5, 2:1-2, 64-65; Neh.7:6-7, 66-67; Zech. 4:9).

(605 BC) 3372: Nebuchadnezzar (605-562 BC) comes to power in Babylon & invades Judah, 1st deport (2 Kings 24:1; Jer. 25:1-3, 8-9, Dan. 1:1-4; Joel 1:6) & defeats Egypt & Assyria (2 Kings 24:1, 7; Jer. 46:1-2).

JESUS' BIRTH & DEATH (map 7)

Daniel's 483 prophetic years, 476 actual (Dan. 9:24-26)

Begin Church Age, Jews denied, Gentiles grafted in

LUKE ROAD →

......Mattathias   Maath   Naggai.....Heli   Joseph

Artaxerxes (465-425) allows Jews to return to Jerusalem to rebuild the temple.
Ezra leads the return of exiles and a national revival where the people repent
(Ezra 7:7, 11-23; 8:32; 9:9, 13-14; 10:2-3; Neh. 8:9; 10)

Artaxerxes decrees for rebuilding Jerusalem walls,
led by Nehemiah (Neh. 1:1-3; 2:1, 4-5; 6:15)

459 BC
3518 yfc

430 BC
3547 yfc
approx. end of OT

446 BC
(Hellenist Period begins)

Greek
Conquest
333 BC
3644 yfc

Jewish
independence
164 BC
3813 yfc

Roman
conquest
63 BC
3914 yfc

3727 yfc abt.
250 BC: Septuagint
(trans. of Pentateuch
to Greek)

3827 yfc abt.
150 BC

3877 yfc abt.
100 BC

MATTHEW ROAD →

Achim   Eliud   Eleazar   Matthan   Jacob   Joseph
(Mark 1:2-4; Luke 1:1-17, 36)

14	Maccabees bring independence (164 BC to 63 BC)
15	Pharisees Period (2nd century BC to 2nd century AD)
16	Sadducees Period (1st century BC to 1st century AD)

3500
3600

No year zero →

5 BC: Jesus' birth
(Matt.1:18-25, 2:1-11; Luke 1:26-33, 2:1-12)
John the Baptist's birth

30 AD
Jesus' death*

Jesus begins
ministry^
27 AD

4000
4046 yfc
4066 yfc
4076 yfc: end of scripture

70 AD: 2nd temple destroyed by the Romans (Dan. 9:26, Luke 21:20-24)
90 AD: Hebrew bible canonized
100 AD about

4100
4200

400 AD abt.: Vulgate trans. to Latin
476 AD: End of West Roman Empire
1382 AD: Wycliffe trans. Vulgate to Eng.
1453 AD: End of East Roman Empire to Turks
1517 AD: Start of Reformation
1611 AD: King James V. translated To English
1750 AD: abt.: Challoner version of Douay Bible
1883 AD: RV bible printed
1901 AD: ASV Bible printed
1941 AD: Confraternity version of Bible written
1947 AD: Dead Sea scrolls discovered
1952 AD: RSV bible printed
1989 AD: NRSV Bible printed

Israel restored
as a nation
1948 AD
5924 yfc

5900
6000
5985 yfc
2009 AD
5769 Jew

* Matt.27:1-37; Mark 15:1-38; Luke 23:1-48; John 18:28-40, 19:1-30
^ Matt. 4:1-17; Mark 1:9-15; Luke 3:23

2009 to the End Times (map 8)

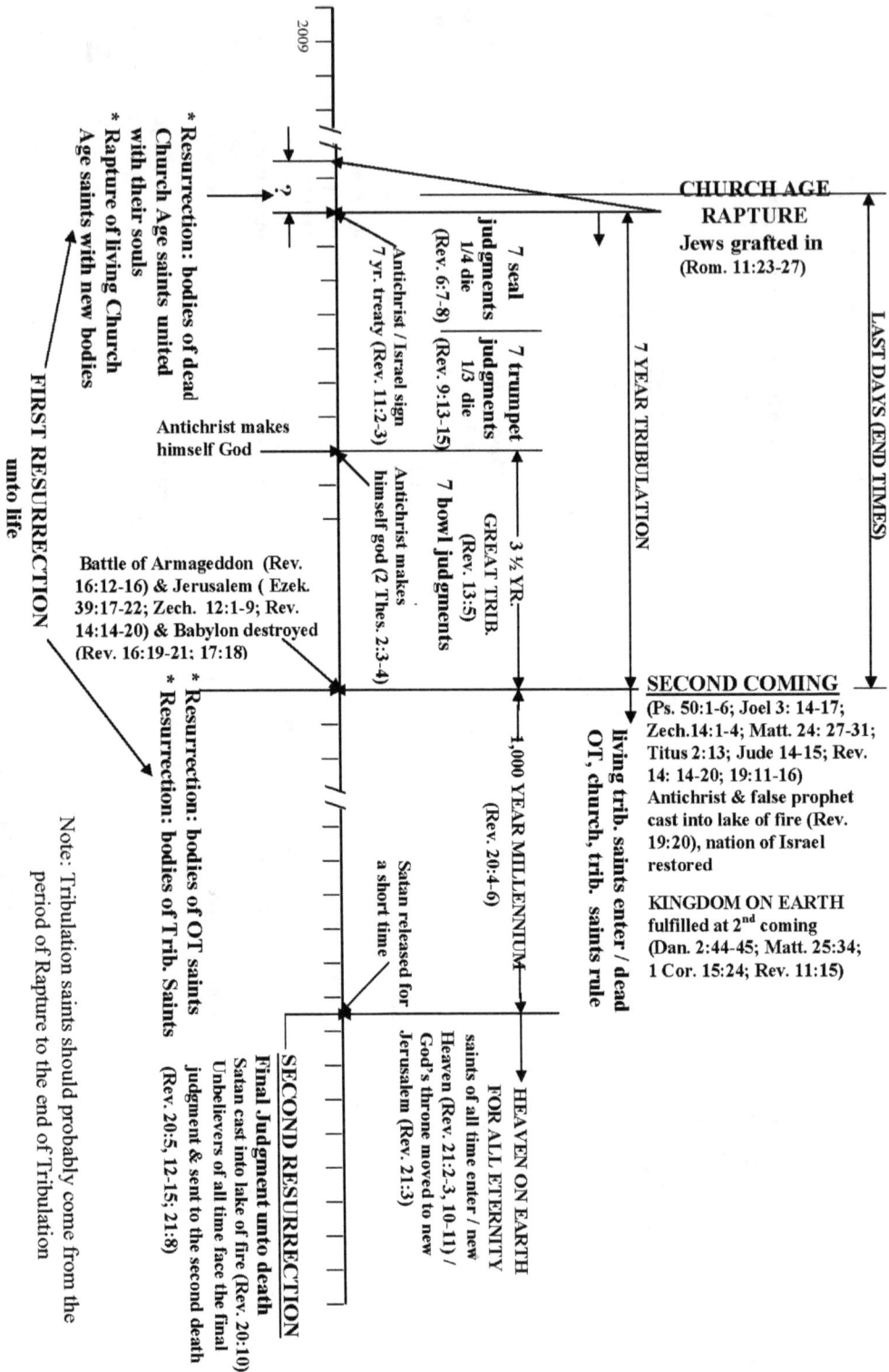

2009

CHURCH AGE RAPTURE
Jews grafted in (Rom. 11:23-27)

LAST DAYS (END TIMES)

7 YEAR TRIBULATION

* Resurrection: bodies of dead Church Age saints united with their souls
* Rapture of living Church Age saints with new bodies

FIRST RESURRECTION unto life

Antichrist / Israel sign 7 yr. treaty (Rev. 11:2-3)

7 seal judgments 1/4 die (Rev. 6:7-8)

7 trumpet judgments 1/3 die (Rev. 9:13-15)

Antichrist makes himself God

Antichrist makes himself god (2 Thes. 2:3-4)

7 bowl judgments

3 ½ YR. GREAT TRIB. (Rev. 13:5)

Battle of Armageddon (Rev. 16:12-16) & Jerusalem (Ezek. 39:17-22; Zech. 12:1-9; Rev. 14:14-20) & Babylon destroyed (Rev. 16:19-21; 17:18)

* Resurrection: bodies of OT saints
* Resurrection: bodies of Trib. Saints (Rev. 20:5, 12-15; 21:8)

SECOND COMING
(Ps. 50:1-6; Joel 3: 14-17; Zech.14:1-4; Matt. 24: 27-31; Titus 2:13; Jude 14-15; Rev. 14: 14-20; 19:11-16) Antichrist & false prophet cast into lake of fire (Rev. 19:20), nation of Israel restored

KINGDOM ON EARTH fulfilled at 2nd coming (Dan. 2:44-45; Matt. 25:34; 1 Cor. 15:24; Rev. 11:15)

living trib. saints enter / dead OT, church, trib. saints rule

1,000 YEAR MILLENNIUM (Rev. 20:4-6)

Satan released for a short time

SECOND RESURRECTION
Final Judgment unto death
Satan cast into lake of fire (Rev. 20:10)
Unbelievers of all time face the final judgment & sent to the second death

HEAVEN ON EARTH FOR ALL ETERNITY saints of all time enter / new Heaven (Rev. 21:2-3, 10-11) / God's throne moved to new Jerusalem (Rev. 21:3)

Note: Tribulation saints should probably come from the period of Rapture to the end of Tribulation

MORMON CHRONOLOGY (map 1a)

Note: dates in ( ) are per Book of Mormon

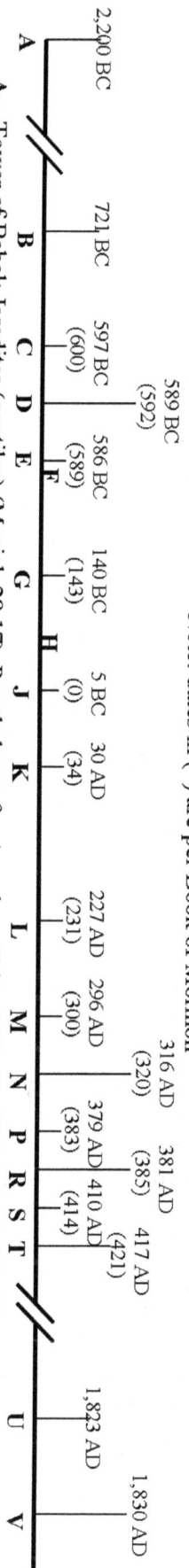

| A | | B | | C | D | E | F | G | | H | | J | K | L | M | N | P R | S | T | | U | V |

| 2,200 BC | 721 BC | 597 BC (600) | 589 BC (592) | 586 BC (589) | 140 BC (143) | 5 BC (0) | 30 AD (34) | 227 AD (231) | 296 AD (300) | 316 AD (320) | 379 AD (383) | 381 AD (385) | 410 AD (414) | 417 AD (421) | 1,823 AD | 1,830 AD |

A—Tower of Babel: Jaredites (gentiles) (Mosiah 28:17). People leave for Americas (Ether 1:33, 41-43; 2:5-7, 16; 6:5, 12).

B—Assyrian invasion. Nation of Israel carried away and dispensed throughout the world-the 10 lost tribes per Christian bible.

C—Hebrews, led by Lehi, leave Jerusalem for the wilderness to escape the Babylon threat (1 Nephi 1:4; 2:1-4; 17:43; 2 Nephi 29:13; Alma 26:36-lost tribes.). Lehi records history and Nephi abridges it and adds more.

D—Hebrews leave the wilderness for Americas (1 Nephi 17:4, 8, 14; 18:4, 8, 23). The people separate into two groups: Nephites and Lamanites.

E—Babylonians conquer the nation of Judah and carry many to Babylon, but some leave and sail for the Americas (Omni 1:15-16).

F—Nephi writes of Joseph in Egypt prophesizing the coming of a prophet (Joseph Smith) to reveal God's covenants with the Hebrews (2 Nephi 3:5-9) and that the words of the Book of Mormon will be delivered to him in the latter days (2 Nephi 27:6, 9, 12).

G—The Church of Christ is formed (Mosiah 18:17). Nephites are more righteous than Lamanites.

H—Nephites battle the Lamanites up to the coming of Christ. Many Lamanites are converted (Alma 17-19; 23:6-13; 26:3-4, 15). Lamanites become more righteous than the Nephites (Helaman 4:23-26; 6:1-2, 30-36; 7:6, 24-27).

J—The birth of Christ.

K—Christ crucified and resurrected and visits the Nephites to deliver the news of God's redemption plan (3 Nephi 11-30) as prophesied (2 Nephi 26:1; Alma 16:20). The name, Church of Christ, is given (3 Nephi 27:3-10).

L—People separate into two church nations: Nephites and Lamanites (2 Nephi 5:5, 14; Jacob 1:13; 4 Nephi 1:35-36). Up to this time, the people were divided, those following Nephi and those following Laman and others.

M—Nephites and Lamanites again become wicked (4 Nephi 1:45).

N—Ammaron hid all the engraved plates of the people's history (4 Nephi 1:48-49).

P—Mormon, a prophet and historian, abridged the plates (Mormon 1:1-4; 2:17-18; 4:23; 5:9) and hid them in New York State during the last battles with the Lamanites and gave a few to his son Moroni who added the Book of Moroni (Mormon 6:6).

R—Lamanites destroy Nephites (Jacob 3:3-5; 7:24; Enos 1:24; Omni 1:5; Words of Mormon 6:1, 11; 8:1-3).

S—Jadedites destroyed (Alma 37:21-31; Ether 15; Moroni 1:1-2).

T—Moroni abridged and sealed 24 gold plates of Jaredite history (Mosiah 8:5-9; Alma 37:21; Ether 1:2; 4:4-6; 15:33; Moroni 1:1) to be hidden until the gentiles repent (Ether 13:1-2; 15:25-31).

U—Moroni resurrected and appeared to J. Smith. The hidden plates were delivered to him in 1827 and he finished translating them in 1829. God provided for 11 persons to witness the plates before they were taken away.

V—Book of Mormon published, and Church of Jesus Christ of Latter Day Saints was started.

1

ORIGIN TO NOAH

(reference road map 1)

Our journey starts with creation. God, by His word, created the heavens and the earth, vegetation, and all the other physical wonders of the universe (Gen. 1; Psa. 33:6-9; Prov. 3:19-20; 8:28-29; 30:4; Isa. 45:18; Jer. 10:12; 51:15; John 1:1-3; Heb. 11:3; Rev. 4:11; Song 9:1–apocrypha). All this creation was inanimate--it had no life. To this handiwork, God added all the fishes, birds, and animals (Gen. 1:20-25), but these animated beings could not worship Him or have communion with Him--they did not possess souls. God, a God of unlimited love, desired a relationship with His creation, so He created man in His image (Gen. 1:26-27; Col. 3:10), possessing morality, knowledge, holiness, righteousness, and a sense of awareness of himself, his environment, and his creator, all to a limited degree--lower than the angels (Psa. 8:4-6; Heb. 2:6-8). Because God did not want a puppet-following, He gave man a free will and the ability to reason so he could make decisions on all matters within his nature, including the will to obey or disobey Him. This is the covenant God made with mankind: to give him dominion over His creation (Gen. 1:28; Psa. 8:5-6; Heb. 2:7-8) in return for his obedience (Gen. 2:16-17). Even though God knew, as I believe, man would disobey Him before He created him, He created him anyway. Since God is omniscient as we understand, He could have by His own will purposely conceded this foreknowledge, even Lucifer's disobedience, without diminishing His glory.

Adam,[1] the first human, was created and placed in the Garden of Eden after all other creations of God. The ruling line on the road map starts with Adam. God then gave Adam a mate, **Eve**. Man was made perfect in the image of God (spiritually). God commanded Adam and Eve to eat all that they desired from the garden except the fruit from the *Tree of the Knowledge of Good and Evil* (Gen. 2:9, 15-17). But Eve was tempted by Satan, the author of sin and now adversary of God; she then convinced Adam to eat the apple from this tree (Gen. 3:1-7).

God made a perfect world made imperfect by sin.[2] This worldly imperfection manifests itself in many ways: painful childbirth (Gen. 3:16), useless weeds interfering with man's toil (Gen. 3:17-19), problems with wild animals, natural disasters, sickness, disease, and shorter life spans, etc.

Science and religion have differed on the Biblical story of creation and the age of human life: religion giving the age of mankind and that of earth as about 6,000 years and science giving the age of mankind as at least 10,000 years and that of the earth from radiometric testing as four to five billion years.[3] Bible scholars argue that God's day can be interpreted as any number of years (thousand, million?) and cite Psalm 90:4 and 2 Peter 3:8 for credibility. See also the "Introduction" and "Preface" for the possibility here of a gap in creation and other later gaps, some large, in the chronological events reported in Scripture. Gaps would make it impossible to determine from Scripture the ages of humans or the earth. These ideas cannot be proven, so we must put our faith in God and accept Scripture as it is given to us and wait until we are in Heaven to learn this mystery.

It is not in the scope of this book to investigate the various theories of creation. We must keep our minds on the goal at hand: to investigate through Biblical chronologies, genealogies, and history, God's plan for providing mankind with the redeeming Messiah. Although creation studies can be interesting and thought-provoking, they do not usually enhance our understanding of God's ultimate plan for our salvation. Knowledge of God's plan should be our top priority, and it will be so with the guidance of the Holy Spirit.

From the beginning, persons who had faith in God had hope for life after death (Job 14:14; 19:25-27; Psa. 17:14-15; 49:15; Isa. 26:19). This hope is still in effect today, although the original sin by Adam and Eve changed God's plan. Because their original sin begat universal sin (Rom. 5:12), a temporary system would be necessary throughout the Old Testament to cover these sins until they could be paid for by Messiah. God had this plan in mind from the beginning (John 1:1-5; 2 Tim. 1:8-9). He gave mankind the Old Testament in preparation of the coming Messiah (2 Tim. 3:16).

We interrupt our chronology to present some of the Messianic Messages that are given in the Old Testament and confirmed in the New Testament that illustrate God's plan from the beginning. Let us keep these facts in mind when traveling along our road to the Messiah. Remember to check the "Introduction" for an explanation of the two dating systems we will be using in this text and for a rule for converting from one system to the other.

The Messiah Messages

- ✔ <u>Adam, father of Mankind</u>. Jesus was called the second Adam (1 Cor. 15:45; Rom. 5:19).
- ✔ <u>Abel chosen over Cain</u>. God chose to accept Abel's offering, the first of his flock, because he pleased God and was righteous by his faith. He chose to reject Cain's fruit offering because he was self-willed and let sin control his life (1 John 3:12), for God, even at this early stage, required animal sacrifices. Abel obeyed this command but not Cain (Gen. 4:3-7; Heb. 11:4). This is the first instance of the blood sacrifice; it would have to sustain mankind until the ultimate sacrifice provided by the Lamb of God. Christ's sacrifice would provide for the forgiveness of sins for those who would accept His offer (Rev. 5:12).
- ✔ <u>Sacrifice of Isaac</u>. Abraham's sad willingness for 3 days to sacrifice his only son at that time is likened to Jesus' 3 days in the tomb (Gen. 22:1-13).
- ✔ <u>Christ called Shiloh</u>. A specific person, Messiah, shall lead God's people (Gen. 49:10).
- ✔ <u>Passover</u>. This yearly celebration by the Jews of their deliverance from the Death Angel in Egypt was a foreshadowing of the Messiah who would redeem mankind from its sins. They were protected by the blood of the lamb that was put on their doors just as Jesus, the Lamb of God, would give His blood as a ransom for many (Exod. 12).
- ✔ <u>Christ the Star</u>. A star shall come out of Jacob, a scepter out of Israel (Num. 24:17-19).
- ✔ <u>Christ the Apostle</u>. Messiah shall lead us and be our minister (Heb. 3:1).
- ✔ <u>Christ the mediator of the new covenant</u>. Jesus is the go-between advocate between man and God (1 Cor. 11:25; 1 Tim. 2:5; Heb. 7:22; 8:6; 9:11-15; 12:24; 1 John 2:1). In Old Testament times, before the advent of Messiah, God communicated with the people through prophets and faithful leaders. They were judged by their faith in God and His plans for them.
- ✔ <u>Jesus' coming, ministry, New Covenant, etc</u>. Many mentions are made of the coming Messiah in Psalms, Isaiah, Micah, and Malachi, and specifically in Daniel 9:25 and confirmed in the New Testament.
- ✔ <u>Christ the Servant</u>. He shall serve mankind with salvation (Zech. 3:8; Matt. 12:18; 20:28; John 13:1-5; Phili. 2:6-8).
- ✔ <u>Jesus' fulfillment of the New Covenant</u>. Jesus replaced all previous covenants with His sacrifice for our sins (Matt. 26:28; Luke 22:20; 2 Cor. 3:6; Gal. 3:16-17; Heb. 7:22; 8:6-10; 9:15; 13:20).

Archaeological Findings

Archaeologists' findings, especially in the twentieth century, are continuing to verify Biblical narratives. Babylonian and Assyrian digs have yielded writings about the creation that are remarkably similar to the Biblical account. These digs have also revealed stories of original sin, the Garden of Eden, and the Tree of Life. Diggings around the area of Mesopotamia, the cradle of civilization in the Middle East between the Tigris and Euphrates Rivers, show layers of pure clay about 8-11 feet thick between layers of debris-filled clay. This evidence suggests a sudden onset of water that washed over soil embedded with evidence of previous civilizations. Debris-filled deposits were then set upon this layer of pure clay suggesting a restart of civilization at least in this area.[4]

Many civilizations provide variations to the story of the flood: Babylonians, Chinese, Greek, Roman, American Indians, Peruvians, Hindus, Assyrians, Persians, Indians, and Brazilians, among others (about 70 in all).[5] These stories suggest common origins. Some scholars claim the flood was localized in Mesopotamia, but Scripture states otherwise: God wanted to destroy all man except Noah (Gen. 6:7-8; 7:1), all animals and birds were saved from extinction (Gen. 7:2), and water was above all mountains (Gen. 7:19).

Until recently, it was commonly believed that the writings of the Old Testament civilizations did not occur until later in Old Testament history, suggesting their early stories were the product of generations upon generations of stories handed down orally until handwriting would be invented long afterward. This thinking denied the possibility that early writings could have been written by eye witnesses: Adam, Enoch, Noah, Shem, Abraham, Isaac, Jacob, etc. Archaeological findings keep presenting evidence that the date of the first writings should be pushed farther back in history.[6] We may learn one day that writing, at least in picture form, dates to antiquity. The Hebrew language, a Semitic language, was developed by about 1,500 B.C.; the Syrians invented an alphabet sometime later.[7] Future findings are sure to enlighten us further on the identity of some, most, or even all of the Old Testament authors. See also the chapter "The History of the Bible" for further discussion.

Enoch, the seventh person on our road map, was a special man of God because of his faith. He did not die but was taken up to Heaven by God (Gen. 5:24; Heb. 11:5). The importance of Enoch in God's Plan is evident if we identify him as one of the two witnesses that God will call forth to prepare for Messiah's second coming (discussed later).

The Flood

The grace of God was on **Noah** (Gen. 6:8), for God made a covenant with him (Gen. 6:18) to keep him safe in the ark and to never again destroy the earth with water (Gen. 9:9-17). Before the flood, mankind lived in perfect harmony with all animals, birds, fish, and insects; after the flood, they would fear man (Gen. 9:2). Noah had many children--see Genesis 10 for the origin of the nations.

Noah was 500 years old when he begat Shem, Ham, and Japheth (Gen. 5:32) even though the actual birth order was Japheth, Shem, and Ham. Shem was listed first because he would carry the blood line to Messiah. Shem was born two years after Japheth in 1558 yfc.

The date of the flood is established as 1656 yfc when Noah was 600 years old (Gen. 7:6; Josephus: Antiquities I, 80-82), and Shem was 100 years old, two years after the flood (Gen. 11:10). These facts establish his birth year as 1558 yfc. From the time of the sons of Shem, Mesopotamia (Iraq today) would become the cradle of civilization spawning the nations of Babylon, Syria, and Assyria, among others.

Shem would be the instrument of God to carry the genealogy from Noah to Abraham along **Chronology Turnpike**. Ham, cursed by Noah for making fun of his nakedness (Gen. 9:21-27), would father the nations of Amorites, Canaanites, and Babylonians, among others (see map 2); all of whom would play important roles in the development of the Hebrew nation. Japheth would become the father of many Caucasian (Gentile) races of Europe and Asia (Gen. 10:2-5), possibly the method by which the early Old Testament stories traveled to all parts of the world. Ham's descendants, from the seed of his son Cush and grandson Nimrod, would become slaves to Japheth's descendants (Gen. 9:26-27). Nimrod would build the Tower of Babel from whence the Babylonian nation would rise (Gen. 10:6-10; 11:9).

Between Arphaxad, son of Shem, and Peleg, son of Eber; we suspect, as mentioned earlier in the "Introduction" and "Preface," gaps in chronology, possibly large gaps as we see noted on our road map. For the sake of continuity and simplicity, we choose to not speculate on any of these possible major gaps on the road map.

Let us look at the chronology road map. Notice the span of 1,056 years from Adam's to Noah's births and that Noah is the tenth significant person in the chronology. Each year-bar along the route represents the birth of the person directly after the bar; e.g., Seth was born in 130 yfc, Jared in 460 yfc, and Lamech in 874 yfc. We are only interested in the span of years from the birth of a person to the time when the next person (son of the previous father) in the genealogy would be born. The chronology progresses from father to son to grandson, etc. In many cases, the later death of significant persons is also noted. For example, Noah was born in 1056 yfc, and his son Shem was born in 1558 yfc to continue the genealogy. Then Noah died in 2006 yfc. This event appears only as a note on the road map. Biblical reference verses are given on the road map for the reader's further verification of the facts. Additional verses will usually be given in this commentary to establish context. Sometimes verses can be meant to be speaking of more than one period of time or event.

Often in these circumstances, the verses will speak of both Old Testament and New Testament events but may also give reference to eschatological events. It is suggested that these verses be read along with this text.

Let us look at the road maps and discuss some of the significant items. On road map 1, we find the continuing chronology of the genealogy that will take us on a journey along Chronology Turnpike to the Messiah. Between Adam and Noah, only Seth and Enoch are of much interest since the Bible says very little about the others.

To prepare for the next chapter on the chronology after Noah, turn to road map 2. We find the dates of the deaths of the persons of Noah's lineage to Abraham plus Sarah, wife of Abraham and mother of Isaac. Some important events are also shown: the era of the destruction of Sodom and Gomorrah, the flood, the covenant with Abram for the building of the Hebrew nation, the covenants with Isaac and Jacob, the era of the Tower of Babel, and the date of the move to Egypt. Notice the square information signs that provide additional information concerning the brothers of Shem, Abraham, Isaac, and Jacob. These brothers became the fathers of many different nations many of which would oppose the Hebrew lineage throughout the ages. Of importance to the future destruction and dispersion of the Jewish nation are:

Ham, brother of Shem—father of the Babylonian Empire, invaders of Judah.

Asshur, brother of Arphaxad—father of the Assyrian Empire, invaders of Israel.

Of importance today are the following races that oppose Israel today:

Ham, brother of Shem—fathered the nation of Egypt.

Ishmael, brother of Isaac—fathered the nation of Arabia.

Let us go back and address the question, "Where did Cain find a wife?" Cain and Abel were the first sons of Adam and Eve. After Cain slew Abel, he objected to his banishment by God (Gen. 4:14) complaining that everyone who found him would kill him. Who were these people since Adam, Eve, and himself were the only humans at that time? We do not know when Cain killed Abel. I suppose Cain could have been referring to the future when more siblings and their children would populate the earth or that the slaying occurred after Adam had more children. Whatever the case, God does not reveal the answer to this trivial question, and we should not waste our time on it.

Perhaps he was looking to the future when his future siblings would populate the earth, and they would marry among themselves and with himself and his children. There was plenty of time for this to happen because of the long lifetimes God provided so the earth could be populated:

Adam lived 930 years
Seth lived 912 years
Enos lived 901 years
Kenan lived 910 years
Mahalalel lived 895 years
Jared lived 962 years
Enoch—n/a
Methuselah lived 969 years
Lamech lived 777 years
Noah lived 950 years.

2

NOAH TO ISRAEL'S MOVE TO EGYPT

(reference road map 2)

Scripture chronology and genealogy are quite precise from creation through Noah to the birth of Nahor's son, **Terah,** in 1878 yfc, and not surprisingly, most if not all chronologists agree. We shall see that the first of seven common points where chronological disagreements occur in this presentation starts at this point in time:

1. Terah's age at Abram's birth.
2. Number of years Israel lived in Egypt.
3. The exodus route.
4. Placement of Joshua's lifetime and the 8 year Syrian servitude.
5. Fitting the judges into their time frame.
6. Fitting the kings into their time frame.
7. Jesus' ancestry.

Throughout the rest of this work, when approaching these controversial periods, the reader will be alerted by a stop sign, , on the road map and in the text.

Terah's age at Abram's Birth. Terah had three sons: **Abram,** Nahor, and Haran (Gen. 11:26) listed in that order. The *Living Bible* states that this occurred up to the time he was 70 years old; in other words, all three sons were born on or before he was 70 years old. The *King James Bible* and the *NLT Bible* state that this occurred when he was 70 years old, meaning he was 70 years old when his first son was born, and the other two sons followed some time later. The *NIV Bible* states that Terah gave birth to the three sons after he was 70 years old. For the same reason that Noah's middle son, Shem (Josephus: Antiquities I, 143), was listed first (Gen. 10:1) because he would carry the blood line to Messiah, so also is Abram, although the youngest, listed first. Therefore, the order of birth would be: Haran, Nahor, and Abram (when Terah was 130 years old). Also, Haran had died before Terah (Gen. 11:28), suggesting that he was the oldest. The KJV, NLT and NIV viewpoints that Terah was older than 70 (130 years actually) when Abram was born is preferred and is justified as follows.

According to Scripture, Terah left Ur of the land of the Chaldees and headed toward Canaan. Early in his journey, Terah settled in the city of Haran of the Chaldees; then Terah died when he was 205 years old (Gen. 11:31-32; Acts 7:4; Josephus: Antiquities I, 152). After Terah's death, God instructed Abram (now age 75) to leave Haran and move to Canaan (Gen. 12:1-5; Josephus: Antiquities I, 154). We are left with several possibilities:

(1) Terah begat Abram at 70 years of age and died at 145 years old (70+75) according to the Living Bible and the Samaritan Pentateuch (detailed later). But we must ignore Genesis 11:32 that gives a lifespan of 205 years. Justification by some scholars for this interpretation cites Abram's surprise when God promised him a son when he was 100 years old (Gen. 17:17)--he wouldn't have been surprised since his father had a son at 130 years.

(2) Terah begat Abram at 130 years of age (60 years after turning 70) and died at 205 years of age (130+75) when Abram was 75 years old. This interpretation, although making it harder to fit later time frames, is preferred because it does not ignore any Scripture. One final note: Flavius Josephus gives Terah's age at Abram's birth as 70 years and his age at his death as 205 years

(1.6.5 Antiquities). This would require that Terah, at 145 years of age, left Haran with Abram at 75 years of age and moved to Canaan and died 60 years later. Since Genesis 11:32 tells us that Terah died in Haran, this would require that we ignore Genesis 12:1, 4, an inappropriate action!

In a nutshell:

	Terah's age	
	At birth of Abram	at his death
Samaritan Pentateuch (a)	70	145
Josephus (Antiquities I, 149, 152) (a)	70	205
Living Bible	70	145
KJV, NLT, NIV Bibles-*my choice*	130	205
(a) nonscriptural		

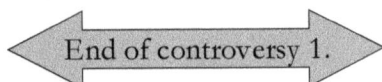

◄ End of controversy 1. ►

God called Abram out of paganism (Gen. 12:1) to become the first patriarch in 2083 yfc, a most important date as we shall see. God told him to move to Canaan, and Abram obeyed without question (Gen. 12:1). Because of his faith (Gen. 15:6; Rom. 4:1-5, 9, 13; Gal. 3:6), God made the **first covenant** with Abram to father a great nation in a promised land (Gen. 12:2, 7; 17:7-8) where his descendants would be His chosen people (Deut. 14:2; 29:13; Psa. 105:6, 43; 106:5). God repeated this promise to Abram a year later (Gen. 13:14-16; 15:18) and also promise him and his descendants (Gal. 3:16-17) an heir (Jesus). In 2107 yfc, God repeated the covenant, this time making it a covenant in which his descendants' parts of the contract would be to obey Him (Gen. 17:9-10; Deut. 28:1-2). In return, they would be God's chosen people and He would provide all their needs because Abram's faith made him righteous (Gen. 15:6; 17:7; Lev. 26:44-46; Judg. 2:1; Rom. 4:3, 13; Gal. 3:6; James 2:21-23). At this time, God changed Abram's name to Abraham (Gen. 17:5) and from hence his descendants would be called Hebrews.

Abraham begat the second patriarch, **Isaac**, in 2108 yfc (Gen. 21:1-5) as God had promised (Gen. 17:15-19) to continue his lineage. Abraham was again blessed after God tested him with the sacrifice of this son, but God halted this sacrifice because of Abraham's faith (Gen. 22:1-2, 10-12, 16-18). This ultimate sacrifice foreshadowed the perfect sacrifice that God would make by giving His only Son for our sins. God has and does give us clues to coming events by often foreshadowing these events. Muslims distort the Bible by identifying Ishmael as the son offered as a sacrifice (Quran 37: 101-102). God repeated or reminded many of their generations afterward of related promises to Moses, David, and Solomon concerning the entering of the Promised Land and the keeping of the royal and blood lines to Messiah (Gen. 17:7; Exod. 6:4; 32:10, 13; Deut. 1:8; 6:10; 30:20; 34:4; 2 Sam. 23:1, 5; 2 Kings 13:23; Psa. 89:3, 28, 34-37; 105:8-11; 132:11-12; Ezek. 16:59-60).

God confirmed His covenant with Abraham, passing it on to Isaac (Gen. 26:1-5) in 2193 yfc. Isaac's brother Ishmael was denied this honor even though he was 13 years older than Isaac. Ishmael married an Egyptian (Gen. 21:21) and would settle in the Wilderness of Paran and become the father of the middle-eastern countries of Arabia and Midian:

```
Abraham:
Hagar (wife)      Keturah (wife)        Sarah (wife)────► Isaac
   │                  │
   ▼                  ▼
Ishmael             Midian────►Midianites (often called Ishmaelites even though Ishmael & Midian
   │                           were half-brothers).  They dwelt between Shur & Kadesh-Barnea
   │                           (Gen. 25:17-18; Judg. 8:22-24; see also Map A)
   │
   └────────► Arabians and Ishmaelites
```

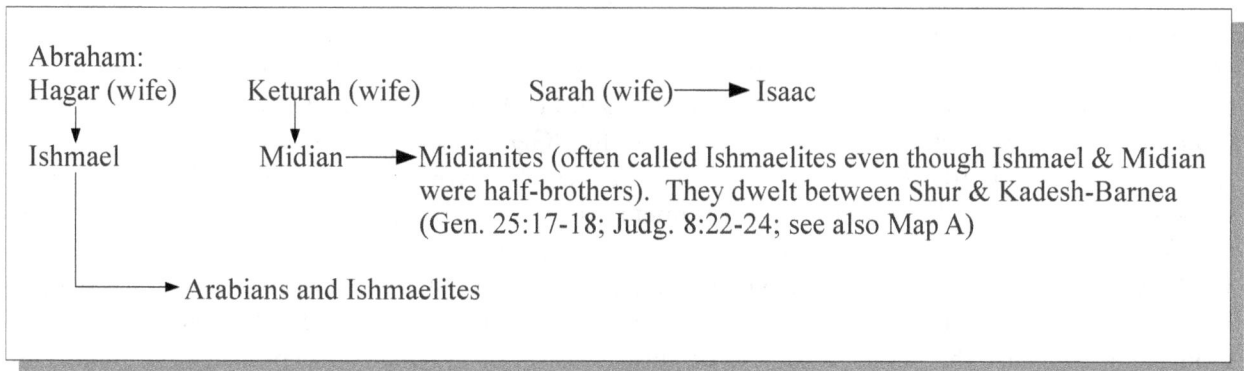

God promised Ishmael that He was going to make him into a great nation (Gen. 16:10; 17:20; 21:14-18), but this was not a covenant. The covenant was reserved for Isaac (Gen. 17:21). This nation, Arabia, although of the same Semitic heritage as the Israelites, was looked down upon by them as an inferior, impure race because Ishmael was born from Sarah's Egyptian maid, Hagar (Gen. 16:8; 21:9; 25:12). This tension exists today as foretold by God (Gen. 16:11-12).

Abraham raised his nephew Lot because Lot's father, Haran, died young (Gen. 11:27-28). Lot moved to Sodom (Gen. 13:12), a wicked city later destroyed (with Gomorrah) by God (Gen. 19:24-29), where only Lot and his two daughters were saved. Lot fathered the eventual nations of Moab (Gen. 19:37; Deut. 2:9) and Ammon (Gen. 19:38), both given to him by God (Deut. 2:9, 19). Moab was located east of the Dead Sea (Salt Sea) and south of the land of the Amorites and north of Edom. Ammon, was located east of the land of the Amorites (see Map A).

In 2168 yfc, Isaac had twin sons **Jacob** and Esau. Jacob, the third Patriarch, would continue the blood line of God's chosen people. Esau, the oldest (Gen. 25:24-26), had the right to his father's birthright and blessing. However, God chose Jacob over Esau even before they were born because He chose to (Mal. 1:2-3; Rom. 9:10-15), and this came true when Esau sold his birthright to Jacob (Gen. 25:27-34), and Jacob tricked Isaac into blessing him instead of Esau (Gen. 27:1-40). We see that Esau sinned because he took his responsibilities lightly and never truly repented although he rued his actions (Heb. 12:16-17). It is very dangerous to put off God's calling and to treat lightly the things of God. Esau would father the nation of Edom, a land given to them by God (Deut. 2:5) in the mountainous region of Mt. Seir and located south of the Dead Sea along the Arabah[8] (Gen. 36:9; Deut. 2:22; Josh. 24:4) (see Map A and Map B).

Esau, who took heathen wives (Gen. 26:34-35), would also become the father of the Amalekites, (Gen. 36:12, 15-16; 1 Chr. 1:34-36) a nomadic people who lived south of Canaan (Num. 13:29) and north of the Gulf of Aqabah and east of the Wilderness of Shur (Gen. 36:12). They would become one of Israel's worst enemies (see Map A).

In 2238 yfc, God repeated the covenant to Jacob when He spoke to him in a dream from a ladder that stretched from the earth to Heaven; it was filled with angels (Gen. 28:10-15; 35:12). Some time later, Jacob was on his way to meet Esau but was fearful of him because he had stolen his birthright and blessing. An angel came and wrestled with Jacob who would not let go until the angel blessed him (Gen. 32:24-26). The angel did bless him and changed his name to Israel (Gen. 32:27-28; 35:10). From this time forward, Jacob's descendants would be called "Israelites."

Israel would have twelve sons (Gen. 35:23-26) and settle in Canaan (Gen. 37:1). Because of jealousy, the eleven brothers of **Joseph** sold him to the Ishmaelites who in turn sold him into slavery to Egypt (Gen. 37:19-28) where he rose to a high position (Gen. 39:1-2; 41:37-44). His interpretation, in 2289 yfc at the age of thirty (Gen. 41:46), of Pharaoh's two dreams of good crops for seven years followed by seven years of famine endeared him to Pharaoh. He was put in charge of the project to save crops during the years of plenty (2289-2296 yfc) to provide for the famine (2296-2303 yfc) (Gen. 41).

Two years into the famine, in 2298 yfc, Israel sent his remaining sons to obtain food in Egypt where they would eventually meet Joseph. He invited them to come to Egypt to live (Gen. 45:6-9; 46:5-7). We can see God's plan being worked out for the preservation of His people even though His chosen Jacob was not always upright as we have seen: he cheated Esau and deceived his father), but God counted Jacob's faith (Heb. 11:21) and prayer life (Gen. 32:9-10). God called the famine for this specific reason (Psa. 105:16-17). God seldom interferes with world events directly. It is His way to work His will through the actions of man, sometimes using wicked persons for His purposes. When faithful people do His will, they are rewarded now and/or in Heaven (Gen.15:1; Matt. 5:12; 6:1; Luke 18:28-30; Heb. 10:35; 11:26) as was Noah, the patriarchs (Joseph the fourth), etc. Israel moved to Egypt in 2298 yfc when he was 130 years old (Gen. 47:7-9) and lived there for 17 years (Gen. 47:28). God seems to realize that Jacob needed to be shown his sin of moving to Egypt instead of putting his trust in Him. Joseph fathered sons Ephraim and Manasseh while in Egypt. Although Joseph would not head a tribe as did his brothers, his two sons would. Joseph demonstrated his faith in God's plan for the nation of Israel when he gave instructions to carry his bones with them when they would leave Egypt (Gen. 50:25).

3

EGYPTIAN LIFE AND THE EXODUS

(reference road map 3)

Egypt, located south of the Mediterranean Sea, was a nation formed from tribes around 3100 B.C. through battles and conquests. Leaders (pharaohs) gained power and came to be seen as humans dwelt within by the sun god Ra (or Re). Because the pharaohs of the time were of Semitic descent, they treated the Israelites as equals at first, allowing them their own land and worship practices. Egyptians practiced polytheism, a worship of many gods: birds, animals, reptiles, etc. They believed in an afterlife and embraced a story of creation. After Israel grew in size, the Egyptians became worried about their threat and therefore enslaved them, forcing them into long hours of strenuous work.

②   **Number of years Israel lived in Egypt.** From reading Exodus 12:40-41 alone, one might conclude that Israel was in Egypt for 430 years. However, Galatians 3:16-17 (and also agreeing with Josephus [Antiquities II, 318]) and with the Samaritan Pentateuch and Septuagint, detailed later), specifies that the 430 years originated from the time (1894 B.C./2083 yfc) Abram moved to Canaan as God had instructed. The 430 years ended when Israel left Egypt, and God gave the Ten Commandments in the same year (1464 B.C./2513 yfc). Also, Genesis 15:5-7, 13-16 says that God told Abram that his descendants would live 400 (430 rounded off) years (4 generations) in a foreign land, first in Canaan and then in Egypt. Note that Abram's home land was Ur (Gen. 11:27-31).

According to Jewish tradition and Josephus (Antiquities II, 318), Israel was in Egypt for 215 years, arriving there in 2298 yfc. Genesis 15:13-16 could also refer to the times Israel would be in servitude: to Egypt (215 years), Babylon (70 years), and the 111 total years they were under foreign rule during the Judges rule (8+18+20+7+40+18), a total of 396 years, rounded off to 400. Note that Genesis 15:16 tells of the Amorite nations finally being punished for their iniquities against Israel. Later, during the Judges reign, we will see that one of these nations living in the Amorite territory, Ammon, was defeated by Jephthah in 2878 yfc ending its 18 year reign of the eastern part of Israel. That eighteen year Ammonite rule coincided with the 40 year Philistine occupation in the western part of the nation of Israel. This 40 year rule would end in 2900 yfc, the 396th year of occupations by foreign nations. Refer to chapter 4 for details.

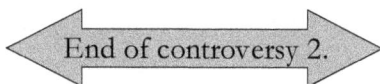

◄ End of controversy 2. ►

The next part of God's plan was to rescue His people from their slavery in Egypt by calling on Moses, from the tribe of Levi, to physically deliver them from bondage (Exod. 2-13) just as Christ would later do, only in a spiritual sense. The journey from Egypt to the Promised Land should have taken less than a year to complete. Instead, it took 40 years because of the Israelites' disobedience to God. Let us relive this journey. At certain points, a time note will indicate the length of time from leaving Egypt.

The Exodus (reference Map A and Map B)

- March 31/April 1 (1464 B.C.) or the first Jewish month, Abib (or Nisan) 15: Leave Egypt from Ramses to Succoth (Exod. 12:37, 40-41; Num. 33:3-5) and on to Etham (Exod. 13:20).

- Travel to the Red Sea, more likely the Suez Canal area of today (Exod. 13:18). Historians generally agree on at least three possible or logical crossing points, all being at some point along the present day Suez Canal or the northern tip of the Gulf of Suez. Some would have Israel taking the north-most crossing point, an easterly route south of the Mediterranean Sea, a more direct and logical route. However, this account is not according to Scripture and is rejected in favor of the southern route taken from one of the three crossing points (Exod. 13:17-18). God parts the sea and Israel crosses (Exod. 14:21-27; Num. 33:8).

- At the Wilderness of Shur (Exod. 15:22), northeastern border of Egypt. At Marah, Moses cures the bitter waters (Exod. 15:22-25; Num. 33:8).

- At Elim (Exod. 15:27; Num. 33:9).

- At the Wilderness of Shin (Sin) (May 1, two months). God provides manna and quail (Exod. 16:1-15; Num. 33:11). Travel to Dophkah and then to Alush (Num. 33:12-13).

- At Rephidim. Moses provides water by striking a rock with his staff as God commanded (Exod. 17:1-6; Num. 33:14). Amalekites attack but are utterly destroyed (Exod. 17:8-14).

- At Mt. Sinai (Horeb) (about three months) (Exod. 19:1-2; Num. 33:15): the exact location is still unknown. God reminds Israel of the covenant He made with Abraham and makes another covenant with them, the Mosaic (or Sinai) covenant (Exod. 19:3-8). This covenant was different from that with Abraham. The Abraham Covenant was unconditional for him because of his faith--God promised to raise a great nation from him and provide a messiah who would come from his lineage. The Sinai Covenant was conditional with Israel--God would be their king if they would obey Him (Exod. 19:5-6; Deut. 7:12).

  The Ten Commandments and Book of the Law (Pentateuch) are given (Exod. 20:3-17, 23-26; 21:1-24:4; 24:12; 31:18; Deut. 5:1-22) and sealed with the blood of sacrificed animals (Heb. 9:18-25), a precursor to the Lamb of God's once-for-all-times final sacrifice for mankind's redemption, the Final Covenant. Instructions for the tabernacle are given (Exod. 25:8-9; 26:1-27:19). Because Moses is a long time in returning, the people become impatient and convince **Aaron**, brother of Moses, to create a golden calf for them to worship, an indication that they had brought with them from Egypt the idea of idol worship (Exod. 32:1-6). God wants to destroy the nation completely and start over by making Moses' descendants His special people (Exod. 32:7-10), but Moses asks for and receives mercy and forgiveness for the people (Exod. 32:11-14). But God seems to want to cease leading the people Himself, seemingly putting an end to the tabernacle building where He was to live among the people. Instead, He decides to send an angel to lead them (Exod. 32:34; 33:1-3). Through Moses' pleading, God relents and agrees to lead them Himself (Exod. 33:12-17; 34:9-10; 40:34-36).

  The Sinai Covenant is expanded (Exod. 34:10-29): God will lead the Israelites in their conquest of the Promised Land in return for Israel's obedience in driving out all the inhabitants; they should worship only Him, and they must obey all the commands of the Law. Aaron and his family (of the tribe of Levi) are made perpetual priests (Exod. 28:1; Num. 3:10; 25:10-13); the office would be passed down from generation to generation (Exod. 29:29). The tribe of Levi (Levites) is ordained for tabernacle service and as substitutes for the first-born sons of the people because they obeyed God (Exod. 32:26-29; Num. 3:5-13; 8:5-6, 16-19; Deut. 10:8). Instructions to build the Ark of the Covenant are given by God (Exod. 25:10-22).

- 2514 yfc: Still at Mt Sinai, the tabernacle is completed (March 15, 11.5 Months) (Exod. 40:17), and a census is taken (April 15, 12.5 months) (Num. 1:1-2). The Ark will be kept in the tabernacle (Exod. 26:33-34) while Israel camps and be at the head of the column when Israel travels. God provides a cloud to lead them (Exod. 40:38; Num. 9:15-23; 10:34). God commands that daily animal sacrifices be made in the courtyard and presented to God in the Holy Place to cover the sins of the people (Lev. 6-9; Heb. 9:6, 25) and also a yearly animal sacrifice be presented to God in the Holy of Holies (Lev. 16:1-19; Heb. 9:7). Use of this tabernacle was a showcase of the heavenly system (Exod. 30:1, 7-9; Psa. 141:2; Rev. 8:3-5).

- At Taberah (Num. 10:33; 11:1-3, omitted from 33:16) where God provides quail. At Kibroth-hattaavah (Num. 11:33-34; 33:16). At Hazeroth (Num. 11:35; 33:17). These must have been either overnight stays or walk-through areas (Num. 9:17-21; Exod. 40:36-38) since Numbers 10:11-13 makes no mention of it.

- Overnight stays and/or walk-through areas (Num. 33:18-34; Deut. 1:2).

- 2514 yfc: In the Wilderness of Paran (May 5, 13 months) at Ezion-geber (Num. 10:11-12; 12:16; 33:35). Levis are given to God for tabernacle assistance (Num. 18:6). They are not to own any land: God is their inheritance (Num. 18:20).

- 2514 yfc: At Kadesh-barnea (about 90 miles south of Jerusalem) on the borders of the Wilderness of Zin and Wilderness of Paran, south of the Promised Land, Canaan (Num. 13:26; 20:1; 33:36, Deut. 1:19-21). God commands that the people go and possess the land He has given to them, but Israel refuses to enter because they are afraid of the inhabitants (Num. 13:1-33; 14:1-10; Deut. 1:19-32⁹). God promises to allow only **Joshua** and Caleb to enter Canaan because they were willing to attack. The Israelites must wander in the wilderness 40 years (Num. 14:22-24, 30, 33; Deut. 1:34-36) (reference Map B). Moses is also not allowed to enter Canaan because he erred in his leadership (Deut. 1:37; 3:25-26; 4:21).

- Still at Kadesh-barnea. The Israelites change their minds and send an army north to start the conquest of Canaan against God's orders. They are defeated by the Canaanites and Amalekites and chased to Hormah (Num. 14:40-45; Deut. 1:41-44).

- 2514 yfc: The Israelites start their wanderings for 38 years between Kadesh-barnea and Ezion-geber in the area of Mt. Seir, i.e., west side of the Arabah that extended into the Wilderness of Paran (Num. 33–38 years between vv. 36 & 37; Deut. 1:45-46; 2:1, 14) (see Map B).

- 2552 yfc: The people head north back to Kadesh-barnea (About April 15, 39 years) (Num. 20:1) where they do not find water and complain to Moses and Aaron (Num. 20:2-6). Moses and Aaron displease God when Moses strikes a rock with his rod for water instead of speaking to it as God had instructed (Num. 20:7-11). They would not be permitted to enter the Promised Land (Num. 20:12). God also punishes Moses because of the refusal of the people to enter Canaan and probably Aaron because of the golden calf incident (implied). Edom (south of the Dead Sea) and Moab (east of the Dead Sea) refuse Israel's entry through their lands (Num. 20:14-21; Judg. 11:16-17). Moab would later be cursed by God (Deut. 23:3-6).

- 2552 yfc: Israel heads east and then south to Mt. Hor on the west side of Edom (Num. 20:22; 21:4; 33:37). Aaron dies (July 15, 39 years) (Num. 20:25-28; 33:38-39; Deut. 10:6).

- Canaanites hear of the Israeli approach and attack but are defeated (Num. 21:1-3; 33:40). Israel travels south along the Arabah Road toward the Red Sea (actually the Gulf of Aqabah) to go around Edom (Num. 21:4; 33:41-42; Deut. 2:1-7) and then head north through the eastern borders of Edom and Moab. Some accounts have Israel traveling from a route further westward on its northward journey through Edom and toward Moab, a route along the Arabah (on the east side, west side, or through it). This route seems unrealistic because of its close proximity to the recent southern journey from Kadesh-barnea to go around Edom. The chosen route raises the questions: (1) why did not Edom object to this route also as they recently had done when Israel was at Kadesh-barnea? Was it because the eastern border of Edom was less fortified than the western border and thus less defensible? (2) Why did not Israel head north-east from Kadesh-barnea to Moab, a direct route, instead of heading south and then north on a route so close to their previous southern journey? It was because they wanted to evade Edom (Num. 21:4). (3) Why did Edom, only a short time later, allow them to go through their land? Was it because the more easterly route to Moab was less threatening to them and/or they were in an inferior military position there? There is no doubt about which route was taken if the exact locations of Punon, Oboth, and Ije-abarim can be determined.

- Israel travels through Oboth and Ije-abarim to the south side of Brook Zared (Zered) (39 years) (Num. 21:10-12; 33:41-44; Deut. 2:7-8, 14).

- 2552 yfc: The journey continues north across Brook Zared along the eastern border of Moab to across the Arnon River, called Wadi Mojib today (39 years) (Num. 21:13; Deut. 2:24). The Amorites are defeated: King Sihon at Jahaz (Num. 21:21-26; Deut. 2:24-34; Judg. 11:19-22) and King Og of Bashan at Edrei (Num. 21:31-35; Deut. 3:1-10; 4:44-47).

- God shows Moses Canaan from Mt. Nebo, east of the Jordan River (Num. 27:12; Deut. 3:27; 32:48-49) and commissions Joshua to replace him (Deut. 3:28; 31:3, 7).

- On westward to Shittim (Acacia) in the Plains of Moab (east side of the Jordan River opposite Jericho) (Num. 22:1) where Israel defeats King Balak of Moab (Num. 22; 23; 24; 25:1).

- God makes an unconditional covenant (the Promised Land Covenant) with the people to take into the Promised Land. He would love and bless them and deliver the land into their hands, making them into a great nation (Lev. 26:3-13). Their part of the bargain would be: destroy all the inhabitants and their idols and altars, do not worship idols or make sacrifices to them, do not intermarry with the inhabitants, make no covenants, tithe their crops and obey, worship, and love Him (Exod. 23:32-33; 34:12-17; Num. 33:50-53; Deut. 6:10-19; 7:2-5; 8:1, 18; 9:5; 10:12-13; 11:1, 8; 12:1-5, 13; 13:4, 17; 14:22-23; 19:8-9; 20:16-20; 28:1; 29:12-15; 30:18-20; 31:20-23). God foretells that they will not keep the covenant (Deut. 4:25-28; 17:14; 28:36, 46, 49; 29:25-28; 31:15-16, 20) for which they will be punished, but God will still be true to His word. Moses foresees the Jewish dispersion (Deut. 28:64-65).

- Midian (east of Edom) is destroyed because of intermarriages and adultery with the Israelites and idol worship (Num. 25:1-9; 31:1-8). This happened after Balak was defeated since Numbers 31:8 tells of Balaam[10] being killed upon the destruction of Midian. The Midianites had settlements around the Plains of Moab and mixed with the Moabites, Amalekites, and Ishmaelites (Num. 22:1-4; 25:1-6).

- 2553 yfc: Moses dies (Deut. 34:7-8), and Joshua takes command (Deut. 34:9; Josh. 1:1-2). The tribes of Reuben, Gad, and the half tribe of Manasseh settle on the east side of the Jordan River in Amorite territory (Num. 32:1-5, 33; Josh. 13:7-8; 14:3; 20:8). Finally, Israel crosses the Jordan River into the Promised Land and into Jericho (40 years) (Josh. 3:1, 16).

End of controversy 3.

Israel's journey to and arrival in the Promised Land, a land flowing with milk and honey (Deut. 8:7-9), is sometimes compared to man's relationship with God--we must be willing to enter this relationship with Him by faith and let Him lead us into unknown ministries (wander for 40 years and then enter Canaan by faith) in order to receive salvation (rest in Canaan). God would remind the nation of His covenant with their fathers Abraham, Isaac, and Jacob many times before their entry into Canaan (Deut. 1:8; 4:31; 6:23; 7:8; 10:11; 11:9, 21; 26:3, 15; 31:7; 34:4).

As we have seen, God warned Israel to completely drive out the inhabitants and destroy their idols. He knew if they didn't, they would surely mix with them, intermarrying, and eventually worshipping their idols. Israel did sin by worshipping idols, intermarrying with heathens, and not completely driving all the inhabitants out of Canaan for which they were punished (Lev. 26:14-41; Judg. 2:2, 11-14; 3:6-8; 4:1; 6:1; 10:6-9; 13:1; Psa. 106:32-42; Hosea 11:2-7) but not to the point of destroying them (Lev. 26:42-45). God warned that He would make the land desolate because of their sins, and Palestine is for the most part a land of desolation today (Deut. 29:22-27). But we shall see in chapter 18 that the land will be restored to its glory and beyond when Jesus returns to set up His eternal Kingdom on earth.

Canaanite was a general name for all the inhabitants of the land: Canaanites, descendants of Canaan, son of Ham, in the east and in the west; Hivites, Perizzites, Amorites, Jebusites (in Jerusalem, Josh. 15:63), Hittites, six nations in all (Exod. 3:8, 17; Deut. 20:17; Josh. 5:1; 9:1-2; 11:3; 12:7-8) whose territories continually varied. Baal was their principle god and Ashtoreth, his wife, the principal goddess. Baal was a nature god who controlled all the agricultural processes, since agriculture was the main occupation of the people. There were many sub-Baal gods, usually with hyphenated names; their cities were attached to the name Baal. Farming was new to the Israelites: they had been strictly herdsmen. Israel would eventually integrate the worship of Baal into the worship of Yahweh. It would take some time, with the urging of the prophets through the coming Judges period, to recognize that Yahweh also controlled the seasons, soil, rains, etc. However, the Israelites' trust in following the one true god, Yahweh, would waver as we shall see through the judges period and the reigns of kings until apostasy would result as Moses predicted (Deut. 31:29). Baal worship ceremonies consisted of wild orgies and infant sacrifices—why God wanted these heathens destroyed!

God told the Israelites that He would help them drive out the Canaanites, quickly at first (Deut. 9:3) and then slowly (Exod. 23:29-30; Deut. 7:22) so the land would not become barren from overuse and the animals would become too plentiful to control. It was up to Israel to remain faithful to God's leading by not making any peace treaties with the nations and to not allow them to live among them (Exod. 23:32-33; Judg. 2:2) lest they adopt the nations' pagan practices. If they should disobey, they would face severe punishment (Deut. 29:18-23). Israel began by obeying God's instructions. They completely destroyed Jericho (Josh. 6) but sinned when Achan kept some loot for himself instead of letting it go to the tabernacle treasury (Josh. 7:1). Therefore, God let them be defeated by the Amorites at Ai (Josh. 7:2-5). After Israel atoned itself (Josh. 7:10-25), God led them to a mighty victory (Josh. 8).

Next, Israel was tricked by the people of Gibeon into signing a peace treaty—Joshua failed to inquire of God (Josh. 9). God did not count this against them after they went back to obeying Him by exterminating all the other peoples (Josh. 11:16-19). It took Israel, led by Joshua, six years to conquer the land of Canaan (Josh. 14:7, 10; Acts 13:19) in 2559 yfc. This period of six years of wars is determined from Joshua 14:7 where we find Caleb was one of the spies sent out in 2514 yfc to check the Promised Land. Then 45 years later, (vv. 10-12) Canaan was conquered in 2559 yfc and Caleb asked for his portion of land. The conquest was accomplished by fighting the central campaign around Jericho first, as just previously mentioned, probably to split the land in half. Then the southern campaign was waged (Josh. 9) and finally the northern campaign (Josh. 11). God gave instructions on the division of the land among the twelve tribes (Josh. 13:7-33; 14:1-5). The tribe of Judah inherited the southern border (Josh. 15:1-12). The tribe of Simeon was given land inside the southern border of Judah (Josh. 19:1-9) and would play only a small role in Jewish history. This insignificant inheritance was probably punishment for the time the tribe of Simeon took vengeance on the village of Shechem for the rape of Dinah (Gen. 34).

The land of Canaan included what many today call Palestine and Syria rather than the small tract of land actually inhabited by the Canaanites. But Israel had disobeyed God by not driving out all the inhabitants of Canaan (Judg. 2:2) whereby God rescinded his offer to help them do so (Judg. 2:3). After Joshua's death in 1399 B.C. (Judg. 2:8), Israel would experience twenty years (some say 1-25 years) of peace. God had promised to give them rest from their wars (Josh. 22:4). During Joshua's and the elders' lifetimes, including the rest period, Israel obeyed God (Josh. 24:31; Judg. 2:7-9). After their deaths, Israel began to sin (Judg. 2:10-14) and disobey God by not completely destroying the rest of the Canaanite nations (Judg. 1:21-36; 3:5-7). The Israelites would be conquered by the Syrians, descendants of Aram (Gen. 10:22), Shem's oldest son, because of their sins (Judg. 3:8).

④ **Placement of Joshua's lifetime and the 8 year Syrian servitude.** There exists differing views of these two periods. Let's review some Scripture references before we decide:

- Joshua was an adult before the 40 years of wandering began (Num. 13:1-3, 16).
- Joshua succeeded Moses after the 40 year wandering ended (Josh. 1:1-2).
- Joshua was an old man before the conquest of Canaan was complete (Josh. 13:1-7). Josephus says he was 85 years old when Moses died. Israel finally conquered Canaan and had rest (Josh. 22:4).
- Joshua lived a long time, to a very old age (Josh. 23:1-2), after conquering Canaan and warned Israel that God would not protect them from their enemies if they mixed with heathens and worshipped their gods (Josh. 23:6-13).
- Israel obeyed God throughout Joshua's lifetime while living among their enemies in Canaan (Judg. 3:1-5) and continued to do so until all the elders that witnessed God's miraculous deliverance of Canaan had died (Josh. 24:31; Judg. 2:7).
- Joshua lived 110 years (Josh. 24:29; Judg. 2:8).
- After the elders died, Israel stopped following God (Judg. 2:10-13), so He delivered them to their enemies, (Judg. 2:14; 3:6-8) the Syrians.

From these facts and in conclusion, Joshua lived a long time during the period of peace that followed the conquest of Canaan (about nineteen years). Then followed about a year during which the last of the elders died, all during the time when Israel obeyed God. Only when they stopped obeying Him did He let them be sold into servitude to the Syrians,[11] worshippers of Baal, a common god to them. The Syrian servitude could not have occurred during Joshua's lifetime or the elders' lifetimes since they were obeying God. Some chronologies insert a short period of rest with Joshua dying after the Syrian servitude. Scripture says no to this idea, having the Syrian servitude occur after Joshua's lifetime--Joshua 24:31 and Judges 2:6-8 would need to be ignored. Finally, don't confuse Joshua 14:10 as a basis for establishing Joshua's birth. This verse is being spoken by Caleb, not Joshua.

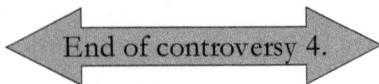

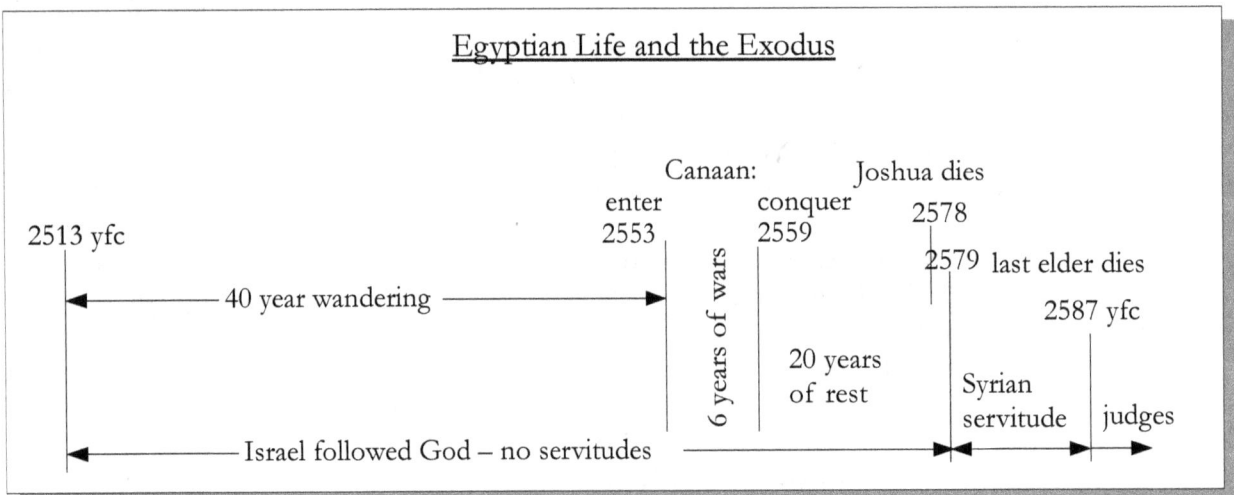

End of controversy 4.

Egyptian Life and the Exodus

2513 yfc

40 year wandering

Canaan: enter 2553

6 years of wars

Canaan: conquer 2559

20 years of rest

Joshua dies 2578

2579 last elder dies

2587 yfc

Syrian servitude

judges

Israel followed God – no servitudes

4

THE YEARS WHEN JUDGES REIGNED

(reference road map 3)

As foretold by God, He would send judges (military and spiritual leaders) who He would lead by the Holy Spirit (Judg. 3:9-10; 6:34; 11:29; 13:24-25; 14:5-6) to rescue His people time and again from their enemies only to have them revert back to disobedience (Judg. 2:15-20). Once a judge delivered them from their enemies, they remained free until that judge died (Judg. 2:18). The period of time that judges reigned is quite controversial.

5 **Fitting the judges into the time frame** Acts 13:17-20 states that judges reigned for about 450 years until Samuel. This period of time would be impossible to fit into the timetable even if we consider Joshua as a judge. We know from 1 Kings 6:1 and as shown on road map 3: from 2993 yfc minus 2513 yfc, that Solomon built the temple in his fourth year of reign, 480 years after the exodus. The conservative calculation for the period of the judges would be:

480 years, exodus to start of temple building by Solomon	
-40 " wandering in the wilderness	
-80 " reigns of Saul and David	
- 4 " of Solomon's 1st 4 years	
356 years of judges rule	

The only way to squeeze 450 years into 356 years is to assume major overlaps of reigns. Scripture might hint at some overlaps but not of this magnitude.

I believe a more plausible interpretation of Acts 13:17-20 comes from most English translations from the Greek text: the NASB, NIV, RSV, ESV, and all Catholic bibles: these interpretations place the 450 years not near the end of v. 20 as given but in v. 19 or at the beginning of v. 20. This placement identifies the 450 years as that period of time from which God made His covenant with Abram in 2107 yfc to the time (2559 yfc) when Israel completed the conquest of Canaan, divided the land, and began their rest from war--452 years actually (see road maps 2 & 3). Then God gave the people judges until Samuel.

The period of the Judges started after the eight year Syrian servitude in 2587 yfc (Judg. 2:13-16; 3:8-9) when the first judge, Othniel, delivered them. The end of this period would come 360 years later in 2947 yfc (derived from the start of the kings rule in 2909 yfc) with the death of the last judge, Samuel (1 Sam. 25:1). Samuel's death must precede King Saul's because 1 Samuel 7:13 says the Philistines did not invade Israel again during Samuel's rule: the Philistines attacked Israel shortly after Samuel died (1 Sam. 28:1-3), and Saul was killed about two years later in that war (1 Sam. 31:6). Thus, Samuel would rule 38 years into Saul's political reign of 40 years (see road map 3).

The period of the Judges' reign must now fit into the time frame: end of the Syrian servitude in 2587 yfc to Samuel's death in 2947 yfc--360 years. If we are to take literally the given lengths of reigns in Scripture, then some overlapping of reigns will be necessary or some of the reigns, especially the 80 year and three 40 year reigns, must be taken figuratively since the number 40 is sometimes used in Scripture as a round number to depict a generation. The exact fit of the reigns of Samson, Samuel,

Deborah and Eli are also open to debate. From the information given in Scripture plus some logical assumptions, let us follow this history of the judges (all years are yfc):

2587–**Othniel** (1st judge) frees Israel from the Syrians (Mesopotamians) and rules for 40 years (Judg. 3:9-11). The Israelites had begun marrying into pagan families and worshipping their gods shortly after Joshua's death resulting in the Syrian servitude.

2627–Moab servitude of eighteen years begins (Judg. 3:12-14) because Israel once again sins.

2645–**Ehud** rescues Israel from Moab (Judg. 3:15) and begins his 80 year reign (Judg. 3:30).

2725–**Shamgar** begins a very short reign (Judg. 3:31). Israel again does evil (Judg. 4:1) so God delivers them to the Canaanites (Judg. 4:2; 5:6-7).

2725–**Deborah** begins her 40 year reign. A 20 years servitude to Canaan begins (Judg. 4:3-4) while Israel is at peace (no wars) during her reign (Judg. 5:31). Another possibility is that the 20 year servitude occurred before Deborah's reign (2725-2745), but this would require her 40 year reign to follow (2745-2785), and more overlapping of reigns would be required later. Verse 4 contains the critical information for making a determination of the two possibilities: Deborah judged Israel <u>during</u> or <u>after</u> the 20 year period of servitude to Canaan. We have chosen the former.

2745–Deborah recruits **Barak,** her military leader, to free Israel (Judg. 4:6, 10-24).

2765–Again Israel sins by worshipping other gods, so God lets them be harassed by the Midianites, Amalekites, and Arabians for seven years during which time they will be in servitude (Judg. 6:1-3).

2772–**Gideon** frees Israel from the Midianite captivity and begins a 40 year reign (Judg. 6:13-16; 8:28). The tribe of Ephraim becomes jealous of Gideon's defeat of their oppressors without being asked for their help (Judg. 8:1).

2812–**Abimelech** begins a three year reign (Judg. 9:1-6, 21-23, 54). The reference in v. 6 of Abimelech being made king probably is a precursor of the coming kings' rule.

2815–**Tola** begins a 23 year reign (Judg. 10:1-2).

2838–**Jair** begins a 22 year reign (Judg. 10:3).

2839 about–**Eli**, more notably a priest, begins a 40 year co-reign (1 Sam. 4:15, 18).

2860–A Philistine servitude of 40 years begins. The Philistines were a seafaring people probably from the area of Greece on the northern shore of the Mediterranean Sea. They were a pagan people (chief god was Dagon) who arrived in the Holy Land about the time of the Israelites. The Philistines had control in the area west of the Jordan River & Dead Sea (Judg. 10:6-8; 13:1; 1 Sam. 4:1). An Ammonite servitude of eighteen years begins in the area east of the Jordan River & Dead Sea (Judg. 10:7-9). This is the year that Jephthah (next judge) rebukes the Ammonite claim to the land taken from King Sihon 300 years earlier (Judg. 11:12-26). There is no conclusive evidence that the eastern and western captivities were coincidental. An equal argument could have the eighteen year eastern captivity start in 2860 yfc as above and the 40 year western captivity occurring later during Samson's rule. This scenario would require extensive overlapping of later judges' reigns and later occupations or a shortening of some other event(s) such as assigning 145 years for Terah's age instead of 205 (see stop sign #1). The Philistines probably took control of the area of the Holy Land at the southwestern border of Israel off the east coast of the Mediterranean Sea. The Ammonites, located along Israel's eastern border, probably controlled that area east of the Jordan River and parts of Benjamin, Ephraim, and Judah on the west.

2878–**Jephthah** frees Israel from the Ammonites in the <u>east</u> and begins a six year reign (Judg. 12:7). The tribe of Ephraim becomes jealous of Jephthah for not asking for their aid in the battles with the Ammonites (Judg. 12:1). This attitude would later bring war between them: Jephthah's defeat of Ephraim would weaken them considerably so they never would regain their stature after the future time of King David. Ephraim's attitude would later help precipitate the differences between tribes in the north and those in the south that would result in the split of the kingdom. The priesthood is taken from Aaron's lineage by God and given to Samuel, another Levite, because of Eli's and his sons' sins (1 Sam. 2:22-24, 27, 30-36).

2879–**Samson** begins a 20 year reign in the west during the Philistine occupation (Judg. 15:20; 16:30-31). He will be the first Hebrew to voluntarily die for his people. His death is possibly a foreshadowing of, although imperfect example of, Christ's destiny to die for the people. Eli dies (1 Sam. 4:1, 15-18), and Israel brings the Ark from Shiloh to Ebenezer where it is taken by the Philistines for seven months, first to Ashdod, then to Gath, then to Ekron (1 Sam. 4:3-5, 17-22; 5:1, 8, 10; 6:1).

2880–The Ark is sent back to Israel at Beth-shemesh because of the Ekronites' fear of God's wrath (1 Sam. 5:10-12; 6:2, 13). But God smites 50,070 (70 by Josephus[12] and some Hebrew manuscripts) Israelites because they looked into the Ark (1 Sam. 6: 19). Because the people of Beth-shemesh felt inadequate with the Ark, they sent it to Kirjath-jearim (or Baalah or Baale) of Judah (1 Sam. 6:20-21; 7:1).

2884–**Ibzan** succeeds Jephthah in the east and begins a seven year reign (Judg. 12:8-10).

2891–**Elon** succeeds Ibzan in the east and begins a ten year reign (Judg. 12:11-12), probably a one or two year co-reign with Samuel (his successor) in his tenth year.

2899–Samson dies (Judg. 15:20).

2900–The Ark has been in Israel at Kirjath-jearim for twenty years, when **Samuel** begins his 47 year reign over all Israel (east and west) after the Philistine occupation ends (1 Sam. 7:1-2, 6; 12:11). Although he was mostly a spiritual leader and prophet (Acts 3:24), he also performed a judges' duties for which many give him that title. He did not act as a military leader as did the previous judges. He was the first to establish schools for the prophets. The Philistines will never again enter and invade Israel during Samuel's rule (1 Sam. 7:13), but they often will skirmish with them outside their borders (1 Sam. 9:16; 10:5; 13:5, 17). The Ark will remain here until David brings it to Jerusalem during his rule (2 Sam. 6:1-12; 1 Chr. 13:5-7, 13-14; 15:1-3), and Solomon places it in the temple he will complete in 977 B.C. (1 Kings 6:37-38; 8:1-4; 2 Chr. 5:1-9).

2901–**Abdon** begins to co-reign for eight years with Samuel (Judg. 12:13-14).

2909–Saul becomes king and will rule for 40 years (1 Sam. 8:5; 10:1; 11:15; Acts 13:21).

2943–Samuel appoints his sons judges (1 Sam. 8:1) who will become corrupt (1 Sam. 8:2-3).

2947–Samuel dies. He was a judge to the end (1 Sam. 7:15; 25:1).

Samuel's death ended the reign of judges, two years before the peace with the Philistines ended when Saul was killed in battle (1 Sam. 28:1-3; 31:6).

◄ End of controversy 5. ►

As we have seen, the period of the Judges was like a roller coaster ride: Israel would sin resulting in God's punishment (servitude to other nations); God would send a judge to lead them to freedom and peace, and then Israel would eventually go back into sin, and the cycle would start all over again. Finally, with the help of Samuel's sons, Israel would sink so low as to completely give up their trust in God and ask for a king like the other nations. So God reluctantly gave them their wish (1 Sam. 8:4-22). He did this because it was better than the low condition they had reached with the judges.

From Israel's entry into Canaan to the coming exile of the Hebrew tribes, God would warn the nation many times of their fate for not obeying Him (Lev. 26:14-33; Deut. 4:23, 27; 11:28; 28:64; 1 Kings 9:6-7; 2 Chr. 24:20; Isa. 39:6; Jer. 5:15; 11:17; Ezek. 5:10, 14-15; 6:9; 12:15; 16:41; 22:15; 39:23; Hos. 1:6; 9:17). However, God in His wisdom provided the Law, rituals, and earthly judges to lead Israel in ways they could understand from their culture so they might learn God's ways through experience and thus submit themselves to His will. This gradual learning process was meant to keep the people from becoming discouraged, but they would still often revert back to the pagan practices they learned from their neighbors. I believe this is why, as we shall see shortly, God will concede Israel a king to lead them, because He knew they would be easier to lead if they had a king to follow like their neighbors—God would work His will through the kings.

A case could also be made for many judges ruling concurrently in different areas of Canaan over a much shorter period on time. Going back to controversy 2, we determined that Israel lived in Egypt 215 years. If we change this time span to 430 years as some chronologists do, we must subtract 215 years from some other period—the rule of judges would seem to be as good a choice as any. That leaves 145 years (360-215) of judges' rule. Of course the placing of the exodus through judges would require a shift on our road map. As one can see, Biblical chronology is not an exact science or even close to it, so I do not claim to be any wiser in this matter than any other chronologist.

Before leaving the Judges, a very brief review of the priesthood seems appropriate here. As mentioned earlier, God gave the priesthood to Aaron's family and promised that his family would be priests forever. He was succeeded in 2553 yfc by his sons, Eleazar and Ithamar (Exod. 6:23-25; Num. 3:1-4; 1 Chr. 24:1-2). The Eleazar line held the title of priest until Eli (from the Ithamar line) became priest and judge in about 2839 yfc. Eli's evil sons were made priests after his death in 2879 yfc. Because of them and Eli's failure to successfully correct them, God told Eli He would eventually end their line of priests and give it to Zadok of the line of Eleazar (1 Sam. 2:12, 30-31; Ezek. 44:15; 48:11). This prophecy would come true when King Solomon would replace Eli's descendant, Abiathar, with Zadok as priest (1 Kings 2:26-27, 35) and all Eli's sons would die in battle (1 Sam. 4:11). After Eli's death, Samuel became the last judge, the first prophet, and was also a priest[13] (1 Sam. 7:9; 9:11-19). Having the priesthood and judgeship temporarily come together in him may have been a foretelling of Christ's coming to permanently and everlastingly fuse these two positions into one (1 Sam. 1:3[14]). Often, Scripture is given in reference to the time when the Scripture was written, and in other instances the Scripture is eschatological--it references events during the last days or is meant for both times. Hebrews 2:17; 3:1; 5:5-6, 10; 7:11-17 refer specifically to Jesus' priesthood.

5

THE YEARS WHEN KINGS RULED

(reference road maps 3-6)

Israel had in **Saul** the king they had asked for. He militarily defended Israel from the Philistines, Amalekites, Ammonites, Moabites, Edomites, and Zobahites (Deut. 25:17-19; 1 Sam. 14:47; 15:2-3, 7). He would be followed by his son David, also a great military leader, who would defeat the Philistines (2 Sam. 5:17-25; 8:1; 21:15-22), Moabites (2 Sam. 8:2), Zobahites (2 Sam. 8:3), Syrians (2 Sam. 8:5; 10:17-18), Ammonites (2 Sam. 8:12; 10:8, 14), Amalekites (2 Sam. 8:12), and Edomites (2 Sam. 8:14). Then David's son, Solomon, would follow, being a peaceful king who would build the temple. This royal line of kings would be led by the Holy Spirit when they would allow God to lead them (1 Sam. 10:10; 16:13). Probably the most controversial task was the placement of the individual kingly rules into the established time frame These rules are accurately given in Scripture with a few exceptions. One problem was determining the span of years involved in the time frame when Kings ruled the Jewish nation. The many reasons that chronologists disagree was discussed at the first five stop signs on our road map. It is not surprising then that there exist so many chronological interpretations. It is important to use Scripture as the primary source of information and only to use other sources to justify or fill in gray areas. Never is Scripture to be contradicted by other sources or to be ignored!

6 Fitting the kings into the time frame

The start of the Kings period can be established from Samuel's death in 2947 yfc. Israel was at peace with the Philistines during Samuel's reign (1 Sam. 7:13). This peace ended shortly after Samuel's death with another Philistine invasion (1 Sam. 28:1-3). Two years later, Saul was killed in battle (1 Sam. 31:6; Josephus: Antiquities VI, 378). Since Saul ruled for 40 years (Acts 13:21), the year 2909 yfc (2949-40) is established as the start of the kings' rule. We can also arrive at the same date by adding 480 years to the exodus date (2513 yfc) giving us the date Solomon began building the temple (2993 yfc) and subtracting 84 years (40 for Saul's rule, 40 for David's rule, four years into Solomon's reign) giving 2909 yfc (1 Kings 6:1; 2 Chr. 3:2) as we saw earlier.

David (2 Sam. 5:3-5; 1 Kings 2:11; 1 Chr. 29:26-27) and **Solomon** (2 Chr. 9:30; 1 Kings 11:42) each ruled for 40 years. After Saul's death in 2949 yfc, it took the ten northern tribes about five years to rid themselves of the influence of the Philistines during which time Israel in the north had no king, while David ruled over only the Judean confederacy in the south (2 Sam. 2:11). In 2954 yfc, Abner, Saul's army commander, made Ish-bosheth, son of Saul, king over the eleven tribes in the north (2 Sam. 2:10) with David still ruling in Judah. Ish-bothesh ruled for two years until he was murdered in 2956 yfc (2 Sam. 4:7-8),[15] then David took control of all Israel, both north and south. He secured Jerusalem and made it the capitol in obedience to God's will (2 Chr. 6:5-6).

Because of David's faith, although he would sin as we shall see later, God made an unconditional covenant with him to provide Israel with an endless line of kings through his blood line (2 Sam. 7:12-16; 1 Kings 11:36; 1 Chr. 17:11-15; 2 Chr. 21:7; Psa. 132:11). God also made a conditional covenant with David's son Solomon and his descendants (1 Kin. 2:4; 1 Chr. 3:10-16) who would break it. God, as we shall see, will eventually take the line of ruling kings away from Solomon's lineage (1

Kings 11:34), but, because of His covenant with David, it will be restored in Messiah through a continuing royal blood line.

During both David's and Solomon's rules, the Egyptian, Babylonian, and Assyrian empires would be in decline only to later reappear. In the year 3029 yfc (948 B.C.) at Solomon's death, the kingdom split (1 Kings 11:1-9, 35-36) as God's first punishment for his sins of marrying foreign women and worshipping their idols (reference Map C). God gave one tribe, Judah, to Solomon's son, Rehoboam, as He promised for David's sake (2 Sam. 19:41-42; 1 Kings 11:11-13, 34, 36). The tribe of Benjamin would also give its allegiance to Rehoboam (2 Sam. 20:1-2) who helped divide the kingdom when he heeded his counselors' poor advice (instead of seeking God's will) to increase the people's workload (1 Kings 12:1-17). These two tribes formed the southern nation of Judah, sometimes referred to as Jerusalem (Zion) its capitol. The other ten tribes were taken from Solomon's family blood line and given to Jeroboam, son of Nebat, an Ephrathite (1 Kings 11:26; 2 Kings 23:15; 2 Chr. 13:6), one of Solomon's servants, a non-family member (1 Kings 11:11, 31). These ten tribes formed the northern nation of Israel, sometimes called Samaria its capitol (made during the rule of Omri). It is an historical fact that the northern nation of Israel was conquered by the Assyrians in 721/722 B.C.[16] This date establishes a span of 226 years in which nineteen kings ruled in the north. Scripture gives enough information to produce a chronology through this period although some overlaps and gaps are necessary. The 2 Chronicles account is concerned only with the ages of the kings when they ascended the throne and their length of rule whereas the 2 Kings account places the kings of Israel relative to the kings of Judah and vice versa.

Several controversial points about the placement of certain kings need to be clarified to justify the reasoning behind their particular placements:

> Hoshea took the throne in (KJV) or after (LB) Jotham's twentieth year (3241 yfc) of sole rule (2 Kings 15:30). Hoshea ascended after (LB) or in (KJV) the twelfth year of Ahaz in 3248 yfc (2 Kings 17:1). A logical explanation of this discrepancy would be to place a seven year gap between Pekah and Hoshea, probably because of the tumult that existed.

> Hezekiah ascended the throne in (KJV) or after (LB) the third year of Hoshea in 3251 yfc (2 Kings 18:1). Either "in" or "after" can be used to satisfy 3251 yfc.

> Azariah co-ruled in Judah nineteen years with Amaziah (3171-3190 yfc) and then began his sole rule in (KJV) or after (LB) the 27th year of Jeroboam II in 3190 yfc (2 Kings 15:1) and ruled 33 more years (3190-3222 yfc). The nineteen year co-rule is necessary to fit in the future ascensions of Zechariah and Menahem in Israel. Zechariah ruled six months in KJV or after (LB) the 38th year of Azariah in 3209 yfc (2 Kin. 15:8): Menahem ascended after (LB) or in (KJV) the 39th year of Azariah in 3210 yfc (2 Kings 15:17).

> Jeroboam II, after an eleven year co-rule (3164-3175 yfc) with Jehoash, began his sole rule in Israel in (KJV & LB) the fifteenth year of Amaziah in 3175 yfc (2 Kings 14:23). He solo ruled for thirty more years to 3205 yfc. Therefore, with the preceding placement of Zechariah, a four year gap (3205-3209 yfc) is necessary to have the aforementioned Scripture verses agree.

We can see God's plan for mankind being worked out according to His will in this developing scenario with the Israelite nation. Our road map shows the two divided nations of Israel and Judah taking separate routes. Looking ahead, we will see that the southern kingdom of Judah would sometime please God, while the northern kingdom of Israel angered God continuously; none of their kings would try to eliminate idol worship. The priests and Levites would flee from Israel to escape the persecutions of Jeroboam (2 Chr. 11:13-16), and Israel would never worship in Jerusalem again. In order to appreciate the different paths these two nations would take, we offer a brief evaluation of the rule of each king. Reference Map C for the split kingdom.

Israel (mixed heathen blood line):

Jeroboam I: Set up idol worship in his kingdom, probably to discourage his people from going to

Jerusalem to worship and appointed evil men as priests (1 Kings 12:28-30; 13:33; 14:16; 15:30). God foretold his sons' deaths (1 Kings 14:10-11) and they did die (1 Kings 15:25-29).

Nadab: Continued his father's sins (1 Kings 15:25-26).

Baasha: Killed Nadab and all Jeroboam's family (1 Kings 15:27-29) and led the people into idol worship for which he was punished by God (1 Kings 16:1-4, 12-13).

Elah: Same as his father Baasha (1 Kings 16:12-13).

Zimri: Killed Elah and his family (1 Kings 16:9-12) and led the people into idol worship (1 Kings 16:18-19).[17]

Omri: Led the people into idol worship (1 Kings 16:25-26).

Ahab: Same as Omri (1 Kings 16:30-33; 21:26). Had Naboth killed (1 Kings 21:1-16).

Ahaziah: Led the people into idol worship (1 Kings 22:51-53; 2 Kings 1:16).

Jehoram (Joram): Led the people into idol worship (2 Kings 3:1-3).

Jehu: Killed Joram of Israel (2 Kings 9:24) and Ahaziah of Judah (2 Kings 9:27) and worshipped idols (2 Kings 10:31).

Jehoahaz: Led the people into idol worship (2 Kings 13:1-2).

Jehoash (Joash): Led the people into idol worship (2 Kings 13:10-11).

Jeroboam II: Led the people into idol worship (2 Kings 14:23-24).

Zechariah: Led the people into idol worship (2 Kings 15:8-9).

Shallum: Killed Zechariah (2 kings 15:10).

Menahem: Killed Shallum and destroyed the city of Tiphsah and all its inhabitants (2 Kings 15:14, 16) and led the people into idol worship (2 Kings 15:18).

Pekahiah: Led the people into idol worship (2 Kings 15:23-24).

Pekah: Killed Pekahiah (2 kings 15:25) and led the people into idol worship (2 Kings 15:28).

Hoshea: Killed Pekah (2 kings 15:30) and led the people into idol worship (2 Kings 17:6-7).

<u>Judah</u> (descendants of Solomon, 1 Chr. 3:10-16):

Rehoboam: Practiced idol worship and moral sins (1 Kings 14:21-24), showed his self-will by fortifying his kingdom (2 Chr. 11:5-12) instead of trusting God, married many wives (2 Chr. 11:18-21), and built shrines to the idols in the hills (1 Kings 14:23).

Abijam: Same as Rehoboam (1 Kings 15:1-3).

Asa: Morally good. Destroyed the pagan altars and idols but failed to remove the shrines in the hills (1 Kings 15:9-15; 2 Chr. 14:2-5; 15:8).

Jehoshaphat: Obeyed God and led Judah back from apostasy but didn't destroy the idol shrines (1 Kings 22:42-43, 46; 2 Chr. 17:3-4; 20:32-33).

Jehoram: Led the people into idol worship (2 Kings 8:16-18) and killed all his brothers and many leaders (2 Chr. 21:4). He was married to Athaliah.

Ahaziah (Jehoahaz): Was evil (2 Kings 8:26-27; 2 Chr. 22:2-4). He was the only surviving son of Jehoram & Athaliah.

Athaliah: Killed all the children of her son, Ahaziah (her grandchildren) except for Joash (2 Kings 11:1-3) and led the people into idol worship (2 Kings 11:13, 16, 18).

Jehoash (Joash): Mostly good but didn't destroy the idol shrines (2 Kings 12:2-3; 2 Chr. 24:1-2). He was the son of Ahaziah.

Amaziah: Mostly good but didn't destroy the idol shrines, bought back idols from war, and did not always act from a righteous heart (2 Kings 14:1-4; 2 Chr. 25:1-2, 14).

Azariah (or Uzziah): Mostly good but didn't destroy the idol shrines (2 Kings 15:1-4; 2 Chr. 26:3-4). Entered the Holy of Holies and burned incense on the altar (2 Chr. 26:16-19).

Jotham: Pleased God but didn't destroy the idol shrines (2 Kings 15:32-35; 2 Chr. 27:1-2).

Ahaz: Led the people into idol worship and sacrificed his children to idols (2 Kings 16:2-4). He had a heathen (Assyrian) altar built (2 Kings 16:10-14; 2 Chr. 28:1-4).

Hezekiah: Removed shrines to the idols and obeyed God (2 Kings 18:1-7; 2 Chr. 29:1-2; 31:1).

He repaired the temple and reorganized the Levis and rites (2 Chr. 29:3-5, 21, 25-26).

Manasseh: Rebuilt shrines and altars to the idols in the temple, sacrificed his children, practiced magic and the occult (2 Kings 21:1-7), and committed many murders (2 Kings 21:16; 2 Chr. 33:1-7). His was the most evil rule and resulted in God's first indictment against Judah with the foretelling of the Babylon invasion that He would permit.

Amon: Led the people into idol worship (2 Kings 21:19-22; 2 Chr. 33:21-23).

Josiah: Pleased God and repaired the temple (2 Kings 22:1-6; 2 Chr. 34:8-13). He led Judah to repentance, postponing their destruction (2 Kings 22:18-20), and destroyed all traces of idol worship (2 Kings 23:4-15; 2 Chr. 34:1-7).

Jehoahaz (Shallum): The son of Josiah (1 Chr. 3:15). His was an evil rule (2 Kings 23:31-32).

Jehoiakim: Puppet king of Egyptian Pharaoh Neco. His was an evil rule (2 Kings 23:36-37; 2 Chr. 36:5; Jer. 26:20-23). He burned the scroll containing God's warning of the coming Babylonian invasion (Jer. 36:29). For this act, God would end the line of kings sitting on the throne after his eleven year rule (Jer. 36:30). He was a son of Josiah (1 Chr. 3:15).

Jehoiachin (Jechoniah /Coniah): His was an evil rule (2 Chr. 36:9). Although he was a son of Jehoiakim (Jer. 22:24), he was considered an illegitimate king (Jer. 36:30; 37:1), and his son would never sit on the throne (Jer. 22:24-30).

Zedekiah: The last son of Josiah (1 Chr. 3:15). He refused to listen to Jeremiah's message from God instructing him not to resist the Babylonians (2 Chr. 36:11-12; Jer. 32:1-5; 37:1-2). He was appointed king of Judah by Babylon—not anointed by God (2 Kings 24:17; 1 Chr. 3:15).

We can see how the nation of Israel was not committed to God; not one of their nineteen kings was righteous. They were idol worshippers and murderers their entire existence. Their fate was predetermined by Solomon's sins, and they would head down the dead-end street to destruction in 721 B.C. when they would be invaded and carried into exile by the **Assyrians** (2 Kings 18:9-12) led by King Shalmaneser, as God had warned (Amos 6:14; 9:8-9). The Assyrians (with Babylon, Iraq today) originated in the upper Mesopotamian plain around 3000-2500 B.C.[18] and rose to world power about 744 B.C.,[19] their chief god being Ashur. In 734 B.C., Israel would unite with Syria to fight the threat of Assyrian expansion. Israel sought the aid of Judah, but Judah sought help from Assyria who would defeat Syria and then Israel in 721 B.C. (see Map D). A lot of speculation, nothing conclusive, has been found to explain the final destiny of the ten lost northern tribes. We do know that they intermixed with the Assyrians and other surrounding peoples, some of them evolving into the Samaritans (discussed later). Speculation and fact has these tribes being dispersed throughout Assyria, Chaldea, Egypt, Media, and Palestine and eventually migrating throughout Europe and Asia and eventually the whole world. It is not unreasonable to imagine that some of the Israelites would return from their exile with their Judean brothers to Jerusalem after the future Babylon exile ended. However, many verses in Scripture tell of the ultimate return of all the united nation of Israel to the new Jerusalem in the Promised Land at the end of the world as it is today (Jer. 23:8; 30:3, 10; 31:4-10; 32:36-40; 33:7; Hos. 3:4-5; Zech. 10:6, 9-10). The final dispensation of the twelve tribes would have the greatest number going to Babylon, Syria and Egypt as God had promised to save a remnant of the Jews (Ezek. 5:10; 6:8; 11:13-16; 14:22).

We are now ready to present the rationale behind the placement of the many kings into our time frame. We know for sure that King Jehu of Israel and Queen Athaliah of Judah ascended to their thrones in the same year, 861 B.C., because Jehu killed both of their predecessors at about the same time (2 Kings 9:24, 27; 2 Chr. 22:9). The relationship of the exile of the northern nation of Israel in 721 B.C. to the chronology of the Judah kings is paramount. Hoshea, the last Israel king, ruled for nine years (2 Kings 17:1), ascending to the throne in 729 B.C. (721+8) during the twelfth year of Ahaz's rule in Judah. This gives us a starting point for the Judah kingly chronology. However, according to how one chooses to account for a few confusing or vague scriptural situations, some co-rules are required. But 2 Kings 15:30 has Hoshea seemingly ascending seven years earlier, in 736 B.C., in the twentieth year of Jotham's rule in Judah. This suggests that, since he killed Pekah for the throne, that tumult or in-fighting occurred for these seven years (736-729 B.C.), thus the gap in the rules between Pekah and Hoshea. Also in 2 Kings 15:30, 33, only three verses apart, gives Jotham's rule as twenty years and sixteen years respectively. This is explained by his 4/5 year co-rule with Ahaz (741-736 B.C.). Points of reference are given here on the road map as quick reference notes to show the position of the kings relative to their peers.

Much research through various Bible versions and scholarly writings has been necessary to answer some seeming vagueness in Scripture. The most glaring example of vagueness occurs in the verses concerning the rule of Jeroboam II. In 2 Kings 14:23, we are told he ascended the throne in the fifteenth year of the rule of Amaziah of Judah. In 2 Kings 15:1-2 we learn that King Azariah (or Uzziah) of Judah ascended the throne in the 27th year of Jeroboam's rule. Since Azariah's rule supposedly followed the 29 year rule of Amaziah, then Amaziah would have ascended the throne in Jeroboam's fourteenth year (29-15) not his 27th year. This information results in a thirteen year difference, actually eleven according to ascension customs (see the "Introduction"). One possibility is to introduce an eleven year gap between the Judah kings. This choice does not work well within the time period allocated to the ensuing kings. There is no indication in Scripture of any wars or power struggles occurring at that time. A more likely scenario is to have Jeroboam II ascending in the fifteenth year of Amaziah's rule (3175 yfc) to satisfy 2 Kings 14:23 and co-ruling with Joash for eleven years before (a total of 52 years) to satisfy 2 Kings 15:1-2 where Azariah begins his solo rule in Judah for 33 years. This necessitates his nineteen year co-rule with Amaziah. We see also that Jehoash (Joash) also co-ruled for two years in Israel with Jehoahaz to satisfy 2 Kings 14:1. Jeroboam II's 41 year rule is assumed to have started the year he started his co-rule with Jehoash in 3164 yfc as has been the practice when co-rules exist. This choice produces a four year gap before the next king, Zechariah (or Zachariah), the explanation being that Israel was in turmoil after Jeroboam II's death and a power struggle ensued (2 Kings 15:10-15). Almost as likely a possibility (in my opinion) would be to date Jeroboam II's rule as starting when he began his solo rule in 3175 yfc. This choice would result in co-rules with Zechariah, Shallum and Menahem, but this has not been the practice when dealing with co-rules. We must remind ourselves again that scriptural writers were not so much concerned with chronologies and genealogies as with revealing God's plan for our salvation.

It was with great difficulty that it became necessary to include two gaps in the Israel kingship, but they seem to be the best answer to the problem of trying to agree with Scripture while fitting the rules into the allotted time frame. Keeping in mind the different dating systems used in Judah and Israel at different periods in history, I have taken a literal interpretation of the dating records given in Scripture so they agree with the "points of reference" given in Scripture (see the road maps). Although the existence of gaps seems to be an assumption on my part, it is highly likely that since Pekah was killed by pro-Assyrian forces in Israel and the Assyrians were constant threats during the gap (736-729 B.C.), it took seven years to overcome the chaos before Hoshea took the throne (2 Kings 16:1-17:1). Therefore, I will leave the gaps as such rather than to speculate since I have faith that the end result (agreement with fixed, known dates) has been achieved, i.e., the placing of the Assyrian and Babylonian exiles.

Now that the year of Hoshea's ascension has been established as 729 B.C., the rest of the Judah kings must fit the 143 years remaining to the exile of Judah to Babylon in 586 B.C., an historical fact.

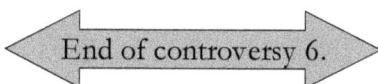

⬅ End of controversy 6. ➡

With the exile of Israel, the survival of the Israelite nation would rest with the nation of Judah, inheritor of the kingly (royal) line and blood line from Rehoboam, grandson of David, for David's sake. As we have seen, the most fatal sin of these kings was their failure to completely destroy the shrines (in the hills) to the idols (Deut. 12:2-3). This condition provided the opportunity for idol worship and the temptation to intermarry with heathens. God never accepts sin although sin is often reported in scripture. Judah had steadily been abandoning worship of only Yahweh[20] who had delivered them so many times. Assyria had continued to be a threat to Judah, but in 712 B.C., God delivered them from their oppressors. I give this date so it agrees with Scripture--the deliverance occurred in the fourteenth year of Hezekiah (2 Kin.18:13; 2 Chr. 32:1; Isa. 36:1) even though many of the historical works say 701 B.C.

The drifting toward polytheism reached its peak with the rule of King Manasseh but would be rectified by King Josiah who would lead a revival in Judah to repentance as foretold centuries before in 1 Kings 13:2. In 622 B.C., a scroll was found with the writings of the "Book of the Law" (2 Kings 22:3-8; 2 Chr. 34:8, 14). It had been several-to-many generations since the people, led by their kings, had been reading God's Word, for the discovery came to them as a surprise (2 Kings 22:12-14). Unlike so many generations before, the people repented and Josiah started the repair of the temple (2 Kings 22:3-7; 2 Chr. 24:4). This turnaround delayed God's punishment for past sins (2 Kings 22:18-20; 2 Chr. 34:27-28), but Judah would very soon revert to their sinful ways as Jeremiah prophesied from 628 B.C. to the coming Babylonian invasion in 605 B.C. (Jer. 25:3, 9).

After Josiah's death in 609 B.C. at the hands of the Egyptians (2 Kings 23:29-30; 2 Chr. 35:20-24; Jer. 46:1-2), religious life deteriorated in Judah during the evil rules of the final four kings, Zedekiah being the last. Judah again drifted toward polytheism, but the Yahweh-only party still prevailed, reinforced by the prophets Jeremiah and Ezekiel. When they prophesied that God would allow an invasion to punish them for their apostasy,[21] false prophets lulled the people into a sense of security by convincing most of them that God would not do such a thing to His chosen people. It would seem that the royal line of kings and the blood line from David had been broken. But we shall later see how God has had it in His plan to preserve both lines to Jesus through Zerubbabel.

Even though Judah met the same fate as their brothers in Israel, they succeeded in preserving the Messianic line in contrast to Israel's debauchery, scheming, and murders. This should serve as proof of God's protection of Judah so His plan could be carried forth.

6

THE PROPHETS

(reference the diagram at end of this chapter)

We interrupt our journey through the kings rule and the coming exiles to present the prophets that ministered to the northern and southern nations and then to the exiles. Much could and has been written by Biblical scholars about the prophets: their historical significance and their influence on the Jewish nation. It is recommended that these works be sought out if a more advanced history is desired. Our goal has been and continues to be to keep our focus on God's plan, so we will only present the highlights of the most significant prophets.

God saw fit to communicate with His people through His prophets, led by the Holy Spirit (Deut. 18:15, 18-22; 34:9; Ezek. 11:5; Micah 3:8; 2 Peter 1:20-21), after the Hebrews decided they wanted a king to lead them like the other nations (1 Sam. 8:4-5). Through the first three kings: Saul, David, and Solomon, the Israelites generally kept their faith in God but slowly gave in to their sinfulness. Finally, when the kingdom split in 948 B.C. because of this apostasy, the ten northern tribes of Israel completely abandoned their faith in God when King Jeroboam I set up calf-worship as the national religion. Later, Baal-worship was added. God in His mercy had warned Israel of the consequences of breaking their covenant as we have seen.

The priests were just as bad as the people if not worse because they were to be protectors of the faith. God would warn them of the graveness of their sins through the earlier oral prophets and then of their doom through the writing prophets and later during the critical period approaching the Assyrian invasion in 721 B.C. (Jer.5:23-27; 11:1-13; Lam. 1:8-9, 18; Ezek. 16:59). Judah had a much farther way to drop out of God's grace because they started out, after the kingdom split, on a spiritual plane that was much higher than was Israel. It would take them longer to slide into the same sins as their brothers, Israel. However, in 586 B.C., they would meet the same fate with the Babylonian invasion, but, using the prophets as messengers, God would save a remnant of His people so the kingship line would continue until the final and everlasting king, Jesus, would take the throne. This plan of God's would also be the fulfillment of His promise to the Gentile peoples to add them to the Kingdom (Isa. 42:1; 49:6; 66:19; Matt. 12:18, 21; Acts 11:18; 14:27; 15:3; 26:23; 28:28; Rom. 3:29; 11:11; 15:12). This period would experience the greatest prophetic activity.

The first prophets were oral communicators, thus the term *Oral Prophet*. The *Writing Prophets* followed later. The oral prophets were just that--they did not record their prophecies—they spoke them. Their basic message was in chastising the people on their apostasy in order to bring them to repentance. The writing prophets' books all appear in the Old Testament. During their period, it seems that God had given up on bringing the nation to repentance, for their central message was prophesying on the destruction of the nation, but they also provided messages of redemption in the far future. We will cover all the prophets but will give only brief mention to some of the lesser known.

ORAL PROPHETS

The oral prophets included Nathan, Ahijah, Iddo, Jehu, Elijah, Elisha, Obed, Shemaiah, Azariah, Hanan, Jahaziel, and Huldah. Following is a listing and brief commentary on four of the most influential oral prophets:

Nathan. Prophesied during the rule of David (2 Sam. 7:2).

Ahijah. Prophesied during the rules of Solomon and Jeroboam I (1 Kings 11:29). He continued the work of Nathan in bringing a sensible worship to the people. After Samuel had started schools at Ramah for the prophets (1 Sam. 19:19-20), they continued the leadership of these schools.

Elijah. Prophesied during the rules of Ahab (1 Kings 17:1), Ahaziah (2 Kings 1:1-4), Jehoram, and early in Jehu's rule in Israel (1 Kings 19:14-16). He took a stand against Jezebel, wife of Ahab, and her attempts at encouraging the worship of Baal. He did not die but was taken up to Heaven (2 Kings 2:1, 11). His messages emphasized Israel's need to repent.

Elisha. (872-816 B.C.): Prophesied during the rules of Jehoram, Jehu, Jehoahaz, and Jehoash in Israel (1 Kings 19:16; 2 Kings 3:1, 10-13; 13:14, 25). He encouraged Jehu to carry out religious and political reforms to cleanse the nation of its wickedness: Jehu killed King Ahab's 70 sons, his wife, and the rest of his family, friends, and officials (2 Kings 10:5-7, 11, 17), killed King Ahaziah of Judah and his 42 sons (2 Kings 9:27; 10:13-14), and killed King Jehoram of Israel (2 Kings 9:24), but he did destroy almost all traces of Baal including the priests (2 Kings 10:23-28). Elisha, more than any other prophet, was a man of miracles (2 Kings 4:1-7, 14-17; 38-44; 5:9-10).

From about 65 years before Israel was exiled to Assyria, the writing prophets appeared as God's messengers. The first four: **Isaiah**, **Jeremiah**, **Ezekiel**, and **Daniel** are considered *Major Prophets* because of the length of their Old Testament books. Following is a listing and a brief commentary on these four major prophets and some of the twelve minor prophets. The last twelve books in the Christian Old Testament Bible are by the *Minor Prophets*. They are combined in the Hebrew Scriptures into one book titled "The Twelve." Those prophets not commented on are Joel, Obadiah, Nahum, Habakkuk, and Zephaniah. Refer to the pictorial presentation of these more influential prophets at the end of this chapter.

MAJOR WRITING PROPHETS

Isaiah (740-700 B.C.). Prophesied from the death of King Uzziah, (Isa. 6:1) and during the rules of Jotham, Ahaz, and Hezekiah, and possibly early Manasseh (2 Kings 21:10-11; Isa. 1:1). He was primarily concerned with Judah. He saw the destruction of Israel in 721 B.C. by prophesying in Isaiah 7:8 that the ten tribes of Israel would lose their identity in 65 years, foresaw the deliverance of Judah from the Assyrian threat in 712 B.C. (Isa. 36:1, 37:33-36), Jerusalem's destruction in 586 B.C. by Babylon 100 years before (Isa. 3:1; 5:13; 13:1, 5; 39:1-7), and deliverance from Babylon (Isa. 47:4-15). He also prophesied about the Messiah's birth and death (Isa. 7:14; 9:6; 11:1-5; 28:16; 49:1-9; 50:6; 52:13-15; 53:3-12), John the Baptist (Isa. 40:3), Jesus' Second Coming (Isa. 9:7; 24:21-23; 26:19; 32:1-8; 35:1-7; 40:9-11; 42:1-4), and the establishment of a powerful Israel in the Millennium (Isa. 2:2-4; 4:2-6; 10:20-23; 11:11-16; 14:1-2; 43:6). He also saw the rise of Persian king Cyrus 140 years in advance (Isa. 41:2; 44:28; 45:1-4, 13), the destruction of Babylon by the Medes 150 years in advance (Isa. 13:6, 17-22), the promise to the Gentile nations (Isa. 56:3, 6-8), the rise of the Assyrians (Isa. 14:24-25), and the Tribulation period (Isa. 24:1-12).

Jeremiah (627-575 B.C.). He presented oral messages probably from the latter part of Manasseh's rule (2 Chr. 33:18-19). His written prophecies would start in the thirteenth year of Josiah's rule in 628 B.C. (Jer. 25:3) and continue through the Babylonian exile in 586 B.C. (Jer. 1:1-3) and some time beyond (2 Chr. 36:11-12; Jer. 39:11-14; 40:1). He warned Judah of the coming Babylon invasion and the need for them to repent but to no avail (Jer. 3:12-13; 4:1-2; 5:19; 7:1-7; 9:13-16; 13:19; 21:1-6; 24:4-5; 27:6), a 70 year servitude to Babylon (Jer. 25:9-11), and also their return (2 Chr. 36:22-23--the Babylon return; Jer. 29:10-14--the eschatological return). Many false prophets would appear opposing Jeremiah, telling the people that everything was fine and assuring the people that God would not let Babylon invade them (Jer. 5:11-13; 7:4; 14:13-15; 20:6; 26:7-8; 27:14; Lam.2:14; Ezek. 12:24). Jeremiah also warned Judah not to resist the invasion (Jer. 21:8-10; 27:11-12), for God was going to exile them to Babylon for their own good (Jer. 24:4-5). Jeremiah went to King Zedekiah to warn him of the coming invasion but was rebuked (Jer. 32:2-5; 37:1-2). Some of the people wanted to flee to Egypt, but

Jeremiah, instructed by God, told them not to (Jer. 42:1-19), because God was shortly going to destroy Egypt and many Judeans who fled there; He fulfilled this in 568 B.C. (Jer. 43:8-12; 44:1-14; 46:19-26; Ezek. 29:2-3, 8-9; 31:10-12; 32:2, 11). However, many did not listen and did flee to Egypt (Jer. 43:4-7) where many would die by the sword and some would escape (Jer. 44:1, 8, 13-14, 26-28). But God would not abandon them forever and promised the nation that He would make a new covenant with them in the future (Jer. 31:4, 7, 10, 31-33; 32:40; 33:15) to replace the old covenant made with Abraham because of the sins of the nation (Jer. 11:10-11). This new covenant would be delivered by the Messiah, Jesus. With all the bad news Jeremiah brought with his prophecies, the Hebrews still recognized the validity of his warnings and had his writings canonized.

Ezekiel (593-560 B.C.). He was also a priest. He was exiled to Babylon in the third deportation in 597 B.C. until about 560 B.C. He warned the people of Judah's destruction (Ezek. 6:1-7; 11:15-17) and then prophesied about Jerusalem's restoration in the Millennium (Ezek. 6:8-10; 11:16-17; 14:22; 16:53, 63; chapter 36; 37:15-28). He received from God the specifications to rebuild the temple and the rules for worship (Ezek. 40-46). Chapters 47-48 of the book of Ezekiel deal with the end times.

Daniel (605-533 B.C.). He was exiled to Babylon in the first deportation in 605 B.C. and rose to a high office because of his wisdom in interpreting dreams (Dan. 1-6). He reported visions about the near future and also of the end times (see chapter 18) comparable to the Book of Revelation (Dan. 7-12). During the rule of Darius the Mede, he was thrown into the lions' den (Dan. 6:1-23) because he prayed only to God, stirring the political jealousies of his contemporary rulers. As God often foreshadows New Testament events with Old Testament events, so likely He did here: Daniel's time in the lions' den foreshadows Christ's time in the tomb, Daniel being delivered as would Christ and Daniel serving his sentence to satisfy worldly law as Christ served His sentence to serve the spiritual Law. Three of his friends were thrown into a fiery furnace, but prevailed because they would not bow down to the king's statue (Dan. 3:9-28). He remained in Babylon until at least 536 B.C. (Dan. 10:1). Daniel, instead of being considered one of the four Major Prophets as in the Christian Old Testament, was not grouped with the prophets in the Hebrew Bible. He was grouped in the "History" section of the Hagiographa (sacred writings), the third division of the Hebrew Scriptures. Also in the group were Ezra-Nehemiah (one book) and 1 & 2 Chronicles (one book). Each of these three books was canonized separately, Daniel sometime after 167 B.C., the supposed date of its writing by some modern scholars. Tradition has the book being written by Daniel.

MINOR WRITING PROPHETS

Jonah (785-770 B.C. about). He ministered to Israel during the rule of Jeroboam II (2 Kings 14:23-25). Unlike the other prophetic authors, he reported on his experiences that would affect future events: sent to Nineveh (capitol of Assyria) to warn them of the consequences of sin. Jesus would liken Jonah's three days in the large fish to His entombment for three days (Matt. 12:39-41).

Amos (770-758 B.C. about). He prophesied during the rules of Azariah (or Uzziah) of Judah and Jeroboam II of Israel (Amos 1:1) until at least 758 B.C.--verse 1:1 says two years before the earthquake. According to Josephus, the quake occurred when Uzziah became a leper and his son Jotham became co-regent in 756 B.C. (2 Chr. 26:16-21; Antiquities 9.10.4). Amos was from Judah but prophesied doom for Israel because of the social injustices and corruption in the land (Amos 5:1). He also offered a word of hope (Amos 9:8-12).

Hosea (773-720 B.C.). He prophesied during the rules of Hoshea, Uzziah, Jotham, Ahaz, Hezekiah, and Jeroboam II (Hosea 1:1). He chastised Israel for apostasy, idol worship, and foretold about 25 years in advance of the Assyrian invasion of Israel from the north (Hos. 8:9; 9:3; 13:16) and also of a restored Israel (Hos. 14:4-8). God used Hosea to literally live a life of example; e.g., he commanded Hosea to take a wife of ill repute (Hos.1:2) just as God's bride, Israel, was committing adultery with idols (Ezek. 16:13, 17; Hos. 4:11-14). His wife would leave him (Hos. 2:5) as Israel was doing, but Hosea would take her back after she suffered for her sins (Hos. 2:6-13; 3:1-2) as Israel will with the dispensations. Because of her sins, Hosea would not be intimate with her for a while (Hos. 3:3) just as

God would take away Israel's kings and sacrifices in the temple (Hos. 3:4) and refuse to deal with them for a while until they returned to Him (Hos. 3:5).

Micah (750-705 B.C.). He prophesied during the rules of Jotham, Ahaz, and Hezekiah. His condemnation of Israel and Judah (Mic. 1:5) was accompanied by hope for their future (Mic. 2:12-13; 4:1-2; 5:3, 7-9; 7:18-20).

Haggai (520-516 B.C.). He prophesied from the second year of Darius I of Persia (Hag. 1:1; 2:18-19) to the time of the returning Jews and encouraged them in the temple rebuilding.

Zechariah (520-516 B.C.). He prophesied from the second year of the reign of Darius I of Persia (Zech. 1:1) to at least his fourth year (Zech. 7:1). He inspired the Jews that were returning to Jerusalem to rebuild the temple and prophesied about sin, God's judgment, and the future, i.e., the coming of the Branch, Jesus (Zech. 3:8; 6:12). A promise was given to the Jews for their final restoration in the end times (Zech. 8:2-8) and to the Gentile nations (Zech. 2:11-12; 8:22-23). Chapters 9-14 of Zechariah deal with the end times.

Malachi (450-430 B.C. about). He prophesied during a period of spiritual lowness due to the corruption of the priests, neglect of the temple, and sins. The coming of John the Baptist (Mal. 3:1) and the Tribulation period (Mal. 4:1-6) were foretold.

THE WRITING PROPHETS

note: the years shown are years of the prophets' influences

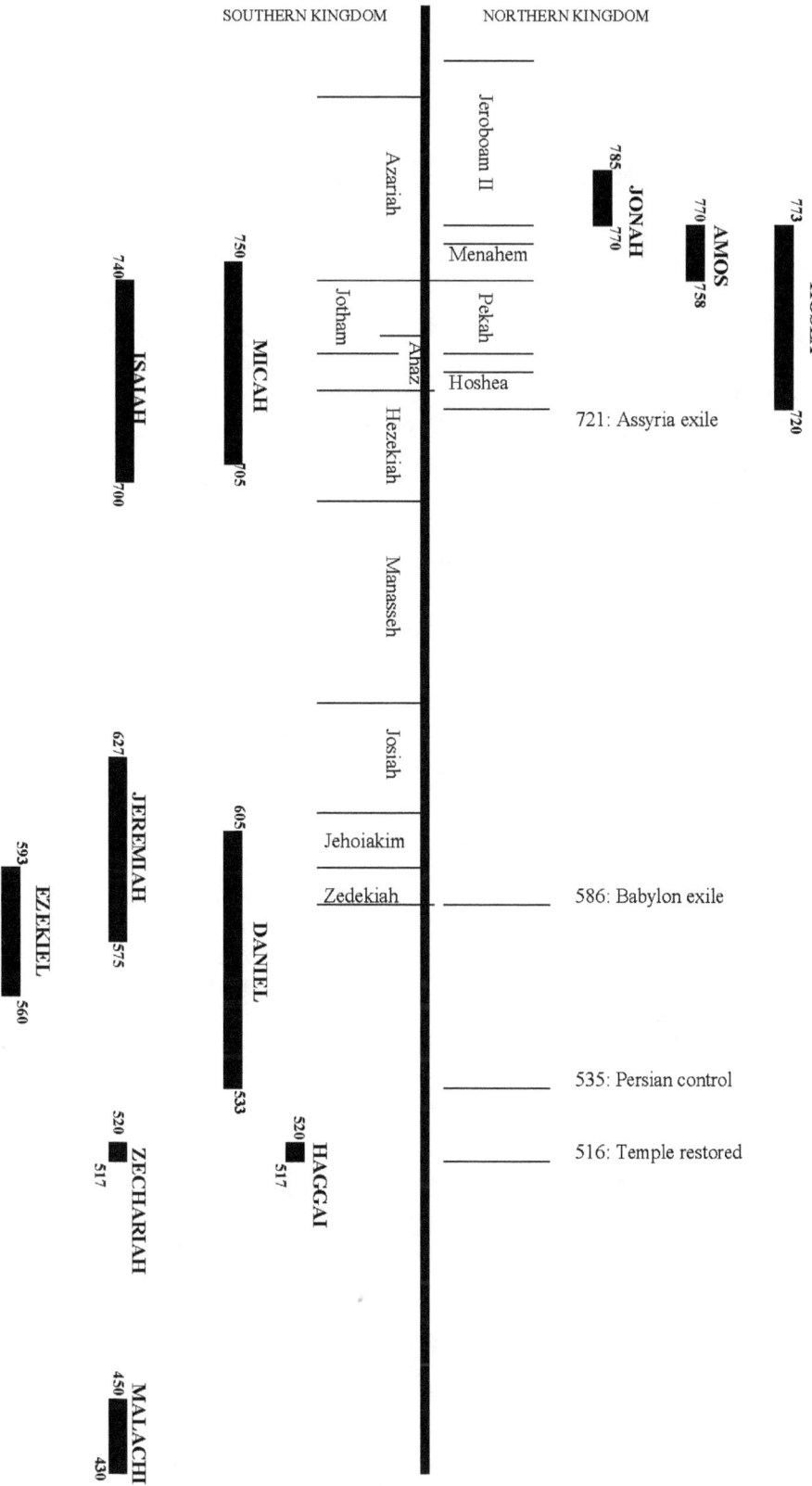

SOUTHERN KINGDOM | NORTHERN KINGDOM

Azariah

Jeroboam II

Menahem

Jotham

Pekah

Ahaz

Hoshea

Hezekiah

721: Assyria exile

JONAH 785–770

AMOS 770–758

HOSEA 773–720

ISAIAH 740–700

MICAH 750–705

Manasseh

Josiah

Jehoiakim

Zedekiah

586: Babylon exile

JEREMIAH 627–575

EZEKIEL 593–560

DANIEL 605–533

535: Persian control

516: Temple restored

HAGGAI 520–517

ZECHARIAH 520–517

MALACHI 450–430

7

THE GENEALOGY OF JESUS

(reference road maps 3-7)

So far, we have traced Jesus' future royal (kingly) blood line from Adam through the patriarchs, judges, and kings. Before progressing any farther, let us regress on our road map to the life of Jacob who would father the Israelite tribal nation through his twelve sons, any one of which could have continued the blood line to Messiah. As we had seen, Jacob was the son of Isaac and the grandson of Abram. In 2083 yfc, God had promised to make Abram and his descendants into a great nation. In 2298 yfc, Jacob had moved his family to Egypt to live. From here, we will take a detour from **Chronology Turnpike** onto **Genealogy Boulevard** (the blood line route) and discover how God would keep His promises by overcoming many obstacles in the way of His plan. See road map 3 and keep the verses of Luke 3:23-38 at hand for reference.

Jacob had twelve sons: ten would become namesakes of a tribe of Israel. An eleventh son, Levi, would be the father of a long line of tabernacle assistants to the priests. A twelfth son, Joseph, would father sons Ephraim and Manasseh who would be the heads of the eleventh and twelfth tribes.

Jacob's sons (1 Chr. 2:1-2) (by birth order)	Tribes
Reuben	Reuben
Simeon	Simeon
Levi (tribe given to God)	n/a (Moses' tribe)
Judah	Judah (David's tribe)
Dan*	Dan
Naphtali	Naphtali
Gad	Gad
Asher	Asher
Issachar	Issachar
Zebulun	Zebulun
Joseph (his 2 sons made tribes)	Ephraim (Joshua's tribe)
	Manasseh
Benjamin	Benjamin (Saul's tribe)

Perez (Phares)†
Hezron (Esrom)
Aram (Ram)
Amminadab
Nahshon (Naason)
Salmon (Salma)
Boaz (Booz)
Obed
Jesse
David (Israel's 2nd king)

*Rev. 7:5-8 omits Dan probably because they were the 1st tribe to worship idols (Judges 18) but Rev. 21:12 honors them
†Messianic inheritance: Gen. 49:8-10; 1 Chr. 2:3-15; Matt.1:3-6; Luke 3:31-33; Heb. 7:14

Jacob seems to elevate Joseph's sons Ephraim & Manasseh as equal or better heirs than Reuben and Simeon (two oldest sons of Jacob) by his adoption of them as sons (Gen. 48:3-5) rather than grandsons as was the custom sometimes in those times to consider grandchildren and sometimes more distant relatives as sons. This was sometimes done for the purpose of bestowing the birthright and/or blessing on a younger son, e.g., Cain and Seth, Ishmael and Isaac, and Esau and Jacob. Reuben, the oldest son of Jacob, had rights to the birthright--a double share of his fathers wealth and blessing (Deut. 21:17), but it was taken from him and given through Joseph to Ephraim and Manasseh because Reuben had slept with his father's wife and was unruly (Gen. 35:22; 49:3-4; 1 Chr. 5:1-2). Ephraim and Manasseh would become the eleventh and twelfth tribes, Ephraim the younger given the greater blessing (Gen. 48:17-20; Deut. 33:17), for Ephraim's name would become synonymous with the ten Northern tribes of Israel (Hosea 11:8). So Ephraim and Manasseh received the material blessing. Even though Joseph, first-born of Rachel, could or should have received the blessing of the right to the messianic lineage, he was bypassed for Judah as Jacob foretold (Gen. 49:8-10), possibly because of his concern for Benjamin in Egypt. So we see that Judah, the fourth born son of Jacob, would receive the spiritual blessing (1 Chr. 5:2) and carry the messianic lineage, Reuben being disqualified because of his sin as previously mentioned. Simeon and Levi were also disqualified probably for their parts in the massacre of the males of Shechem (Gen. 34; 49:5-7).

Saul, Israel's first king, was a descendant from the tribe of Benjamin from whence the title line could have continued. He started his rule by obeying and pleasing God, but because of his self-will, he started to disobey God as God knew beforehand (Gen. 49:10): he consulted a medium (1 Chr. 10:13), made an unauthorized burnt offering (1 Sam. 13:8-14), saved the spoils of war (1 Sam. 15:2-3, 9-11; 28:18), and his family broke the Gibeonite treaty (Josh. 9; 2 Sam. 21:1-2). These sins led God to take the earthly kingdom throne from him and his lineage and give it to David of the tribe of Judah (1 Sam. 15:23-24, 28; 28:16-17) as shown in the previous illustration. Notice also on the road map that the blood line bypasses Saul. Therefore, the descendants from the tribe of <u>Judah</u> would carry the <u>title and blood lines</u> through David, the **Davidic Covenant** (2 Sam. 7:12-16; 1 Chr. 28:4; 2 Chr. 13:5; 21:7; Isa. 55:3; Jer. 23:5; 33:20-22; Matt. 1:20-21; 9:27; 12:23; 22:42; Mark 12:35; Luke 1:27, 68-69; John 7:42; Rom. 1:3; 15:12; 2 Tim. 2:8) to our Savior instead of the tribe of Benjamin.

God promised David that his family would rule forever (not like Saul) and that his son, Solomon, would build Him a temple (2 Sam. 7:12-16; 1 Chr. 17:11-14; 22:9-10; 28:4-8). But David also sinned: he caused Uriah to be killed in battle so that he could have his wife (2 Sam. 11:2-17). However, unlike Saul, David would admit his sin, seek forgiveness, and repent (2 Sam. 12:13; Psa. 51). God did not kill him or take the kingdom away from him but punished him with evil that would follow him from other nations (e.g.: Ammonites) and his own house for the rest of his life (2 Sam. 12:9-11). Probably the greatest punishment to come to David would come from his son, Absalom, who would rebel and war against him, resulting in the death of this beloved son (2 Sam. 17:26; 18:6-7, 16-17). Despite his sins, God saw righteousness in him because of his faith and promised that his family, starting with his son Solomon, would produce an eternal line of kings (although the royal line would temporarily find no king on the throne as we shall see) culminating with the final king (Jesus) who would rule forever, thus including His promise to David in the new, **Final Covenant** (2 Sam. 7:12, 16; 1 Kings 2:4; 8:25; 9:5; 11:36; 1 Chr. 22:8-10; 2 Chr. 7:17-18; Psa. 89:3-4, 27-29, 34-37; 132:11; Isa. 9:6-7; 11:1, 10; Mic. 5:2, 4; Acts 13:22-23). God promised David that, for his sake, even though his son Solomon would sin against Him, that He would show mercy on him and his descendants (2 Sam. 7:14-15). God blesses penitent people in spite of their sin! Even with God's forgiveness of our sins, we must still suffer the consequences of our foolish actions (Gal. 6:5). Later in life, David's pride would again lead to God's punishment. God, angry with Israel, moved David to sin (using Satan's urgings) by taking a census, a worldly, prideful act (2 Sam. 24:1; 1 Chr. 21:1). God used this event to humble David into repentance (2 Sam. 24:10) and punished him by sending a pestilence (2 Sam. 24:15).

David had sons Nathan and Solomon (who inherited the throne) (1 Chr. 14:4). God promised to pass the blessings of the Davidic Covenant, a kingly dynasty leading to the Messiah, to Solomon and his descendants if they would follow Him as David did (1 Kings 2:4; 9:4-5; 2 Chr. 7:17-18). David's was an unconditional covenant promise spanning to Messiah but dependent on the individual faithfulness of Solomon and his descendants. But Solomon sinned: he married foreign wives and worshipped their idols (1 Kings 11:1-8) and thus would suffer God's wrath (1 Kings 9:6-7; 11:11-12; 2

Chr. 7:19-20). It seems odd that a man who had asked God for wisdom instead of material blessings or power should turn completely from his earlier virtues. Likely the achievement of wealth and power led Solomon into pride and self-will resulting in his forbidden marriages to foreign wives. Solomon had not truly repented nor exhibited sorrow for his sins as did his father David. His personal punishment would come with the split in the kingdom in 3029 yfc: the ten northern tribes of Israel being taken from his family rule (1 Kings 11:13) (a dead-end street named **Israel St.**, ending with the Assyrian invasion) and the two southern tribes going to his son, Rehoboam, for David's sake (the title road and the blood line named **Judah Ave.**). Judah Ave. is therefore a continuation of Chronology Turnpike representing the Davidian <u>title route</u> and the Judean <u>blood route</u> to Jesus (Matt. 1:7-12). God reveals that an end will come to the rules of kings sitting on the throne in Judah after Jehoiakim,[22] but the royal line will continue. A stem (root, symbol of Messiah) will emerge from Jesse to lead the Jews and Gentiles to salvation although the title line would be diverted from the last king of Judah, Zedekiah, because of the continuing disobedience of Solomon's descendants. But David's blood line would be continued through Jehoiakim's son Jehoiachin (Coniah) and continue to Jesus, the final king to sit on the throne for ever (Isa. 11:1, 10; Rom. 15:12).

Nathan would also carry a blood line to Jesus (Luke 3:27-31). Thus our road map shows **Nathan Ave.**, the other blood line, deviating from Chronology Turnpike (the blood and title lines) which split into Israel St. and Judah Ave.

As we look back in review, we see the hand of God working through the lives of humans to provide them with a redeemer. He started with promises to Abram, Isaac and Jacob, then through Jacob's son, Judah, through the period in Egypt, the period of Moses and the judges, and then the period of the kings. When the kingdom split, the northern nation of Israel was left without a blood line or title line that reached back to God's chosen lineage.[23] Their nation would end in 721 B.C. The southern nation of Judah would continue Solomon's rule and blood line through his son Rehoboam (1 Kings 11:12-13, 43). We see from the road map that the Judean blood line continues on to Jesus congruent with the royal line, although the line of kings sitting on the throne will cease temporarily. We see that the one line from Nathan, son of David, is strictly a blood line whereas the Judah line is a royal blood line.

⑦ Jesus' ancestry

Both lineages (Nathan's and Judah's), through Jewish marriage customs, converge on **Zerubbabel**, a leader of the Jews who returned to Jerusalem from Babylon to rebuild the temple (Ezra 2:1-2; 3:2), as shown on road map 6. From Zerubbabel comes another split in the genealogy, this time along **Luke Road** and **Matthew Road**, each providing a blood line to Jesus. Here is where more confusion arises: determining the parents and children of Zerubbabel:

Ezra 3:2, 8; 5:2- -Shealtiel (or Salathiel) fathered Zerubbabel (or Zorobabel).					
Hag. 1:1, 12------ "		"	"		
Matt. 1:12-13---- "		"	"	who fathered Abiud.	
Luke 3:27--------- "		"	"	" "	Rhesa.
1 Chr. 3:19-2-----Pedaiah		"	"	" "	7 sons and a daughter, Shelomith.

First, Zerubbabel's Father. There have been several theories to explain the seeming contradiction that gives Shealtiel and Pediah as Zerubbabel's father. One explanation is that Pediah was the actual father and Shealtiel was <u>considered</u> as a father by Jewish marriage customs (Gen. 38:8; Deut. 25:5-6; Mark 12:19), part of the Law and prevalent in the Near East. We start with King Jehoiakim's sin of destroying the scroll containing God's warning to Judah to repent before the Babylon invasion in 586

B.C. God foretold that, because of this sin, his title line would end after his eleven year rule (Jer. 36:30) and it did when his son, Jehoiachin (or Jechoniah or Coniah), took the throne for three months of evil rule. This rule was considered <u>not valid</u> as told in Jeremiah 22:30 when God told Jeremiah to <u>record</u> Coniah as childless, not that Coniah <u>was</u> childless. Thus, God's decree that no son of Jehoiakim[24] would sit on the throne is valid since his son Coniah was illegitimate according to the Jews, and Zedekiah was not anointed of God to rule. Therefore, Solomon's descendants' ruling from the throne ends, but the royal blood line continues—no king will sit on the throne after Jehoiakim until Jesus. God, as He said He would, would preserve Solomon's throne forever (1 Chr. 17:12-14), for David's sake, to the time when Messiah would come. Solomon's royal blood line through illegitimate Coniah thus bypassed Zedekiah and continued the Davidic Covenant through Zerubbabel. God carried out His punishment of Coniah by rejecting his sons (1 Chr. 3:17-18) for kingship, for Zedekiah, uncle of Coniah,[25] was appointed king by Babylon (2 Kings 24:17; 1 Chr. 3:15). For this reason is Coniah <u>recorded</u> in Matthew 1:11-16.

Following is a graphic display of the lineage from Josiah through Jehoiakim and on to Coniah. Note two Zedekiahs: one a son of Josiah and one a son of Jehoiakim.

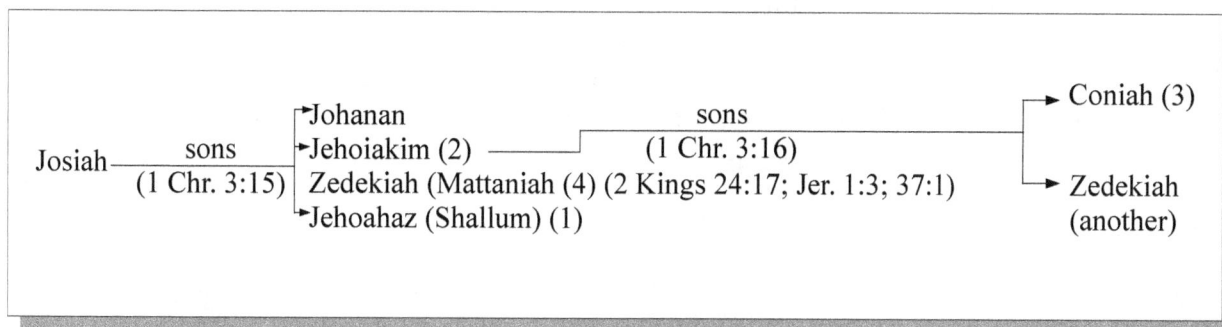

As we propose, Coniah later married the widowed daughter of Neri (from the blood line of Nathan).* She had a son brought into the marriage, Pedaiah. Coniah and Neri's daughter had a son, Shealtiel (or Salathiel) making Pedaiah and Sheatiel brothers (half-brothers as we recognize today) according to Jewish Levirate marriage law,[26] and Coniah became a son of Neri (son-in-law as we recognize today). Therefore, when Pedaiah married Shealtiel's widow, their son Zerubbabel obtained two fathers: an actual father (Pedaiah) and a legal (according to Jewish customs) father (Shealtiel). Remember that God considered Coniah childless for the purpose of preventing Jehoiakim's descendants from occupying the throne, not that God would bring an end to the title line since it would be reestablished with Jesus. The royal blood line would pass through Coniah and his son, Shealtiel (Matt. 1:12), according to Jewish marriage law.

Therefore, Pedaiah married Shealtiel's widow, and they had a son, Zerubbabel. Thus David's royal blood line, now a non-ruling line, continued with Pedaiah the actual father providing Shealtiel with the son (through his wife) to carry the blood line. We see on the road map the royal blood line from Coniah to Shealtiel by virtue of Pedaiah's seed. Thus we have the blood lines of both of David's sons, Solomon and Nathan, converge on Zerubbabel as I think is fitting.

---

* From this point, we will combine scripture with Jewish tradition while making some likely assumptions as we attempt to provide logical chronological genealogies.

We have already identified Coniah as the father of Shealtiel. Two other Biblical verses throw confusion on this status: Luke 3:27 lists Neri, and 1 Chronicles 3:17 lists Assir (son of Coniah) as the father. Coniah, Neri, and Assir can all be considered as the father because of the Jewish genealogy custom of not recognizing women and using the term "son" through several to many generations. As we can see, God's hand has been working, especially at this critical point, to preserve Solomon's royal line (because of David) as He promised in 1 Chronicles 17:12-14. The blood line continued through Zerubbabel from Pedaiah's mother, daughter of Neri, to carry the royal line to Messiah, preserving the Davidic Covenant.

Another explanation[27] is offered starting from Coniah (1 Chr. 3:17). In the KJV Bible, Assir is given as a son of Coniah and father of Shealtiel, but in the Living Bible, Coniah is given as the father of Shealtiel. In both versions of Matthew 1:12, Coniah is given as the father of Shealtiel. This situation makes Shealtiel either a son of Coniah or a grandson (sometimes considered as a son in Hebrew genealogies). If we assume that Pediah (actual father of Zerubbabel) died, then Shealtiel (oldest son of Coniah) could have adopted Zerubbabel. Therefore, we have both Pediah and Shealtiel as the father of Zerubbabel.

Now, Zerubbabel's Children. From Zerubbabel to Jesus, more controversy arises. Matthew 1:13-16 gives the genealogy to Jesus from Zerubbabel's son (grandson as we shall see), Abiud (shown on the road map as Matthew Road), and Luke 3:23-27 gives the genealogy from Zerubbabel's son (son-in-law as we shall see), Rhesa, shown on the road map as Luke Road.

Abiud and Rhesa are not listed as sons of Zerubbabel in the 1 Chronicles 3:19-20 report leading one to believe that his seven sons that are recorded did not qualify or were rejected from the genealogy. That would leave Zerubbabel's daughter, Shelomith, with the honor. Let's suppose she married Rhesa making him a son-in-law to Zerubbabel. He would be considered as a son (according to Jewish customs) with Shelomith being ignored in the genealogy as was customary in Biblical times to omit women from genealogies in favor of their husbands. Now let's suppose that Rhesa and Shelomith had a son, Joanna, through whom the blood line to Joseph would continue. Thus the Luke line is given credibility. Either Shelomith had a second son, Abiud, or he was a direct son of Zerubbabel. If Abiud was a second son of Shelomith, he would be a grandson of Zerubbabel making the Matthew account wrong. If he was a son of Zerubbabel, then the 1 Chronicle account is incomplete. If we use the argument that Shelomith was ignored in the genealogy in favor of her husband, Rhesa, then Abiud would still be Zerubbabel's grandson, in this case through Rhesa. There is no conclusive evidence in Scripture for accepting either case or that there are any other circumstances. For now, the explanation will be that Abiud was a second son of Shelomith and Rhesa, and that Shelomith is omitted from the genealogy with no deference to Rhesa. Thus, the royal blood line continues with Abiud to Joseph, and the Matthew line is given credibility. The following graphic display should more clearly illustrate this situation.

```
                  ┌─── 7 sons (disqualified, 1 Chr. 3:19)
Zerubbabel ───────┤
                  └─── Daughter (Shelomith) ──────┐
       In-laws                    M              ├─── Joanna (son) ──► Luke line continues
                                                  │                      to Joseph
                Rhesa ─────────────────────────────┴─── Abiud (son) ──► Matt. Lines continues
                                                                          to Joseph
```

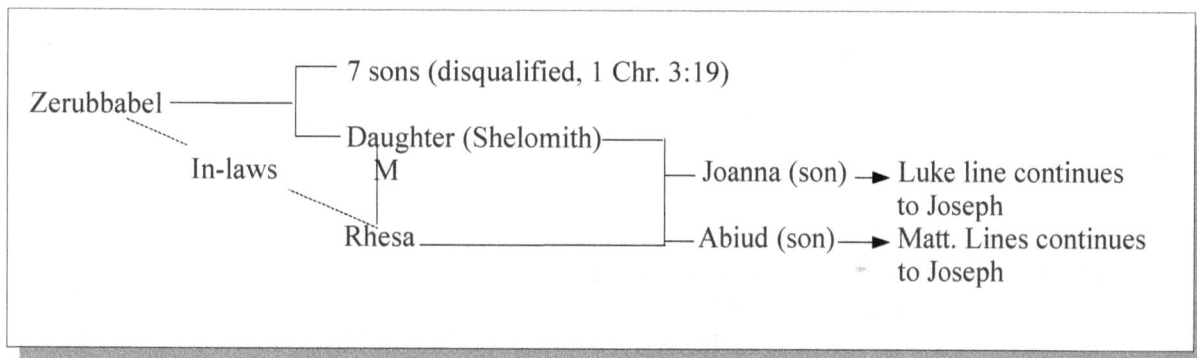

Now both genealogies converge on **Joseph**, Jesus' worldly father as shown on our road map with the two routes taken from Zerubbabel.

First, let us look at the two scriptures providing the genealogy of Jesus: Matthew 1:2-16 and Luke 3:23-38. We can break down these two accounts as follows:

Matt. 1:2-6------Abraham to David & Solomon (Chronology Turnpike:
                     Title Line)
       7-12------Solomon to Zerubbabel (Judah Ave.)
      13-16------Abiud to Jesus (continuation of Judah Ave.-Matthew Rd.)
Luke 3:23-27------Jesus to Rhesa (blood line, continuation of Nathan Ave.-Luke Rd.)
      27-31------Zerubbabel to David (Nathan Ave.)
      32-34------Jesse to Jacob (Genealogy Blvd.)
      34-38------Isaac to Adam (Chronology Turnpike)

As we see, the Matthew account originates with Abraham and follows the royal blood line through the kings and then through the royal descendants to Jesus. Matthew was a Jew writing from a Jewish perspective for Jews looking for their messiah. He would naturally want to trace Jesus' genealogy to Abraham, father of the Jewish nation.

The Luke account originates with Adam and follows the blood line from David's son, Nathan, paralleling the royal line and also leading to Jesus. This is the non-royal blood line. As most scholars agree, Luke was a gentile writing for gentiles. Luke would have been interested in showing that Jesus came for all peoples.

Each genealogy names a different father for Joseph (father of Jesus): Matthew names Jacob and Luke names Heli. There have been many explanations produced over the centuries seeking to provide an explanation.

One theory[28] (the one I prefer) states that the Luke line gives the lineage from Rhesa to Heli as Mary's blood line, and the Matthew line gives the lineage from Abiud to Jacob as Joseph's title line, Mary being the unnamed daughter of Heli and Joseph being the son of Jacob (and also son-in-law of Heli). Therefore, the blood lines are continued: Joseph is given as Jacob's son in the Matthew account (actual parent) and also given as Heli's son in the Luke account (son-in-law through marriage), Mary not being mentioned because of the usual custom of that time of omitting women from genealogies. In this case, the Luke blood line is continued through Mary to Jesus, but the Matthew blood line ends with Joseph because of the virgin birth—God is Jesus' father. This theory fits well when we consider that Matthew mentioned three women in his account: Ruth and Rahab in v.5 and Mary in v. 16, whereas Luke excluded all women from his account, but silently recognized Mary as the mother of Jesus and Joseph (as was supposed) the legal father of Jesus.

```
Luke line...................Heli ———— daughter ————→ Mary (not named)
Maternal line                                          |      (actual mother)
                    (Son-in-law)................        M ————————————————→ Jesus
                                                        |
Matt. Line..................Jacob ———— son ————→ Joseph (legal father)
Paternal line
```

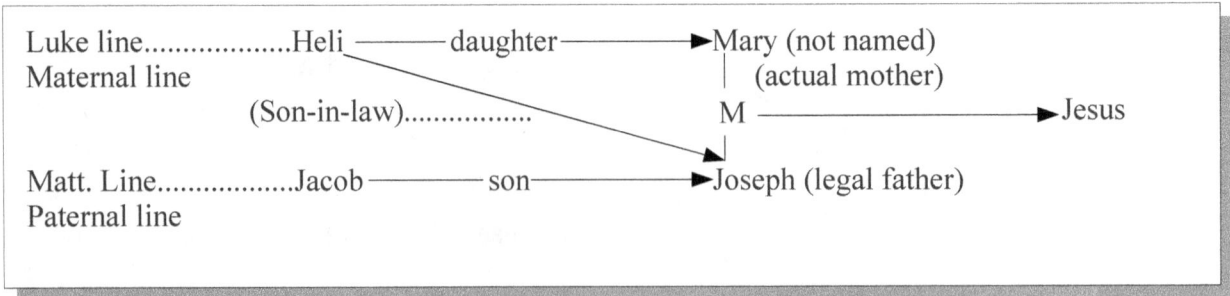

Another theory,[29] similar to that just presented, gives Mary as the daughter of Jacob in the Matthew line and Joseph as the son of Heli of the Luke line. Joseph is the legal father of Jesus in the Luke line and Jacob is the grandfather of Jesus in the Matthew line but listed as Jesus' father because of Hebrew habit of omitting women (Mary here) in genealogies.

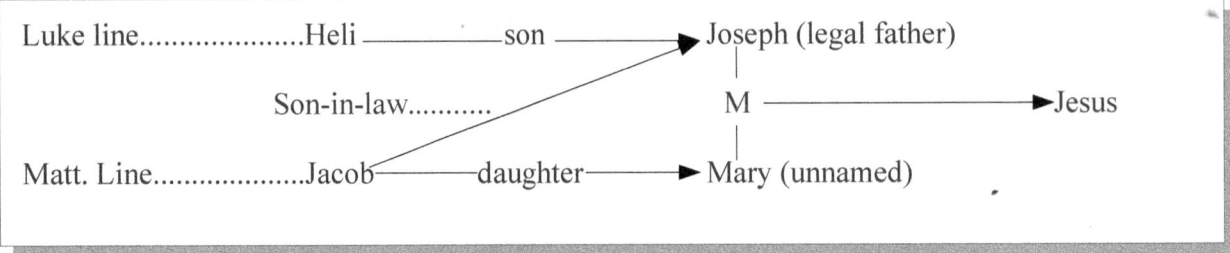

```
Luke line.....................Heli ———————— son ————→ Joseph (legal father)
                                                          |
                    Son-in-law...........                 M ———————————————→ Jesus
                                                          |
Matt. Line...................Jacob ———— daughter ————→ Mary (unnamed)
```

Still another theory (I have a hard time accepting) has Jacob having an unnamed daughter (again because of Jewish genealogy customs) in the Matthew lineage. This daughter marries Heli and they have a son named Joseph. Joseph would therefore be a son of Heli and grandson of Jacob, but he would be considered as a son because of the absence of the unnamed daughter in the genealogy. Joseph, having two fathers--Heli and Jacob--then marries Mary, an outsider. In this case, the Matthew and Luke blood lines would converge on Joseph and then on to Jesus. But because of the virgin birth to an outsider, Mary, one could argue that since Joseph had no contribution to the divine birth, the blood line to Jesus would end here thus invalidating God's promise to David that Messiah would come from the seed of Jesse. But God can raise seed as He wills. The Holy Spirit might be a substitute for Joseph's actual seed. So we must also consider this possibility.

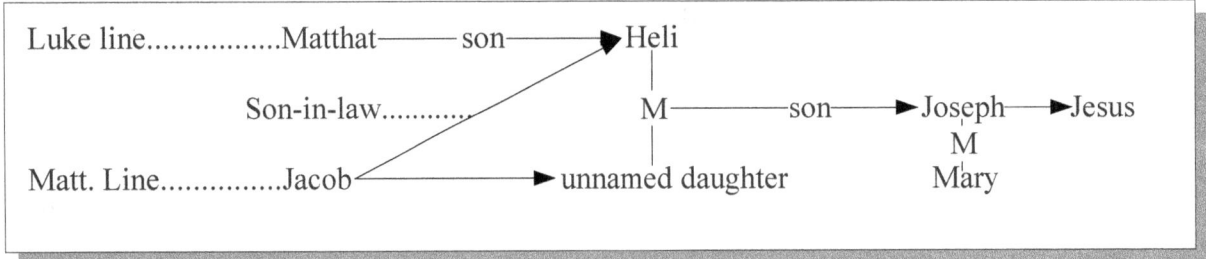

```
Luke line.................Matthat ———— son ————→ Heli
                                                    |
                 Son-in-law...........              M ———— son ——→ Joseph ——→ Jesus
                                                    |                 M
Matt. Line...............Jacob ————————→ unnamed daughter          Mary
```

In all cases, Joseph is not the paternal father of Jesus (only the legal father)—God is His father.

As an afterthought, the Hebrews took great care to pass on genealogies to ensure the purities of their family lines, for God had commanded them not to intermarry lest their spouses would lead them to worship other gods. We see an example of the detail with which genealogies were preserved in the second chapter of Ezra and the importance of keeping the race pure (vv. 59, 62). Since it had been about 400 years after the last writing in the Old Testament (Malachi), Matthew was most likely inspired by God to include Jesus' genealogy in his writing. It was important to prove that Jesus was the promised messiah, a descendant of David of the tribe of Judah.

We take it by faith that it is not important how the blood and title lines to Jesus were preserved, but that they were preserved because God said they would! This is the second critical time when God needed to rescue the royal line to Jesus as Israel's final, everlasting king, the other being with Zerubbabel's parents.

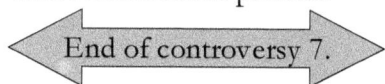
End of controversy 7.

8

THE BABYLONIAN OCCUPATION (605-535 B.C.)

(reference road map 6 & Map E)

From here, world history will be integrated into our story to provide a worldly background to the events leading to the Messiah and the following development of His Church. World history as it is taught in our schools should be called "worldly history," for little is ever mentioned of the spiritual history that paralleled and inspired it.

Around 650 B.C., Babylon (Iraq today) allied itself with the Medes to combat the threat of the Assyrians. By 625 B.C., the Babylonian Empire, with capitol city Babylon, became a major force in the Middle East[30] and in 612 B.C. became a world power with its conquest of Assyria (modern day Iraq, Syria, Lebanon, and Israel). Babylon, Daniel's *First World Power* (Dan. 2:37-38; 7:1-23), was a nation that originated in southern Mesopotamia and developed from the Chaldean dynasty (627-539 B.C.) in the region northeast of Palestine on the east side of the Arabian Desert between the Tigris and Euphrates Rivers. Babylon practiced polytheism, their most prominent gods being Ishtar, who was similar to the Canaanite Astarte, Goddess of Fertility and the Heavens, Marduk (also known as Bel, a parallel to the Canaanite Baal). They embraced stories about creation and the flood including the building of an ark.

As discussed earlier, God's covenant at Sinai with the Hebrews was conditional on their obedience to Him. When they broke the covenant with their disobedience before and during the wanderings and in the Promised Land during the judges and kings reigns, they were scattered around the world as punishment, and world power was given to the Gentiles, i.e., Babylonians, as foretold in Deuteronomy 28:47-54, 64 and by Solomon (1 Kings 8:46) and Jeremiah (Jer. 9:13-16).

Nebuchadnezzar (605-562 B.C.), son of Nabopolassar, founder of the Chaldean dynasty, came to power in Babylon in 605 B.C. (Jer. 25:1, 9-11; Dan. 1:1-2) in the third or fourth year of Jehoiakim's rule and invaded Judah, carrying off some of the population (2 Kings 24:1; Dan. 1:3-4) as prophesied (Isa. 1:9; Jer. 25:1, 8-9; Joel 1:6). This was the first of seven deportations followed by the second invasion in 599 B.C., the third in 597 B.C., and the fourth in 588 B.C.[*]

In 586 B.C., Jerusalem with its temple was destroyed,[31] and the fifth deportation was carried out (2 Kings 25:8-9; 2 Chr. 36:17-20; Jer. 39:1-2, 8-10; 52:12-16) ending Zedekiah's reign. The temple destruction marked the end of the *first temple period* (977-586 B.C.). Babylon would eventually be used by God, as prophesied by Jeremiah and Ezekiel, to punish many nations who had sinned against the Israelite nation in one way or another. In 312 B.C., Edom would be destroyed as prophesied (2 Chr. 20:22; Isa. 34:5-6; Jer. 27:1-7; 49:7-22; Ezek. 25:12-14; 35:2-9; 36:5; Joel 3:19; Amos 1:11-12; Obad. 1, 15[32]), ending the legacy of Esau's ancestry. God's punishment would be inflicted because: they had sided with Babylon during the siege and occupation (Jer. 49:7-22), they had revolted against Israel (2 Kings 8:20-22; 2 Chr. 21:8-10; 28:16-21), they had refused Israel entry through their land on their exodus journey (Num. 20:14-21; Judg. 11:16-17; 2 Chr. 20:10), and they had opposed Israel's kings: Saul (1 Sam. 14:47), David (2 Sam. 8:13-14), Solomon (1 Kings 11:14-18), Jehoram (2 Kings 8:20-22), and Ahaz (2 Chr. 28:16-18). In 568 B.C., Egypt would be conquered by Babylon as prophesied (Jer. 43:9-13; 44:30; 46:13, 18-26; Ezek. 29-31; Joel 3:19) because they had reneged on their promise to provide lasting help to Judah during the Babylonian invasion and because pharaoh had claimed to be a god. Joel 3:19 provides further doom for Egypt during the end times. The Ammonites, as prophesied

---

[*] See the graphic in chapter 9.

(Jer. 27:1-7; Ezek. 21:28-32; 25:1-7; Amos 1:13-15), would be conquered by Babylon because they had rejoiced in the destruction of Judah by Babylon and because of their opposition to: Jephthah (Judg. 10:6-11:33), Saul (1 Sam. 11:1-11), David (1 Chr. 19:1-15; 20:1-3), and Jehoshaphat (2 Chr. 20:1, 22). The Moabites, as prophesied (Jer. 27:1-7; Ezek. 25:8-11; Amos 2:1-3), would also be conquered by Babylon because of their contempt for Israel (2 Chr. 20:1, 22).

Because of their attempts at destroying God's people, the Philistines, as prophesied (Ezek. 25:15-17; Amos 1:6-8), would be destroyed for their actions during the rule of Judges Shamgar, Samson, and Samuel (Judg. 3:31; 13-16; 1 Sam. 7:7-14), and Kings Saul (1 Sam. 14:1-23), David (2 Sam. 5:17-25; 8:1), Jehoshaphat (2 Chr. 17:10-11), Jehoram (2 Chr. 21:16-17), Uzziah (2 Chr. 26:6-7), and Ahaz (2 Chr. 28:16-18). Destructions against Phoenicia (Tyrus) for breaking a treaty with Israel (Ezek. 26; 27:1-11; Amos 1:9-10) and against Syria for their harsh treatment of Israel (Amos 1:3-5) were also prophesied and fulfilled.

The conquest was completed with the last two invasions: the sixth in 586 B.C. when the temple was destroyed and the seventh in 583 B.C. The prophet Daniel, who was exiled to Babylon in the first deportation, had foretold of Babylon's future defeat by the Medo-Persian Empire (Dan. 2:37-39).

The life of servitude in Babylon awakened the Israelites to seek after God's forgiveness. During this period, Judaism developed as the religion of Judah. Since the Israelites were separated from Jerusalem, the only place where sacrifices were allowed to be made, a non-sacrificial form of worship developed which is still practiced today.[33] Although they lost their sovereignty, the Israelites would prosper as farmers and more notably as merchants and traders, occupations that would be passed down from generation to generation. From this point in history, anti-Semitism would rear its ugly head because of their culture and their successes (Esth. 3:8-13). Because they were denied their normal worship in the temple in Jerusalem, the Babylonian captives retained their faith in Yahweh by worshipping in their homes. Later, synagogues would be built for worship.

God will not forget His chosen people as we shall see. By His love and faithfulness, He will sustain the Israelites during their captivity (Lam. 3:22-23). He will bring them back from Babylon (Ezek. 20:41-44[34]) and, looking far into the future, will join together Judah and Israel to set them above all nations in the Millennium (Lev. 26:5-6; Deut. 30:3; Isa. 11:11-16; 35:1-10; 43:5-6; Jer. 3:18; 23:3-8; 24:5-7; 30:3, 10; 32:37; Ezek. 20:34, 41-44; 28:25; 34:13, 23-24; 36:22-28; 37:10-28; 39:25-29; Hos. 1:11; 3:4-5; Joel 3:1-2, 7; Amos 9:14-15; Zech. 14:1-2, 11; Rom. 11:26-27).

9

THE PERSIAN, GREEK, AND ROMAN OCCUPATIONS

(reference road maps 6 & 7)

The Persian Occupation (535-333 B.C.) (reference Map G)

About 559 B.C. while the Israelites were under Babylonian control, Persia (Iran today) was emerging as a world power.

Persia practiced a religion called Zoroastrianism[35] from its founder Zoroaster. Their tradition says that he had a calling through a vision. He established his religion in Persia through the conversion of Prince Vishtaspa. Polytheism, practiced up to this point, was eliminated. Zoroastrianism was a belief in one god--the impersonal good spirit Ahura Mazda. Among their other beliefs were: a bad spirit-- Angra Mainyu, afterlife, heaven, hell, occult practices, magic, and final judgment. After Zoroaster's death, Persia lapsed back into polytheism: ascribing assistant gods to Ahura Mazda and also adding ceremonial rituals to their worship.

Led by Cyrus (the Great) in 549/550 B.C., the Persians invaded and conquered the Medes.[36] The two nations would blend together unlike most conqueror/conquered nations (Dan. 5:28; 6:8, 12; 8:3, 20), but the Medes, being ruled by Darius the Mede,[37] would always be subordinate to the Persians. The Medes under Darius conquered Babylon in 539 B.C.[38] (Dan. 5:30-31; 9:1) as God had earlier said would happen (Isa. 13:17, 19-21; 21:2; Jer. 51:11, 28-29; Dan. 2:39). Many historians question Darius' role, if any, in the siege of Babylon, giving credit to Cyrus instead as predicted about 140 years in advance in Isaiah 41:2; 44:28; 45:1-4, 13. The Medes, still subject to Persia, i.e., the Medo-Persian Empire, the *Second World Power* of Daniel (Dan. 2:39), jointly ruled with them over Babylon. Israelites were treated well and allowed to worship as they pleased. The following verses, when referring to the first year of Darius or the first year of Cyrus, mean the first year they controlled Babylon.

In 538 B.C., Cyrus issued a decree that permitted the Israelites to return to Jerusalem to rebuild the temple (2 Chr. 36:22-23; Ezra 1:1-3; 5:13; Isa. 44:28; 45:1). It is likely that the prophet Daniel brought to the attention of Cyrus the words of Isaiah's prophecy concerning the defeat of Babylon at his, Cyrus', hands.

Evidently only a small number of Israelites quickly left Babylon in 538 B.C. for Jerusalem (Ezra 1:4), and it would take two years to gather a large contingent (about 50,000), led by Zerubbabel and Ezra, to leave to rebuild the temple (Ezra 1:5; 2:1-2, 64-65; 5:2; Neh. 7:6-7, 66-67; Zech. 4:9). The land of Judah would thereafter become known as "Judea" which encompassed most of the area west of the Jordan River. Work would start a year later in 535 B.C. (Ezra 3:8), 70 years after the Babylon occupation (Jer. 25:11-12; 29:10; Dan. 9:1-2). But interference by the Samaritans, because the Israelites had turned down their offer to help, put a stop to the rebuilding program for fifteen years to the second year of Darius in 520 B.C. (Ezra 4:4-5, 24; Hag. 1:14-15). The temple was finally completed in the sixth year of Darius in 516 B.C., 70 years after it was destroyed by the Babylonians in 586 B.C. (Ezra 6:14-15; Zech. 1:12, 16). Thus we have two significant 70 year periods of Jewish history: from 605-535 B.C.[39]–the period of Babylonian captivity and 586-516 B.C.–the period when the Israelites were without a temple.

After the Hebrews returned from Babylon, they would for the most part never return to idol worship. They would continue in their growing understanding of the coming Messiah, most likely influenced by the recent writings of Daniel and the coming revival led by Ezra and the leadership of

Nehemiah. Their understanding would lead them to believe the Messiah would come in power to deliver them from their oppressors and restore them to their former glory. This belief is still prevalent today. Entering the fifth century B.C., the Hebrews would be called "Jews."

See the following illustration for a pictorial view of these time periods.

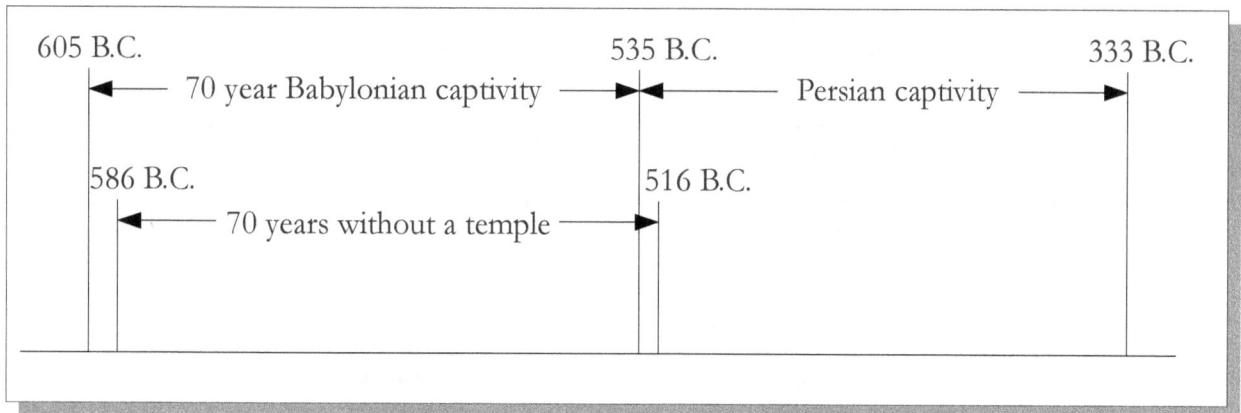

In 459 B.C., the Persian king Artaxerxes, in his seventh year, decreed that the remnant of Jews still in Babylon could return to Jerusalem to rebuild their temple that had been neglected for almost a hundred years. Led by Ezra, a priest of the lineage of Aaron (Ezra 7:1-5), a national revival with repentance resulted because of the sinful lives led by the Jews (Ezra 7:7, 11; 8:32; 9:9, 13-14; 10:2-3; Neh. 8-10). Ezra translated the Book of the Law into the language of the local population free of the Chaldean dialect. The reading and studying of Scripture led to interpretations being added by the religious leaders. Thus was born the order of **Rabbis** along with the growing tradition they attached to the Law. See the chapter, "Bible History," for further details. In 446 B.C., Artaxerxes decreed that the Jerusalem Jews, led by Nehemiah, could rebuild the walls of the city (Neh. 1:1-3; 2:1, 4-5; 6:15).

The fall of the Medo-Persian Empire to the Greeks was foretold by Daniel (Dan. 2:39).

The Greek Occupation (333-63 B.C.) (reference Map H)

From 750-650 B.C., Greece, center of the Macedonian Empire, was transformed from an oligarchy to a monarchy. They practiced polytheism, their chief god being Zeus. In 480/479 B.C., Greece was attacked at Athens by Persia (under Xerxes, or Ahasuerus) and Carthage. The Greeks prevailed, resulting in immense national pride that would be a major factor in Greece's later rise to world power. In 333 B.C., Alexander the Great (356-323 B.C.) of Macedon, Greece, the *Third World Power* of Daniel (Dan. 2:39), drove the Persians and Medes out of Asia Minor, Syria, and Judea on his way to Egypt determined to establish Greek culture in all his territories (1 Macc. 1.1; Josephus: Antiquities 12.1.1) as foretold by Daniel (Dan. 8:3-8, 20-22; 11:2-3). Alexander took control of Judea in 322 B.C. Because of the fair treatment of the Jews by the Greeks (also called Macedonians or Hellenes), there arose a class of people called **Hellenists** They were pro-Greek Jews who adopted Greek customs and integrated the Greek language and customs with their own, were worldly, intellectual, and believed less and less, as time elapsed, in spiritual matters or their own religion. Classical Greek became transformed to a new dialect called "common Greek" or Koine. Up to this time, property was privately owned. Property would later come under the control of kings, temples, and other important persons.

After Alexander conquered Egypt and died in 323 B.C., the rule of the vast Greek empire was divided into four parts (Dan. 11:3-4; Josephus: Antiquities 12.1.1). The rule of the eastern part of the empire was split between Syria (the Seleucid dynasty, 300 B.C. about-64 B.C.), descendants of Aram, son of Shem (Gen. 10:22), and Egypt (the Ptolemy dynasty, 323 B.C.-30 B.C.) as foretold about 200 years before by Daniel (Dan. 11:2-15). Judea was located between these two sections: Syria to the north and Egypt to the southwest. The Promised Land has been, from the earliest of times, a strategic location for trade routes in the Middle East. The Seleucid and Ptolemy dynasties fought for it, Rome later would covet it, and today it is still a prize territory and will be even more so in the latter days. For the next century and a half, these two powers would vie for superiority (Dan. 11:5-20).

At first Judea came under Syrian control, but in 301 B.C. control went to Egypt. Antiochus III, The Great (223-187 B.C.), the sixth Seleucid king of Syria retook control of Judea from Egypt in 199/198 B.C. He was succeeded by Seleucus IV, Philopater (187-175 B.C.). Antiochus (IV) Epiphanes (8th Seleucid King) (175-163 B.C.) started his rule in 175 B.C. (1 Macc. 1.10; Josephus: Antiquities XII, 234) as prophesied by Daniel (Dan. 11:21-35) and immediately faced resistance from the aged priest Mattathias (1 Macc. 2.1-27; Josephus: Antiquities XII, 265-285; Wars of the Jews I, 34-37).

Mattathias' family would come to be known as **Maccabees**, a priest-king reign also known as the **Hasmonean Dynasty** (after the great grandfather of Mattathias). This dynasty would last until the fall of the Greek Empire unless the priestly period is consider, when they would be ousted by Roman king Herod the Great. Epiphanes permitted the sale of the high priesthood to Jason, brother of the high priest, Onias, further angering the Jews (2 Macc. 4.7-8). Jason at once began the process of converting the Jewish population to the Greek way of life: the Hellenization of Judah (2 Macc. 4.9-15; Josephus: Wars I, 34-35). Three years later, Jason was also sold out in like manner by Menelaus (2 Macc. 4.23-26) who remained in power despite his wickedness, especially against his own people (2 Macc. 4.50). During this period, Jews were constantly fighting among themselves about the high priesthood and with the Samaritans (Josephus: Antiquities XII, 237-264). This disorder was probably an influential factor in the degree of oppression that was inflicted on Judea by her captors.

Antiochus IV Epiphanes entered Jerusalem in 167 B.C. and desecrated and robbed the temple (1 Macc. 1.20-24; Josephus: Antiquities XII, 246-247) and two years later ransacked and plundered Jerusalem (1 Macc. 1.29-35; Josephus: Antiquities XII, 248-256) in an attempt to further establish the Hellenistic society and destroy the Jews and their religion (1 Macc. 1.41-53; 2 Macc. 6.1-11). This action outraged the Jewish population, especially the Maccabees, led by Mattathias. He led a Jewish revolt from 167-166 B.C. (1 Macc. 1.54-64) which would become a prelude to the later Jewish Wars (66-70 A.D.). The present day Hanukkah holiday celebrates this revolt. Mattathias officially ruled in Judea one year, 166 B.C. (1 Macc. 2.69-70; Josephus: Antiquities XII, 279). In 166 B.C., Judas Maccabaeus (1 Macc. 2.49; 3.1; Josephus: Antiquities XII, 285), son of Mattathias, became the family head (166-160 B.C.), led a revolt, and resisted the Syrians for three years (1 Macc. 3.1-4.61; Josephus: Antiquities XII, 287-XIII, 57). In 164 B.C., the Jews finally achieved their religious independence, rebuilt the altar and walls of Jerusalem (1 Macc. 4.36; 2 Macc. 10.1-2), and were allowed to worship and make sacrifices in the temple. In 160 B.C., Judas signed an alliance treaty with the Romans because of the evident power of their rising empire (1 Macc. 8). The struggle for political independence continued after Judas' death with his brother Jonathon (160-142 B.C.) (1 Macc. 9.28-31; Josephus: Antiquities XIII, 46-61; Wars I, 48-49) and then with another brother, Simon (142-134 B.C.) (1 Macc. 13.41-42; 16.14-16; Josephus: Antiquities XIII, 194-200; Wars I, 50-53), until in 142 B.C. the Jews secured their peace with a treaty signed with the Seleucid king, Demetrius II. John Hyrcanus, son of Simon, continued the rule (1 Macc. 16.23-24; Josephus: Antiquities XIII, 225-229; Wars 1.2.3). He was followed by Aristobulus (64-63 B.C.) (Josephus: Antiquities XIII, 301; Wars I, 70) who came to power 474 years (Josephus: Wars I, 70)[40] after the Jews returned to Jerusalem from their Babylonian captivity. He ruled about one year until the Romans got control of Judea.

The Maccabeans were supported by the **Hasidim**, a conservative, very orthodox, and puritan element in Jewish society. Shortly after the Maccabean revolt, the Hasideans evolved into a society of people called **Pharisees**[41] who separated themselves from the Hellenists. The Pharisees (Josephus: Wars II, 162-163) were a society of zealous students and teachers, being strict adherents of the Law and rituals. They were progressive in worship and made additions to the Torah, expanding it, adding commentaries to it, and adding new laws. Modern Judaism, from the leadership of the Rabbis, traces its roots to the Pharisees.[42] Their ranks (Josephus was one) included lower class scribes, lawyers, rabbis, and priests. They accepted the new Messianic ideas, resurrection, angels, and final judgment and strongly resisted Hellenism.

The Hellenists would later develop into a new group called **Sadducees**[43] (Josephus: Wars II, 164-166) who would exist from the first century B.C. to the first century A.D. They became a Jewish society of educated, wealthy, and aristocratic high priests who were pro-Roman, admirers of Greek philosophies, pompous, and aloof to the Jewish population they looked down on. They were responsible for the temple management and worship rituals; did not believe in resurrection, angels, spirits, or predestination (only in man's will), and recognized only the **Judah Pentateuch** (not the entire Torah)--see later the chapter on the development of the Old Testament.

Another Anti-Hellenist group that emerged as a Maccabean offshoot was the **Essenes** (Josephus: Wars II, 160-161). They distanced themselves from the politics of the Sadducees and Pharisees and even withdrew to the wilderness to escape the evil society around them shortly after 150 B.C. They settled themselves mainly around the city of Qumran and lived on a hilltop south of Jericho under cliffs bordering the northwestern shore of the Dead Sea where they led an ascetic, monastic life studying Scripture and other books. They embraced the teachings of John the Baptist and Jesus and were extremely rigid in discipline and enforcement of the Law. They believed the temple worship to be corrupt, were preparing for the Messiah in their day, and limited Jesus' influence; they did not recognize Him as Messiah. They were the only Jewish group not condemned by the early Christians. Three contemporary writers during the Essenes period: Josephus (37-100 A.D.), Pliny (23-79 A.D.), and Philo (20 B.C.-50 A.D.) wrote about them. The Essenes were the true apocalyptic Jewish writers. They are generally given credit for the writing and/or copying of some or most of the Dead Sea Scrolls that, along with fragments of all the Old Testament books except Esther, included non-canonical writings.

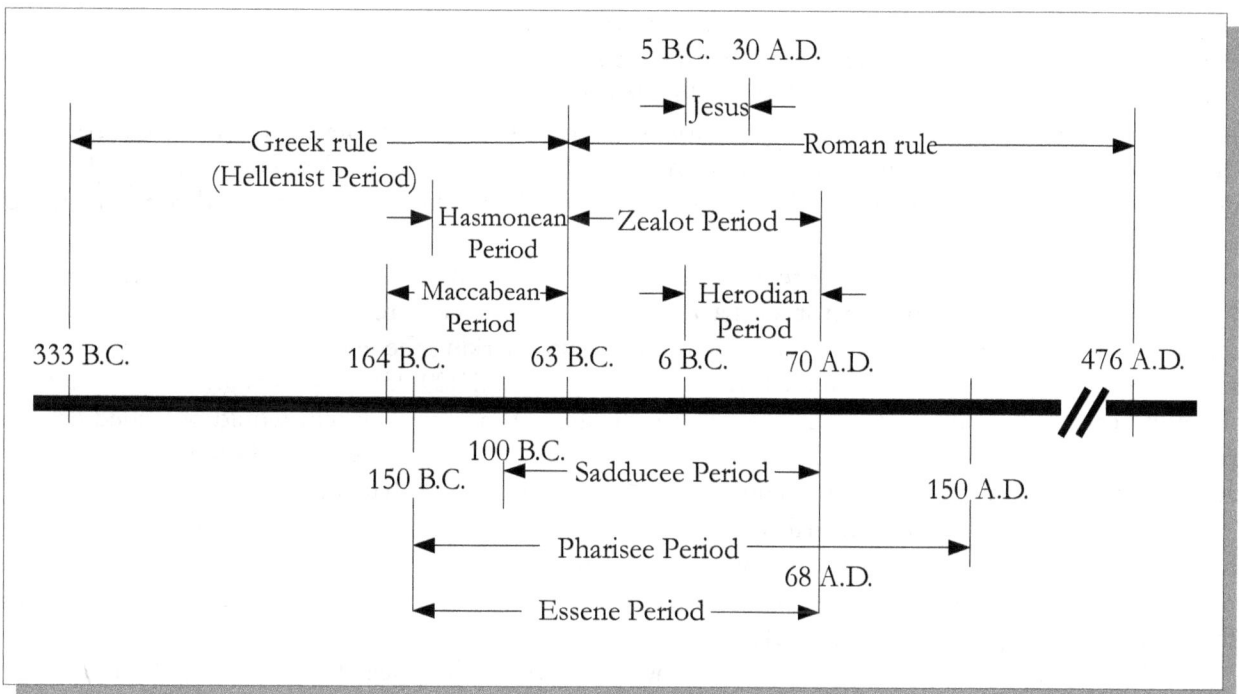

During the time of the Pharisees and Sadducees, some educated Jews called **Scribes** devoted much of their time to studying, interpreting, and copying Scripture writings and were used as legal recorders among other things. The work of these Scribes probably started during the early days of the kings. After the exile, they became expert in civil and religious law. They were instrumental in developing Jewish oral laws and tradition, becoming arrogant in their power and esteem.

The Roman Occupation (63 B.C.-476 A.D.) (reference Maps J & M)

The empire had its beginning with the growth of Rome from the merging of several groups of people in the sixth century B.C. In the third century B.C., Roman imperial control expanded throughout and around the Mediterranean area where polytheism was practiced. Romans took Greek gods and renamed them, e.g., Zeus was renamed Jupiter. Priests conducted the worship ceremonies and rites. Pontiffs oversaw the priests in this state-run religion where images began to be placed in their temples. Eventually, about 150 B.C., this state-run religion lost its appeal to the masses resulting in the educated intellectual class transforming the religion to emperor worship where the emperor was recognized as a god.

In 63 B.C., the Romans, under Octavian Augustus, sent General Pompey to settle ongoing disputes of religious matters between the Maccabean successors (with Sadducee support) and the Pharisees that had evolved into a power struggle and a civil war. The result was Jerusalem's destruction and Roman, the *Fourth World Power* of Daniel (Dan. 2:40), occupation of the Holy Land. The idea of the coming of a messiah to save the Jews from their unacceptable condition would gain increased popularity during the Roman rule giving impetus to apocryphal writings--See the chapter, "The History of the Bible." More Jews than ever, were optimistic that God would save them by sending a messiah in the end times, necessitating a change in the world order.

After the Romans took control of the Jews' lives, two politically involved religious groups emerged: the **Herodians** and the **Zealots**. The Herodians, established about 6 B.C., were a sect of rich and political Jews who were supporters of Herod the Great.[44] The Zealots probably emerged shortly after 63 B.C. from the Pharisees who they thought to be too tolerant of Roman rule. They were enthusiastic for rebellion against the extremely oppressive Roman rule under Florus and believed that their opposition might speed the coming of the Messiah or result in the Messiah being found in their midst (Josephus: Wars II, 280-410). The Zealots led the Jewish rebellion in 66 A.D.[45] that started the Jewish Wars that freed Jerusalem from the Romans. The Essenes are believed to have taken some of the Jewish manuscripts to caves in Qumran in 68 A.D. while fleeing the Roman advance. After the destruction of Qumran, a remnant of Essenes held out until 73 A.D. when they would commit suicide at Masada rather than surrender.

In 22 B.C. Herod the Great rebuilt the temple to appease the Jews. In 70 A.D., the Romans, led by Titus, son of Roman emperor Vespasian (69-79 A.D.), recaptured Jerusalem and destroyed the temple for the final time. It was never to be rebuilt again, marking the end of the third temple period as Jesus prophesied (Matt. 24:2; Mark 13:14;[46] Luke 19:43-44; 21:20-23). Josephus gives 1.1 million as the number of Jews killed. From this time forth, the animal sacrificial system would be ended except for Christ's appointed sacrifice on Calvary. Both the Herodians and Zealots would disappear sometime after the temple destruction. It has been supposed by some thinkers that Judas Iscariot was a member of the Zealots, expecting the Messiah to rise to worldly power and deliver them. When this did not happen, he became disillusioned and betrayed his master, possibly to force Jesus into starting a revolution. Even His disciples became dismayed when He had not returned in three days to deliver them from their oppressors (Luke 24:21).

The Sadducees, with their priests and sacrifices, would disappear forever. Only the Pharisees, with their Rabbis, would last longer (until about 150 A.D.), the rabbis still being active today. This loss of the Jews as a nation resulted in the final dispersion of the people to foreign lands. It would not be until 1948 when they would be partially united in their homeland in preparation of their final unification at Christ's Second Coming.

We now present a graphic display of the history of the three temple periods:

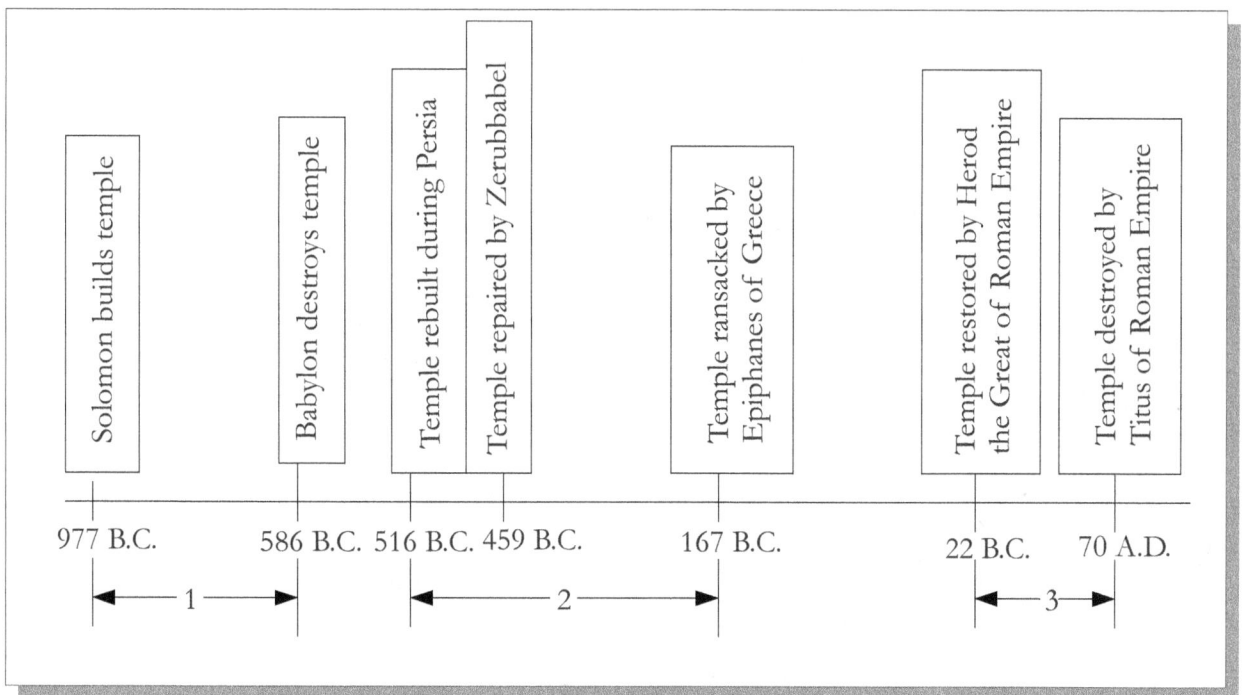

```
Solomon builds temple

Babylon destroys temple

Temple rebuilt during Persia

Temple repaired by Zerubbabel

Temple ransacked by Epiphanes of Greece

Temple restored by Herod the Great of Roman Empire

Temple destroyed by Titus of Roman Empire
```

977 B.C.   586 B.C. 516 B.C. 459 B.C.   167 B.C.   22 B.C.   70 A.D.

|←— 1 —→| |←——— 2 ———→| |←— 3 —→|

The Roman Empire, actually the western part, which was the most influential, was able to survive by keeping its army politically divided while the bureaucracy was made strong and unified. As the empire grew, so did the bureaucracy and army grow in order to keep control of the government. Jews became eyed as threats even to the point where Judea, along with surrounding territories, was renamed "Palestine" by the Romans around 135 A.D. To finance this empire and keep its army and courts solvent, taxes were raised. The middle class and peasants saw more and more of their properties being confiscated by the emperors and large land owners to pay their taxes. Government offices began to be passed down to family members resulting in a rich aristocracy. In this prelude to the coming Middle Ages, the peasants came to despise the government officials and aristocrats. Finally, in 476 A.D., the empire became too large and bureaucratic to effectively manage; control of the army was lost and the empire fell. The eastern (Byzantine) part of the empire would stay together much longer because of its secure geographic position; therefore, it depended less on its army for survival.[47] But the invasion in 1453 A.D. by the Ottoman Turks (united Islamic groups) would bring an end to the empire. As the Babylon Empire was the Old Testament symbol of paganism, the Roman Empire became that of the New Testament. See the chapter, "The Development and Growth of the Christian Church through the Middle Ages" for further details.

10

THE HISTORY OF THE BIBLE

We retreat in time to present this most important subject. Christianity recognizes and accepts the Bible as God's inspired word revealing Himself to mankind through the Holy Spirit (2 Tim. 3:16; 2 Peter 1:20-21). The Old Testament reveals God's plan leading up to the coming Messiah, Jesus. The New Testament reveals Jesus as the Messiah and also reveals the development of His church in the early years and the fulfilling of His Kingdom on earth in the end times. The Bible was not written as an historical document; at least that was not the main intent of its writers. Let us be mindful to keep our focus on the development of God's plan for mankind.

The Old Testament writings end around 400 B.C.[48] These writings were a culmination of many authors' writings from as early as Moses and possibly before, even to Noah as some scholars might imagine. Archaeological findings and historical records provide some important information on events that affected the Hebrews. No original Old Testament or New Testament manuscripts have ever been found, only copies.

It would be a gross understatement to say that the Hebrews were good record keepers. Following is a list of their records as mentioned in Old Testament Scripture:

> The Book of the Covenant (Exod. 24:4, 7; 2 Kings 23:2, 21; 2 Chr. 34:30).
> The Genealogical Register (The Book of Shemaiah and Iddo) (2 Chr. 12:15).
> The History of Judah (Iddo the Seer, The story of the Prophet Iddo) (2 Chr. 12:15; 13:22).
> Heroic Ballads (The Book of Jasher) (Josh. 10:13; 2 Sam. 1:18).
> The Book of the Wars of the Lord (Num. 21:14).
> The Book of the Law of the Lord (2 Chr. 17:9; 34:14).
> The Book of the Acts of Solomon (1 Kings 11:41).
> The Book of the Chronicles (Neh. 12:23; Esth. 2:23).
> The Book of the Chronicles of the Kings of Media and Persia (Est. 10:2).
> The Book of the Kings of Israel (2 Chr. 20:34; 33:18).
> The Book of the Kings of Judah and Israel (1 reference in 1 Chr. & 7 in 2 Chr.).
> The Book of the Chronicles of the Kings of Israel (7 refs. in 1 Kings, 11 in 2 Kings, 2 in 2 Chr.).
> The Book of the Chronicles of the Kings of Judah (4 refs. in 1 Kings, 11 in 2 Kings, 1 in 2 Chr.).
> The Life (Acts) of Uzziah (2 Chr. 26:22).
> The Book of the Kings (2 Chr. 24:27).
> The Book of the Prophets or Sayings of the Seers (2 Chr. 33:19).
> The Book of Jehu (2 Chr. 20:34).
> The Book of Nathan the Prophet (1 Chr. 29:29; 2 Chr. 9:29).
> The Book of Samuel the Seer & The Book of Gad the Seer (1 Chr. 29:29).
> Sayings of the Seers (2 Chr. 33:19).

The foundation of the Hebrew Old Testament came from nine volumes in two groupings: (a) The Judah Pentateuch[49] was canonized about 400-500 B.C. (earlier by Moses-2 Kings 23:1-3 or Josiah-2 Chr. 34:29-32)--Genesis, Exodus, Leviticus, Numbers, and Deuteronomy, (b) the former prophets were canonized about 200 B.C.--Joshua, Judges, Samuel, and Kings. Then were added the latter prophets, Isaiah, Jeremiah, Ezekiel, and The Twelve (Minor Prophets), canonized with the former prophets; note: Daniel not included but canonized later. Thus the books of the Old Testament scriptures were put into three categories: the Law, the Prophets, and the Writings. Jesus made references to the Law and the Prophets (Matt. 7:12; 22:40 and Luke 16:16). The prophets, former and latter, would be classified as historical books. As previously stated, all the scriptural Old Testament books were copied, recopied, edited, and reedited from previous written materials based on stories handed down from generation to generation before their final versions were completed. Many modern secular scholars credit the following sources of early scripture writings.

Sources of the Pentateuch

Toward the end of the nineteenth century A.D., secular scholars looking for other possible sources of Scripture began giving main literary strands letter designations to identify various writers other than Moses: scribes or groups of writers they imagine to have possibly written or influenced Old Testament Scripture. These writers, it was observed, used different names for God (J & E), had different writing styles and/or ideologies, and were associated with different periods of history. This attempt was not the only attempt by secularists, as we shall see later, to question Biblical authorships.

J document (Judaic or Jehovistic): Said to have been written by a Judean author about 950-850 B.C. (who referred to God as Jehovah or Yahweh, spelled with a J in German) from oral traditions of Israel about the Egyptian exodus and from Canaanite records before then. These stories included positive stories of creation, the flood, Abraham, Isaac, Jacob, and Moses.
S document (Seir): Some stories are akin to the J document (e.g.: creation, flood) but more of a negative writing in man's relationship to God.
E document (Elohistic): Thought to be authored by an Israelite priest about 750 B.C. (calling God Elohim), similar to J concerning the history from Abraham to Joshua. Unlike J, God limits His face-to-face contact with man through Moses and communicates with the later leaders through dreams and visions.
D document (Deuteronomic code): This would purportedly be the scroll found by Josiah in 622 B.C. (but possibly most or all of the Pentateuch) that led to a religious revival in Judah. Modern scholars attribute its writing to a Judean priest about 650 B.C. It was written in the style of a sermon about the Ten Commandments and the special laws given to Moses from much of the book of Deuteronomy.
P document (Priestly code): Said to have been written by a Judean priest around 450 B.C. about their rules and rituals and the need to keep their race pure from Gentiles.
Other Sources: The Covenant code (1,200-1,100 B.C.), the Holiness code (about 550 B.C.), Original Poems.[*]

Predominant in Genesis, Exodus, and Numbers are J, E, & P, in Leviticus is P, in Deuteronomy is D. A point to ponder: which theory on the authorship of the Pentateuch would you prefer, that of Moses or that of various writers? Consider Deuteronomy 4:25-31: if by Moses—a prophecy, if by many writers—a summary. A few examples supposedly supporting the use of strands: J Document mentions Mt. Sinai (Exod. 16:1; 19:2), whereas the E Document mentions Mt. Horeb (Exod. 3:1; Deut. 1:2) and Reuel (Exod. 2:18) and Jethro (Exod. 3:1) being the same person mentioned by different writers. I prefer the Moses authorship because of the Scriptural references to his authorship (see below) except for chapter 34 on Moses' death.

Sources of the Historical Books

(a) The Former Prophets:
Joshua: Christian scholars give credit almost entirely to Joshua, while secularists base the writing in part on the J, P, and E documents with some additions after 200 B.C.

---

[*] There are a variety of divisions of the sources and dates suggested for each source. This is a very general outline.

Judges: Traditionally, Samuel is given credit although much questioned. Secularists base the writing in part on the E document and sources similar to the J and E documents.

Samuel: Samuel traditionally credited with only the earlier writings of 1 Samuel although secularists base much of the writing on the account of Ahimaaz, son of Zadok, of King David's biography around 950 B.C. and poems from about 1,000-300 B.C. and other accounts from 750-250 B.C.

Kings: Although definite authorship is unknown, Jewish tradition credits Jeremiah with these writings written about 600-250 B.C. The original author used material from A Biography of Solomon, Book of the Chronicles of the Kings of Judah, Book of the Chronicles of the Kings of Israel, and A Chronicle of the Temple in Jerusalem (written by priests). Later editors added biographies of Elijah from about 800 B.C. and Elisha from about 750 B.C.

(b) The Latter Prophets:

As previously presented, they are generally credited with writing all or at least most of their books. Daniel (not listed among them by the Hebrews) was written, as some modern historians claim, by a Jew in Babylon around 167 B.C. At best, this idea seems to have traces of validity only if one accepts the probability that his work was a copy of Daniel's.

As previously stated, the Hebrew Old Testament originally consisted of the Judah Pentateuch (the Law), the first five books of the Old Testament. The writings are traditionally credited to Moses in the fifteenth century B.C.[50] (Exod. 17:14; 24:4-8; 34:27; Num. 33:1-2; Deut. 31:9, 24; Josh. 1:7-8; 8:31-32; 23:6; 1 Kings 2:3; 2 Kings 14:6; 21:8; 23:25; 2 Chr. 23:18; 25:4; 30:16; 35:12; Ezra 3:2; 6:18; 7:6; Neh. 8:1; 13:1; Dan. 9:11, 13; Mal. 4:4; Mark 12:26; Luke 24:27, 44; John 1:45; Acts 28:23; Rom. 10:5; 1 Cor. 9:9). These are the earliest writings. The rest of the Old Testament books (19) were added and canonized by 250 B.C. The Sadducees considered the written Torah complete at this point. The Pharisees and later the rabbinical order added to the Law of the Torah by introducing the oral law which explained the written law, adding comments to the margins of the Judaic literature. This oral law developed a tradition that eventually became more important than the written law given to Moses. This tradition led to pride in the accomplishments of the Hebrews' strict orthodoxy (Matt. 15:4-6). These additions seem to be in defiance of God's order to not add to the Law (Deut. 4:2). Mark 7:8-9, 13 condemns taking tradition over the bible. These writings became known as the **Talmud** which consists of two parts: (1) The **Mishna**, completed about 200 A.D., is considered as the second law, a summary of the rituals of the Law. It explained in finest details the rituals given in the Pentateuch, (2) The **Gemara** is a commentary, or supplemental notes, on the Mishna. There are two Gemaras: the one in Jerusalem (completed probably about the third or fourth century A.D.) known as the Palestinian Talmud and the one in Babylon (completed about 500 A.D. and the larger and more important of the two). The Babylonian Talmud was the major source of Jewish law in the eighth and ninth centuries A.D. The Talmud would be the source of all the traditions that would result in the development of Judaism down through the centuries.

It is recommended that the later chapters on "The Development & Growth of the Church" be frequently referred to for a better understanding of conditions that existed during the interpretations and translations of the Bible. We now present a brief, selected chronological history of the Bible.

Bible Writing Chronology

5th Century B.C. The Law (first five books of the Old Testament) was copied, recopied, added to, edited, and rephrased by priests up to this time and probably canonized about this time. The southern nation of Jews, Judah, and the northern nation, Israel, each had their own version of the Law (Pentateuch). The nation of Israel had intermixed with the Assyrians in northern Canaan and other peoples upon their exile. Their version of the Law became known as the **Samaritan Pentateuch** because it was edited by the Samaritan community.

4th Century B.C. A schism developed between the Jews and the Samaritans because the Jews looked at the Samaritans as an impure race. They rejected the Samaritan version of the Pentateuch. The Samaritans believed they were God's true people because their shrine, erected during the reign of Alexander the Great, was established on God's holy mountain, Gerizim (2 Macc. 6:1-2; Josephus: Antiquities. XII, 1-10; XIII, 254-258), instead of at Shiloh where the Jewish tabernacle was built. This final act influenced or led directly to the religious split between the Jews and Samaritans. Samaritans still recognize only their version of the Pentateuch and are still looking for God's coming to rescue them. The Judah Pentateuch was probably canonized by this time.

Old Testament writings had been completed by this time (about 400 B.C.), but Jewish writers continued to produce writings of their history and teachings until Rome would occupy Jerusalem in 70 A.D. These writings became known as the **Apocrypha**; Jews originally accepted these writings but would later reject them.

Up to 250 B.C. (about). The other books we now recognize as the Old Testament were added to the Law. They included (1) the Prophets: Joshua, Judges, Samuel, Kings, Isaiah, Jeremiah, Ezekiel, and The Twelve (Minor Prophets as one book), (2) writings (Hagiographa): Psalms, Job, Ruth, Song of Solomon, Proverbs, Lamentations, Ecclesiastes, Esther, Daniel, Ezra-Nehemiah, and Chronicles. These nineteen books along with the Pentateuch became the complete Hebrew text of 24 books.[51] They were written and translated in Hebrew and Aramaic languages of the Semitic peoples from the seventh century B.C. to seventh century A.D. Aramaic was the language of commerce in the Babylonian empire, similar to Hebrew and the most common Jewish language after the exile. The many copies that were made resulted in some minor non-doctrinal errors. As we shall see later, steps would be taken to ensure that these errors would not happen again. The responsibility for preservation of the original text would eventually go to the Masoretes, a school of text scholars.

Hellenism had deeply influenced the lives of Greece's captive populations and continued to do so after the Roman conquests. Many Jews lost their ability to read the Hebrew Scriptures in the Hebrew language. Therefore, the Hebrew Scriptures were translated into the more common Greek language. Called the **Septuagint** (sometimes called the LXX), it is a common Greek[52] translation of the Pentateuch from about 280-250 B.C. The translation was accomplished by 70 Jewish scholars[53] who used the most authentic Hebrew manuscripts available. Over the next three centuries, the other nineteen books of the Hebrew text would be translated to Greek.

250 B.C.-100 A.D. Between the Old and New Testaments (about 400-1 B.C.) when prophecies and revelations ceased, Hellenist writers attempted to add to the Hebrew Old Testament texts with their own apocryphal writings known as the Apocrypha. The entire Apocrypha consists of fifteen books: 1 Esdras, 2 Esdras, Tobit, Judith, The Wisdom of Solomon, Baruch, The Letter of Jeremiah, The Prayer of Azariah (Song of the Three Hebrew Children), Susanna, Bel and the Dragon, The Prayer of Manasseh, 1 Maccabees, 2 Maccabees, additions to Esther, Ecclesiasticus (Sirach). Although originally included in the Septuagint, they were all rejected later by the Jews in the first century A.D.[54] as either conflicting with the Hebrew writings or being too fantastic. However, the Apocrypha was not recognized by the early Christian Church.

The Church of England and the Episcopal Church of the United States would later include some readings of apocryphal books although they do not recognize them as fully canonical. The Roman Catholic Church would eventually accept twelve of these writings (excluding 1 & 2 Esdras and The Prayer of Manasseh), calling them <u>deuterocanonical</u>, and include them in all their bibles. The Eastern Orthodox Churches add some of 1 & 2 Esdras, Prayer of Manasseh, 3 & 4 Maccabees, and Psalm 151. The later Protestant churches would question the authenticity of the Apocrypha and only some would include them. Jesus often quoted from the Pentateuch since it was in wide use at that time. Several hundred quotations or allusions in the New Testament are taken from the Septuagint. In Jesus' time, these writings were called "Scripture."

Jesus also called them "The Word of God." Even though the Septuagint contained most of the apocryphal books, there is not one quotation by Jesus or any other person mentioned in the New Testament. This omission gives question, along with their questionable origin, to their authenticity and authority. The Septuagint translation thus contains the Hebrew Scriptures plus the Apocrypha. The Septuagint books, other than the Apocrypha, are identical to the Hebrew Scripture but are in a different order, and some books were divided into two separate books and in one case twelve books. The following illustration compares the books of Christianity with those of Judaism; the numbers in parentheses show the fifteen extra books in the Christian Bible because of splits:

Hebrew OT Books	**Split Septuagint Books**
Samuel	I Samuel & II Samuel (+1)
Kings	I Kings & II Kings (+1)
Chronicles	I Chronicles & II Chronicles (+1)Ezra-
Nehemiah	Ezra & Nehemiah (+1)
The 12 Minor Prophets	12 Individual books (+11)

This gives 39 canonized books in the Septuagint and 24 in the Hebrew Old Testament Scripture. One of the apocryphal books, 2 Esdras, in verses 14:44-48, recognizes the 24 books of the Hebrew Bible plus 70 apocryphal books. The Hebrew Old Testament text had been a work in progress from about the thirteenth century B.C. and was completed and canonized by Jews in this period (250 B.C.-100 A.D.).

70 A.D. Up to this time, the Jews kept a standard version of the Old Testament at the temple in Jerusalem. When the temple was destroyed in 70 A.D. and the standard taken to Rome, the Jews were left without a standard until the later work of the Masoretes.

90 A.D. (about). The Hebrew canonical text was finalized by rabbis ending the possibility of more additions and errors. The basic criteria for canonization was and is whether the writings were inspired of God. The text became known as the "Palestinian Canon" consisting of the 24 Hebrew Scriptural books, the Apocrypha excluded. This is the Hebrew Scripture--the **Torah**, in use today. After the Babylonian exile return, Palestine was undergoing a language transition from Hebrew to Greek. The transitional language that became popular until Greek was Aramaic. It became necessary in the temple to explain in Aramaic the Hebrew Bible readings (paraphrased) and later, in the first century A.D., to have these explanations written. This addition to the Torah is called the **Targums**.

1st Century A.D. to 2nd Century A.D. About 100 B.C., the Hebrews, through the work of many writers, had completed an authoritative Old Testament text, but it still was not deemed good enough to be a standard. New Testament writings, not accepted by Jews, were being written in common Greek by the early Christians after Christ's resurrection until about 100 A.D. when the last New Testament writing, Revelation, would be completed.

2nd Century A.D. The Bible was translated from Greek into Latin, including the Apocrypha. It was translated for the churches in the western part of the empire and became known as the *Old Latin Bible*. The bible was also translated into Syriac, known as the *Peshito Manuscripts*, for the churches of the eastern empire and from these into Arabic, Armenian, and Persian. From the second to eighth centuries, some New Testament apocryphal books were written for, among other reasons, the filling in of the Bible's near silence on Jesus' early life and days between His crucifixion and resurrection and for the support of heretical doctrines. These books provided fantastic and incredibly exaggerated stories directed toward the ignorant and unenlightened masses and were never canonized.[55]

170-200 A.D. Rabbi Judah the Prince decided that it was time that the oral law was written down. Since, according to Jewish history, the oral law was given to Moses on Mt Sinai, it was never recorded as the Covenant Law had been. Up to this time, the oral law was communicated to the people orally by the rabbis. Rabbi Judah the Prince consulted many other rabbis to obtain the most authentic memories as possible.

200 A.D. The work of Rabbi Judah the Prince was completed and was named the *Mishna*. Rabbis realized around 219 A.D. that the Mishna was not enough; they thought it was too complicated for the average Jew to understand. Rabbis met in Jerusalem and in Babylon to discuss the best ways to explain the Laws, the results: the *Jerusalem (Palestinian) Talmud* (about 300 A.D.) and the *Babylonian Talmud* (500 A.D., the largest, simplest, and most popular today). This work combined the written and oral traditions together and is the encyclopedia of all Jewish life.

Near End of 3d Century. Lucian of Antioch began publishing his translation, with extensive editing, of the New Testament from a conglomeration of manuscripts. This version became the standard of the Greek Churches in the east even after Latin translations became available.

325 A.D. about. The Codex Vaticanus was produced. It is the oldest, almost complete extant New Testament manuscript.[56]

393 A.D. The Synod of Hippo canonized the 27 New Testament books and the Synod of Carthage re-canonized them in 397 A.D. and 419 A.D., recognizing divine authorship.

382-405 A.D. The Christian Old Testament and New Testament were translated by Jerome, a Biblical scholar from Dalmatia, to Latin from the Hebrew and Aramaic texts and also some Greek texts. This version became known as the *Latin Vulgate* with the inclusion of the Apocrypha although relegated to secondary text status or appendices; it was non-canonical but fit for reading. The Latin Vulgate would be the official and only Christian bible for about 1,000 years, Christians bringing it to England in the sixth century A.D.

5th to 10th Century A.D. The Jewish community was still without a standard version of the Old Testament. Starting about 550 A.D., a school of Jewish text scholars and scribes, **Masoretes**, would start to accumulate and consolidate all the surviving copies and copies-of-copies-of-copies of the Hebrew Old Testament in an attempt to identify and correct the minor copying errors that had occurred through the centuries and to ensure that errors would not occur again. Several copying improvements were initiated to accomplish this task:[57] (1) Checkpoints were added in the margins of the new copies to prevent future additions and deletions of words, (2) the Masoretes drew up rules for copying texts, (3) because the Hebrew Language had no vowels, they added punctuation marks around 700 A.D. (vowel points) to every word to help standardize pronunciations. The work of the Masoretes is identified as the Masoretic text (Masorah), being the standard source of all future copies including the English versions.

1000-1010. The work of the Masoretes was completed. Their text became known as the *Leningrad Codex* and is still the oldest complete Hebrew bible to survive to date.[58] By this time, Latin had become the most popular language in the western church (Roman Catholic). Only the high church officials and the wealthy laity were schooled in this language, leading the church to fear that the masses were not capable of making accurate interpretations of Biblical writings.

1380-1382. The Old and New Testaments were translated into English by John Wycliffe using the Latin Vulgate. This bible was for the common people, giving them the ability to read and interpret scripture and determine for themselves that Christians had direct access to Jesus.

1415. The Council of Florence condemned the Wycliffe translation.

1517. Start of the Protestant Reformation with a splitting from the Roman Catholic Church.

1525-1526. William Tyndale translated the original Greek and Hebrew New Testament into English. He was forced to leave England for Germany because of the Church's persecution, under papal control, of his translations.

1534. Martin Luther translated the entire Bible to German, excluding the Apocrypha.

1546. The Council of Trent canonized the Apocrypha books of the Latin Vulgate except for The Prayer of Manasseh and 1 and 2 Esdras, relegating them to appendices. The English translation known as the *Douay Version* would be based on this text (1582 New Testament/1609 Old Testament). It contained marginal notes giving Roman Catholic interpretations of controversial passages and is still in use today. The Council also declared the church traditions as equal in importance to the Bible,[59] possibly to counteract the Protestant movement of the Reformation period.

1560. The *Geneva Bible* was written because of the dissatisfaction of the reformists with the Latin translations and their interpretations. It was the first complete bible translation (Old and New Testaments) from the original Greek and Hebrew texts. This first addition contained the Apocrypha, later omitted in some versions. It was the first English bible to number the verses and included excessive marginal notes depicting Calvinistic and Protestant interpretations and therefore was banned from the Church of England.

1611. The *King James Version Bible (KJV)* was translated into English from the Masoretic text by 50 some scholars. The Apocrypha was included as an appendix.

1643. The Westminster *Confession* recognized 39 Old Testament and 27 New Testament books as canonical but declared the apocryphal books not divinely inspired and therefore not canonical.

1749-1752. The *Challoner Version* of the Douay Bible was written.

1883 (about). The *Revised Version (RV) Bible* was printed.

1901. The *American Standard Version (ASV) Bible* was printed.

1941. The text of the Challoner Version was revised resulting in the *Confraternity Version*.

1947. The Dead Sea Scrolls were discovered in the northwest coastal corner of the Dead Sea. They would be excavated from 1951-1958.

1952. The *Revised Standard Version (RSV) Bible* was printed.

1971. The *Living Bible* was printed.

1978. The *New International Version (NIV) Bible* was printed.

1982. The *New King James Version (NKJV) Bible* was printed.

1989. The *New Revised Standard Version (NRSV) Bible* was printed.

It was and has been to the present day the desire of Biblical scholars, because of the many manuscripts discovered over the centuries and up to recent times, to investigate and test scriptural texts for faithfulness to the autographs even after the many translations that appeared after the Latin Vulgate: Egyptian (Coptic), German (Gothic), Roman (Latin), etc. The oldest copies of whole or partial New Testament manuscripts are from the years of 100-500 A.D. Some were copied fastidiously by scribes making their texts extremely accurate with the original manuscripts. Other copies were made by scribes intent on clarifying texts by paraphrase, additions, and deletions, and of course all were susceptible to unintentional errors. Methods and tools were developed to determine the authorships and dates of manuscripts and to test the accuracy of the writings: historical context of the text itself, archeological artifacts discovered with manuscripts, the style of writing, handwriting form, genre, radiocarbon testing, and comparisons to existing canonized texts (usually the Masoretic Texts). These developments, along with careful, open-minded analysis of existing texts, have answered or at least softened secular criticism of seeming discrepancies and errors in the texts.

As we have seen, the Old Testament was a product of the Jewish community and the New Testament was a product of the early church community before it was divided and before it was organized into any particular religion (Protestant, Roman Catholic, Eastern Orthodox). The Old Testament prepared the way for Messiah, and the New Testament revealed God's plan.

For a snapshot overview of Biblical development we present now the following graphic display:

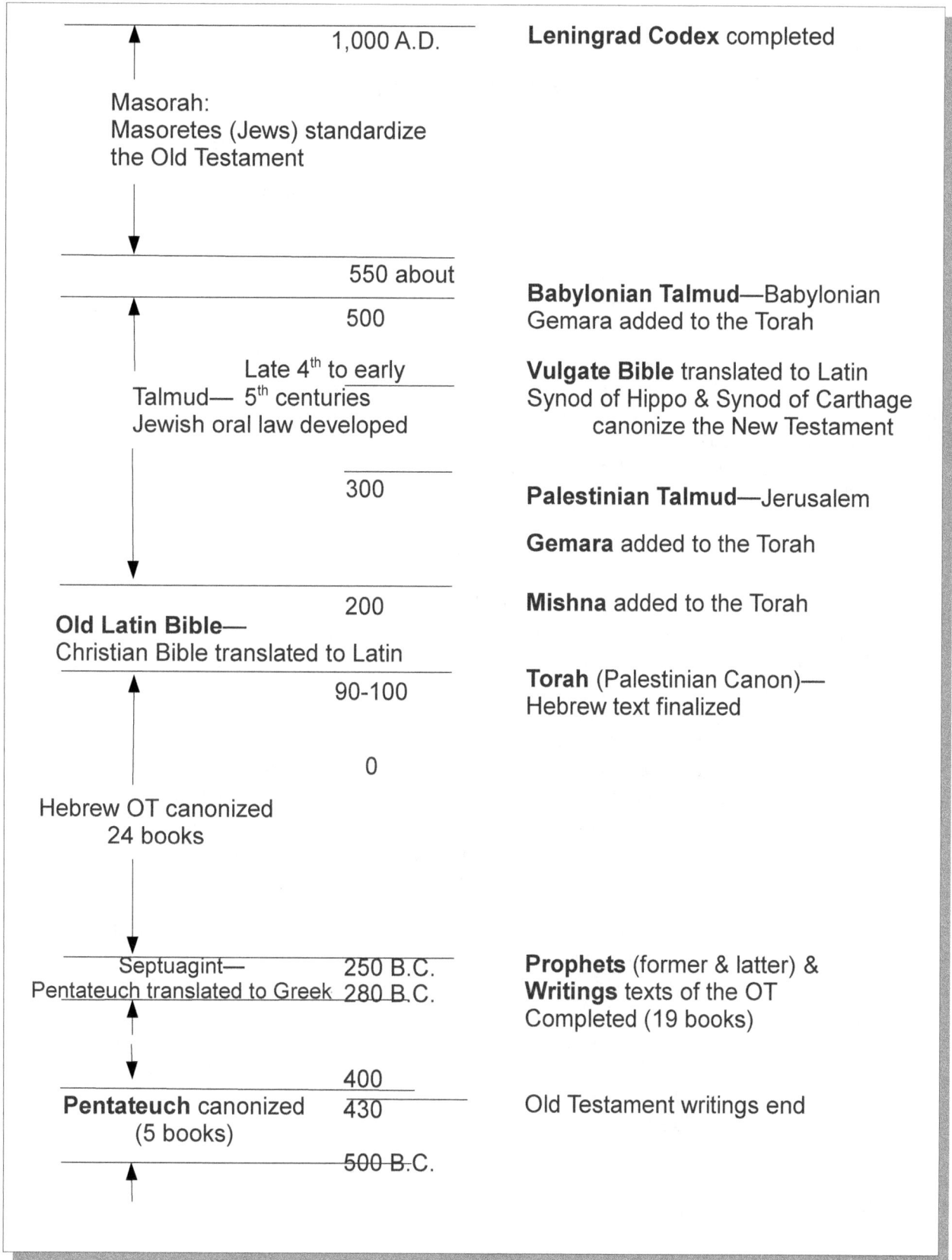

	1,000 A.D.	**Leningrad Codex** completed
Masorah: Masoretes (Jews) standardize the Old Testament		
	550 about	
	500	**Babylonian Talmud**—Babylonian Gemara added to the Torah
Late 4th to early Talmud— 5th centuries Jewish oral law developed		**Vulgate Bible** translated to Latin Synod of Hippo & Synod of Carthage canonize the New Testament
	300	**Palestinian Talmud**—Jerusalem
		Gemara added to the Torah
	200	**Mishna** added to the Torah
Old Latin Bible— Christian Bible translated to Latin		
	90-100	**Torah** (Palestinian Canon)— Hebrew text finalized
	0	
Hebrew OT canonized 24 books		
Septuagint— Pentateuch translated to Greek	250 B.C. 280 B.C.	**Prophets** (former & latter) & **Writings** texts of the OT Completed (19 books)
	400	
Pentateuch canonized (5 books)	430	Old Testament writings end
	500 B.C.	

11

JESUS, THE PROMISED MESSIAH

Throughout the Old Testament, we find evidence of God's plan for mankind. Many persons were made righteous in the eyes of God because of their faith in His promises, although they did not understand exactly how God would accomplish much of it (Heb. 11:11-13). The eleventh chapter of Hebrews presents many of these people and their examples of righteousness obtained through faith: Abel, Enoch, Noah, Abraham, Sarah, Isaac, Jacob, Joseph, Moses, Rahab, Gideon, Barak, Samson, Jephthah, David, Samuel and the prophets. Abraham foresaw the coming of Christ (John 8:56)—the Messiah, Savior, Redeemer. With His coming, man's righteousness manifested itself in faith in the Son of God to save them from their sinfulness (Rom. 3:24; 11:26-27; Gal. 3:13; Eph. 1:5-7).

The covenant with Abram was unconditional; The Sinai Covenant was conditional upon Abram's physical seeds (Jews). The Hebrews broke the covenant: by moving to Egypt (Heb. 8:9) where they were put in bondage, they broke the Sinai Covenant by refusing to enter the promised land, and they broke the Promised Land Covenant. But God would not forget his promise to Abraham and his seed—he would send a Messiah to offer a new plan to Abraham's spiritual seed: Gentiles (Gen. 12:3; 22:18; 26:4; Isa. 11:10; John 10:16; Acts 3:25; 10:44-45; 13:46-47; 15:7-9, 17; Rom. 11:17-18, 25; 15:12; Gal. 3:7-9, 14-17, 28) and Jews in Christ (Jer. 31:31; Rom. 11:26-27; Gal. 3:28-29; Heb. 8:10; 12:23-24). Israel was dispersed throughout the world as punishment for their disobedience (Ezek. 36:19). They had physically returned in part to the Promised Land in 1948 and will eventually re-inherit their land completely after Jesus' Second Coming to finalize the new covenant.

At the advent of Messiah, Herod I (the Great) (37-4 B.C.), son of Antipater an Idumean (Edomite) who was procurator of Judea (Josephus: Wars I, 123), was made governor of Judea, subordinate to Caesar Augustus the Roman emperor (Josephus: Wars I, 386-390). He was called "King of the Jews" (Josephus: Wars I, 282). The territory of Judea was located in the southern portion of Palestine with Galilee in the north and Samaria between the two. Jews were shown favor and were allowed to practice their religion although polytheism existed in the Roman Empire during Jesus' lifetime: Greek God Isis, Yahweh among the Jews, and the Persian God Mithras, to name a few.

Devout Jews looked for the promised savior (Messiah) who would soon come in power and glory to establish a worldly kingdom on earth where they would become rulers instead of captives (Deut. 18:15-19; Dan. 7:13; Acts 1:6). They believed this even though their Torah gave a different picture of Messiah: a peaceful teacher of the Kingdom who would offer Himself as a final sacrifice to save them from their sins (Gen. 49:10-11; Psa. 2:2, 6-12; 22:1-8; 24:7-10; 45:6-7; 68:18; 69:21; 72:10-11; 110:1; 118:22; Isa. 7:14; 8:14-15; 9:2, 6-7; 11:1-5; 28:16; 32:1; 40:10-11; 42:1-4; 49:6; 52:13-15; 53:4-12; Jer. 23:5-6; 33:15-16; Micah 5:2; Zech. 3:8; 6:12-13; 9:9; 11:12; 12:10; 13:1, 7; Mal. 3:1). Jewish religion during Christ's time consisted of a formal tradition with its strict rituals which Jesus criticized (Matt. 15:3, 6, 9; Mark 7:8-9, 13). The Jews were proud of their heritage of being Jews and tried to be righteous by the Law (Rom. 9:30-32; 10:1-3).

The prophet Daniel was more specific on the time of arrival of Messiah: there would be 490 years (70 weeks of years) of further punishment of Judah (Dan. 9:24-27). There are many interpretations of this Scripture—see the chapter "The Kingdom to Come" for this analysis.

Jesus was born in 5 B.C. (one or two years before the death of Herod) in a small town called Bethlehem as foretold (Isa. 7:14; 9:6; Mic. 5:2). Although Herod had restored Jerusalem and the temple (Josephus: Wars I, 401-402), undoubtedly for political reasons and not because of his piety, his evil actions speak for themselves: he feared losing his throne so he had his wife and two sons murdered and also his enemies and the babies of Bethlehem and the surrounding areas to prevent the real King of the Jews, Jesus, from threatening his rule (Matt. 2:16-18) as prophesied (Jer. 31:15).

Jesus, who possessed the Holy Spirit from birth (Luke 1:15; 3:21-22), was a Nazarene (Matt. 2:23; 21:11; John 1:46; 19:19; Acts 24:5). Nazareth was a small town in southern Galilee, Jesus' childhood home (Matt. 2:23; Luke 2:4, 51). He was also a Galilean (Isa. 9:1; Matt. 4:13-16; 21:11; Mark 14:70). Galilee was a territory inhabited mostly by Gentiles north of Judea, west of the Jordan River and the Sea of Galilee. Galileans, like Samaritans, were hated by the Jews. He was called from Egypt (Hos. 11:1)--his parents had moved to save Him from Herod (Matt. 2:14-15).

Little is known from Scripture of Jesus' early life to the time of his anointing (baptism). We do know that even as a young boy He knew who He was and what His mission was. In the story of His parents' visit to Jerusalem and His being left behind at the temple, Jesus states that He was going about His father's work (Luke 2:41-49). John the Baptist (foretold in Mal. 3:1) also knew that Jesus was the Messiah (John 1:29-34). He prophesied His coming (Luke 3:4, 16-18; John 1:6-8, 15-16, 23-27). In 27 A.D. he baptized Jesus (Matt. 3:13-17; Mark 1:2-11; Luke 3:21-22; John 1:29-34), when Jesus was about thirty-one years old (Luke 3:23) to anoint Him for His ministry (Matt. 3:2) and therefore prepared the way for the Church Age to be followed by the eternal *Kingdom of Heaven* on earth. Jesus announced His ministry at the Nazareth synagogue (Luke 4:16-19, 21). This ministry would last for 3 1/2 years. Herod Antipas (4 B.C.-39 A.D.), under Roman Emperor Caesar Augustus, was ruler over Judea at the time. Jesus recruited all His disciples from this region except for Judas.

Jesus had many enemies among the high priests, Scribes, Pharisees, and Sadducees, because they believed Messiah would come in power to overthrow their oppressors, the Romans. They feared that Jesus would draw away many of their flock (John 5:18; 7:31-32, 47-49; 11:47-48). For this reason, they were looking for a reason to rid themselves of Him. After Jesus raised Lazarus from the grave, the **Sanhedrin**[60] called a special meeting, presided over by Caiaphas (18-36 A.D.) the high priest, to discuss the threat of Jesus on the status quo. They agreed that Jesus must die and sent Him to Pontius Pilate, Roman governor of Judea (26-36 A.D.) (Matt. 27:2; Luke 3:1), for trial and execution. Pilate found no guilt, so he sent Jesus to King Herod Antipas, king of Galilee, that he might be relieved of the responsibility of condemning Jesus. Herod only mocked Jesus and sent Him back to Pilate who finally condemned Him (Luke 23:1-24). Under the Romans, Jews were prohibited from putting anyone to death (John 18:31). Led by Caiaphas, they had authority only in Judea, a Roman province, and could only pronounce a death sentence; they needed to convince the Roman authorities to perform executions. Nicodemus, a Pharisee, was also a member of the Sanhedrin. He tried to defend Jesus against the Pharisees before His arrest (John 7:50-51) and provided burial perfumes (John 19:39-40). Joseph, another Sanhedrin, provided Jesus' tomb (Matt. 27:57-60; Mark 15:42-46; Luke 23:50-54; John 19:38-42). The apostle Paul, before his conversion, was a Sanhedrin.

Jesus willingly offered Himself as a sacrifice for the forgiveness of sins (Matt. 9:12-13; 26:53; Luke 19:10; John 10: 17-18; 14:31), for He knew His destiny was to die for the remission of mankind's sins (Luke 18:31-33; John 10:15-18) as Isaiah prophesied (Isa. 53:1-12). He was the final, perfect sacrifice, the Lamb of God (Isa. 53:7; John 1:29, 36; 1 Cor. 5:7; Heb. 9:12; 1 Peter 1:19; Rev. 5:12) whereby everlasting life would be offered to all who would believe in Him (John 8:24), unlike the Old Testament animal sacrifices that were required daily rather than forgive them (Exod. 24:8; Lev. 6-9; Heb. 7:26-28; 9:27-28; 10:1-18). The purpose of adding the Law was to show how sinful we are and in need of a savior (Rom. 3:20; 7:7; Gal. 3:19-25) and to cover sin until a better plan, the new covenant sealed by Christ's blood, would be activated (Heb. 8:7-13). The Law condemned us instead of saving us by baring our sinfulness (2 Cor. 3:6). Jesus did not cancel the letter of the Law (rules)--He fulfilled the spirit of the Law (Rom. 10:4-salvation by faith), living a perfect sin-free life (Heb. 4:15; 1 Peter 2:21-22). When we break only one of God's laws, we are guilty and unfit for Heaven (James 2:10). See the chapter "The Kingdom to Come." Since God is perfect, not capable of sinning (Heb. 6:18), all sins must be paid for. Jesus was that payment, for He was the propitiation for our sins (2 Cor. 5:21; Gal. 3:13; 1 Peter 2:24; 1 John 2:2). He did not contradict the Law as some accused Him (Matt. 5:17; John 8:46) but fulfilled it and was the only one who could keep all of the Law (2 Cor. 5:21; 1 Peter

2:21-23). Jesus was made flesh with all the temptations and hardships that are the lot of the human condition (John 1:14; Phili. 2:5-7; 1 Tim. 3:16; Heb. 2:16; 4:15), but unlike Adam, this second Adam withstood Satan's temptations (Rom. 5:15) so He could seal the Final Covenant at the cross replacing all previous covenants and initiating (establishing, inaugurating) the Kingdom of God (heaven) with the start of the *church age* (Jer. 31:31-34; Heb. 8:6-10; 9:11-15; 10:9-10; 12:24).

Immediately after Jesus gave up the Ghost, the veil of the temple was split (Matt. 27:51; Mark 15:38; Luke 23:45; 2 Cor. 3:14). This veil separated the Holy Place (where priests ministered daily) from the Most Holy Place (Holy of Holies) (Exod. 26:33-34). Up to this time, only the high priest could enter the Holy of Holies to intercede for the people and only once a year on the *Day of Atonement* (Lev. 23:27-32; Heb.9:7). The splitting of the veil symbolizes that God, through Jesus' sacrifice, had opened Himself up to man, eliminating priests and giving man direct access to Him (1 Cor. 11:25; Heb. 9:8; 10:19-20). Christ, by entering the Holy of Holies (Heb. 9:12), became the only mediator between God and man (John 10:1; 14:6; Acts 4:12; Eph. 1:22-23; 1 Tim. 2:5; Heb. 8:6; 9:11-15; 12:24; 1 John 2:1); no animal sacrifices, no rituals, no intermediaries were necessary (Matt. 23:9; Heb. 9:25-26; 10:12). Christ's death established the New Covenant--the testator must die before his will (testament) takes effect (Heb. 9:16-17).

Jesus rose from the grave in three days and would appear to His disciples and many others for the next 40 days (Acts 1:3). Jesus directed His disciples to spread the Gospel throughout the world (Matt. 28:19-20; Mark 16:15; Luke 24:47). Jesus promised that the Holy Spirit would be sent to them to dwell in their hearts (Matt. 28:19; John 7:37-39; 14:15-18, 26; 15:26; 16:7, 13; Acts 1:8; Eph. 3:17) to help and comfort them, which happened at Pentecost ten days after He ascended to Heaven (Matt. 3:11; Luke 12:11-12; John 15:26; 16:7-8, 13; 20:22; Acts 1:5, 8; 8:15-17; 10:44-48) to sit at the right hand of God to intercede (plead) for us (Rom.8:34). The spiritual Church Age is said to begin at Christ's resurrection and the physical Church Age at Pentecost (Matt. 16:18-19; 26:29; Mark 14:25; Luke 22:18; Acts 2:4, 38; Eph. 1:22) when about 3,000 Jews were saved. Satan had power over death up to that time--he authored sin that results in death, but Christ conquered death with His resurrection (Heb. 2:14). From then, true Christians' souls go directly to Heaven upon death, but our souls must wait until the Rapture (discussed later) to be united with our bodies.

The <u>Old Testament saints</u> were still in "Abraham's Bosom"[61] awaiting release. Jesus visited this place right after His crucifixion and took their souls to Heaven (Acts 2:25-27; Eph. 4:8-10), their bodies remaining until the Second Advent. But it seems that many Old Testament saints' bodies were raised (Matt. 27:51-53) at this time and went into Jerusalem to preach.

We offer the following account of some of the titles given to our Lord and Savior:

<u>**Jesus the Prophet.**</u> Jesus was the prophet God had promised (Deut. 18:15, 18; Acts 3:20, 22; 7:37). God had provided prophets to the Jewish nations of Israel and Judah prior to and during their exiles to Assyria and Babylon to warn them of their wickedness and need for repentance. Jesus foretold of His death (Mark 8:31; Mark 10:32; Luke 18:32-33) and resurrection (Luke 24:7), the establishment of His Kingdom with His church (Luke 24:49; Acts 1:8), Peter's denial (Matt. 26:33-34; Luke 22:34), Judas' betrayal (Matt. 26:21; Luke 22:47-48; John 6:70; 13:21) for 30 pieces of silver (Zech. 11:12; Matt. 26: 14-15), His Second Coming (Matt. 24:29-31; Mark 13:24-26), the destruction of the temple (Matt. 23:36; 24:2; Mark 13:2), and the last dispersion of Jews worldwide in 70 A.D. (Luke 21:23-24).

<u>**Jesus the High Priest.**</u> The destruction of the temple in 70 A.D. ended the long line of priests who had ministered in the temple since Aaron's time. The Jewish people would be without a priest until God would provide them with their final high priest like Melchizedek who would minister to them forever (Gen. 14:18; Psa. 110:4; Zech. 6:13; Heb. 2:17; 3:1; 4:14-15; 5:5-6, 9-10; 6:20; 7:1-11, 17; 8:1-5; 9:11; 10:11-14). But Jesus would not come from the tribe of Levi, Aaron's tribe, but from the tribe of Judah (Heb. 7:11-14) as prophesied (Psa. 78:67-68). That system of priesthoods handed down through the family line of Levi failed because it depended on the animal sacrifices for the forgiveness of sins (Heb. 7:27-28), whereas Jesus was the perfect, final

sacrifice, the Lamb of God. Jesus' destiny preceded that of the temporary animal sacrifices. The Law failed to make anything perfect, but Jesus gave a better hope (Heb. 7:19)—His priesthood replaced the old one and the Law (Heb.7:20-22, 24; 8:1-4) with a plan of salvation.

Jesus the Judge. The rule of the Judges began shortly after Joshua's death and ended during the rule of Saul, the first king over the Hebrew nation. The judges had preserved the Israelite nation through the most difficult time of adapting to life in the Promised Land. The judges would rescue the nation time and again when they would stray from their relationship with God. But Jesus would be the final judge to judge the Jews and the Gentiles (1 Sam. 24:15; Psa. 9:7-8; 96:13; 98:9; 110:6; 135:14; Isa. 33:22; John 5:22; Acts 10:42).

Jesus the King. When the Israelites demanded a king (1 Sam. 8:5), God warned them what would happen if they put their trust in a mortal man (1 Sam. 8:11-18). The wicked leadership of most of the kings would eventually lead to destruction of the Jewish nation. The line of ruling Kings from the ancestry of David had ended with the Babylonian exile, but the blood line was continued and the title line of ruling kings interrupted until Jesus came to sit on the Kingdom throne forever. Jesus has been king before, during, and after the rules of the earthly kings (Gen. 49:10; Psa. 2:6-8; 10:16; 29:10; 44:4; 74:12; 84:3; 98:6; Isa. 32:1; 33:22; Jer. 23:5; Matt. 21:5; Luke 19:38; John 12:13-15; 1 Tim. 6:15; Rev. 17:14; 19:16).

Jesus the Messiah. Jesus admitted who He was (Matt. 26:63-64; 27:11; Mark 14:61-62), and the apostle John quoted Jesus as to His being the Messiah (Rev. 22:16).

As we see, Jesus fulfilled all the requirements in God's plan from the beginning. He set in motion (introduced) His Kingdom plan starting with His ministry in 27 A.D. telling of the Kingdom being at hand, that is, time was drawing near to its inception (Matt. 4:12-17; 10:7; 12:28; Mark 1:15; Luke 10:9; 11:20; 17:20). He established His Kingdom plan by sealing the New (final) Covenant with the Holy Spirit (2 Cor. 1:21-22; Eph. 1:13) on His death and resurrection (Jer. 31:31-33; Heb. 2:9; 8:6-13; 9:12, 15-18; 10:16; Matt. 26:28-29; Mark 14:24-25; 15:43; Luke 14:15; 19:11; 22:16-20; 23:42, 50-51; Acts 14:21-22[62]). This covenant was unconditional–offered free to all who would accept it. See the chapter "The Kingdom to Come" for further details regarding Jesus' Second Coming.

God, because of His perfect personality, cannot lie and therefore must keep His covenants. Jesus assured the believers that He was going to prepare a place for them and would come back to redeem them (John 14:2-3). But Jesus promised that until then, He would always be with them. Jesus will develop His Kingdom on earth during the Church Age, for He is the only way to Heaven (John 10:9; 14:6; Acts 4:12). There are many other Old Testament prophecies identifying Jesus as the Messiah:

	Prophecy	Fulfillment
Messiah of the seed of Abraham	Gen. 12:1-3	Matt. 1:1
Messiah from the tribe of Judah	Gen. 49:10	Luke 3:23-33
Messiah to be born in Bethlehem	Isa. 40:3; Mic. 5:2	Luke 2:4
Time of Messiah's crucifixion	Dan. 9:25	Luke 2:1-7
Messiah to be rejected by the Jews	Isa. 53:3	Luke 23:18, 21; John 1:11
Messiah to be betrayed by a friend	Psa. 41:9	Luke 22:47-48
Messiah betrayed for 30 pieces of silver	Zech. 11:12	Matt. 26:14-15
Messiah silent to His accusers	Isa. 53:7	Mark 15:4-5
Messiah spat on and mocked	Isa. 50:6; Psa. 22:7-8	Matt. 26:67; Luke 23:35
Messiah's sacrifice for our sins	Isa. 53:4-5	Rom. 5:6, 8
Messiah to die with sinners	Isa. 53:12	Mark 15:27-28
Messiah to be pierced in His side	Zech. 12:10	John 19:34, 37; 20:27
No bones of Messiah will be broken	Psa. 34:20	John 19:32-33, 36
Messiah to be a humble king	Zech. 9:9	Matt. 21:5; John 12:14-15
Messiah's garments to be gambled for	Psa. 22:18	Matt. 27:35
Messiah forsaken by God	Psa. 22:1	Matt. 27:46

These prophecies about Jesus as the Messiah were out of His human control. No mortal human could have met all the prophetic criteria that Jesus did! God's guiding hand was behind all the circumstances that led to Jesus ministry, death, and resurrection.

Those who accept the Word, Jesus, (John 1:1, 14-15) into their hearts through faith are born again, that is, regenerated (John 3:3) and will be given a new nature (Matt. 5:3-12; 2 Peter 1:2-11) where they will be changed from within. The only requirement is that we have faith in God's plan, repent, ask for forgiveness, and ask Jesus to be the ruler of our lives.

With salvation, each believer is baptized in (with) the Holy Spirit (Matt. 3:11; Luke 3:16; 24:49; John 14:17; Acts 1:5; 8:14-17; 19:6; Rom. 8:9; 1 Cor. 12:13; Gal. 4:6; Eph. 1:13; Titus 3:5) as were the first believers at Pentecost (Acts 2:1-4, 38) and later all believers, Gentiles included (Acts 10:44-48; Rom. 3:29; 11:15-18; 15:8; Eph. 3:6) as Peter mentions (Acts 2:14-21) and Joel prophesied (Joel 2:28-29). Up to the time of Jesus, the Spirit was given only on special occasions and to leaders (Exod. 31:3; Num. 11:17, 29; Neh. 9:20; Psa. 51:11; Ezek. 36:27; Joel 2:28), but after Pentecost, the Holy Spirit would dwell within all believers (John 7:39; 14:17-18). Without possessing the Holy Spirit, one cannot be saved (Rom. 8:9), for those who are saved receive the Spirit immediately (Ezek. 36:27; Titus 3:5). God will do the rest in transforming us, either slowly or immediately, into this new person with new desires for a relationship with Him and will unite us with other Christians (Eph. 4:13, 16). From this point, with the help of the Holy Spirit, new Christians will be led to seeking to learn as much as possible of God's plans for their growth and education through bible study, prayer, worship, and Christian fellowship (Neh. 9:20; 1 Cor. 2:10; 3:18; Eph. 4:14-15; Col. 3:10; Heb. 10:25; 1 Peter 2:2). The Spirit will guide and teach us hidden things (Matt.11:25; John 14:26; 16:12-15; 1 Cor. 2:13-14). This new-found direction leads also to seeking God's will and to becoming a messenger and steward to the unredeemed world (Matt. 28:19-20; Mark 16:15; Luke 24:47-49; John 20:21, 28; Acts 1:8; 10:42; 1 Pet. 2:9; 3:15; 20:24). Thank you Jesus! It is the Christian's responsibility to keep his/her heart pure for the baptism (filling) of the Holy Spirit (Gal. 5:25; Eph. 5:18). This <u>filling of the Spirit</u> (Mark 1:9-10; Luke 3:21-22; Acts 1:8; 4:8, 31; 1 Cor. 12:8-11) is not an ongoing thing as is the <u>baptism in the Spirit</u> at the moment of salvation (Acts 8:14-18; 19:1-6) but the full measure of the Spirit's presence when we ask for it on specific occasions with a clean heart. Because God is holy, He cannot be present in us when sin is present. It is necessary to first confess our sins, repent, and seek forgiveness through prayer and actions in order to prepare our hearts for the Spirits teachings, help, and heart-changing intercessions. However, the Spirit is always in combat with the flesh through which Satan urges (Gal.

5:17), but the Christian must make the decision on who to follow. We are given Christ's righteousness when we walk in the Spirit (Isa. 41:10).

How are we to know if we are living in the Spirit or the flesh? We know by the fruits of our labors (Gal. 5:22-26) which are quite easy to discern: a changed heart manifested in righteous living, joy, peace, patience, gentleness, kindness, faithfulness, meekness, self-control, and love toward the Father, Son, Holy Spirit, and to our fellow man (Matt. 5:44; 22:37-38; Mark 12:29-31; John 13:35; Rom. 5:5; 14:17; 1 Cor. 16:22; Gal. 5:22-23; Eph. 5:9; 1 Thes. 3:12; 1 Peter 4:8; 1 John 3:14; 4:20-21), for love and faith are mutually inclusive (Gal. 5:6, 22). These fruits of the Spirit are usually developed over a period of time. In those times when we give in to the flesh, it is imperative that we confess, repent, and seek and accept forgiveness quickly so we can get back in the Spirit (Gal. 5:16; 6:1). We know of our salvation because we keep God's commandments (1 John 2:3).

If one is not growing in the faith as they know they should, that person is not allowing the Spirit to take hold of their life, a submission that is required for Christian growth. Fellowship among other Christians is an essential part of one's growth in faith and understanding. Each Christian needs all other Christians for support, comfort, and guidance. When we walk in darkness (sin, the flesh) we cannot have a close relationship with God. The longer we are apart from God the larger the gap between us and God becomes until it becomes very difficult to hear His voice.

If you think you do not hear God speaking to you through the Holy Spirit, look at the changes in your life since you gave your life to Jesus. These changes were due to the voice of the Holy Spirit convicting you of your sins and your need to repent, for I believe all good thoughts and urgings come from God even if we do not physically hear His voice (conscience).

Christ existed with God from the beginning (John 1:1). He was made flesh, lower than the angels only so He could make the perfect sacrifice to save us from our sins and thus enter Heaven (John 17:5; 1 Cor. 10:1-4; Col. 1:15-17; 1 Peter 1:19-20; 1 John 1:1-2; Rev. 1:17-18; 13:8), becoming greater than the angels (Psa. 2:7; Heb. 1:4-13).

As we have seen, the ruling line on the road map began with Adam and continued to the end of the rules of the kings, was temporarily interrupted, and then was restarted unto eternity with Christ's kingship. Jesus' blood line was never interrupted, continuing from Adam through Jacob and David and the kings (except for Saul) and then through Zerubbabel along two blood lines.

12

THE DEVELOPMENT AND GROWTH OF THE CHRISTIAN CHURCH THROUGH THE MIDDLE AGES

What's in a name? A name cannot tell us all about an era just as it cannot tell of our personalities. Names for historical periods are attempts at identifying or describing that era. Any particular era of history is preceded by many events leading to its advent. For this reason, it is difficult to determine when an age started and when it ended.

The Middle Ages saw both political and religious changes occurring in Eurasia. Territorial boundaries of the empires were changing and Christendom was undergoing doctrinal changes as it coexisted with Islam and Judaism. Depending on one's perception or goals, there are several accepted periods recognized by historians as the Middle Ages:

476-1453 A.D.:	from the fall of the Western Roman Empire to the fall of the Eastern Roman Empire.
325-1517A.D.:	from Constantine's call for the Council of Nicaea to the Protestant Reformation.
590-1517A.D.:	from Pope Gregory I taking of the papal throne to the Protestant Reformation.
476-1492 A.D.:	from the fall of the Western Roman Empire to the time Spain expelled Jews and Moors, and changes began to take place in Christendom.
500-1500 A.D.:	rounded off dates of the above periods for convenience.

It could also be acceptable to reach back as far as the fourth century, 311/312 A.D. to be exact, and recognize Constantine's act of legalizing the Roman Church as the start of the Middle Ages. I have chosen the 325-1517 A.D. period to define the Middle Ages because it sounds as good as any other choice we might make.

1st Through 7th Centuries

Jesus' followers expected His quick return to powerfully set up His Kingdom, becoming disillusioned after three days (Luke 24:21). Then ten days after Jesus ascended into Heaven, about 120 brethren were meeting when the Holy Spirit descended on them (Acts 2:1-4, 33, 38) as prophesied by Joel (Joel 2:28-29). This day became recognized as the day of **Pentecost**. It fell on the same day as the Old Testament Hebrew festival of the same name. Gifts such as preaching, healing, discerning, teaching, tongues, prophecy, etc., were given to the early church (Rom. 12:4-8; 1 Cor. 12:4-11; Eph. 4:7-12) for the purpose of establishing the church and reaching out to the lost so the church might grow. Jesus came to the Jews first. Once they rejected Him as their messiah, they were cut off and the kingdom offered to the Gentiles (John 1:11; Acts 28:26-28; Rom. 1:16; 11:19). This situation, as we shall see, will last throughout the Church Age (Jews are also invited to be converted), ending with the

Rapture, where the Jews will be grafted back in. Some people say that God replaced the Jews with Christians, but in Romans 11:1, 11-12, Paul states that they may have stumbled and fell (2 Cor. 3:12-15) and the Gentiles given salvation instead, but a remnant of redeemed Jews will be blessed in the last days.

It was and has been in God's plan to withhold His New Covenant from those who are unreceptive to it (Isa. 6:9-10; Matt. 13:10-14) just as He did to the Jews until their coming time, after the Rapture when God will open a remnant's eyes and those who accept Christ as their Messiah and Savior will be saved. We are getting a little ahead of ourselves since we will address these points later.

Up to the middle of the first century, Christians, led by the apostles (Matt. 10:2-4; Mark 3:14-19; Luke 6:13-16; Acts 1:13), were tolerated and given a certain amount of autonomy, for the Roman Empire looked on them as an offshoot of Judaism, a religion they condoned. These early Jewish Christians used the Septuagint bible to spread the Word to the Gentiles.[63] This new expansion movement made Christianity very suspect to the Roman authorities who feared losing control or even anarchy (see Map N). This was probably a major reason why Nero blamed Christians for the fire that burned Rome in 64 A.D.[64] and for the subsequent persecution of Christians. This persecution would continue until Emperor Constantine would eventually legalize the Christian Universal Catholic Church (discussed later).

With the revelations given to Paul, the early church learned that the Kingdom of Heaven was not meant only for Jews. It was always God's plan for salvation to be provided to all mankind (Acts 15:13-17; Rom. 11:19-24; Eph. 2:4-6, 11-19).

In the early years, the church was made up of only Jewish converts who believed their Messiah had come, this being the only difference between Judaism and Christianity at that time. These converts were considered heretics by the orthodox Jews, who believed their messiah had not yet come to deliver them. When Christ was offered to the Gentiles also, a split developed: traditional Jewish Christians believed the Law, especially circumcision, should still be observed, i.e., Gentiles must become Jews (Acts 15:5). Many Jewish converts could not accept that they must be changed from within rather than continuing their outward piety under the Law. Many left the church and returned to Judaism. Eventually, Christians crowded out most of the Jews over this disagreement about the Law's place in God's plan. When the temple was destroyed in 70 A.D., a permanent split occurred between the Jews and Gentiles.

It is important to mention here Peter's role in the development of the early Church. In reference to Matthew 16:13-19, Jesus asks Peter who he thinks He is. Peter answers, "Thou art the Christ, the Son of the living God" (v. 16). To this Jesus answers (paraphrased, v. 18), "Thou art Peter and upon this rock I will build my church, and the gates of hell shall not prevail against it." The interpretation of Jesus' remark to Peter would later contribute, among other differences, to a major division in the church that would climax with the Protestant Reformation (discussed later).

Paul did not seem to put himself or anyone else in a position of power in the early church, for we see in 2 Corinthians 2:8-10 that he sought the decision from the church at Corinth on a matter of discipline rather than making that decision himself. This situation began to change in the fourth century with the introduction of traditional ideas into the organizational structure of the church.

In the second century, many churches with differing interpretations of Scripture sprang up. These heretical sects claimed special knowledge from different apostles and developed written doctrines. To distinguish itself from these sects, the church started to refer to itself as the Catholic (universal) Church with each Catholic Church claiming roots to a specific apostle and ironically, as we shall see later, to Peter only. The Catholic Church also developed its own formal doctrines from the many informal doctrines among the many churches and installed a bishop to head each.

Toward the end of the second century, Christians were living in relative peace among themselves and with their pagan idol-worshiping neighbors because of Rome's preoccupation with defending its territories. To ensure that dissidents would not interrupt or interfere with the plans of the emperors, it was decreed that it was acceptable to worship any god as long as that god was submissive to the Sun god of the Roman Empire. Christians were not generally sought out but if they were arrested and charged with a crime, they were required to recant their faith and worship the emperor and the Roman god.[65] Jews and Christians would feel the brunt of this law through persecution, torture, and even death. These threats would continue on-again, off-again through the first 50 years of the third century. In 202 A.D., Septimius Severus issued an edict that outlawed Christianity and Judaism under the threat of death—usually by being fed to the arena beasts.[66] Most of the rest of the third century saw only sporadic persecutions, but the worst persecutions would occur from the early fourth century to 311 A.D. when churches and books were burned and Christians who refused to recant their faith were tortured, killed and given to slave labor.[67]

During this period of persecution, a controversy developed within the church as to what to do with the apostates, those who succumbed to the Roman threats and recanted their faith. Some held views that they should be forgiven and reinstated into the church. Others, called Donatists, emerged in the third century in North Africa who held that apostates should be excommunicated.[68] They also asserted that any sacraments delivered by an apostate were invalid. Donatists were condemned by the Orthodox Church and seceded in 316 A.D. This schism in the North African church would finally end in the early fifth century through the efforts of Augustine, bishop of Hippo, recognized as the most influential theologian of the Christian Church in the west at this time who held that sacraments offered by unworthy ministers were valid[69]—they were only agents of Christ. His teachings of salvation by grace would become the backbone of the later Reformation.

The **Christian Universal Catholic Church** expanded toward the west where a bishop was the patriarch stationed in Rome and toward the east where four patriarchs headed the church body (see Map N): Constantinople (its headquarters with a universal bishop), Alexandria, Jerusalem, and Antioch, each with a Patriarch (bishop) at the head.[70] All five patriarchs were equal in power and adhered to the same creed but differed in certain racial, philosophical, social, and linguistic ideas. As an illustration of the rift that began developing between the eastern and western churches, Roman bishop Calixtus I (218-223 A.D.) claimed the title "Bishop of Bishops." The religious services of the Church in Rome were conducted in Latin and that of the churches in the east were in Greek. See the display at the end of chapter 16 to follow the chronological development and history of the Christian Church which would be in competition with Islam and Judaism.

In the third century the Roman Empire showed signs of decay as previously presented. From about 295-310 A.D., because Christians refused to worship the Roman gods, they were removed from public office, their land confiscated, and their books and churches burned with many being martyred. However, many succumbed to the persecutions and recanted their faith.

Constantine (306-337 A.D.) became emperor of the western part of the Roman Empire in 306 A.D. and stopped the persecutions in 313 A.D., issuing the Edict of Milan[71] confirming religious freedom. Up to this time, the church that developed from the apostles was not yet centrally organized or ecclesiastical; each congregation was autonomous.[72] In 312 A.D., Constantine held that he had a vision of a fiery cross in the sky and heard a voice say, "In this sign conquer." He believed it meant that God would help him in his conquests if he embraced Christianity. He was converted and legalized Christianity in the Roman Empire. The church was on its way toward unity and hierarchal control. Constantine considered himself the head of Christianity even though Sylvester I (314-335 A.D.) was the bishop in Rome. He gained control of the eastern part of the Roman Empire in 323 A.D.

During Constantine's reign, Christianity became the primary religion of the Roman Empire (see Map N); its popularity attracted the pagan masses that would bring their pagan ideas into the church: use of incense, elaborate vestments, processionals, among others. This church-state would find political influences in church organization, structure, and worship. Before Constantine, civil authorities mostly stayed out of church arguments over theology, but after, the church began to rely on the civil authorities to expediently settle their differences rather than going through the long process of debate. From here, politics in church and government inspired infighting for power and influence among the elite within the church. In 325 A.D., Constantine called all the bishops to the **First Ecumenical Council** of the Church in an attempt to unify the church for the purpose of stabilizing the Empire. This meeting, the **Council of Nicaea I,**[73] was held in Nicaea (or Nicea) to settle the question of Jesus' godly status. Up to this time, a presbyter named Arius was preaching that Jesus was of a <u>different substance</u>, that he was a human created by God. Another group, led by Alexander of Alexandria, Hosius of Cordova, and Athanasius, believed in the orthodox view that Christ was of the <u>same substance</u> as the Father; He always existed. This view was the one held from the time of the apostles. A third group, led by Eusebius of Caesarea, held a middle-of-the-road view that Christ was of a <u>similar substance</u> with the Father. The Council accepted the view that Jesus was the son of God and of the same substance (person); the Father and Son are one (John 1:1-3). They reached this decision through the Council's belief that Scripture was the only basis for truth, and this view was according to Scripture. This decision was accepted by Constantine, for it had the best chance of keeping unity in the church, a main concern of his. Arius would continue his crusade for his viewpoint and Athanasius defended the church's orthodox view. Around 360 A.D. it seemed that Arianism would prevail except for Athanasius' diligent work in preserving the orthodox view. The Athanasian Creed would be required of all church members. The use of images was accepted and the jurisdictions of the patriarchs were defined. Church Councils would continue to be the agency from which differences would be resolved until the later shift of power to the to-be-created papacy—council decrees would need papal approval.

The Church was continually growing farther apart between the east and west up to this time. Constantine, in 330 A.D., moved his capitol from Rome to Byzantium, Greece, which was later renamed Constantinople. This move widened the church differences between east and west. The church was made popular with the pagan population after Constantine's reign. Theodosius (378-395 A.D.), a later emperor, organized the **Council of Constantinople I**[74] in 381 A.D., whereby the Holy Ghost was also recognized as of the same person as the Father and the Son completing the Holy Trinity: one God in three Persons (Matt. 28:19; John 10:30; 14:9-11; 2 Cor. 13:14; Eph. 6:17-18, 23; 1 John 5:7). This council ratified the doctrine of the Council of Nicaea I[75] that Jesus was of the same substance as God and recognized the bishop of Rome as primary in honor—above the bishop of Constantinople.[76]

Theodosius I officially made Christianity the state religion of the Roman Empire in 391 A.D. and forced membership on the population while suppressing all other religions.[77] Thus Christianity became the official religion of the Roman Empire and Latin the church language. These acts marked the beginning of the acceptance of pagans into the church with the church taking on the image of the Roman Empire. The introduction of the rosary, sign of the cross, celibacy, worship of and prayers to saints and Mary, purgatory, extreme unction, mass, and prayers for the dead would be introduced into church dogma during the Middle Ages. The church and state had become partners! Simple worship services would develop into elaborate ceremonies. The title "priest", a Jewish title, would replace "minister" or other appropriate titles.

The fourth century also saw invasions by hordes of barbaric Germans that would split the Roman Empire into east and west in 395 A.D. (see Map Q) as foretold by Daniel (Dan. 2:41). The Visigoths invaded Rome in 410 A.D. but were converted to the church. Vandals invaded North Africa from the Atlantic Ocean to Egypt in 455 A.D. The Visigoths invaded what is present day Spain and south France; the Franks invaded what is present day northern France; the Ostrogoths invaded what is present day Italy and areas northward, among others. However, the church remained the only stabilizing force among the barbarous invaders with the bishops of Rome gaining greater authority in the region.[78] The invasions would continue into the fifth century (see Map P). By now the church had grown in property and converts. The church income came from the masses and from Government grants. Government and church jobs would become very lucrative, especially the bishop positions.

From 325 A.D. to 787 A.D., the church would call seven Ecumenical (universal) Councils for the purpose of shaping the future of the church: two at Nicaea (325 & 787 A.D.), three at Constantinople (381 & 553 & 680-81 A.D.), one at Ephesus (431 A.D.), and one at Chalcedon (451 A.D.). An Ecumenical Council is a special legal meeting of the church hierarchy to discuss doctrine, administration, and discipline usually resulting in decrees being passed with the approval of the assembled members. They are not to be confused with ordinary or regularly scheduled meetings or meetings to resolve emergency situations. Circumstances that might lead to the calling of a council usually involve some form of improvement to the faith or self-defense for preservation of the faith.

In 428 A.D., Nestorius, bishop of Constantinople, started a controversy with his idea (Nestorianism) of Christ's nature—Christ being two distinct persons—rather than one person with two natures. This heretical idea was condemned by the **Council of Ephesus**[79] in 431 A.D.

Roman Bishop Leo I (440-461 A.D.) would, in 445 A.D., claim to be *Primate of all Bishops*, i.e., *Pope*. In 449 A.D., he confirmed the dogma that Jesus' spiritual and physical natures were united in Him who was sinless and divine, so He became qualified to redeem mankind with His sacrifice on the cross and provide God with satisfaction for sin. The **Council of Chalcedon,**[80] led by Leo I in 451 A.D. and allied with Constantine, completed the official establishment of five Sees given jurisdiction throughout the empire: Rome, Alexandria, Antioch, Jerusalem, and Constantinople and gave the patriarch of Constantinople equal status with the Roman patriarch. This council confirmed the dogma of Jesus' nature in agreement with Leo I and approved the **Nicene Creed** which was developed from the Council of Constantinople.

Finally, the western empire fell in 476 A.D. leaving the Roman pope to work political deals which further enhanced his power and further alienated the east (see Map R). The church became a sort of government in themselves, taking the lead in individual morality, laws, culture, education, organization, etc. Territorial controls in the west would eventually go to monarchies in the hands of kings and emperors. The fall of the western empire further increased the tensions between Rome and Constantinople—the east looked to a council of bishops for its organization while the west looked only to Rome (see Map P).[81] The influx of Slavs in the sixth century further isolated the east from Rome. Gregory I (the Great) (590-604 A.D.) is generally recognized by most present day historians as the first bishop with the official title of "Pope" (some claim Leo I: 440-461 A.D.),[82] although the Church in Rome still claims Peter as its first Pope with a continuous line of successors to the present day pope. It is said Gregory, an admirer of Augustine, took a speculation of his on purgatory as fact and made it doctrine:[83] Christians who die without full forgiveness go to a temporary place of punishment (purgatory) until they are purified for Heaven. He also recognized confession, penance, and priestly absolution for the forgiveness of sins that would keep the sinner out of purgatory, and that the living can, through masses and indulgences, help those souls exit purgatory sooner.[84] The mass would soon become a reenactment of the crucifixion.

The **Council of Constantinople II,**[85] with a disproportionate delegation of eastern bishops in 553 A.D. condemned the "Three Chapters" giving fourteen canons as reasons for anathema of Nestorian writings.

The **Council of Constantinople III**[86] in 680-681 A.D., rejected that Christ had only one will and affirmed that Christ had two wills and two natures—human and divine acting in unison.

The **Council of Nicaea II,**[87] in 787 A.D., rejected iconoclasts—those who objected to images in the church.

Islam (reference Map U)

We interject here, for historical reference and its importance in world history, the start and growth of the **Islamic** religion practiced by the Muslim world. Islam began in Arabia where pagans worshipped nature and idols. Arabians were a nomadic tribal people headed by sheiks and descendants of Ishmael, son of Isaac, as we have previously seen on the road map. Mohammed, born about 570 A.D. in Mecca, is recognized as their greatest prophet: He supposedly had, from Islamic tradition, a vision in 610/611 A.D. showing that he should become a prophet of God, greater than Jesus. Muslims cite John 14:16 as referring to the Helper (Comforter) as Mohammed; Christians cite John 14:26 to identify the Holy Spirit as the Comforter who will come in Jesus' name. Also, v. 16 says the Helper will abide with them (believers) forever, but Mohammed wasn't even born yet. Finally, Acts 1:5 says the Helper will come soon, but Mohammed didn't come for 600 years.

Mohammed was disturbed by the idol worship of his community, so he urged Arabs to worship one god. The people of the city of Mecca opposed him, so he went into hiding in the city of Medina in 622 A.D. only to return to Mecca with an army in 630 A.D. to erase the city of idolatry. Muslims count 622 A.D. as the start of the religion of Islam. Muslims believe the angel Gabriel revealed their sacred book, the Koran (Quran), to Mohammed from 610 to 632 A.D. The Koran teaches one god, Allah, a judgment day to come, profession of faith, jihad, five daily prayers, alms, Mohammed as the human prophet promised by God (citing Deut. 18:15-18), and mentions prophets Abraham, Moses, and Jesus (but not as Messiah), et al. The later development of the Sharia, part of the traditional code of Islamic law, would be derived from the Koran and teachings of Mohammed.

Mohammed at first was sympathetic to Jews and Christians, but when they rejected him, he campaigned to his death to unify the Arab tribes under his religion. He gained control over most of Arabia when he took Mecca. After his death in 632 A.D., the Koran was made the official holy book (in 650 A.D.), and his followers (caliphs) ruled and continued the wars to rid the nation of infidels. These wars developed into a religious crusade, a Holy War (jihad) required of Muslims (when necessary) to protect and/or spread Islam (Quran 4:74, 95; 9:20, 111; 47:4; 61:11). By 640 A.D., Muslims controlled Syria and Palestine. Uthman, from the aristocratic Umayyad family, was the first caliph elected in 644 A.D. In 691 A.D., Muslims built their shrine "Dome of the Rock" on the site of the Jewish temple. The empire expanded into Persia, Egypt, and North Africa (Moors or Moroccan Islams) and made inroads into Western Europe with its invasion of the Iberian Peninsula (Spain and Portugal) in 711 A.D. and occupation until 716 A.D. The expansion reached its peak in 732 A.D., but the invasion of France at the battle of Tours resulted in defeat, an event considered by many historians as determining Christianity as the major European religion. Uthman's rule would be handed down through his lineage until 750 A.D. They were political rather than religious in their reigns, ruling more like kings. Because of political and social disagreements with the Umayyads and disputes over nepotism, the Abbasids replaced the caliphs so the center of power shifted to Baghdad.

Two major divisions would emerge in the Islamic community--Sunnites and Shiites. The Islam religion during the ninth century expanded into Persia, Egypt, Syria, Iraq, and Palestine, becoming a major threat to Christianity. Jews, Christians, and Zoroastrians (of Persia: Iran today) were allowed to participate in the Arab society if they had acquired skills that would benefit that society. During this period, the Franks would take control over much of Western Europe. Islam would also become alienated from Judaism because of the Muslim idea of possessing sole truth. The new Arabian religion provided a rallying cry that gave unity to the tribes, and their successes proved to them that Allah was intervening on their behalf. Islamic doctrine says that God is impersonal to man and salvation is obtained through good works and obeying the will of God.

8th Century Through 12th Century

The Turks, who had originated from allied nomadic Germanic tribes, succeeded the Roman Empire in power after the west fell in 476 A.D. They migrated into France.

In 568 A.D., the Lombards, a Germanic people, invaded the northern part of the Byzantine Italian peninsula, establishing the Kingdom of Italy, and would eventually control most of the peninsula by 754 A.D. Pope Steven II sought protection against the Lombards and convinced Frankish king Pippin (or Pepin III {The Short}) for help. In campaigns in 754 A.D. and 756 A.D., he took control of the northern peninsula and in 756 A.D. made a donation of properties in central Italy to the pope, laying the foundation for the pope's temporal power over the Papal States.

Charlemagne (Charles the Great, 768-814 A.D.), son of Pippin and his successor who protected Pope Leo III from Roman accusations of misconduct, defined the lands in central Italy where the Pope would have temporal (secular) power over the Papal States. In 800 A.D., Leo III (795-816 A.D.) conferred the title of "Roman Emperor" (Imperator Augustus) on the Frankish king, most likely to establish his power over the kingship. Thus, the pope became an earthly king and the Holy

Roman Empire[88] was begun, although not officially named as such at this time. The emperor would often be sought to settle theological questions, usually to his own advantage. With this acquisition of power, the western church no longer needed the eastern church for support as it had until 476 A.D., e.g., for the confirmation of its popes. By 800 A.D., the Franks had brought unity back to the old Roman Empire lands and were in control of much of Western Europe: what is now Belgium, France, the Netherlands, and parts of Australia, Italy, Germany, and Spain. But with Charlemagne's death in 814 A.D., the Empire soon started to decay from the divisions among his successors and the emerging invasions by the Scandinavian Norsemen.

With protection from the emperor, the church became more secular in its quest for added influences in the communities as well as with the temporal powers. By the late 800's to the eventual split in the church in 1054 A.D., the office of pope and bishop would be sought after, bought, murdered for, and sometimes appointed by the emperor. Bribery and intrigue characterized this period.

In the east, Photius was assigned in 857 A.D. to the throne in Constantinople. Pope Nicholas I (858-867 A.D.) in Rome decried this appointment as non-canonical claiming only he had the authority to make appointments. Finally in 867 A.D., Nicholas and Photius excommunicated each other. The disagreements between the eastern and western churches did not completely divide them, but the seeds of division were being laid. The **Eastern Orthodox Church** separated itself from the **Western Roman Church** in 869 A.D. after Photius was condemned by the Eighth Ecumenical Council, **Constantinople IV,**[89] and by 1054 A.D. the split would be complete. The catalyst of the schism was the disputes that had been brewing for several centuries: (1) the filioque clause, equating Christ with God, inserted in the Nicene Creed by the western church, (2) the disagreements about jurisdictions, (3) the use of unleavened bread in the Holy Eucharist (mass), and (4) the disputes about papal authority over the eastern churches. These specific areas of contention only served to expose the real (or general) reason for the schism I believe: the quest by the western church for additional powers that would give them authority over all the churches as evidenced by the increased papal powers they garnered in later history.[90]

Leo IX (1049-1054 A.D.) sought to reform the church before it was too late. He was concerned with the influence of the rich and powerful and with the doctrine of celibacy as a means of protecting the church from nepotism.[91] However, Cerularius, the patriarch in Constantinople in the east (1043-1059 A.D.), had his own agenda--ambitions of grandeur, calling himself *Ecumenical Patriarch*, thus claiming to have authority over all the eastern churches. He excommunicated the legates sent to him by Leo X for seeking an accord and was excommunicated himself by the Western Church.[92] How this happened is debatable since Leo died shortly after. Cerularius' opposition to the western church would be considered by many historians as the single most important cause of the split between the eastern and western churches in 1054 A.D. After the split, Cerularius began making temporal (secular) decisions. Before this time, the emperors had the authority in both secular and religious matters; they often looked to the popes with their wealth and power for the support they had over the masses. The popes looked to maintain their status. The conflict between the eastern patriarch and the emperor became a power struggle that ended the alliance between them.

The Greek Church (Eastern Orthodox) would come to dominate the Middle East in competition with Islam, and the Roman Catholic Church (western) would dominate the rest of Europe. There are many differences between the Roman and Greek Churches. To go into detail would go beyond the scope of this work. In brief, we present many of these differences (also similarities) in doctrine with the Roman church, intensified because of language (Latin in Rome and Greek in Constantinople).
Differences:
- No pope or infallibility or Vicar of Christ recognized; authority rests in church councils. The Holy Spirit is the vicar (representative) of Christ (John 14:26).
- No immaculate conception.

- No surplus merits or indulgences.
- No statues allowed.
- No purgatory.

similarities:

- Pictures allowed, and saints are honored.
- 7 sacraments recognized.
- Holy Eucharist performed every Sunday and holy days.
- Belief in transubstantiation—Eucharist[93] bread is changed into the essence of Christ.
- Dead are prayed for, and dead pray for the living.
- Faith and works required for salvation.

Arabians continued their dominance over the Islamic world until 1058 A.D. when the Turks took control. Their rule would treat Christianity even more cruelly. Finally in 1095 A.D., the Crusades were started to wrestle control of the Holy Land (Palestine) from the Muslims. This war, consisting of eight crusades in all, would last until 1272 A.D. and be instrumental in preventing the spread of Turkish rule into Europe. From about 350 A.D. and toward the end of the eleventh century, Jews were tolerated as infidels (rather than heretics) by the Christian churches because they remained inconspicuous and were protected by Roman law. When they were located in numbers, they were all too willing to be subjugated to their captors so they would be permitted to govern themselves. By the early eleventh century, the Jewish population grew to significant proportions in the German area of the Roman Empire. By the twelfth century, Jews were targeted for death and confiscation of their properties. From about the middle of the twelfth century to the end of the Middle Ages, principalities (territories ruled by princes) were the normal type of monarchies that ruled Europe. Education was the primary domain of the church in the early Middle Ages. Bible reading, study, and interpretation were solely in the hands of church leaders, thus grew the traditions of the eastern and western churches. As the end of the Middle Ages approached, education slowly became available to the laity. Questions about Church dogma began growing as the church began to lose more and more of its political power. By the thirteenth century, Jews were basically barred from the trade professions because of usury.

The Crusades

The three major religions: Christianity (east and west churches and later Protestant), Islam, and Judaism had for centuries been alternating between persecution and toleration of each other. Probably no period of history is more likely to have produced controversial analyses than the period of the Crusades and Inquisitions. Some, if not many, historical writings have been tainted by their authors' biases. We will present as unbiased an analysis as possible and, where appropriate, give all sides of the story. Some dates are debatable but generally accurate depending on the availability of historical records.

By the eighth century, Islamic conquests had spread to northern Africa and Spain. Toward the end of the eleventh century, the Muslims controlled 2/3 of the Byzantine Empire (old eastern Roman Empire) except for Greece. Finally, in 1095 A.D., Pope Urban II organized the Crusades[94] to take the Holy Land from the Arabian Islamic Turks, but the army was poorly organized and failed.

1096-1099 (or 1095-1101): The first Crusade, led by the nobles of Europe, took Jerusalem in 1099 A.D. Non-Christians, Jews included, were massacred. The knights were encouraged to join the fighting with the promise of wealth and fame.

1147-1149 (or 1145-1147): The second Crusade, led by King Louis VII of France and King Conrad III of Germany, failed to take the Muslim city of Damascus.

<u>1187</u>: Muslims retook Jerusalem and allowed a degree of freedom to the Jews.

<u>1189-1192 (or 1188-1192)</u>: The third Crusade, called by Gregory VIII, led by Fredrick I of Germany and Richard I (the Lionheart) of England and Philip II of France, failed to take Jerusalem.

<u>1202-1204</u>: The fourth Crusade took and plundered Constantinople, capitol of the Christian Byzantine Empire. Pope Innocent III (1198-1216) encouraged another war in 1209 A.D. against the Cathars (heretic) in southern France (the Albigensian Crusade). This war, waged primarily by secular forces, would lead to the first Inquisition in 1233 A.D. A later children's crusade to the Holy Land failed.

<u>1217-1222</u>: The fifth Crusade was unsuccessful against the Muslims in Egypt.

<u>1228-1229</u>: The sixth Crusade, led by Holy Roman Emperor Fredrick II while under the church's ban, invaded the Holy Land and negotiated control of Jerusalem and southern Palestine with the Muslims. Jerusalem would fall to the Muslims in 1244 A.D.

<u>1248-1254 (or 1249-1252)</u>: The seventh Crusade, led by King Louis IX of France into Egypt, was unsuccessful.

<u>1270-1272</u>: The eighth Crusade, led by King Louis IX of France, failed in its attack into North Africa (Tunis). Prince Edward of England also failed in his attack of the Holy Land.

The crusades had further extended the differences of the west with the Muslims and the Byzantine Catholics.

(13th through 15th centuries)The Papal (Medieval) Inquisition

Constantine's successors believed it to be their duty to protect the church. In the sixth century, cooperation between the church and state in meting out capital punishment for heresy was first suggested. St. Augustine at first rejected this measure but later succumbed to it either by persuasion or because it was so successful in obtaining confessions. From this point onward, "church" will mean the Roman Catholic Church unless otherwise specified.

During pre-reformation times, it was generally accepted by the western church in Rome that orthodoxy should be maintained at all costs, including the use of the death penalty, even more so after the church allied itself with the Roman Empire creating the Holy Roman Empire. In the twelfth century, two groups of believers were questioning many of the doctrines[95] of the Roman Church: (1) Albigenses (southern France, northern Italy, northern Spain)—**Lateran Council III** (1179 A.D.) recognized them as heretics and renewed imprisonment of them and confiscation of their properties[96] (2) Waldenses (southern France, northern Italy)—Pope Lucius III in 1184 A.D. and **Lateran Council IV** (1215 A.D.) declared them heretics[97] and approved the doctrine of transubstantiation, etc..[98]

During the twelfth century, the church held itself innocent of executing heretics because the sentences were carried out by the civil authorities (kings, emperors, etc.) and mobs, although it was the church that rooted them out and they were tried by their bishops. In southern France, heretics were bought before the Episcopal court, tried, excommunicated if guilty, and turned over to the civil authorities for punishment (not capital). Pope Innocent III (1198-1216 A.D.) ascended and would become one of the (if not the) most powerful of all popes.[99] He would claim to be the Vicar of Christ with authority over all the kings of the earth and would decree transubstantiation based on John 6:53-54. He did not attempt to change the laws against heresy.

The church was constantly questioned, sometimes hostilely, on matters concerning the ecclesiastical hierarchy of church officials, the mass, and the sacraments, et al. Two monastic orders were started in the early years of the thirteenth century. The **Franciscan** order was based on a life of poverty for its monks and to preaching. The **Dominican** order was devoted to study, teaching, and preaching. They put professors in the universities and tried to convert Muslims and Jews.

1233: The Dominican Order, mainly, and the Franciscan Order were chartered by the next pope, Gregory IX, as inquisitors probably because of the fact that they were submissive to the church. They answered only to the pope so were in effect, autonomous--an independent court. This inquisition was established mainly in southern France, northern Italy, and Germany for the purpose of reconverting heretics to the Roman Catholic Church. Gregory IX also decreed that life imprisonment and capital punishment not be used for fear that some innocent people might suffer. However, in 1231 A.D., he recanted and gave approval of life terms for confessed and repented heretics and the death penalty for those who did not confess. The accused persons' properties were also confiscated. At the time, the crusade was being directed mainly at the Cathars (also known as Albigenses) of southern France but would eventually include Protestants after the start of the Reformation in 1517 A.D. Defendants at the inquisition were not allowed to know their accusers but could name their enemies in order to nullify their testimonies. The use of torture was officially condemned at first by the church but, according to some historians, it was often used in secret.

In 1259 A.D., Clement IV authorized torture (but with no loss of life or limb) which became more and more prevalent for extracting confessions. Most trials ended with guilty verdicts. The condemned were handed over to the secular authorities for punishment, usually penance, fine, or imprisonment for those who confessed and recanted and burning at the stake for those who refused to if enough evidence was present. The guilty person's property was also confiscated by the local ruler and sometimes shared with the church. Torture would eventually also be directed at the witnesses to extract information about the accused and also to obtain information about the accused person's friends and relatives.

Jews would also be persecuted in the thirteenth, fourteenth, and fifteenth centuries if they interfered with the societies where they were living. In 1290 A.D., they were expelled from England, in 1296 A.D. from Normandy, in 1306 A.D. from France, and in 1492 A.D. from Spain.

Fourteenth and fifteenth centuries: From 1305-1377 A.D., starting with Clement V (1305-1314 A.D.) who was pro-French, the popes resided in France. Clement would reside in Avignon, France, Urban V in Rome, Italy (see Map S). Thus there were two popes, each vying for the support of the masses: Scotland and France supported Clement while England, Scandinavia, Hungary, and Poland supported Urban. Germany was split and other nations often changed sides. Clement named 24 cardinals; 23 were French and several were his relatives. This practice of nepotism would continue into the sixteenth century.

Urban VI (1378-1389 A.D.) was made pope in 1378 A.D. He campaigned against the rich and self-important lifestyles of the bishops, the majority who were French. He appointed many Italian cardinals in an effort to wrest control from the French but made the mistake of continuing nepotism. In protest, the French cardinals elected their own pope, Clement VII (1378-1394 A.D.). This situation alienated the English with the papacy during the Hundred Years War (1337-1453 A.D.) in which the papacy served the interests of France. Neither Clement nor Urban would resign so a new pope could be elected in order to end the schism. Many councils were called to resolve the stalemate, but usually matters were made worse--once three popes claimed the papacy, each claiming roots to Peter.[100] This schism led to the "Conciliar Movement"—the struggle for supremacy between the Church Councils and the Papacy. The **Council of Constance**[101] (1414-1418 A.D.) decreed the Council's authority over the pope. Pope Eugene IV (1431-1447 A.D.) emerged victorious in 1449 A.D., and the power of the councils was taken over by the papacy.

By 1350 A.D., the Ottomans had conquered much of what we know today as Turkey and Greece. The Ottoman state was born between Islamic Arabia and the Byzantine Empire.

The black (Bubonic) plague (1347-1351 A.D.) came upon civilization and devastated the populations and economies of the world. With all the death occurring so frequently, a feeling of pessimism about man's fate came to dominate the world during and after the plague subsided. This feeling of doom would be a significant factor in the people's search for new answers to their destinations. Jews were sentenced to death as Christian communities sought to purge themselves of possible sources of this calamity. The Eastern Roman Empire and its capitol, Constantinople, fell to the Islamic Ottoman Turks in 1453 A.D. The Eastern Orthodox Church became divided along social and national lines: Romanian, Albanian, Georgian, Bohemian, Syrian, Greek, Russian, and Serbian. The recovery from the plague would be followed by a period of economic recovery and a boon in prosperity leading into the sixteenth century.

Nepotism and worldly corruption continued within the church into the fifteenth century.[102] English reformist John Wycliffe and the Lollards (his followers) among others would campaign for changes.

(1478-1820) The Spanish Inquisition

When Ferdinand V married Isabella in 1469 A.D., Spain became united against the Muslim dominance of its nation. Spain was on its way to becoming a wealthy nation due largely to the presence of the Jews who were more wealthy and influential than the national citizenry. This condition produced feelings of jealousy, anger, and anti-Semitism among the population, a typical reaction when a minority group succeeds in a society. Many Jews admitted their conversion to Christianity to escape persecution, but many of those practiced Judaism in secret. In 1478 A.D., their secret was exposed leading Pope Sixtus IV to order the inquisition to eradicate this threat to the faith. The king of Spain was given authority to nominate the inquisitors who would be confirmed by the pope. This inquisition was conducted by Isabella, a devout Catholic, and was thus independent of Rome. It is most likely, I think, that this inquisition was granted for the purpose of purifying the church of heresy (mostly of Jews, to a lesser extent of Islamics, and in the sixteenth century of Protestants). But Ferdinand more likely had other motives, probably wealth and power. Anyone with the least trace of Jewish blood, even if he were Christian, would eventually come under the scrutiny of the inquisition. The concentration of the inquisition would shift from heretic cleansing to ethnic cleansing.

The Spanish Inquisition is famous for the torture employed by the church to extract confessions and the cruelty of the punishment handed out by the civil authorities. The accused were denied counsel and witnesses were kept secret. Those who would not confess their heresy were handed over to the secular authorities to be thrown into a fire and their property confiscated.

The Iberian Peninsula was taken back from the Muslims in the early eleventh century. Jews and Muslims were banned from Spain in 1492 A.D.

It is inconceivable that so much suffering and hatred would be thrust upon mankind by the religions of this period. These acts against God's nature must be condemned regardless of the motives behind them. No justification can be made for people to betray God's will in His name. I believe it is God's will for peaceful coexistence among persons and nations and the peaceful bringing of all mankind into the Kingdom that Jesus inaugurated upon His death and resurrection.

13

THE DEVELOPMENT AND GROWTH OF THE CHRISTIAN CHURCH THROUGH THE PROTESTANT REFORMATION

(16th century)
(Reference Maps K & L)

Up to the sixteenth century, the church was the best haven against the social unrest of the times. The church enjoyed the status of state-church with support from the emperors. When the western empire fell in 476 A.D., the church was there to offer hope and leadership to the masses for the next 1,000 years.

Starting around 1400 A.D. in England, **John Wycliffe** initiated reforms in the Roman Catholic Church. These reforms would eventually lead to the **Protestant Reformation** in 1517 A.D. in Germany with Martin Luther's *95 Theses* protesting against indulgences-for-penance, among other doctrines. The doctrine of Lutheranism would evolve. The resulting split from the mother church in Rome had been developing, as we have seen, over a long period of time because of the corruption within the church, abuse of power, and other disagreements in faith and doctrine from traditions most of which were:

- Questions of Papal authority and infallibility.
- Belief in purgatory (1 Cor. 3:13-15; 2 Macc. 12:40-45 or 12:46 Douay per Roman Catholic Church), a temporary hell for those who die in venial (pardonable) sin. Those who die in mortal (fatal) sin go directly to hell with no chance of redemption. The 2 Maccabees verses cited by the Roman Catholic Church tell of money sent to Jerusalem for the souls of slain soldiers who died and were in purgatory, although Matthew 25:41 and Luke 16:19-31 indicate a permanent punishment with no escape from hell even when one has regrets. This money was for the forgiveness of sins of adultery, but adultery is a mortal sin by Roman Catholic doctrine and dooms the person to hell if not given absolution (forgiveness) before death. The 1 Corinthian verses are interpreted by the Roman Church as a reference to Purgatory while Protestants interpret the verse as speaking of rewards given to saved persons for their works of faith.[103]
- Selling of indulgences to shorten the time of loved ones in purgatory.
- Belief that forgiveness of sins can be had through good works.
- Belief in prayers and sin offerings for the dead in Purgatory (2 Macc. 12:39-45 per Roman Catholic Church).
- Church tradition, as determined by church leadership, given equal (or more) authority as Scripture.
- The stifling of individualism among the masses.
- Images (statues and Pictures) in the sanctuary, holy water, and rosaries.
- Confession and the forgiveness of sins by bishops and priests.
- Prayers to and worship of Mary & saints although Exodus 20:3; Revelation 19:20; 22:8-9 order that angels not be worshiped.

- Priests as intermediaries between God and man (ref. Eph. 1:22; Heb. 7:22-25) and celibacy of the priesthood.
- Five of the seven Sacraments questioned: Confirmation, Penance, Eucharist, Holy Order, and Anointing the Sick. Baptism and Marriage were accepted.
- Effectiveness of the Holy Eucharist as the reenactment of Christ's crucifixion and the changing of the bread wafer and wine into the body and blood of Christ—the doctrine of transubstantiation during Holy Communion. Thus God was made flesh again and died again for the forgiveness of sins during the mass (reminiscent of Old Testament sacrifices?).

Tradition is an important part of all religious groups. It can be defined as beliefs or customs that are developed throughout history. Tradition becomes an important tool through which groups attempt to define their faith. Tradition can provide uniformity and order to worship and beliefs. When any religion takes tradition to excess, it can compromise, replace, or divert the basic messages of the Scriptures.

The church had for centuries before the Reformation made political policy a major priority, sometimes at the expense of spiritual enrichment. Kings, princes, and clergy were considered more important than the ordinary members. Peasants had been protesting for simple and direct sermons, against serfdom, and the right to choose their own preachers. Around the start of the sixteenth century, the church was being questioned about its practices and doctrines by many of its members. The Reformation started in the first quarter of the sixteenth century over religious differences but would come to also include social issues: slavery, individualism, and reforms in the church and government. The Church was now faced with the prospect of winning back Protestant defectors.

A natural tendency of a religious group (church) is to trace its roots back to the apostles, in particular, Peter. Apostolic heritage would provide much credence to a religious group, even to claims of being the one true religion, or at minimum, of superiority over other religions. Most religions do at least recognize their indirect roots to the apostles through the handing down over the centuries of the church leadership. The Roman Catholic Church accepts Peter as its first pope from its tradition, but Protestants maintain that the early church was not organized but was a community of many independent churches (2 Cor. 2:10).

One major area of disagreement that was developing within the Church was the interpretation of Matthew 16:13-19 (see chapter 12). The Roman Church interpreted Jesus' words to mean: (1) He would build His Church on Peter, the rock, (2) the Church is infallible, i.e., it has not committed any errors, because no persons, groups, or nations have overcome it since it still is operating, and (3) Peter and all his papal successors have the power to admit and exclude people from the Church, in effect, authority to condemn them to Hell (v. 19). The reformers interpreted these statements differently, and the church would continue to add to its tradition up to the present day as we shall shortly see.

First, in verse 13, Jesus asks, "Who do men say that I the Son of man am?" Peter answers, "Thou art Christ, the Son of the living God" (v. 16). In verse 18, Jesus counters with, "Thou art Peter, and upon this rock I will build my Church." From the clarification of the Greek words for Peter (petros, a small rock or pebble in the masculine gender) and for rock (petra, a large rock in the feminine gender),[104] the Reformers concluded that Jesus was referring to the rock as the truth of Peter's answer in verse 16 that "He is the Christ." Another interpretation would have Jesus referring to the rock as himself, for He is the cornerstone of the Church. This truthful statement would be the rock that the Church would be built on: "Jesus is the Christ." Scripture tells us that the Church would be built upon apostles and prophets with Christ as the cornerstone and foundation (Psa. 118:22; Isa. 28:16; Matt. 21:42; Mark 12:10; Luke 20:17; Acts 4:11; Eph. 2:19-20; 1 Peter 2:6-7), and 1 Corinthians 3:9-11 names Jesus as the foundation and Christians as the building (Church). Peter had never claimed any special authority only to being an apostle and elder (e.g.: 1 Peter 1:1; 5:1-3), and Paul (writer of 11 letters in the New Testament) had never put that authority on Peter. In fact, Paul seems to have had more authority than Peter, even rebuking him for acting hypocritically toward Gentiles (Gal. 2:11-14).

Jesus had never given more honor to any disciple (Matt. 20:25-28; Mark 9:33-35; 10:35-44). Other interpreters say Jesus was referring to Pentecost when He said He would build His church on Peter because about 3,000 Jews were converted due to Peter's preaching.

Secondly, Jesus' statement that, "The gates of hell shall not prevail against the Church" (Matt. 16:18) was interpreted by the church as "shall not stand against it." Just because the Roman Church has not been overthrown does not prove that the Church is infallible, claimed the reformists.

The Roman Church would later, at the First Vatican Council in 1869-1870 A.D., describe infallibility of the pope as meaning that he could not err in statements of faith and morals while in ex cathedra--sitting on Peter's chair in his official capacity as head of the Church--often citing John 14:16-17. As with all mortals, many errors and moral sins have been committed by popes down through the centuries. But the church would come to recognize that the pope was not unable to sin and that in the cases where moral sins were committed, the popes merely succumbed to temptation--none had violated their infallibility as previously defined. The church would also come to recognize only two infallible statements being invoked: the truth of the Immaculate Conception in 1854 A.D. by Pope Pius IX and the truth of the assumption of Mary's body and soul to Heaven by Pope Pius XII in 1950 A.D. The word "faith" has never been clarified so an understanding can be made as to when the pope has made an infallible statement.

Thirdly, the Roman Church, citing Matthew 16:19, gave Peter and his successor popes the power to admit persons to the Church and to excommunicate them. But the reformers cited verse 19, and also Matthew 18:18 where Jesus said (paraphrase) to all the disciples, "Whatsoever you bind and loose" and not, "Whosoever you bind and loose" meaning that He was not referring to a person(s) that could be bound or loosed but to the Word being bound or loosed. All the apostles, not just Peter, had the power to preach (loose) the Word or to withhold (bind) the Word from the world. All Christians, being successors to the original disciples, were and are able to loose the Word or bind it.

The Roman Church today might counter the Protestant interpretation of Matthew 18:18 as Jesus' commission to priests and bishops to forgive sins also and John 20:22-23 for positive proof. A Protestant interpretation of the John verses recognizes Jesus' charge as a commission to all Christians to lead sinners by the Holy Spirit to the forgiveness of sins by God only, citing Mark 2:7 for proof.

Being commissioned as such to spread the Word, Christians will be judged from the fruits of their work, i.e., their impact on the spread of the Kingdom message through their words, deeds, lifestyle, and stewardship.

Fourthly, the Council of Nicaea in 325 A.D. had created 20 canons; the sixth described the jurisdictions of the patriarchs in Alexandria, Rome, Antioch, Constantinople, and Jerusalem. Nothing was mentioned of any of the patriarchs (especially Sylvester in Rome) as having authority over any other except the bishop of Alexandria who was secondary only to the bishop of Rome.[105]

The Reformation opened the door for free interpretation of Scripture by the individual. The result of this opportunity would lead to a pyramidal splitting of the church down through the centuries because of differences in theology and doctrine (see Maps K & T).

Martin Luther, after receiving his MA in 1505 A.D., entered a monastery in Germany. For two years he struggled with the perception of his unworthiness as a sinner, searching Scripture for answers. He could not come to an assurance that his good works as a monk could bring him redemption as the church was teaching. He was appointed as professor of Holy Scriptures at the local university in 1512 A.D. where he would finally find his solace in Romans 1:17, "Salvation is attained by righteousness through faith" (paraphrased). He now realized that he was right with God, that he was justified by his faith, not by anything he had done but from what Christ had done. He initially wanted to reform the church of its abuses of power and errors. But by 1520 A.D., his work became that of a destroyer of the church, attacking most every tradition from which the sacraments evolved but especially of the idea of the infallibility of the pope and the hierarchy of the clergy over the laity. He denied transubstantiation, purgatory, and the effectiveness of the Eucharist (mass). He was finally excommunicated from the church in 1521 A.D. and would be recognized as the major leader of

Evangelical Lutheranism. Luther's conviction that man is justified only by faith opened the Scriptures to the laity, not just to the clergy to interpret. In 1530 A.D., the "Confession of Augsburg" affirmed many Christian doctrines including Luther's interpretation of grace in salvation and rejection of merits and works earning righteousness—works are a result of righteousness.

Ulrich Zwingli, who would lead the reformation in Germany and Switzerland, began in 1519 A.D. to preach as Luther did, "Justification by faith and the sole authority of Scripture" instead of the church's stance of salvation through the honoring of the sacraments. But he differed from Luther on the interpretation of the meaning of Christ's body and blood in the bread and wine: Luther maintained that this was a physical transformation as a result of the recipient's faith, but Zwingli maintained that this was a spiritual fact. In the 1560's, he, along with John Calvin, John Knox, and Philip Melanchthon, split from Lutheranism and formed the **Reformed Church** in Switzerland and France. **John Calvin** defined the Protestant position with his writings on church discipline. His theology was challenged by Jacobus Arminius, a Dutch theologian in the early seventeenth century, and John Wesley, a Methodist theologian in the mid eighteenth century, among others. See chapter 19 for a more detailed discussion on this subject. Before this, in Switzerland in 1525 A.D., disagreements with Zwingli over matters of church and state and infant baptism (which they denied) had led to the emergence of a new group called Rebaptisers, or Anabaptists.

Because of their passive views concerning adult baptism and ideas of separation of church and state, Anabaptists were severely persecuted by the Protestant and Catholic Churches. They would become distinct from the Catholic and Protestant Reformation churches and separate themselves from society and spread to Holland, England, and Austria.

There developed a division within the Anabaptist movement. One group held a strict belief in separation of church and state, isolation from society and its modernizations, and the practice of shunning whereby excommunicated members were shunned from the congregation until they repented. The other group held more lenient views. Finally in 1693 A.D., the Anabaptists split into two factions: the Mennonites (lenient ones) and the Amish (strict ones).

The struggle between **Lutheranism** and **Catholicism** in German lands provided religious choice in some regions of Europe. The upper, middle, and lower classes were found in either religion. The German princes were equally divided in their religious choices. This was important since the ruling prince usually determined the religion of the land. Many hard-line members began to argue for separation of church and state, reasoning that once a person is converted, they belong to God's community. Since the German converts did not believe in infant baptism, they also became known as Rebaptisers. Western Europe in the sixteenth century found either Catholic or independent Lutheran churches being established.

From 1536-1558 A.D., Protestantism was established in France and Switzerland by John Calvin. France continued to be dominated by Catholics and controlled by the kings, but Calvinists (Huguenots) made inroads in the last half of the sixteenth century even though they were persecuted. Spain and Portugal (under Spanish control) remained Catholic entering the seventeenth century.

England's government in the fifteenth century consisted of the king's council of informal advisors that would develop into a more centralized committee of ministers. As the Reformation approached, a more centralized form of government evolved--the Parliament consisting of a *House of Commons* and *House of Lords*. The king remained the head of government but needed Parliament to enact laws and assess taxes. England converted to Protestantism shortly after the start of the Reformation. In 1533 A.D., King Henry VIII, through an act of Parliament but prohibited by the Roman Catholic Church, obtained a divorce from Catherine. A year later the *Act of Supremacy* removed the authority of the pope and placed it on the English king who became the royal head of the new Catholic (Henrican) Church. This church would last until 1547 A.D. when Protestantism would take control in the name of the English church. Henry laid the groundwork for the later coming of the **Anglican Church**. In 1553 A.D., under (Bloody) Mary, a Catholic, England reverted back again to Catholicism only again to revert back to Protestantism on her death in 1558 A.D. with the ascension of Queen Elizabeth I to the throne.[106]

Elizabeth defined the new Anglican faith (with its Calvinist base) with her *Thirty-Nine Articles of Faith* in 1563 A.D. The Anglican Church would come to be commonly called the Church of England in the seventeenth century. The Puritans among them sought to purify the Church of England from Roman influences and to eradicate the superstition that was prevalent in the Middle Ages.

The sixteenth century saw the Islamic Ottomans migrate eastward and take control of Asia Minor, Syria, and Palestine and southward to conquer Egypt and North Africa (see Map L). The Ottoman expansion would cease in the seventeenth century, a sign that the empire was weakening. Because of increased bureaucracy and arrogance, the empire would start to downsize in the eighteenth and nineteenth centuries.

The doctrine of Lutheranism was defined in 1577 A.D. by the *Formula of Concord*. This marked the establishment of the **Lutheran Church**.

Presbyterianism was organized in Scotland in 1643 A.D. with "The Westminster Confession of Faith" that accepted: Scripture as the only authority with no new revelations or traditions added, predestination, inherited sin, God's grace in salvation, man cannot fall from grace once justified, Christ the head of the church, baptism of babies and adults, the Lord's Supper, and more.

The Church of England would experience many splits over the following decades: Baptists, Puritans, Quakers, Methodists, and Presbyterians all of which would see their ways to the New World.

In effect, the Reformation divided the western church into north/south territories: the Protestant churches dominating the north and the Roman Catholics the south (see Map T).

14

The Roman Inquisition

(16th century to mid 17th century)

In 1542 A.D., Pope Paul III reconstituted the Papal Inquisition by creating the *Holy Office* (or *Congregation of the Inquisition*) to better administer it. It was more commonly known as the *Roman Inquisition.*[107] Its inception was due to the rising number of defections from the church since the start of the Protestant Reformation in 1517 A.D. and the heretical ideas (as determined by the church) being propagated. Up to this time, Protestants were making inroads into England, France, Germany, Switzerland, and even Italy, threatening the very existence of the Roman Catholic Church. The **Council of Trent** (1545-1563 A.D.),[108] consisting of delegates assigned by the pope, met to discuss doctrine. It authorized the use of the inquisition and enacted many reforms, some of which were: rejection of Lutheranism, Jerome's Latin Vulgate Bible declared the official canonical text, church tradition made equal to the Bible in doctrinal matters, and decreed power on the pope over all worldly leaders. Also, 2 Maccabees was canonized into the bible in support of 1 Corinthians 3:13-15 supporting the doctrine of purgatory.[109] As previously mentioned, 2 Maccabees is an apocryphal book not recognized as inspired by Protestants. The 1 Corinthian verses were interpreted by the Roman Church as referring to the loss of salvation when peoples' works are burned by fire, but then they will eventually be saved. Most Protestants interpreted these verses as speaking of people coming before the judgment seat of God to receive their rewards. If they had been true to Christ to the end, they would receive their rewards, but if they had not remained true, their works would be burned, that is, they would lose their reward but not their salvation. Catholic clerics were ordered to preach against Protestants under the threat of being accused as heretics. The **Counter-Reformation** was therefore installed to counteract Protestantism. In 1559 A.D., Pope Paul IV published the first *Index of Forbidden Books* which included the writings of all the reformation writers.

Torture continued to be widely used to extract confessions, and life imprisonment and the death penalty (usually burning at the stake) were punishments expected from the church when heretics were handed over to the state. Persons sentenced to either of these punishments also had their property confiscated even if they were sentenced posthumously. It seems that excommunication would have been a more appropriate punishment to the poor souls who were so harshly treated. It is a church's responsibility to bring souls into the kingdom, not to pass such final judgment that gives up hope of repentance.

The Holy Office was replaced by the *Congregation for the Doctrine of Faith* at the **II Vatican Council** (1962-1965 A.D.). Today, the church admits to the occasional misuse of torture by isolated individuals but maintains that the church had put restrictions on its use and tried to regulate it, although some used it to gain wealth through confiscations, especially during the Spanish Inquisition. The inquisitors were, and are, generally held in high regard by the church because of their integrity, sensibility, and fairness, asserting that because of these qualities, civil judges attached little merit to confessions extracted by torture.

Today the Roman Catholic Church looks back on the inquisitions as having been humanely administered and that the church had never officially sentenced anyone to death but that they had merely excommunicated them and had turned them over to the state, usually with recommendations of mercy. Protestants have alleged, however, that it was well understood at the time by all parties that state authorities were duty bound (under papal thread of excommunication) to carry out death sentences. The church also claims that the Protestant reformers also believed that death was an appropriate sentence for heresy, but evidence seems to come from a few scattered cases. The Protestant Reformation is viewed as an apostasy of the faith by the Roman Catholic Church. Heresy is viewed as a crime by the church that the secular rulers, members of the church themselves, were obligated to punish. Whether or not the inquisitions were justified is a moot point to the church that looked upon itself as protector of the faith.

15

CHRISTIANITY ESTABLISHED IN THE NEW WORLD

(15th through 18th centuries)

Religious history cannot be fairly understood or appreciated as an isolated study. As we have seen up to now, politics is ever so entwined with religion, so making a study of either in isolation is quite difficult and unfair. We will therefore interject secular history with our presentation of the development and spread of religion to the New World in the hope of providing perspective and continuity to this important subject.

European religions and cultures started to expand to the New World about 1415 A.D. through efforts to find a new sea route to the Asian trade markets. The first to do so were the Portuguese, most notably, Vasco da Gama and Bartolomeu Dias who found routes along the west coast of Africa and around the Cape of Good Hope. In 1492 A.D., Spanish explorer Christopher Columbus, seeking a direct westerly route to the Indies, thought he had reached his destination, but he instead landed on the North American continent. Spanish conquistadors would conquer all the areas of Central and South America, most notably Mexico (by Herman Cortez), Peru (by Francisco Pizarro), and Brazil (by Pedro Cabral). Colonization later became a goal of the Portuguese as well as the Spaniards and with it the expansion of Christianity through the efforts of converting the Indian inhabitants of the New World.

North American colonization was initiated by the Spanish along the southern Gulf Coast, but the territories seemed of little value to them, so they concentrated their efforts in Mexico and South America. The French explored the east coast as far north as Nova Scotia and settled in Quebec in the early seventeenth century. In 1598 A.D., King Henry IV of Roman Catholic France endorsed the *Edict of Nantes* granting religious and civil rights to the Protestant Huguenots. The Dutch settled between Delaware and Connecticut and the Swedes around Delaware.

England finally became a player in the exploration and settlement of the New World. Initial explorations by Francis Drake and Walter Raleigh, among others, offered a new chance at life for the poor and the **Puritans** (a religious sect started around 1560-70 A.D.) who did not want to leave the Church of England (Anglican Church) but rather to reform it of its rites, rituals, ceremonies and hierarchy while still giving allegiance to the church. Education would become a focal point in their beliefs, enabling all participants to make logical and meaningful decisions toward their salvation, individualism being of prime importance. They believed in piety (spiritual repentance before conversion), spiritual evidence of conversion, and Christian growth after conversion. The first successful settlement was founded at Jamestown in 1607 A.D. after a perilous start, where starvation, disease, the threat of the Indian inhabitants, and their own inabilities to survive almost destroyed the settlement. Future settlements were granted to individuals by charter with the stipulation that all laws enacted must agree with English law. The Puritans saw this new milieu as their chance for a new beginning with religious freedom.

Another group of separatists, **Pilgrims**, left England around 1620 A.D. and settled in Holland because of their dissatisfaction with the Church of England. They believed basically as the Puritans but sought simplicity in their religion and life. They were against the substitution of a king as the religious head of the church. They left on their ship, the Mayflower, in 1620 A.D. and landed at Plymouth Rock at Cape Cod, Massachusetts. In 1630 A.D., 1,000 persons, mostly Puritans, left England and settled in

Massachusetts Bay. The greatest number of future immigrants to resettle in the new world would come from England. The most powerful nations of the world at that time were France and Iberia,[110] Spain as #1.

By the mid-seventeenth century, Massachusetts had adopted a two-house legislation with a governor elected by church members. About the same time, Puritans gained control of the Mother Land, England, and elected Oliver Cromwell as head. England attempted to protect the government and Church of England with three acts:

The Corporation Act (1661)—required an oath of allegiance to the government and church.
The Five-Mile Act (1665)—made it unlawful for lay persons to preach, allowed only ordained persons through the Church of England, required allegiance to the church and state, outlawed secret religious meetings contrary to the Church of England.
The Conventicle Act (1670)—abolished secret meetings and permitted breaking in and entering.

In 1687 A.D., England (now predominately Catholic and Anglican) passed The "Declaration of Indulgence" giving freedom of religion to nonconformists and canceling oaths of allegiance to the government and church. Migrations to the New World continued with settlements being made in today's New England area, New York, Pennsylvania (by William Penn, a Quaker), Maryland (where Roman Catholics settled in 1634 A.D.), with a melting pot of other nationalities with their religious affiliations intermixing. The myriad of small colonies that were springing up, each with their English-style two-house legislature and governor accountable to England, presented a control problem for mother England. She would attempt for the remainder of the seventeenth century to enact policy geared to increase control of colonial trade and to consolidate all the colonies under English rule through stiffer charter requirements and dissolution or changes made to existing ones.

The *Thirty Years' War* (1618-1648 A.D.)[111] was fought throughout Europe over minor religious differences and political aggression (or the fear of). The Peace (Treaty) of Westphalia[112] ended this war and effectively collapsed the Holy Roman Empire by curtailing its secular control over the Christian world, establishing international sovereignty and equality among the states and establishing binding international treaties. France won a decisive battle against Spain in 1643 A.D. at Rocroi and war with Spain would continue until 1659 A.D. By then, France had succeeded Spain as the dominant European nation for the remainder of the seventeenth century. In 1685 A.D., Louis XIV revoked the Edict of Nantes and declared France entirely Catholic.

England took full control of the territories east of the Mississippi River in the eighteenth century with the French controlling Canada. The English colonies in the south, because of the short supply of labor, began importing slaves from Africa and the West Indies. Europe was relatively peaceful during the eighteenth century, and Roman Catholics would be restricted and discriminated against by the mostly Protestant colonies until the revolution. For the purposes of raising revenues from its colonies, England imposed several taxes:

- Sugar Act of 1764 A.D.--tax on sugar, rum, and molasses imports.
- Stamp Act of 1765 A.D.--stamps made a requirement on all legal documents and papers.
- Townsend Act of 1767 A.D.--taxes on many imports into America.

The cry of "Taxation without representation" quickly led to repeal of these taxes because of the hostilities they aroused among the colonists. In 1773 A.D., the British gave a monopoly to the East India Company on tea exported to the colonies resulting in the Boston Tea Party, a retaliatory act. England closed the port until the cost of the tea was paid. Another bone of contention was the presence of British troops in America, viewed by the thirteen colonies as a strategic British tactic in case of revolt. In 1774 A.D., the colonies boycotted British goods and formally required England to correct the wrongs it had imposed on the colonies. With the threat of the British presence, the threat of taxes, and most importantly, repression of religious freedom (the Anglican church was the English state religion), the colonies began readying themselves for war. The first confrontation came at Lexington, Massachusetts in 1775 A.D. Although they were defeated at the battle of Bunker Hill (actually nearby Breed's Hill) in Boston, the colonies won the respect of France for their ability to inflict heavy casualties on the British. The colonies also gained confidence that they could fight against such a formidable foe. Finally, the colonist's victory at Saratoga in late 1775 A.D. convinced France the colonies could win the war. For fear of a victory by their enemies, the British, France agreed to ally itself with the colonies. The battle of Saratoga would become viewed by later historians as the turning point in the American Revolution. After defeating the English, Congress endorsed the colonies' Declaration of Independence on July 4, 1776.

The colonies finally obtained independence with a treaty signed with the British on September 3, 1783 A.D. The drawing up of the Constitution would be completed in 1787 A.D. Of main concern of the founding fathers was the protection of individual rights against governmental authority. For this reason, a balance of power was established between the federal, state, and local authorities. The Roman Catholic Church would find a marked increase in membership in the centuries following the revolution. By the late seventeenth century, the **Church of England** had established itself in the southern colonies of the New World and grew until the American Revolution. But church membership became suspect during these times of difficulty with the British. The Anglican Church was divided and seemed dead at war's end, but in 1783 A.D., it would emerge as the **Protestant Episcopal Church** (now known as the Episcopal Church) and become independent in 1789 A.D.

16

MAJOR PROTESTANT DENOMINATIONS IN THE USA

(18ᵗʰ to 21ˢᵗ centuries)

We have seen that <u>Christianity</u> is the name attributed or claimed by: The Roman Catholic Church, the Eastern Orthodox Churches, and the Protestant Churches. All these religions worship the same God but in different ways with some major differences in theology as previously noted. The greatest divide exists between the Catholic churches and Protestant churches.

It is beyond the scope of this work to try to validate or deny any aspirations of superiority by any one religion. The beliefs of any religion should stand on the merits of its agreement with Scripture. If we are to believe that the Bible is the inspired word of God (2 Peter 1:20-21), then we must accept the fact that it is sufficient for leading us to salvation. Tradition, with its developing dogmas, cannot add anything to what Christ has already done for us (Matt. 15:3; Mark 7:9; Col. 2:8).

The major <u>world religions</u> that worship one God (monotheism) today are:

- Christianity--Christ is recognized as the Messiah through whom redemption is obtained.

- Judaism--same God as Christians except Messiah has not yet come to free the nation of oppression. Salvation comes through obedience to the Law. Jesus recognized only as a prophet, but some Jews will eventually accept Jesus, especially in the last days.

- Islam--Salvation is obtained by obedience to the laws given to Mohammed and the lesser prophets and to good works. Jesus is recognized only as a prophet, citing Deuteronomy 34:10 as if it were written after Jesus' lifetime. We use the term "religion" loosely here when in fact, Islam is actually a movement or in many cases a form of government.

The differences between these religions are so vast that wars and persecutions have resulted among all of them. Ecumenism, even between Catholics and Protestants, is almost impossible because of the differences in basic theologies and doctrine dealing with the road to Heaven. The most that can be expected is to obtain coexistence. However, God can save souls across the church lines, for salvation is about giving one's life over to Christ through individual faith regardless of church affiliation. But Christianity and Islam are dedicated to converting the world to their religion, Christianity mostly through peaceful works today (but sometimes of questionable motives in the past) and Islam, by persuasion and by radical force through any means to its end if necessary. Judaism is smug in its religion and would prefer to keep God all to itself. Jesus, the son of God, the Messiah, is the barrier that separates Christianity from all other religions as mentioned in Scripture as a stumbling stone (Isa. 8:14; Matt. 21:42; Mark 12:10; Luke 20:17; Rom. 9:32-33; 1 Cor. 1:23; 1 Peter 2:8). All three religions recognize the same god but differ in theology, but Christianity is the only religion recognizing Jesus as Messiah and part of the triune God.

Because of the encouragement for individualism and free interpretation of Scripture from the Protestant Reformation, many different Protestant denominations evolved from the days of Calvin and Luther. We have already presented the Roman Catholic Church as much in detail as the scope of this work will allow but before we continue, first a few words about the **Ecumenical Councils** after the first seven. The last two Councils are identified as **Vatican Councils** conducted by the Roman Catholic Church. The Vatican Councils were Ecumenical councils held long after the Protestant Reformation. Special details will be given to some of the more important Councils.

8th Ecumenical Council , Constantinople IV (869-70). It condemned Photius. (Adrian II presided). See also chapter 12.

9th Ecumenical Council, Lateran I, (1123).

10th Ecumenical Council, Lateran II, (1139).

11th Ecumenical Council, Lateran III, (1179).

12th Ecumenical Council, Lateran IV, (1215). It decreed 70 reforms and was presided over by Innocent III. It accepted transubstantiation and decreed for confessions at least yearly.

13th Ecumenical Council, Lyons I, (1245). Deposed Holy Roman Emperor Fredrick II; ordered a new crusade (7th) under St. Louis. It was presided over by Innocent IV.

14th Ecumenical Council, Lyons II, (1274).

15th Ecumenical Council, Vienna, (1311-1312).

16th Ecumenical Council, Constance, (1414-1418). It attempted to end the schism between the Eastern Orthodox and Roman Catholic Churches and was presided over by Gregory XI.

17th Ecumenical Council, Basle, (1431-37), Ferrara (1438-1439), Florence (1439-1445).

18th Ecumenical Council, Lateran V, (1512-17).

19th Ecumenical Council, Trent, (1545-1563). Measures were presented to defend against the Protestant Reformation. See also chapter 14.

20th Ecumenical Council, the First Vatican Council (1869-1870).[113] It was presided over by Pius IX. The Eastern Churches were invited, but no representatives attended. Its accomplishments were:
- The dogma of the infallibility of the pope was confirmed when in ex cathedra, while exercising his office as the shepherd and teacher of all Christians by virtue of his supreme authority; he defines a doctrine in matters of faith and morals.
- All the popes are successors from Peter and inherit his authority.
- Anathema (excommunication) for all who oppose church doctrine.
- The Roman Catholic Church has authority over all other churches.
- Salvation depends on the acceptance of all church decrees and doctrine.
- The pope has authority over Ecumenical Councils.
- Accepted seven sacraments necessary for salvation.
- Accepted purgatory, images, indulgences, traditions, transubstantiation, prayers to saints.

21st Ecumenical Council, the Second Vatican Council (1962-1965). Modernization of the Church and attempts at the unification with the Eastern Orthodox and Protestant churches were major reasons for this council. All the Eastern Orthodox Churches sent representatives except the Greek Orthodox Church. Its major accomplishments were (see also chapter 14):
- Changes in the practices of the Sacraments.

- Mass in the vernacular with congregational singing.
- More participation in the Mass by the laity.
- A more acceptable attitude toward non-Catholics.
- Regret for the actions that led to the East-West split. Rescinded Cerularius' excommunication by Leo IX.
- Changed the name of the *Holy Office* to *Congregation for the Doctrine of Faith*.

A brief review of the histories of some of these major Protestant religions with their respective theologies is now offered. We group these churches as Christian in the sense that they recognize Jesus as the Christ although some scholars adhere to a much stricter definition depending on their faith. Any religion that contradicts or adds/subtracts from scripture is viewed as a cult by most Biblical scholars (2 Cor. 11:4, 13-15) as is the case with the Mormons and Jehovah's Witnesses.

Baptists

They had their start as British Separatists in the early seventeenth century. They opposed the Church of England more strongly than the Separatists and differed with them and other Arminian theologists concerning baptism (reserved only for confessed, of-age believers) and prevenient grace (instead, believed in common grace that restrains sins and shows us our need for redemption). John Smyth, a Separatist living among the Mennonites in Holland, received his inspiration for the Baptist movement. Smyth organized the first Baptist Church in England in 1609 A.D. Separation of church and state was a major principle of this faith. By 1641 A.D., two Baptist churches were established in the New World, the first by Roger Williams in 1639 A.D. in Rhode Island.

Much of their beliefs had their roots in Calvinism and "saving grace" theology that draws sinners to faith in Jesus for salvation. In 1845 A.D., Southern Baptists seceded from the organization because of organizational differences and because of the slavery controversy.

Baptists have maintained a democratic individualism, each church being independent of any other and each individual being independent concerning matters of faith. However, they have been united by agreement with certain principles of faith: sole infallible authority of the Bible and its validity as the word of God with no new revelations or tradition to be added, immortality after death, separation of church and state, the redemption of believers, predestination, the Lord's Supper, and adult baptism by immersion after confession of faith, among other things. Southern Baptists are more conservative in theology than their northern counterparts and are more Calvinistic in their faith.

The first African-American Baptist church was organized in 1773 A.D. As the Civil War approached, African-Americans belonged to either the Baptist or Methodist Church, but after the war, the more democratic and simplistic Baptist faith became more attractive to them.

Presbyterians

John Calvin laid the foundation of this denomination during the Reformation, and John Knox organized the church in Scotland and the British Isles. Calvin could not accept the strict and rigid forms of worship in the Roman Catholic Church. Churches were also established in England, Ireland, Germany, France, the Netherlands (Dutch), and Switzerland. British Presbyterians fled to the New World with the Pilgrims in 1620 A.D., the remaining Presbyterians stayed with the Church of England. In Calvinist thought, God is the supreme ruler of the universe with man being completely dependent on Him. Presbyterians are highly concerned with a strict form of an organized hierarchal structure, individual interpretation of Scripture, and the education of the clergy and laity. They use the Book of Confessions containing nine creeds: the Apostles Creed and the Nicene Creed being two of them.

Lutherans

Lutheranism began in the early years of the Reformation in Germany from the results of the works of Martin Luther, Ulrich Zwingli, John Calvin, Philip Melanchthon, and John Knox (see chapter 13 for their works). Luther rediscovered the Bible after centuries of church discouragement of private Scripture reading by the laity. He centered church doctrine with salvation through faith because of his revelation of righteousness through faith from which he felt reborn. Lutheranism became a disparaging catch word by Luther's enemies to describe the movement away from the Roman Catholic Church. The movement broke into two branches: Evangelical Lutheranism led by Luther and Melanchthon and the Reformed Church led by Calvin, Zwingli, and Knox. After spreading into much of Europe, the church would migrate to the New World in Delaware in 1638 A.D. The church grew along the Atlantic coast from New York to Georgia and then westward; the need to organize became apparent. Over the years, the church made great efforts at unification. All the Lutheran churches are built on Luther's idea of justification by faith in Jesus—affirmed in 1530 A.D. by the "Confession of Augsburg," the Bible as God-inspired, the Apostles Creed, the Nicene Creed, the Athanasian Creed, sacraments of baptism (infants and adults), the Lord's Supper, secular works, rites, traditions are dead, inherited sin, God's grace in salvation, and a rejection of transubstantiation, among other things.

Mennonites

The first community of Mennonites originated from the Anabaptist movement in Switzerland in 1525 A.D. and quickly spread to Holland (Netherlands, Dutch) and northern Germany in 1530 A.D. They disagreed with Zwingli on his soft stance against the unification movement of church and state. They denied infant baptism, so they were known as Anabaptists (or Rebaptists). The movement was named after Menno Simons, a converted Roman Catholic priest who established more congregations in Holland. The movement spread slowly (because of their isolationist views) to England and then to the New World during the eighteenth century. The first settlement in the New World was at Georgetown, Pennsylvania in 1683 A.D. and spread to Ohio, Virginia, Indiana, Illinois, and then on to Canada and westward. Mennonites believe in separation of church and state, Christ as the son of God, redemption through Jesus, repentance, salvation by conversion, baptism (usually by pouring) after confession of faith, and no oath-taking, among other things.

Mennonites also felt the pangs of division among their ranks. Hans Reist, a Swiss elder, was very influential in the Anabaptist movement, but some of the brethren considered him too liberal in his isolationist views and the matter of shunning. One such leading Swiss member was Jacob Amman who called for Mennonite reform near the end of the seventeenth century.

United Church of Christ

This denomination is the product of the union in 1957 A.D. of three churches: the Congregational Church, the Christian Church, and the Evangelical and Reformed Church.

The **Congregational Church** originated in England with the Pilgrims and migrated to the New World on the Mayflower in 1620 A.D. They joined with the Puritans of the Massachusetts Bay colonies around 1636 A.D. Their faith encourages independence of a believer's local church, Jesus as the son of God and savior, witnessing to the world, teachings of the truth from the Holy Spirit, the individualism of each member, and unity across denominations, among other things.

The **Christian Church** began from secessions from the Methodist, Baptist, and Presbyterian churches around the turn of the nineteenth century. They believe in Christ's authority, the Bible as God's word, individual interpretation of Scripture, and unity among Christians, among others.

The **Evangelical and Reformed Church** started in 1934 A.D. from the union of the Evangelical Synod of North America and the Reformed Church in the United States with roots from Calvin, Zwingli, and Melanchthon. Their beliefs include: the Bible as final authority, infant baptism (usually), the Lord's Supper, doctrine as given in the Heidelberg Catechism, Luther's Catechism, and the Augsburg Confession, among other things.

The United Church of Christ allows the autonomy of individual churches; they can continue with their beliefs and disciplines.

Amish

This group resulted from the split, led by Jacob Amman, with the Mennonites in Switzerland in 1693 A.D. See "Protestant Reformation" and "Mennonites" previously given. This split was the result of differences in the matters of shunning and separation from society (isolationism) including government. In the first half of the eighteenth century, most Amish migrated to Holland because of cultural persecutions and influence and for religious freedom and later to the New World along with German immigrants. No matter where they settled, the Amish were always faced with the influence of the secular world, especially in matters of religious doctrine which led to their lifestyle. One such influence was the evangelical movement in the New World. Evangelicals believed in an instantaneous conversion experience accompanied usually by strong emotions, a sign that the converted had truly made a decision for Christ. The Amish however believed in growing spiritually over a period of time into salvation from their reading of the Word and their prayers.

With the opportunities of better farming (the usual occupation) and the influences of surrounding Christian churches, the Amish migrated westward to Western Pennsylvania and Ohio during the first half of the nineteenth century. From its disorganized unity of congregational churches that were autonomous with no hierarchical structure, there developed a semblance of unity later in the century--leaders, sometimes roving, appeared in these close-knit communities. From home meetings, worship in the latter half of the century gave way to church building meetings; each church congregation was still independent from any other church congregation.

Due to the continuing influence of the growing society around them, many Amish individuals became more open-minded to ideas that many of their Mennonite brothers and sisters had succumbed to. There began developing a schism among the ranks of the Amish: one for traditional values (conservatives) and one toward liberalism. Finally, around 1870 A.D., these two factions split, the traditionalists becoming known as the *Old (order) Amish* and the liberals as *Amish Mennonites*.

Amish Mennonites continued their drift toward modernization approaching the twentieth century. Their lifestyles were becoming more progressive and their religious structure more organized with formal teaching either in their parochial schools or in state schools, closely imitating the old Mennonites. Through the first half of the twentieth century, many Amish Mennonites would join Mennonite churches until about 1940 A.D. when all were integrated in.

Because of social and political pressures, the Old Order Amish in the first half of the twentieth century would expand westward and into Canada. WWI and WWII found the Amish in perplexing situations, both legal and social because of their defiance of the draft, for they were pacifists. The Amish were given the status of "conscientious objector" which somewhat eased their situation, but many youths succumbed to the cultural pressures put on them at their non-fighting assignments. Public education was also a problem for the Amish in the twentieth century. Until the middle of the twentieth century, Amish permitted their children to attend public school until the eighth grade or age fourteen. When states tried to force age fifteen or sixteen, the Amish took a stand and were granted farming exemptions. When states started consolidating one-room schools, the Amish built their own parochial schools. Their curriculum usually consisted of the three R's and practical vocational studies. Other troubles arose with the social security system in the form of social insurance and the pension system. The Amish disagreed with these programs because of their dogma of separation of church and state. The federal government eventually exempted the Amish.

Church services today are held in members' homes on a rotating basis with each congregation electing its own preachers from their ranks. These chosen preachers receive no formal education; they must study scripture on their own with the guidance of older preachers and bishops. They receive no pay for their services. From the ages of sixteen to the early twenties, each person must make a decision on joining the church. When they do (90% usually do),[114] they are baptized into the church. This decision demands a lifetime commitment to obey the church and to cede individuality for the benefit of the community, a one-for-all and all-for-one doctrine. They are to remain meek, honest, self-controlled, quiet, humble, gentle, and simple. They believe in a literal interpretation of Scripture. Their salvation comes from living a bible-centered life with obedience to the Word of God.

In the second half of the twentieth century, the Amish, because of the rising costs of land ownership, began to migrate to the factories or went into home businesses, where many of their ranks succumbed to the pressures of modernization because of their neighbors' influences.

United Methodists

John Wesley had a religious experience at a Moravian prayer meeting in London in 1738 A.D. where he became impressed with their assurance of salvation. He received his assurance through the reading of Romans 8:16 where the "spirit bearing witness" meant to him: assurance in the heart of the believer that they have been redeemed. Wesley came to realize the meaning of being justified by faith-- a conversion of the heart resulting in holiness of character and rightful living. His future ministry would stress the free-will, heartfelt religious experience of salvation evidenced by an emotional reaction, although he would also recognize the need for formality in worship. The on-fire John Wesley, with his brother Charles and a friend, George Whitefield, tried to live their faith within the Church of England, but the church had become staid and formalized; they were never satisfied that the church's teachings led to salvation. Because of their efforts for spiritual renewal within the church, they were eventually barred from its doors. They started the first Methodist church in London in 1740 A.D. The church attracted mainly the lower class; the staid upper class ridiculed them because of their station in life and their zeal for preaching and converting souls.

Wesley believed in different kinds of God-given grace: (1) Prevenient grace that is given to the individual at birth that points us to accept saving grace that leads to salvation and lasts to the first instance of one's recognition and desire for a relationship with God, (2) Converting (saving) grace that provides justification and a new heart, (3) Sanctifying grace that enables one to mature as a Christian, and (4) Glorifying grace that takes us into the presence of God. Wesley also added that the means of grace consisted of two overt, required acts on one's part: (1) Works of piety: prayer, the Lord's Supper, bible study, fasting, and Christian fellowship that bring us closer to God and (2) Works of mercy: financial and spiritual support, aid, comforting, and encouraging that provides evidence of our love of God and fellow man. These works do not earn salvation but are for spiritual growth and maintenance and are results of faith. For further Wesleyan theology and especially as it differed from Calvinistic theology, see Chapter 13.

The new denomination found its way to the New World in 1766 A.D. thanks to the leadership of John Wesley. It was established in 1784 A.D. as the Methodist Episcopal Church, incorporating Wesley's *Articles of Religion* which he adapted from the Church of England as his own. He revised the order of worship for more balance between evangelism directed at the congregation and that directed at those outside the flock (outreach evangelism).

The church would thrive in the cities but especially so in the small towns and rural areas. Small group meetings and riding ministers took the revivals to the edges of the frontiers, identifying the Methodist methods of reaching the people. In the nineteenth century, the small group meeting gave way to larger camp meetings and then to even larger meetings as church buildings became larger.

Between 1813 A.D. and 1817 A.D., many African-American groups formed their own independent churches, and in 1830 A.D. a group calling itself the Methodist Protestants broke away from the main church because of political differences. In 1844 A.D., the church split further, because of the slavery issue, into the northern body and the southern body. Finally in 1939 A.D. they were reunited along with the Methodist Protestants into the Methodist Church.

In 1968 A.D., the Methodist Church merged with the Evangelical United Brethren Church (whose doctrine was nearly identical) forming the United Methodist Church. The church recognizes the Apostles Creed (by some), the Confession of Faith, the Book of Discipline, the Methodist Articles of Religion, and in matters of faith: the Trinity, Scripture infallibility, free will, justification by faith, conversion and repentance, baptism of children and adults (usually by sprinkling), the Lord's Supper (open to all), freedom of Scripture interpretation, resurrection with future rewards, and punishments, among other things. The Wesleyan tradition is steeped in evangelism and missions. Membership is by confession of faith or letter of transfer from another church.

Episcopal Church

As previously discussed in chapter 15, the Protestant Episcopal Church (better known today simply as the Episcopal Church) emerged from the Church of England in 1789 A.D. Their faith recognizes the Apostles Creed and the Nicene Creed, the Articles of the Church of England (except the 21st article) with some changes, and belief in: personal faith, liberty in worship, religious freedom, baptism by immersion or pouring, the Lord's Supper, and penance, among other things.

Christian Church (Disciples of Christ)

This denomination started in the United States in the early nineteenth century from the works and ideas of Thomas Campbell: salvation not dependent on church affiliation or church titles, individual actions are more important than creeds, authority had no place in the church, individual faith, baptism by immersion, the Lord's Supper every Sunday, the intellect of the mind in faith rather than in emotionalism, freedom of Biblical interpretation, and no formal worship, among other things. In 1968 A.D., for the purpose of efficiency, the loosely tied individual churches were organized into a more centralized form of government.

Churches of Christ

Because of the questions about church government, they broke away from the Christian Church (Disciples of Christ) after the Civil War. They are more conservative and believe in: only Scripture-based theology, no creeds, simple worship with no musical instruments, conversion, the Trinity, the virgin birth, the resurrection of Christ, and the Bible as God's revealing word (the only source of truth), among other things. They are nondenominational with no governing body or clergy. A vigorous prayer life with Bible study and church attendance is stressed. Membership is by individual faith in Jesus as the son of God, repentance, confession of faith, and baptism by immersion.

Church of Jesus Christ of Latter-Day Saints (Mormons)

In 1823 A.D., Joseph Smith, said to be a prophet, was supposedly visited by the spirit of Moroni, son of Mormon, and shown hieroglyphic plates written by many prophets and historians of previous generations, the most notable being Mormon, Moroni, and Nephi. These records were said to be buried in New York State. They told of the true ancestors of the American Indians as Hebrews who fled Jerusalem in 600 B.C. to escape the Babylon threat and eventually sailed to the Americas. Mormons cite John 10:16 to identify these people as the ones Jesus referred to as "other sheep in His fold" although other Christian denominations recognize that Jesus was referring to the gentiles, soon to be called to the church.

In their eyes, God's plan seems to have taken a parallel course in the New World. This remnant of God's people eventually separated into two peoples about 227 A.D.: Nephites and Lamanites. After Jesus' resurrection, He supposedly visited the Nephites to deliver the news of God's plan for redemption and named the church the Church of Christ (not to be confused with the Churches of Christ). The Nephites and the Lamanites were constantly at war. In about 316 A.D., all the hieroglyphic plates were hidden until they came into the hands of Mormon in 379 A.D. during the last battles between the Nephites and the Lamanites. Finally in 381 A.D. the Nephites were destroyed. Mormon abridged the plates and Moroni added the Book of Mormon before the plates were hidden in New York State. Also told was a history of the original inhabitants of the Americas--gentile peoples called Jaredites who left the Tower of Babel around 2,200 B.C. and sailed to the Americas only to be destroyed about 410 A.D.

Smith translated the hieroglyphics in 1829 A.D. into the Book of Mormon, considered by him to be a supplement to the Christian bible which he believed had been corrupted over time. The book contains many verses and passages similar or almost identical to those in the Old and New Testaments. It presented the errors of the extant churches (the Gentile church of Satan as they said), identified the new revealed church (Church of Christ) as the true church, and identified Jesus by name as the Messiah 600 years before His advent. The book was published in 1830 A.D., and the Church of Jesus Christ of the Latter Day Saints was started soon after. Some of the tenets of the church are similar or identical with that of Protestantism: birth, crucifixion, resurrection, and the second advent of Jesus, faith in Christ and repentance for redemption and final judgment, baptismal immersion, gifts of tongues and prophecies, the Lord's Supper, and the twelve tribes of Israel being united in the last days. Some major differences with Christianity: the origin of God's church, Jesus was created by God and was the first human to achieve god status as is possible with any man, church leaders are prophets who can add to existing writings and make interpretations, the laity are not permitted to make interpretations, their other books supersede the bible where contradictions arise, and continually changing doctrine. See map 1a for a chronological presentation of the religious development of the Mormon faith.

Smith also wrote two other books of equal authority: *The Book of Doctrine and Covenants* and *The Pearl of Great Price*. Smith claimed that John the Baptist bestowed the "Priesthood of Aaron" on him and Peter, James, and John bestowed the "Priesthood of Melchizedek" on him. At his death, the *Quorum of the Twelve Apostles* was made the head of the church with Brigham Young as its president. Smith moved the church to Salt Lake City, Utah in 1847 A.D.

Jehovah's Witnesses

They were officially known as such in 1931 A.D. but trace their origins from 1872 A.D. in the United States. The congregation (they never use the word "church") was organized by Charles Russell and consisted of circuits (many groups in a specific area) ministered to by traveling ministers (all believers are ministers, no clergy recognized). Spreading of the Word is accomplished by house-to-house witnessing and the distribution of published works from their journal *The Watchtower*. They believe God created a good world that was turned bad by Satan and that Jesus, created by God and not divine, came in 1914 A.D. to defeat Satan and establish His rule. He sent out the Witnesses in 1918 A.D. to spread the Word. Satan's defeat will occur at the battle of Armageddon when Jesus will lead His angels. The righteous living and the resurrected dead will populate the world (the unrighteous dead will remain so). The 144,000 mentioned in Revelation 7 and 14 will rule with Christ in Heaven. Witnesses reject the teachings in all churches as non-scriptural, and condemn governments and businesses as tools of Satan. They refuse to work in government, salute flags, and to go to war. Among their beliefs: Jesus was not resurrected physically but as a spirit creature, no eternal punishment for lost souls (they simply die, the end), no trinity, salvation through works rather than by grace through faith, all Christianity is wrong--they are right, and only their interpretations of scripture are valid.

Seventh-Day Adventists

Adventism began in the early nineteenth century in Europe and the United States under the leadership of William Miller (1782-1849 A.D.), a Baptist minister. Adventism was not a church but a movement within the existing Protestant churches of the time. The faith recognizes Saturday as the Sabbath and rests heavily on the prophetic books of Daniel and Revelation as interpreted by Miller--Christ's Second Coming (Advent) would occur 2,300 years after 457 B.C. (our timetable says 459 B.C.--see Map 7) when the command was given to rebuild Jerusalem. Miller interpreted the 2,300 "days" mentioned in Daniel 8:14 as representing years and that the countdown would start at the same time that the 70 weeks of years mentioned in Daniel 9 would, in 457 B.C. when the rebuilding of Jerusalem began with the temple reconstruction, counting the temple rebuild as the start of the Jerusalem rebuild as mentioned in Daniel 9:25. This reasoning set the date of Christ's Second Coming to Earth to cleanse it (the sanctuary mentioned in Dan. 8:14). The calculation set the date between March 21, 1843 (if year zero is counted: 2,300-457) and March 21 1844 (if year zero is not counted as in the Gregorian calendar: 2,300-456). When these dates passed without incidence, October 22, 1844 was given as the revised date of the Second Coming. When that prediction failed; many people left the movement.

One group that remained, the Seventh-Day Adventists, justified the original date given by Miller, admitting to his error in interpreting Daniel 8:14 and reasoning that Christ <u>had</u> come, but that the sanctuary mentioned refers to the Heavenly, not Earthly sanctuary. That is, Christ has already entered the Most Holy Place, the sanctuary in Heaven, and will cleanse the earthly sanctuary at His Second Coming. Some of their beliefs are: the dead are in a state of unconsciousness waiting to be resurrected at the Second Coming, the righteous will partake of the Millennium (Pre-Millennialism), the Bible as God's revelation about Himself, prophecy, Saturday as the seventh day of the week—the Sabbath, and baptismal immersion, among other things.

Ellen White (1827-1915 A.D.), one of the founders in 1863 A.D. of the official church, is revered as a prophet to this day because of her reported visions and writings on prophetic subjects. Her many writings are considered authoritative by most members but not on equal footing with Scripture, although some members disagree.

Pentecostal Church

Pentecostal is the term applied to many different sects and religions in America and identifies their fire for the Pentecostal experience (very emotional). Many of its members came from the Methodist and Baptist Churches. Included in their numbers are the Church of God and the Assemblies of God. They believe in: the Trinity, Biblical infallibility, salvation through Jesus, the son of God, the work of the Holy Spirit, baptism (usually by immersion), healing, and speaking in tongues, among other things.

The Eastern Churches

Photius condemned the western Roman church for adding the word "filioque" to the Nicene Creed thus saying that the Holy Spirit came from the Father <u>and</u> Son rather than from only the Father as the Eastern Church believed. This difference was an important factor among the many differences between the two church bodies, producing ill will that would eventually help lead to the decisive split between the two in 1054 A.D. (see chapter 12). The Eastern Orthodox Churches (sometimes referred to as the Greek Churches) accept the declarations of the first seven ecumenical councils from 325 A.D. to 787 A.D. In general, it can be said that the Eastern Orthodox Churches became the Christian religions of the Middle East and European Slavs, while the Western Church (Roman Catholic) became the religion of Europe and the New World that it shared with Protestants.

The Eastern Orthodox Church became divided along social and national lines (see chapter 12), many of them migrating to the New World. Their denominations generally believe: the Bible as the basis for doctrine, observance of the Nicene Creed without the word "filioque," the same seven sacraments as the western church, transubstantiation, and reject: the pope as Vicar of Christ, church infallibility, surplus merits of the saints, indulgences, carved images (but accept pictures), and purgatory (but pray for the dead), among other things. Their services are very ritualistic.

Secular Influences

We have seen that orthodox theology and conservatism became dominant with the Protestant Reformation, but during the eighteenth century "Enlightenment Period," liberal theological ideas emerged with the questioning of Scripture and church tradition.[115] From the mid eighteenth century to the turn of the twentieth century, liberalism became stronger with its questioning of the Bible's authority.[116] Secular thinking, with its humanistic ideas (no God or Heaven, provable worldly realism instead of invisible spiritual things, science instead of religion, reason over faith, philosophy over theology) began to infiltrate intellectual minds. Those who, through their pride in their own intellects, rejected spiritual truths and substituted only those things that could be observed and proven, infected the masses with their worldly philosophies, embracing man as the only source of truth. Worldwide socialism has been and is their agenda as they elevate man to be the solution to improve the human condition. We need only to look at the many anti-religious changes that have been made in our society since then to know that the world is on a dangerous course toward the end times. Supposedly wise thinkers such as Darwin, Freud, Marx, Lenin, etc., have blinded many eyes to the truth. Let us remain fast in our faith no matter how tempting today's false prophets make their worldly knowledge seem. In response to this secularism at the turn of the twentieth century, fundamentalism (belief in creationism and a literal interpretation of Scripture) again strove to defeat this enemy of God's plan.[117]

Christian Church History

30 A.D.--Apostles go into the world to spread the Word

100+ A.D. about--**Western Church** in Rome under a bishop (Latin)--**Eastern Churches** (Greek) under 4
        patriarchs

330 --   "   "   "   "   "   "   " --Emperor Constantine moves the capitol from
                                                        Rome to Constantinople (Greece)

378-395--Emperor Theodosius (378-398) officially makes Christianity the state religion

395--The Roman Empire divides between east and west further depleting the influence of Rome
        Western Church under a bishop in Rome ◄──► **Eastern Churches** under 4 patriarchs in Alexandria, Antioch,
                                                                Constantinople (hdqs.), Jerusalem

445--Leo I (Roman bishop) claims "Primate of all Bishops" (pope)

476--Western Roman Empire ends

604--Gregory I (590-604) generally recognized as the first pope

630--Islam started

774--Charlemagne recognizes the pope's temporal power over
      the papal states. The pope becomes an earthly king.

867--Pope Nicolas I (858-867) & Photius, patriarch of Constantinople,
      excommunicate each other

869--Christianity split begins:

Roman Church ◄───────────► Eastern Orthodox Churches
In Rome (pope)   Hdq. in Constantinople (4 Patriarchs)

1054--**Split in Christianity is complete**

1198--Pope Innocent III (1198-1216) most powerful pope

1400--Eastern Churches divide along social lines

    Reforms initiated by John Wycliffe in England

1453--Eastern Empire falls to Islamic Ottoman Turks

1500------------

Bohemian | Syrian | Greek | Russian | Serbian | Romanian | Albanian | Georgian

1517--**Protestant Reformation** from Roman Church----see next exhibit
              started in Germany by Martin Luther (95 Theses)

1536--
                             Protestantism established in France
                             & Switzerland by John Calvin

1558--

1559--Church of England groundwork laid by King Henry VIII

1563--Queen Elizabeth finally establishes the Church of England
                    with her "39 Articles of Faith", excomm. from RCC in 1570

1577--Lutheranism doctrine defined by the "Formula of Concord"

1612--Baptists founded by John Smyth in England

1620-1636—Pilgrims & Puritans settle in New World

1639--First Baptist Church founded in America in Rhode Island
              by Roger Williams

1662--Puritans forced out of England & are absorbed by Baptists,
              Quakers, Presbyterians among others

1664--Lutheran Church is established in America in New York

1681--First Quaker settlement established in America in Philadelphia,
              Penna. by William Penn

1710--

1739--Influx of Scotch-Irish
          Methodism founded by John Wesley.   Presbyterians to America
          Break from the Church of England

1744--

1750--

1766--Methodism established in America

1806—Holy Roman Empire dissolved

2009--Roman Catholic   Protestant   Eastern Orthodox Catholic

Anabaptist Movement away from Protestantism

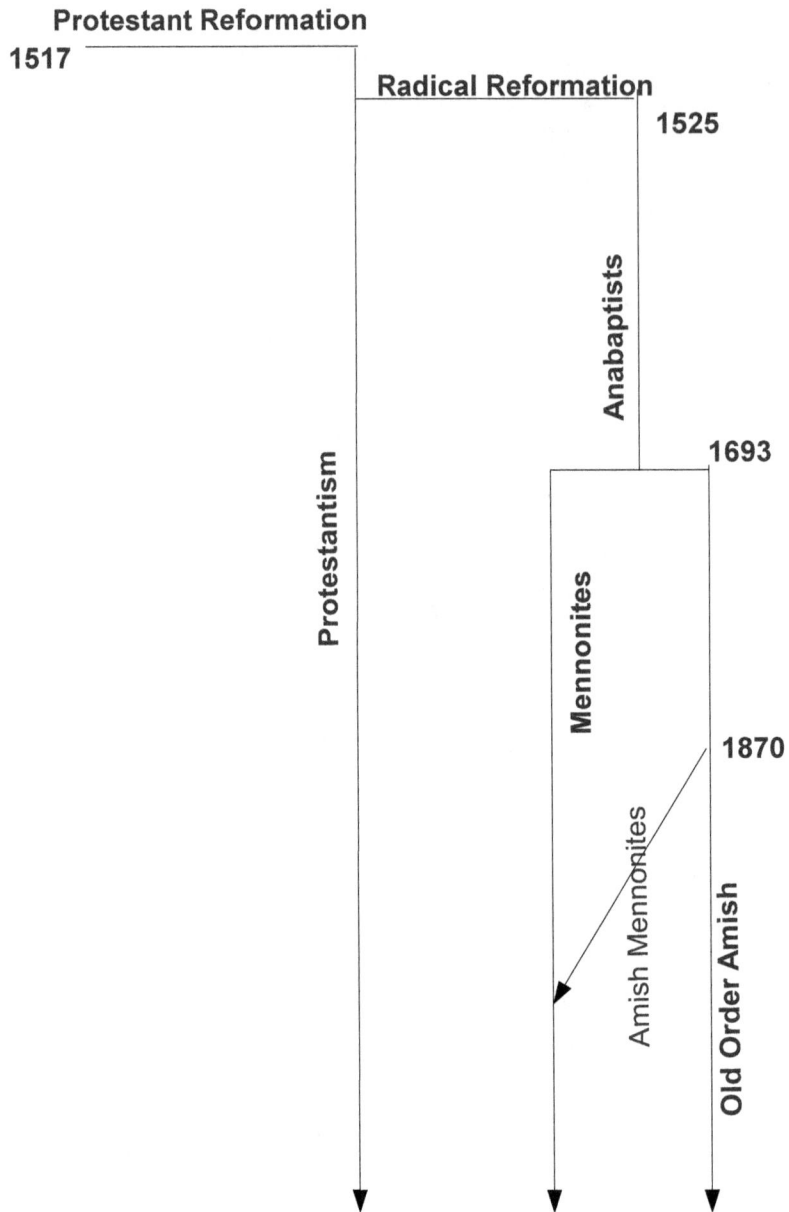

Protestant Reformation

1517

Radical Reformation

1525

Anabaptists

Protestantism

1693

Mennonites

1870

Amish Mennonites

Old Order Amish

17

LATER JEWISH HISTORY

Since Old Testament times, the Jewish people have been discriminated against and harassed, sometimes to the point of attempted extermination by Muslims, Gentiles, and especially power hungry dictators through the crusades and Middle Ages, even into the present age. It has been God's will to preserve a remnant of Jews since 586 B.C. when they lost their sovereignty to Babylon. This, God has done because of His original covenant with Abraham. This covenant is still in effect today and will be finally realized when Jesus returns to deliver God's final covenant and to gather His saints, both Jews and Gentiles alike who have accepted Him as their personal savior (Jer. 31:31-34; Ezek. 36:22-27—these verses are often also interpreted as God redeeming Israel from the Babylonian captivity).

In mid-1500 A.D., the Ottoman Turks won Muslim Arab favor in Palestine. In 1909 A.D., Jews began returning to Palestine to establish a homeland. Finally in 1917 A.D., the British took control of Palestine from the Turks, promising independence to Jews and Arabs. This truce never developed because of the constant disputes between them. The United Nations offered a plan for dividing the land in 1947 A.D. The Jews accepted this offer, but the Arabs refused. Israel declared its independence in 1948 A.D., the first step in God's plan to restore Israel to glory in the Promised Land (Psa. 126:1-2; Isa. 43:1, 5-6; Jer. 31:4, 8; Ezek. 11:17, 19; 37:5-8, 19-21). Jeremiah 31:7-8 and Ezekiel 37:9-11 foretell of the final restoration in the Millennium. In 1967 A.D., Israel gained control of all Jerusalem in the *Six-Day War*. There has been a constant struggle for dominance between these two nations since, resulting in wars, attacks, and counter-attacks. God has told us that Israel is His chosen nation, and that He will bless those who bless Israel and curse those who afflict Israel (Gen. 12:3; 1 Kings 8:53). God has promised in His covenants to give Israel a permanent possession in the Promised Land and that will complete His plan for Israel when He breathes life (spiritual) into them at Christ's Second Coming (Ezek. 37:6) when Jerusalem will belong to Him forever (2 Chr. 6:6; 7:16; 33:7). The ceding of the Gaza strip in 2005 to the Muslim world is a step backward and must be very disturbing to God as foretold in Joel 3:2. In the meantime, God is busy in His plan of gathering His people (Jer. 16:14-15).

18

THE KINGDOM TO COME

(reference road map 8)

Christians have for centuries been expecting and often unrealistically trying to predict the return of Jesus in the end times (last days) as has been foretold. This futile attempt, in reality, has no merit, for those things are left only to God, who's year could mean a thousand years (Psa. 90:4; 2 Peter 3:8) or more. Scripture gives only <u>signs</u> of when this will occur, and that is the only thing that needs to be known. The Book of Daniel provides some interesting foresight on God's timetable for dealing with Israel, Christ's ministry, and the end times. Of course, God's initial dealing with the nation of Israel and Christ's ministry is past history; the end times are yet to come.

In the 490 year prophecy of Daniel (Dan. 9:24-27), he foretells of a period of 483 years (7x7 + 62x7) and then 7 more (v. 27), when God would deal with Israel as a nation for their iniquities (v. 24). Bible scholars have generally placed the start of the 483 year period at the year a decree was issued to rebuild Jerusalem. There are four decrees identified in Scripture that were issued after the destruction of Jerusalem:

> 538 B.C.—Cyrus' decree (2 Chr. 36:22-23; Ezra 1:1-4; 5:13) to rebuild the temple.
> 520 B.C.—Darius I decree (Ezra 4:24; 6:1, 6-12) to rebuild the temple.
> 459 B.C.—Artaxerxes I decree to Ezra (Ezra 7:7-26) to rebuild the temple to 27 A.D.
>   when Christ begins His ministry.
> 446 B.C.—Artaxerxes I decree to Nehemiah (Neh. 1:1; 2:1-8) to rebuild Jerusalem.

As we can see, only the decree to Nehemiah in 446 B.C. deals with rebuilding Jerusalem (v. 25) and Messiah's crucifixion (v. 26). This period extends 483 continuous prophetic years to Christ's crucifixion in 30 A.D. From this information, the period 446 B.C. to 30 A.D., agrees with this prophecy. But this seems to be only a 476 year span (with no year zero):

> 446 B.C. to 1 B.C. = 446   years (ascension year counted as yr. 1)
> 1 B.C. to 1 A.D.   =   1   year (no year zero)
> 1 A.D. to 30 A.D. =   <u>29</u>   <u>years</u>
>   476   years total (see road map 7)

But this is not the 483 years of scripture. The explanation for the difference lies in the difference between the lunar and solar calendars. The Old Testament Hebrews adopted a calendar based on twelve months, each of which consisted of a lunar cycle of 29 ½ + days giving a year of 354 1/3 days. To compensate and bring into agreement with the astronomical seasons (solar calendar), they added a thirteenth month to seven out of every nineteen years resulting in a year of 365 ¼ days. In general, Biblical accounts, when given as factual information, use the solar calendar, i.e., the adjusted lunar calendar. However, the 483 year time span is based on a prophetic year of 360 days as in Revelation 12:14 where 3 ½ years (time + 2 times + ½ time) = 42 months (Rev. 13:5) = 1,260 days (Rev. 11:3). We convert the 483 prophetic years to solar years as:

483 years (times) 360 days/year (divided) by 365 1/4 days/year = <u>476 years</u>, the solar calendar.

Therefore, the 483 prophetic years given in Scripture spans 476 years on today's solar timetable.

In any case, God was dealing (being involved) with the nation of Israel for these 483 prophetic years (time of the Jews) no matter how we may try to pinpoint the actual times. Christ's crucifixion concluded this period, ushering in the **church age** at His resurrection where God would cease dealing directly with the Israel nation and instead deal with the Gentile nations (Heb. 9:15). The 490 year period will be completed when God again will deal with the nation of Israel during the seven year Tribulation.

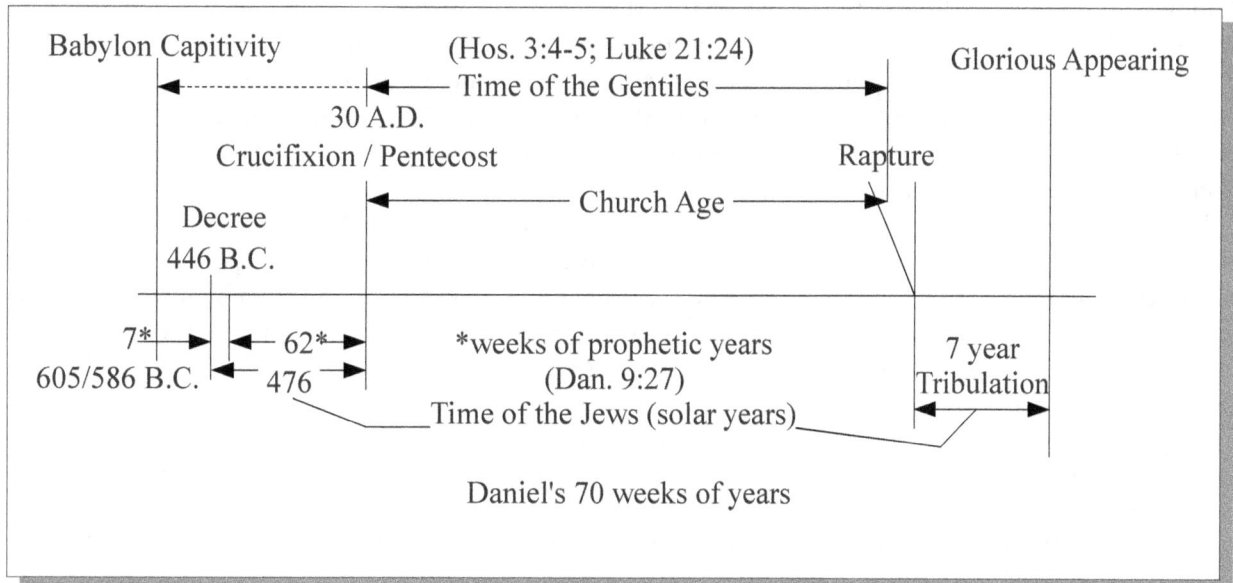

Daniel's 70 weeks of years

The 69 weeks of years (483 lunar years) of Daniel 9:25 are divided into continuous weeks of years of 7 and 62, the reason of which is not clear, except that some scholars count the first 7 weeks of years (49 years) as the time (446-397 B.C.) to rebuild Jerusalem (Neh. 3:6).

Christ came to earth to issue in the church age where God's plan of salvation (for Jews and Gentiles alike) would be provided through His death for our sins (Isa. 55:1-7; 56:1-7; 2 Cor. 5:21; Gal. 1:4). The timetable for the last days started ticking at this time (Acts 2:14-21; Heb. 1:1-2; 1 John 2:18). Jesus was the mediator of the *New Covenant* that completed and replaced the imperfect Sinai covenant (1 Cor. 11:25; 1 Tim. 2:5; Heb. 7:22; 8:6; 9:15; 12:24) that was ineffective because the Israelites broke it by not trusting God (Deut. 29:25-28; Jer. 11:10; Ezek. 44:7). As mediator, Christ became the go-between providing mankind with direct access to God. Those who come to Christ for salvation are given access to the Kingdom of Heaven. Christ earned this honor by freely giving Himself as the perfect sacrifice for sins and shedding His innocent blood for our redemption (Isa. 55:3; Jer. 31:31-34; 32:40; 33:14; Ezek. 16:60; Matt. 26:28; Mark 14:24; Luke 22:20; Rom. 11:26-27; 1 Cor. 11:25; Heb. 7:22, 27; 8:13; 9:12-26; 10:10).

Scripture speaks of the *Time of the Gentiles* (Hosea 3:4-5; Luke 21:24). Some would place this period from the Babylon conquest in 586 B.C. or from the first invasion in 605 B.C., which I do not believe, to the Rapture (which I believe) when the *Fullness of the Gentiles* is realized, that is, when the last Gentile will be saved, reasoning that God is dealing with the church up to this time and dealing with the nation of Israel during the Tribulation. Others would have the Times of the Gentiles extended to Christ's Glorious Appearing, but I don't believe Christians will endure the Tribulation. We will be presenting these subjects shortly.

With Messiah's crucifixion in 30 A.D., God temporarily ceased dealing directly with the nation of Israel but began another phase of His plan to bring all mankind, converted Jew and Gentile alike (Gal. 3:28), into the Kingdom of God. The first part of this plan was the establishment of the Church

Age where Gentiles were grafted into the Kingdom (John 10:16; 1 Peter 2:9-10). This Church Age will last until Christ's coming to rapture His church whereupon He will once again deal with the Jewish nation during the Tribulation period. In the meantime, Jerusalem has been and will continue to be trampled upon by the Gentile nations (Luke 21:24). This phase has already been presented and is a work-in-process. The souls of all believers during the Church Age go directly into God's presence upon their death (2 Cor. 5:6-9; Phili. 1:21-25). They will be given heavenly bodies at the Rapture. The next phase will be the end times that we will deal with now.

Jesus instructed His disciples on what the end times would be like and how they and all believers should react before His coming (Mark 13:5-23). He warned of the signs that would appear preceding the end times: false prophets (Matt. 24:5, 11, 24), wars and rumors of wars, earthquakes, famines, and pestilence (Matt. 24:7). He also told them that the gospel must first be preached to all the nations (Mark 13:10; Col. 1:23), and that the time of the end is unknown by all except God (Mark 13:32; Acts 1:6-7). Therefore, we must watch for these signs only to help us prepare for that day and not waste our time trying to predict the date. Malachi says that Elijah must appear before Messiah (Luke 1:13-17; Mal. 3:1; 4:5-6). Jews interpret this prophecy as speaking of the time when Messiah will come to deliver them from their oppression and overthrow the world system, but Christians look to John the Baptist for the fulfillment of this prophecy (Matt. 11:11-14; 17:11-13) even though John denied that it was him (John 1:21). Actually he may have meant that he was not Elijah in the sense that the Jews thought of his coming, or else he didn't really know that he was. Another sign worthy of our attention is the fact that the Jerusalem temple must be rebuilt, probably sometime before the start of the Tribulation. This is so because we learn from Rev. 11:1-2 that Jerusalem and undoubtedly the temple will be destroyed sometime during the 3 ½ years of the Great Tribulation.

There are several events we learn from Scripture that must occur before this age will be replaced by Heaven on earth:

> First Resurrection (includes the rapture of the church—the 1st phase of second coming).
> Seven year Tribulation period.
> Glorious Appearing of Christ—the 2nd phase of the second coming (advent)
> Millennium period.
> Second Resurrection.

The placement of these events at the end times has been debated for centuries:

- Pre-Tribulation (rapture),
- Mid-Tribulation (rapture),.
- Post-Tribulation (rapture).
- Pre-Millennium (Glorious Appearing).
- Post-Millennium (Glorious Appearing)--church will rid the world of evil through witnessing bringing about the Kingdom on earth for 1,000 years, then Christ will return..
- Amillennium—occurring now, church replaces Israel through the Second Coming.

Many attempts have been made through the centuries to place these events in various combinations in the end times, e.g., pre-tribulation/pre-millennium, post-tribulation/pre-millennium. Each has been presented with scriptural backing supporting their views. With merely one interpretation change in any one of these positions, the whole theory begins to unravel. Therefore, I do not put a lot of faith in trying to validate any of these theories, but since I must choose one, I prefer the **Pre-Tribulation (rapture)/Pre-Millennium (Glorious Appearing)** combination because Revelation 4:1 presents future events as given by Christ to John. Since Revelation 3:22 is the last mention of the church until chapter 19, it seems to follow that chapters 4-18 deal with Israel from the Rapture to the Glorious Appearing. This situation also fits well with Daniel's 490 year prophecy.

The Pre-tribulation theory offers a consoling prediction for Christians, for it spares Christians from the terrible torments the Tribulation will bring as is clearly stated in Scripture (1 Thes. 1:9-10; 5:9; Rev. 3:10).

As is evident, the biggest differences of opinion lie with the time when the church will be raptured and the time of Christ's *Glorious Appearing*, both events being part of the Second Coming. Only the Pre-Tribulation/Pre-Millennium theory will be presented for I believe it best fulfills all the Scriptures of Matthew 24-25; Mark 13; Luke 21:5-13, 25-28; and Acts 2:16-21 as interpreted as follows and is the chronology that is easily presented on our road map. It is important to recognize the difference between the Rapture and the Glorious Appearing since both are phases of the Second Coming. The Rapture concerns Christ's return only to the clouds for His church, initiating the Tribulation period, whereas the Glorious Appearing occurs at the end of the Tribulation period to fulfill the Kingdom promises. Most times, Second Coming verses refer to the Glorious Appearing, but sometimes to both events, e.g.: Matthew 24:36-44, 50; 25:13; Mark 13:32; Luke 17:34-36; 1 Thessalonians 5:1-4; and Revelations 3:3; 22:7, 12, 20. When the context of a verse includes the church, we can be assured it is speaking of the Rapture, but when Israel is being spoken of we know the second phase, the Glorious Appearing of the Second Coming is being presented. This problem disappears when we combine the post-tribulation rapture with the pre-millennium Glorious Appearing.

Many events are to occur after the Rapture:

> 7 seal judgments, 7 trumpet judgments, 7 bowl judgments.
> Prophecy of 2 witnesses for 3 ½ years, Battle of Armaggedon.
> Tribulation period of 7 years, the last 3 ½ years being the *Great Tribulation*.
> Jerusalem attacked and ransacked, Antichrist, and the false prophet times.
> Christ's Second Coming, the Glorious Appearing.
> Millennium period.
> Second Resurrection.
> Final judgment
> Heaven on Earth established for eternity

First Resurrection (of the Righteous unto life) in 3 Phases:

1. The First Fruits Resurrected First: First, Christ (Acts 26:23; 1 Cor. 15:20, 23; Col. 1:18; Rev. 1:5) came to conquer death not to destroy it (Romans 8:23, James 1:18), for that will come on His return. Christ's resurrection has already occurred, ushering in the church age; the faithful will follow (James 1:18) in like manner at the rapture. Upon Jesus' ascension, it seems many Old Testament saints' bodies were raised from the grave (or Abraham's Bosom, discussed later) and went to Heaven with Him (Matt. 27:51-53). The bodies of the rest of the Old Testament saints still wait in Abraham's Bosom to be resurrected at the Glorious Appearing of Christ.

2. The Church Age Rapture: This is the first phase of Christ's return (or Second Coming) this time only to the clouds (1 Thes. 4:17). It ends the Church Age and is the beginning of the end times. Nonbelievers will not understand this disappearance of the believers (1 Thes. 4:13-17). Jesus will come before or at the start of the seven year Tribulation to redeem Christians (church age saints) from the horror of the Tribulation as Pre-Tribulationists believe (Luke 21:34-36; 1 Thes. 5:9-11; Rev. 3:10-11) and as shown by the indefinite time span on the road map. Scripture seems to say that the rapture will occur sequentially as follows:

(a) First the dead in Christ, (Christian Jews and Gentiles), will rise to meet Jesus in the air (John 14:1-3; 1 Cor. 15:23, 52-53; Col. 3:3-4; 1 Thes. 4:14-16). These dead are the resurrected bodies of the souls of the saints who had died during the church age (from the crucifixion to the rapture) and had accepted Christ to save them.

(b) Then the living in Christ, the present day Christians of the church, will immediately rise to meet Jesus in the air (1 Cor. 15:23, 52; Col. 3:3-4; 1 Thes. 4:17).

These two rapture events will find us given new heavenly, powerful, incorruptible bodies (Rom. 8:23; 1 Cor. 15:35-44, 47-54), not given to marriage (Luke 20:35), superior or equal to angels, and eternal (Luke 20:36; 1 Cor. 6:3; 2 Cor. 5:1; Phili. 3:20-21; 1 Peter 1:3-4; 1 John 3:2). As we shall later see, we will return in these bodies with Christ at His Glorious Coming (Jude 14). This ends the Church Age as presented in Revelations 2-3, when God is dealing with the Gentiles. The Jewish nation will be grafted back in and given seven years (the Tribulation period) to accept Jesus as their Messiah. Chapters 4-22 deal with the events to occur after the Rapture of the church. Directly after Christ claims the living and dead saints of the church age, He will sit on His *Judgment Seat* to judge and reward their works of service they performed on earth and reward them accordingly (Rom. 14:10; 2 Cor. 5:9-10; Rev. 22:12—this verse sometimes is attributed to the Glorious Appearing): those who were faithful servants will be given leadership roles in the coming Millennium, and those who were lax in their service will have their rewards lessened or taken away because of their apathy, laziness, or lack of works, but they will not lose their salvation (Matt. 6:20; 1 Cor. 3:10-15; 2 Tim. 4:8; Titus 3:8; 1 Peter 5:2-4--to pastors).

The last book of the New Testament, Revelation, deals specifically with the last days. I prefer to interpret this book literally in most cases, as I believe it was meant to be when the context tells us so, instead of using the often misunderstood and confusing allegorical (symbolical) method because of its possibilities for ambiguity.* Chapter 1 is an introduction. Chapters 2-3 deal with the seven churches which can be taken as the seven churches of John's day or seven symbolic churches that will appear during the church age, or could be references to individual Christians. Laodicea is the last church and most typical of churches today--neither hot nor cold.

The Tribulation Period, Daniel's seventieth week (a seven year period for the "time of the Jews") will begin after the Rapture (directly or later) of the living and dead church age saints, i.e., the Gentiles that God dealt with. See the previous illustration "Daniel's 70 weeks of Years." The church will escape this difficult period just as Noah escaped the flood (Gen. 7:1) and Lot was spared from the destruction of Sodom (Gen. 19:22-30) although Post-Tribulationists would disagree. Likewise, God will probably spare the church so only the unrighteous will be destroyed. Satan at this point must be going to realize the seriousness of his position and will pull out all stops to spoil God's plan of grafting Jews back in. Satan (the dragon as described in Rev. 13:2, 4) will try to copy and counteract God--he will empower a mortal human, **Antichrist** (the beast as described in Rev. 13:1-4), as God did with Christ and will promote a **False Prophet** (the second beast as described in Rev. 13:11-18) to honor Antichrist as God does with the Holy Spirit for Christ.

God vs Satan

Christ vs Antichrist

Holy Spirit vs False Prophet

Antichrist is being restrained, probably by the church, until God's appointed time, but this restraint will be taken away after the Rapture (2 Thes. 2:6-7). Some interpret these verses as identifying

---

* But God's plan may purposely be ambiguous at times because he keeps hidden some prophecies so that they may be revealed at the proper time in the future.

the Holy Spirit as the restrainer, but if this were so, no one could be saved during the Tribulation, for repenting hearts are wooed by the Holy Spirit. The beginning of this period will find God grafting the Jews back into His Kingdom plans (Ezek. 34:11-13; 39:22-29; Rom 11:17-27). Also at the beginning of this period, Antichrist (Son of Perdition) will be released on the earth (Rev. 6:1-2, the first seal judgment) and be revealed (Mark 13:14-could also apply to the temple destruction in 70 A.D.; Dan. 8:23-25, 9-12; 2 Thes. 2:8-9) and make a seven year treaty with Israel, promising peace (Dan. 9:27; 1 Thes. 5:3) with the gentile world in his quest for world power (Dan. 9:27). As we see, Antichrist must precede Christ (2 Thes. 2:3-4), and the city of Babylon must be rebuilt, for Scripture tells us it is going to be destroyed (Rev. 16:17-19; 18:1-24). Antichrist will probably center his empire in Babylon because of its strategic location. This seven year period pertains to God's dealings mostly with Israel (refer back to Daniel's seventieth week). God's angels will seal[118] 144,000 (either literal or figurative) converted Jews in the early part of the Tribulation and they will witness to those unbelieving Jews left after the Rapture, giving them one last chance to repent so none may be lost (Acts 3:25; Rev. 7:1-4; 14:1-5) before He returns in glory to fulfill His Kingdom promise. Although I have opted to show the tribulation period as God's time to deal with Israel, I believe God could, if that is the plan he chooses, also offer salvation to those gentiles who missed the rapture. A remnant (1/3) of Jews will survive the Tribulation period (Jer. 30:3, 7; Zech. 13:8). The old covenants with the patriarchs will be replaced with the **New Covenant** after Jesus comes to Rapture the church so Jews can be grafted back into God's plan (Heb. 8:7-10). Those other untold numbers of people saved by the testimony of the 144,000 witnesses will also be sealed for protection from the judgments that follow although many of these saints will be martyred, waiting in Heaven to be avenged (Rev. 6:9-11; 17:6; 20:4), for God has the power over life and death (Deut. 32:39; Job 1:21). But they will be raised and blessed at the glorious coming of our Lord at the end of the Tribulation (Rev. 7:9-14; 14:13).

Seven seal and seven trumpet judgments will be sent on mankind during the first 3 ½ years of the Tribulation to bring people uncommitted to Antichrist to repentance. However, Antichrist will break the seven year treaty with Israel in midweek (after 3 ½ years) initiating the **Great Tribulation** period (Jacob's trouble: Jer. 30:7) of 3 ½ years (Dan.[119] 7:25; 12:1, 6-7, 11;[120] Matt. 24:15; Rev. 11:3; 12:6, 14; 13:5-7). Satan and his demons will be cast out of Heaven (Rev. 12:7-9, 12-13) from where they, up to this time, had access to the heavenly throne to accuse the saints throughout the ages (Job 1:6-12; 2:1-5; Rev. 12:10). They will wreak havoc on mankind (Rev. 12:12-13).

Antichrist will desecrate the temple in Jerusalem and set himself up as king and god above all as Antiochus Epiphanes had done in 169 B.C. by offering a pig on the altar of the temple (Dan. 11:31, 36-39; 12:11; Matt. 24:15; 2 Thes. 2:3-4; Rev. 13:5-7). Great persecutions (judgments) will occur (Matt. 24:21; Mal. 4:1)--Jews fleeing for their lives to the Gentile nations for God's protection (Jer. 30:4-7; Dan. 12:1; Rev 12:6, 14). The false prophet will appear sometime, probably early in the last half of the Tribulation, wielding religious and economic power and enforcing allegiance to the Antichrist (Rev. 13:11-18; 16:13). People will be required to worship an image of Antichrist with the threat of death if they decline. They will also be required to make an irrevocable decision to accept the *Mark of the Beast* so they can buy and sell, thus sealing their fate for eternity or face martyrdom for rejecting it (Rev. 6:5-6; 14:9-11). Could Revelation 12:14 refer to the United States (eagle) as giving refuge to the Jews? Revelation 7:9-14 gives a glimpse of the Gentile survivors and/or martyrs (since the Jews are being protected) from the Tribulation. We see in Revelation 6:10-11 these saints asking God when their revenge will come. Don't be confused by this chronology. Remember that these saints' souls went to Heaven as soon as they died (as all people after Christ), and they were/are waiting for their new bodies to be resurrected for eternity.

Two special witnesses will appear, probably at the start of the Great Tribulation, to preach repentance for up to 3 ½ years (Rev. 11:3-4). I believe these two will be Enoch and Elijah since they were taken up to Heaven without dying (Gen. 5:24; 2 Kings 2:11; Heb. 11:5)–their death will come during the Tribulation (Rev. 11:5-7). Some would identify Moses as one of these, but Moses had already died; why would he have to die again? The seven bowl judgments, probably announced by the seventh trumpet and included in it (Rev. 16), will be inflicted on mankind without a call for repentance. I have presented the seal, trumpet, and bowl judgments as consecutive events; others have viewed them as congruent. Persecutions will become increasingly worse throughout the Great Tribulation, but those who endure will be saved (Matt. 24:13). The last great war, the battle of **Armageddon** (Isa, 34:1-10; Joel 3:9-14; Zech. 14:1-5, 11; Rev. 16:12-16; 19:19-21), will be fought probably at the end of the Tribulation, being so terrible that it will have to be shortened by Jesus' Glorious Appearing (Mal. 4:1-2) lest all mankind perish (Matt. 24:22). This battle is not to be confused with the battles described by Ezekiel 38 & 39. The Ezekiel chapters are open to debate by scholars as to the identity of Gog and Magog and when these battles will be fought: (1) before the Rapture, (2) during the Tribulation, (3) after Christ's Glorious Appearing but before the Millennium, or (4) after the Millennium.

Those (including myself) who accept (1) recognize Russia as the probable or possible *King of the North* (Dan. 11:40-45; Ezek. 38:5-6, 15) that will attack Israel with its Arab allies of probably or possibly Persia (Iran), Ethiopia, Egypt, and Libya, among others (*King of the South*), shortly before the Rapture. These forces will be drawn by God to Israel to show His power to the heathen nations (Ezek. 38:16, 23). He will do so with an earthquake, pestilence, and confusion (Ezek. 38:18-22); killing 5/6 of Israel's attacking enemies (Ezek. 39:2). Since it will take Israel seven years to burn all the weapons of this war (Ezek. 39:9), it seems likely that this war will precede the Rapture by seven or more years. The elimination of the Russian and Arab threat could be the catalyst that brings Antichrist to power as world leader.

Those who accept (2) would require that Antichrist be involved with the Ezekiel wars, since his appearance will signal the start of the Tribulation period. It would be required that these wars be fought during the Great Tribulation, since Antichrist will promise peace until it is broken just before the Great Tribulation. If these wars will be fought in the second half of the seven year Tribulation period, the burning of the arms will infringe on the Millennium period which I feel is unlikely.

Those who accept (3) would require a gap between the Glorious Appearing and the Millennium to include all of the seven years required to burn the weapons of war or some part of it. It does not seem fitting that this activity would be likely in this period of peace and Messiah's rule.

Those who accept (4) cite Revelations 20:7-9 as the same battle described by Ezekiel. But this is a different battle. The Ezekiel battles draw Israel to God before the Millennium period and the Revelation battle comes after the Millennium.

The battle of Armageddon will conclude the Tribulation period as we suppose. This battle will be Antichrist's (with Satan's backing) last desperate attempt to prevent Christ's return. The *King of the East* (probably China or some other eastern bloc of countries) and the *King of the West* (probably or possibly the European bloc allied with other western countries, hopefully without the support of the U.S.A), led by Antichrist, will meet in Israel (Rev. 16:12-16) for control of the world by setting up an indestructible government. It is assumed that Antichrist will prevail in this battle and take control of Palestine for one hour (Rev. 17:12) with the ten nation confederation who will give their complete allegiance to him (Rev. 17:12-13). This government will allow Antichrist to continue his control over Babylon, the revived Holy Roman Empire, possibly the seventh empire of Revelation 17:10.[121] But their rule will be short-lived, for they will make war with the Lamb (Rev. 17:14) to destroy Jerusalem (Zech. 12:1-9; 14:1-2). The Lord will completely destroy this Revived Roman Empire symbolized by the harlot city of Babylon (Hag. 2:21-22; Zech. 14:3-4, 9; Acts 3:20-21; 15:13-18; Rev. 16:19; 17:1-5; 18:1-3, 21).

Near the end of the Tribulation, a wonderful event will take place in Heaven. Christ will have already gathered the remainder of His church at the Rapture, so a wedding (Matt. 22:1-4; 25:1-13; Rev. 19:7; 21:9) is going to be given with a feast (supper)—as prophesied by Isaiah (Isa. 25:6-9) to follow as we shall shortly see. The parable given by Jesus in Matthew 25:1-13 for preparing for the Kingdom gives us a clue to the time of the marriage. Since there will be no need to prepare for the Kingdom after Jesus' Glorious Appearing, it must occur before that time. One could make a case for the wedding to occur at the time of the Rapture, but that would require either a seven year gap between the wedding and feast, or that the feast would last through the tribulation. Neither of these scenes seems appropriate. Therefore, it seems likely that the time of the wedding be near the end of the Tribulation. Christ will be the bridegroom (Isa. 61:10; 62:5; Matt. 9:15; 22:2-3; 25:1; John 3:29) at this wedding and the Church will be the bride (Isa. 61:10; John 3:29; Eph. 5:25-30).

3. The Glorious Appearing of Christ: the *Day of the Lord* includes the Rapture (the first phase of the Second Coming), Tribulation period, and the Glorious Appearing (the second phase of the Second Coming when Christ will return at least seven years after the rapture of the church, i.e., at the end of the Tribulation as foretold by Joel 2:30-32). Specifically, the *Glorious Appearing* (or *Blessed Hope* or *Revelation)* will find Christ coming, this time to earth to fulfill His Kingdom promises of the New Covenant for Israel (Lev. 26:39-46; Isa. 40:9-11; Dan. 2:44-45; 7:14; Amos 9:11-15; Matt. 25:34; 1 Cor. 15:24-25; Titus 2:13; Rev. 11:15) for Jesus will come as a thief in the night (Matt. 24:44; Luke 12:40; 1 Thes. 5:2-4; 2 Peter 3:10; Rev. 3:3; 16:15)--some would attribute some/all the verses of this sentence to the Rapture and/or Glorious Appearing depending on their interpretation of the chronology of end time events, but we need not argue this point. Jesus' coming will be in power and visible glory (Isa. 66:15; Matt. 16:27; 24:27-31; 25:31-46; 26:64; Mark 13:24-27; 14:62; Luke 17:24; 21:25-28; Acts 1:11; Rev. 1:7; 6:12-17; 14:14) to end the present age and usher in the new Kingdom on earth. He will end all earthly rule and authority (1 Cor. 15:24-25). Jesus will be accompanied by angels and the resurrected saints of the church (Zech. 14:5; Matt. 13:41, 49; 16:27; 24:31; 25:31; Luke 9:26; Col. 3:4; 1 Thes. 3:13; 2 Thes. 1:7-10; Jude 14-15) and the Old Testament and Tribulation saints (Ezek. 37:12-14) to issue in the Kingdom of Heaven (or God) on earth (Gen. 49:10; Isa. 9:6-7; Jer. 31:31; Dan. 2:44; 6:26; 7:13-14, 27; Hosea 3:4-5; Mic. 4:7; Luke 1:32-33; John 14:1-3; Acts 1:6-7; Rev. 11:15). Jesus will be their promised king from the line of David (Hos. 1:10-11; 3:4-5), a kingship unfilled since the last legitimate king, Jehoiakim, in 597 B.C.

The Antichrist (beast) and the false prophet (second beast) will be cast into the lake of fire (Hell) (Dan.7:11; 2 Thes. 2:8; Rev. 19:19-21; 20:10). The Second Coming will result in the resurrection of the rest of the righteous, leaving only the unsaved in Hades (Mark 13:27):

> (1) *OT saints* who were under the Law, saved by grace (Isa. 26:19-21; Ezek. 37:12-14; Dan. 12:2-3), their bodies resurrected from Abraham's Bosom and united with their heavenly souls which Jesus took to Heaven at His ascension.
>
> (2) *Dead Tribulation saints*—Bodies of those Jews (and possibly gentiles) who accepted Jesus as Messiah and who remained faithful during the Tribulation will be resurrected and united with their heavenly souls (Dan. 12:2—1,000 years separate the resurrection of these righteous from that of the unrighteous; Rev. 6:9-11; 20:4).

Christ will also separate and judge the living Israeli and Gentile nations, the righteous people will enter the Millennium (Matt. 13:36-38, 49; 16:27; 25:31-40), the unrighteous being cast into a furnace (Hell) (Matt. 13:39-43, 49-50; 25:41-46; Luke 9:26). Note that the 1,290 days of Daniel 12:11 (Great Tribulation) could allow 30 days to judge the nations between the Tribulation and the Millennium.[122] The 144,000 Jewish preachers and the souls they save (Rev. 7:4-8; 14:1-here, some say these are different people from those of Rev. 7:4-8,[123] that they are Christian converts) and the living survivors of the Tribulation who will have accepted Christ and the martyred Tribulation saints (Rev. 7:9-14) will enter the Millennium (Isa. 66:8; Jer. 31:33-34; Dan. 7:9-18; Joel 3:12-17). Revelation 7:13-17 tells of the future glory of the Tribulation saints (those martyred and in Heaven and those that enter the Millennium).

There are many Scripture verses not yet mentioned foreseeing the Second Coming: Num. 24:17-19; Job 19:25-27; Psa. 22:26-31; 72:1-17; 89:27; 102:16; 110:1-7; Isa. 2:2-4; 59:20; Joel 2:1-11—may also be the coming invasions of Israel and/or Judah, 2:30-32; 3:12-17; Amos 1:2; 9:11-15.

Millennium Period.

As previously mentioned, Christ will subdue all nations at His Glorious Appearing. Satan's hands will be tied for 1,000 years (Rev. 20:1-2), and Christ will rule (Isa. 9:6-7; Rev. 2:27; 12:5; 19:15-16) with the first resurrected saints as kings and priests (Dan. 7:18, 22, 26-27; Matt. 19:28-29; Eph. 1:10-12; Rev. 1:6; 2:25-26, 28-29; 3:5, 12-could be in new Jerusalem after the Millennium; 3:21; 5:8-13; 20:4-6; 22:4-5).

A marriage feast will be held in Heaven to celebrate the wedding of Christ with His church (some say Israel) (Matt. 22:1-14; Luke 14:15-24; Rev. 19:6-10). This supper will likely last during the entire Millennium period. It should be noted that Matthew 22:1-14 probably refers specifically to the feast but also speaks of the wedding that must precede it. Guests to this feast will likely be the Old Testament and Tribulation saints who will have been resurrected at the Glorious Appearing. They cannot be the Church, for the Church will already have been raptured.

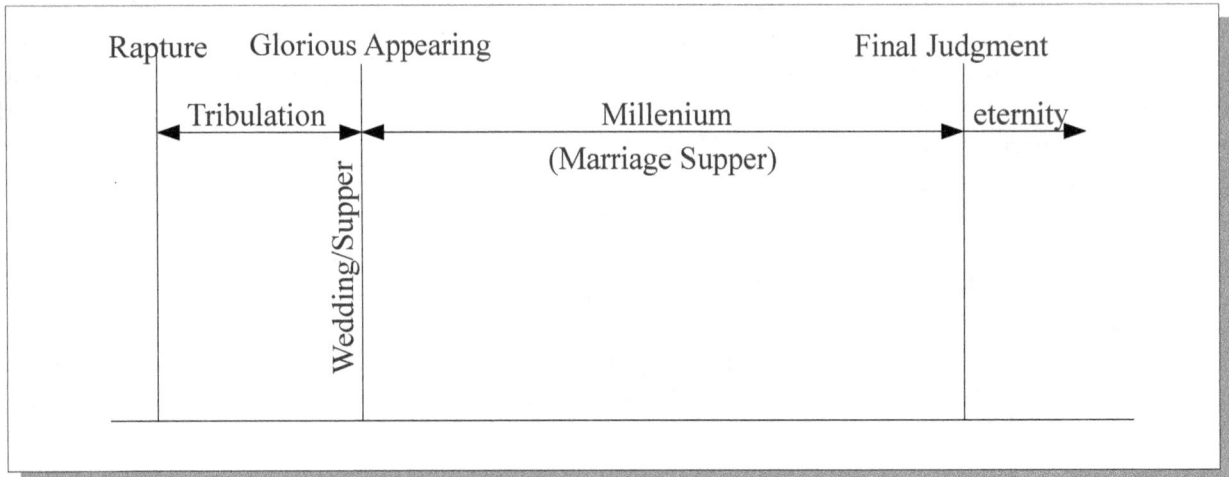

At the start of this period, resulting from Christ's Glorious Appearing, the nations of Judah and Israel will be united (Deut. 30:1-10; Isa. 11:11-13; 43:5-7; Jer. 16:14-15; 23:3-6; 24:6-7;[124] 30:10-11; 31:31-34; 32:37-42; 33:14-16; Ezek. 11:16-20; 14:22; 36:24-28; 37:16-28; Joel 3:20-21; Amos 9:14-15; Zeph. 3:19-20; Mark 13:26-27; Rom. 11:25-27) in the Holy Land with Christ ruling from Jerusalem (Ezek. 43:7; Dan. 7:13-14; Rev. 11:15; 12:5) with David's assistance (Jer. 30:9; 33:15; Ezek. 34:23-24; 37:24-25; Hos. 3:5) and Jesus' disciples over the twelve tribes (Matt. 19:27-28; Luke 22:29-30), a final fulfillment of the covenants with Abraham and David. The Jewish nation will be given a new heart and spirit (Isa. 4:3-6; Jer. 24:7; Ezek. 36:24-29; Heb. 8:10; 10:15-16) and prosper in their homeland (Isa. 9:7; 26:15; 35:1-10; 65:17-25; Ezek. 34:27; 36:29-37; Joel 3:18) made into a Garden of Eden (Psa. 67:6; 72:16; Isa. 4:2; 32:15-18; 35:1-2, 6-7; 51:3; 55:13; Ezek. 36:30-36; Joel 2:23-26). They will be a light unto the gentile nations (Isa. 60; 62), given the greatest honor among nations (Isa. 49:22-23; Hag. 2:6-9). Jerusalem will be the center of the world (Isa. 2:2-3; Zech. 8:22; Rev. 15:4). The Gentiles will also come to worship God and be at peace with Israel (Psa. 46:9; 72:7; Isa. 2:4; Mic. 4:3-4). The saints will be given dominion over the new earth (Rev. 2:26) with all animals being tamed and in harmony (Isa. 11:6-9; 66:22-24; Ezek. 34:25, 28; Isa. 65:25; Hos. 2:18). Although originally created lower than the angels, the saints will be given a higher standing now (1 Cor. 6:3) but under Christ who also had been given a lower standing than angels during His time in the flesh (Heb. 2:9). Gentile leadership will probably differ from that of the Jews. Believers entering the Millennium will have children who will need to make a decision for Christ. These people will be dealt with at the Second Resurrection.

Near the end of the Millennium, Satan will be released from the pit and will return to earth to deceive the people in a last-ditch effort to prevent God's plan for the fulfillment of His Heaven on earth (Rev. 20:3, 7-9). Satan with his fallen angels and unredeemed humans will wage a final battle against Israel at Jerusalem, but they will be defeated and cast into the lake of fire (2 Peter 2:4; Rev. 20:10), probably a more severe Hell--one for eternity.

Second Resurrection (the unrighteous unto death) and Final Judgment.

Those of all times who died in the faith will have already been resurrected unto everlasting life by the First Resurrection and will not experience the second death (Rev. 2:11). They will be joined by the living Millennium saints who will have endured to the end to begin the eternal Kingdom of Heaven on earth (Rev. 3:21). The bodies of those dead Millennium saints and all those dead unsaved people of all time (Obad. 15-16; Rev. 20:5–1st sentence; 11-13) will be raised and united with their souls to face the final judgment (Dan. 12:2--1,000 years between the First and Second Resurrections) along with the living unsaved Millennium people. These groups will be separated and judged and held responsible; the unsaved group will be judged (Jude 14-15) from two books[125] and cast into the lake of fire--the second death (Matt. 25:41, 46; Rev. 20:13-15; 21:8) unto everlasting separation from God (2 Thes. 1:8-9). The saints will be revealed from the Book of Life (Psa. 69:28; Dan. 7:10; 2 Cor. 5:6-10; Rev. 3:5; 13:8; 17:8; 20:12, 15; 21:27) from the beginning and enter eternity in the Kingdom on earth in the presence of God (Matt. 25:46) just as the flood foreshadows this final judgment.

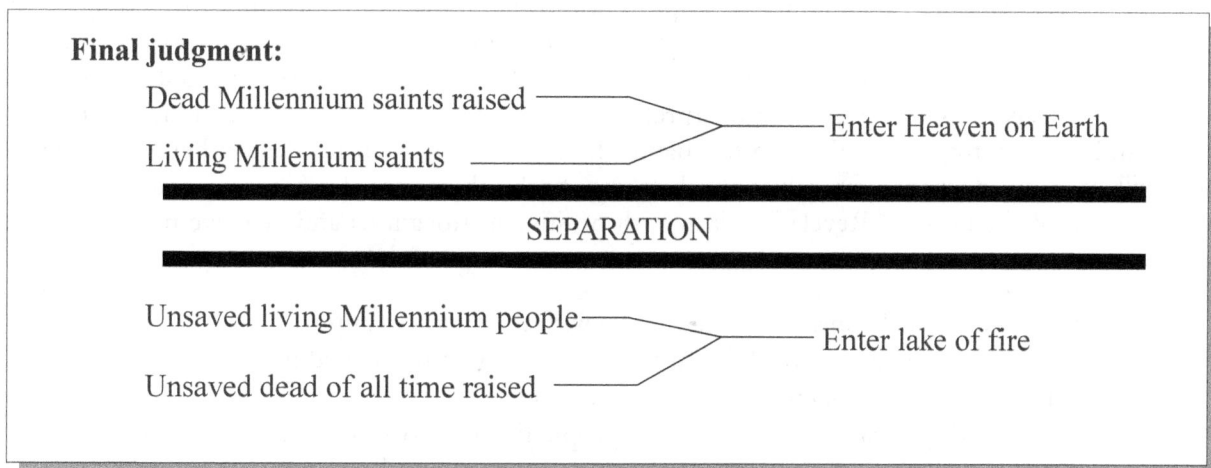

Final judgment:

Dead Millennium saints raised ———— ⟍
                                        ⟍———— Enter Heaven on Earth
Living Millenium saints ————————— ⟋

SEPARATION

Unsaved living Millennium people ——— ⟍
                                        ⟍———— Enter lake of fire
Unsaved dead of all time raised ————— ⟋

Heaven on Earth

All the saints of all time will enter the new Heaven on earth (Isa. 65:17; 2 Peter 3:13; Rev. 21:1, 10-11; 22:3-5) serving God for all eternity because of what Christ has done through His death, resurrection, return, and final judgment. Death, the last enemy of the Kingdom, will be destroyed (1 Cor. 15:26; Rev. 21:4). A new Jerusalem will be created on earth for God's throne, for God will live on earth and be visible to all the saints (Isa. 65:18-19; Zech. 8:3, 8, 22; Rev. 21:2-3, 10, 22;[126] 22:1-5). There will be no more weeping or sorrow, no pain or death (Isa. 33:24; 65:19; Rev. 21:4). There will be no more seas (Rev. 21:1) or need for a temple, for God will dwell among His people (Rev. 21:22) and be their light—there will be no need for the sun or moon for the glory of God will lighten the earth and Christ will be the light (Rev. 21:23-25).

I have not to this point quoted many scripture verses, preferring that the reader open God's word for himself. Now I feel the urgency to quote Revelation 22:18-19 in reference to the Book of Revelation:

For I testify unto every man that heareth the words of the prophecy of this book, if any man shall add unto these things, God shall add unto him the plagues that are written in this book: and if any man shall take away from the words of the book of this prophecy, God shall take away his part out of the book of life, and out of the holy city, and from the things which are written in this book (KJV).

I provide this quote because of its stern warning and extreme consequences to anyone who adds or subtracts from the prophecy of the Book of Revelation (also consider Deut. 12:32). So serious is this warning that I have chosen, rather than risk the possibility of errors, to not expound or present as fact any interpretations that might lead to false doctrine. My prayer is that if I have misrepresented this book in any way that detracts from the Lord's basic message of salvation and especially in the end times, that He will correct me that I may reconsider any or all parts of my work.

No one can foresee for certainty with 100% accuracy the sequence of events in the end times, for God has not yet revealed all that is to be revealed on these matters. These details will be made more certain as history unveils more agreement with Scripture. Instead, we need to concentrate on the true meaning of Scripture as it pertains to the requirement for eternal life with God: His plan of grace from the beginning to offer redemption to sinners through the belief in and commitment by faith to Jesus Christ as savior and Lord. For this matter, there is no interpretation; God has clearly given us all the information we need (John 3:3, 36; 5:24; Acts 2:21; 15:11; Rom. 1:17; 3:24, 28; 4:4-5, 21-24; 5:1, 9; 10:9-10, 13; Gal. 2:15-16; Eph. 2:8-10; Phili. 3:9; Titus 3:5-7).

The most important message of Revelation is to watch and be ready for Christ's coming (Luke 12:39-40, 45-47). All events mentioned in Scripture will come to pass, although they may not be in the same order that we expect. As I said before, and I do not mind repeating because of its importance-- God wants that we understand the basic message of salvation and worship of Him only. Errors and misunderstandings of minor events or interpretations, provided they do not detract from truth, are understandable and forgivable; they do not damn the soul, for they do not lead others astray where they will lose their chance at salvation. Looking back, there are four recognized systems of interpretation of the book of Revelation each with positive justifications and negative possibilities for their positions:

✓ Preterist—deals with Christianity's struggles with the Roman Empire.
✓ Historical—a general view of the church's history and on to the end times.
✓ Futurist—mostly a prophetic view of the end times.
✓ Spiritualist (Allegorical, Symbolic)—not a prophetic or historical book but a symbolic one applicable to all times, dealing with the struggle between good and evil.

Various combinations of these interpretations account for the five theories of end time events we have just presented in this chapter, any one of which can provide insights rather than facts.

A final word before we leave this most important subject. The idea of life after death had very early beginnings, I would think, from the time of the first man, Adam. Genesis 25:8 and Job 19:25-26 seem to hint at this fact. As the nation of Israel developed after Abraham, so did the Jews' idea (tradition) of Hades (Greek) or Sheol (Hebrew) or later that of the Christians (Hell). Hades became known as the temporary holding place where people went after they died. Sometimes in Old Testament Scripture, Hades is another word for the grave, where mortals are destined after they die (Psa. 55:15; Prov. 15:24; Isa. 14:9). Hades was (is) a two-tiered abode: the upper tier, called the *Paradise of God* or *Abraham's Bosom,* was for the saints and the lower tier for the lost. This was the place where the body and soul up to the establishment of the Church Age went, until they would eventually be resurrected to life or judged unto death (Luke 16:22; 2 Peter 2:4-9).

Up to the time of the flood, only eight persons (Noah and his family), were righteous enough in faith to be saved. God had destroyed the bodies of the unrighteous people, and their spirits were sent to the two-tiered Hades. Jesus went to Hades during his entombment days to announce His victory over death to these <u>lost souls</u> (Psa. 16:10; Matt. 12:40; Eph. 4:8-9; 1 Peter 3:18-20; 4:6). There are at least two interpretations of why Jesus visited Hades: (1) to offer hope to the lost spirits—

possibly because they never had the Law to guide them? This seems to be mere speculation and as far as I can determine, non-scriptural and (2) the one I believe to be scriptural: to seal their judgment. Jesus took all the souls of the <u>Old Testament saints</u> to Heaven during his time in the tomb, some in their resurrected bodies (see the chapter, "Jesus, the Promised Messiah"). The bodies of the rest of the Old Testament saints remain in Abraham's Bosom until they will be resurrected at the Glorious Appearing, and all the lost Old Testament persons remain there (1 Peter 3:18-20) until they are resurrected and united with their souls at the second resurrection for final judgment (Dan. 12:2, 13). I cite Luke 16:19-31 as evidence of a lost Old Testament rich man speaking from this place of torment and righteous Lazarus being in Abraham's Bosom (ref. also Luke 13:25). These verses verify the finality of death; there will be no second chance after death to accept Christ as Savior and Lord (Prov. 29:1; Luke 13:23-28). There are some exceptions to the fate of the Old Testament saints: Enoch and Elijah who did not die but were taken body and soul directly to Heaven because of their faith (Gen. 5:24; 2 Kings 2:11; Heb. 11:5-6). The preceding presentation is for enrichment only and is not to be taken as theology or hard fact.

Generally speaking, <u>after Jesus' resurrection</u>, the spirit of deceased believers goes directly to Heaven (2 Cor. 5:6-9; Phili. 1:21-25), the body to the grave (John 3:13; Acts 2:29-34; 13:36) and the souls of the unbelievers goes directly to the lower abode of Hades, the body to the grave (Luke 16:19-31; Rev. 19:20-20:15). Unlike Christ, whose body did not decay but was taken up to Heaven with His spirit, the spirits of the saints must wait until their new, perfect bodies are resurrected and united with their spirits in the end times. Let us trace from the material already presented, the journey of the human body and soul after death as best I can determine from Scripture. The following graphic display is offered to present the subject of body and soul destiny in a clear and compressed manner with the idea of giving a snapshot view for easier edification. Some sequences of events may vary from those presented depending on one's interpretation of Scripture. But the bottom line of this analogy, the one I hope to convey for spiritual edification, is that all souls of all time will eventually face God, some to eternal fellowship with Him and some to eternal damnation (John 5:28-29). How we derive the sequence of events is important only in the sense of leading us in the right direction. Let us continually keep this idea in mind and stay focused and prepared for that day--our death or the Second Coming of Christ.

Two-tiered Hades

Saints' bodies & souls in "Paradise Of God" or also called "Abraham's Bosom" Evidently, Saints are not aware of the other Side (Job 14:10-12, 21-22; Psa. 146:4)	**Lost People of all time** Souls and bodies tormented in lower part Of Hades—a temporary holding place Until the Final judgment. Evidently, lost Souls are aware of the joys of the other side (Ecc. 9:5-6, 10; Luke 16:19-31)

AFTER JESUS' MINISTRY:

BELIEVERS:

UNSAVED:

FIRST RESURRECTION:

Up to 2nd RESURRECTION:
body and soul go to grave (Hades)

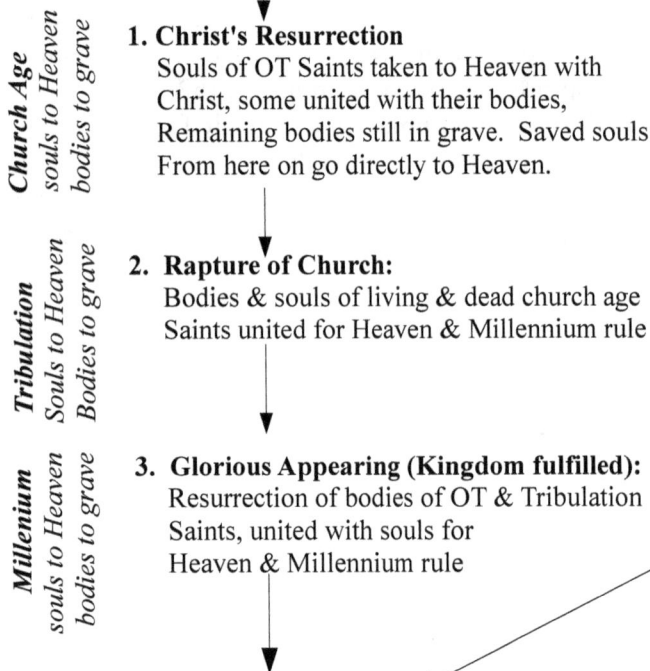

Church Age
souls to Heaven
bodies to grave

1. Christ's Resurrection
Souls of OT Saints taken to Heaven with
Christ, some united with their bodies,
Remaining bodies still in grave. Saved souls
From here on go directly to Heaven.

Tribulation
Souls to Heaven
Bodies to grave

2. Rapture of Church:
Bodies & souls of living & dead church age
Saints united for Heaven & Millennium rule

Millenium
souls to Heaven
bodies to grave

3. Glorious Appearing (Kingdom fulfilled):
Resurrection of bodies of OT & Tribulation
Saints, united with souls for
Heaven & Millennium rule

SECOND RESURRECTION:
final judgment: unbelievers separated from Saints,
Their bodies and souls united & cast into Hell &
HEAVEN ON EARTH:
Dead Millennium Saints raised & united with souls.
Saints of all time enter ─────────────────► **Eternity**

As we have seen in the Old Testament, God made two unconditional covenants with individuals —one with Abraham and one with David. These covenants were made with individuals who had proven their faith in God. Abraham showed his faith by obeying God by moving to an unfamiliar land and his willingness to sacrifice his son.[127] David showed his faith by obeying God with the defeat of the Philistines and their giant (1 Sam. 17:1-50) and his trust in God during the war campaigns.

God also made an unconditional covenant with the Israelite nation as they prepared to enter Canaan (Promised Land Covenant), a covenant that will be completed when Israel is restored in the Promised Land in the end times. The ultimate covenant (Final [New] Covenant) was made for Jews and Gentiles with Christ's sacrifice on the cross and will be completed in the end times. God made this one final, everlasting covenant with all mankind to replace all the other covenants through faith in what Christ had accomplished on the cross.

In review, God's plan for the Kingdom from Christ's ascension can be summarized as follows:

- ✓ Kingdom <u>introduced</u> at Jesus' baptism.
- ✓ Kingdom <u>prepared</u> during Jesus' ministry: Jesus often mentioned, "The Kingdom is at hand" and "The Kingdom is like…"
- ✓ Kingdom (new, final covenant) is <u>established</u> (initiated, inaugurated) and sealed with the blood of the Lamb preparing the way for the Church Age.
- ✓ Church Age started:
  - o Spiritual Church Age—at the Resurrection.
  - o Physical Church Age—at Pentecost.
- ✓ Church developed through the Church Age, ends at the Rapture.
- ✓ Kingdom <u>fulfilled</u> at the Second Coming.

19

FINAL COMMENTS

We have seen that original sin put a barrier between God and man—man lost his closeness and relationship with God and his dominion over the earth. Satan took control (Luke 4:6) or so he thought. Satan has a claim on the world (Job 1:6-8; Luke 4:7-8) only as far as God permits, as Jesus recognized, and also power to inflict the fear of death (Heb. 2:14-15). Satan's sins came from his pride in being the most beautiful and wise of God's angelic creation. It is possible that Satan believes all his lies. I suspect that he understands he is already defeated (Matt. 8:28-29), but his evil and prideful nature prevents his surrender to Christ—he wants to take us with him.

God had a plan from the beginning to provide a way to reunite us with Him. Man had to be taught from generation to generation in ways they would understand. God has predestined some (Rom. 9:11-15; 1 Peter 1:1-2) for salvation--those ordained to fulfill His Kingdom plan. To start with, He chose the Hebrews to be the caretakers of this plan, starting with the initial covenant with Abraham. Throughout Old Testament times, He gave them the Law to guide them and rituals and sacrifices to cover their sins (not to take them away) and tide them over until the final covenant would take effect at Christ's second coming. They were saved by faith in God, but confession and repentance were necessary when they apostatized (2 Chr. 7:14; Isa. 55:7; Jer. 3:12-13), just as forgiveness has been given to all Christians throughout the Church Age when they accept Jesus as the son of God. The Law wasn't a means of salvation, for it could save no one; it only identified sin (Rom. 3:20; 7:7). Jesus taught that the Law attempted to change the individual from the outside, while salvation changes one from within.

Since Adam and Abraham, redemption was and is still possible through our Redeemer who has existed from the beginning (John 17:5). When we are born into the world, we inherit a dead and evil nature (Rom. 3:23). We find life only in Christ (John 5:24; Eph. 2:1-5; 1 John 3:14; 5:4). The individual was and is redeemed by his/her faith in our Redeemer and not on church affiliation. That which is reported in the Old Testament leads to the fulfillment of this final covenant. Jesus the Christ--the Messiah--has and will fulfill all that was predicted about Him by the prophets. We are warned to beware of false prophets who will try to lead us in different ways (Matt. 7:15; 24:11, 24; Mark 13:22; 2 Peter 2:1; 1 John 4:1) and also to respect and love our spiritual leaders: pastors, elders, etc. (1 Thes. 5:12-13).

Instead of the Old Testament ritual of continual animal sacrifices for sins, Jesus offered himself as the one final sacrifice for our salvation (Rom. 5:8). All He requires is that we repent, believe and confess through faith that He is the resurrected Son of God (Matt. 10:32; Mark 16:16; John 1:12; 3:16, 36; 5:24; 6:40, 47; 20:31; Acts 16:31; 26:20; Rom. 10:9; 2 Cor. 7:9-10; 1 John 5:1), confess that we are sinners, ask and thank Him for forgiveness, ask Him to come into our hearts, and dedicate our lives to Him with the help of the Holy Spirit He promised to send to seal us (2 Cor. 1:21-22; Eph. 1:13-14; 4:30). This conversion of the heart (Matt. 18:3; John 3:3; 1 Peter 1:23) changes us into new creatures in Christ (Ezek. 36:25-27; 2 Cor. 5:14-17) and leads us to willingly do good works (Rom. 2:6-7; Eph. 2:10): good works are required of the Christian (Matt. 3:10; Luke 3:9; Acts 26:20; Titus 3:8), enhances faith (James 2:20, 26), and is the result of salvation and not the cause. Faith and works are therefore mutually inclusive, but faith must precede works for works to be counted as a blessing (James 2:14-17). As we have seen, the requirements of the Law can only be fulfilled by walking in the Spirit, for we cannot sin when we are in the Spirit (Rom. 7:6; Gal. 2:20-21). The working of the Holy Spirit cannot be obtained while we are walking in the flesh, since the Spirit cannot abide in us under this condition (Rom. 8:4). Only by faith through the grace of God and our love for our Lord and others (Matt. 22:37-39) can we please God and receive His blessings for our good works (Gal. 3:11-12; Heb. 11:6). We cannot repay Jesus for His sacrifice or retain or prove our salvation to ourselves or others.

Christians, by the gift of grace from God (Rom. 3:23-26; 6:23), are justified and made righteous only through Jesus' faith and their faith in Him (John 1:12; 3:16; Acts 13:39; Rom. 3:28; 4:5; 5:1-2, 9; Gal. 2:16; 3:24; Eph. 2:8-9) and not in the Law or works (Rom. 10:3). The Holy Spirit prepares the sinner's heart and convicts him/her of the need for a spiritual renewal thus paving the way for their acceptance of the Word (Jesus) and repentance. As we pray, the Holy Spirit leads us in what to pray for, making intercessions to Jesus for us (Rom. 8:26; Eph. 6:17-19). It is the sinner's responsibility to act on this witnessing (an act of free will) not just believe (Rom. 10:13; Rev. 3:20), for Satan also believes in God (James 2:19). We must be very careful not to substitute for prayer: tradition, our works, or rituals—especially when they are repetitive.

Works without faith cannot be effective (Rom. 4:4-5; 11:6), works being the <u>product</u> of that faith, for faith without works is dead (James 2:17). Therefore, putting our trust in the Law and doing good works in itself cannot save us; we are now under the New Covenant that requires faith through grace. This grace is the unearned favor given by a superior (God) to an underling (mankind). God provides grace first; we accept it by free will through faith or reject it.

Those who perform good works from their own wills may receive only worldly rewards, e.g., wealth, fame, recognition, and honor from man. Those who do their work in Jesus' name (Col. 3:17) through and by the power of the Holy Spirit will receive their rewards (fellowship and communion with God and other Christians) in this life (Jer. 17:10; Luke 18:29-30) and the afterlife (Isa. 40:10-11; Matt. 5:12; 6:1-6; 10:41-42; Luke 18:28-30; 1 Cor. 3:8; 2 Cor.4:17; Eph. 6:8; Col. 3:23-24; 1 Tim. 6:19; Heb. 10:35; 1 Peter 1:4; 5:4; Rev. 11:18). It is well known that the writer James stressed works more than any other writer. Some believe he contradicts Paul who stressed faith alone to be required for salvation. James also believed this fact about faith but tried to show that Christians were also expected to perform works through the gifts given them from God for God's glory (Eph. 4:11-12; 1 Peter 4:11); We can understand this truth by remembering that Paul directed his ministry toward nonbelievers while James directed his toward Christians (James 1:21-22; 2:14, 24) who add earthly and heavenly rewards with their works.

Active Christians are urged to direct their labors first toward the works of salvation and the glory of God's Kingdom (Matt. 5:16; John 6:27; Gal. 6:8; 1 Peter 2:12), especially through their witnessing (Matt. 10:32; Luke 11:33; 12:8; John 15:26-27; Acts 5:30-32; Eph. 6:18-20), evidenced by the fruits of their labor (Matt. 7:16). To be passive in our work, that is, to hide from our responsibilities to God and not be a doer, is to sin (James 1:22-25; 4:17) as Jesus told in two parables (Matt. 25:14-29; Luke 19:12-26). We are also to not act hypocritically (James 1:26-27). For all those who share in the Kingdom of God shall be judged by God for the things done while in their earthly bodies. Christ will, on His return, bring their rewards according to their good works (Rev. 22:12).

Christians are not to partake of sinful lifestyles–grieving the Holy Spirit–which will not only jeopardize their future but also most likely influence unbelievers away from the Kingdom (Eph. 4:30; 5:11-15; 2 Peter 3:14)--a negative witness. Sin is defined in James 4:17 as anything we do that we know is not righteous (paraphrased). Christians are in jeopardy of losing some or all of their rewards for living in the flesh (Matt. 6:20; 1 Cor. 3:10-15; 2 Cor. 5:10; Rev. 22:12). That can only mean that some will have larger blessings in Heaven because of their faithful work during their time on earth (1 Cor. 15:39, 41). These rewards will probably be the higher honors given to them in their closeness to God, whether in praise, administration, or in leadership. God blesses individual believers with gifts that are to be used in their good works (1 Cor. 12:1-11; Eph. 4:7). He knows we cannot carry out His will without the help of the Holy Spirit. Some works (finances, maintenance, serving, etc.) may seem as merely secular duties, but they are just as important as spiritual duties, for they free ministers and leaders for ministries.

Satan is real and will do all in his power to destroy God's plans and our lives as Christians (Isa. 14:12-14; Mark 1:13; 4:15; Luke 13:16; 22:31; Acts 5:3; 1 Cor. 7:5; 2 Cor. 2:11; 1 Thes. 2:18; 1 Pet. 5:8). We are warned in Scripture that the world will persecute us for our witness but God has promised us His protection for our place in the Kingdom (Prov. 29:25; Isa. 41:10, 13-14; 1 Cor. 10:13; 2 Cor. 12:10; 2 Tim. 1:12; Jude 24; Matt. 5:10-12; Luke 12:4-5; 2 Tim. 2:12). It is helpful for Christians to keep their eyes and ears on world events as they unfold in fulfillment of prophecy, for Satan knows if he could wipe out the Jews, he could claim himself more powerful than God. Satan could prove God to be less than omnipotent with this accomplishment, for he would be able to prove God wrong, the God who promised to protect and deliver Israel. Although Satan is presently (and since original sin) "prince of the power of the air" (Eph. 2:2) and ruler of this world (Job 1:6-8; John 14:30; 2 Cor. 4:3-4; Eph. 6:12) and is more powerful than mankind (Eph. 6:11-12), he is not omnipotent (Job 42:2; Psa. 33:6-9; Matt. 19:26; Rev. 19:6), omnipresent (Psa. 139:7-10; Jer. 23:23-24), or omniscient (Exod. 3:7; Job 37:16; Psa. 69:5; 139:1-6; 147:4-5; Prov. 15:3; Matt. 10:29-30; John 21:17; 1 John 3:20) as is God, for he can do only that which God allows him to do (Job 1:10-12; 2:3-7). Therefore, we can put our trust in Jesus for strength to overcome the evil temptations of Satan (Luke 22:31-32). If we resist with the help of the Spirit and submit ourselves to God, Satan will flee from us (Matt. 17:18; James 4:7; Zech. 3:1-2).

It is eagerly expected that this Biblical work will help to lead others to our Lord and also to give inspiration to Christians for the study of the Bible's Word (for Jesus is the Word, the Truth, John 1:1; Rev. 19:13) and have a more meaningful devotional experience. A word of warning: a strictly secular bible study (without prayer) will give only limited insights into God's plan for life. Bible study can give useful information for enhancing the revelations that come from God through devotional readings and prayer (Matt. 26:41; Luke 18:1). Let us continually pray for forgiveness (1 John 1:9-10). Be aware of the proper attitude and spiritual condition necessary for prayer: we must come to the Lord with a clean, pure heart–right all wrongs we have against others (Matt. 5:23-14; 6:14-15)–so God will more readily hear us, we must confess our sins, ask for and accept forgiveness that Jesus has already paid for, and be repentant (Psa. 66:18; Prov. 28:13; Luke 18:13; Acts 3:19; 1 John 1:9).

Since no one will know the time of Christ's Second Coming, I hope this work will help someone to prepare for this day. Not ever hearing the Word (Scripture) or being witnessed to is no excuse for never committing one's life to Christ. God has provided evidence of himself through the majesty of His creation and has instilled the sense of His existence in each individual (Ecc. 3:11; Rom. 1:18-20; 2:12-15). The Holy Spirit is constantly urging (some would identify this as conscience) all of mankind to come to God (John 16:7-8; Acts 7:51; 1 Cor. 2:12-14) whether or not they are aware of this fact or ever had the opportunity for a direct encounter with the facts of God's salvation plan. Jesus' statement of the great commandment demanding love toward God and mankind (Matt. 22:36-40) gives the basic criteria for Christian living from the earliest of times (Matt. 25:37-40; 1 John 4:20)— The Old Testament saints were redeemed because of their faith (Heb. 11) even though they knew not about Messiah's coming but had faith in God's plan for them.

There are several theologies about salvation that have been put forward over the centuries after the Protestant Reformation. We present those ideas of John Calvin, Jacobus Arminius, and John Wesley, among many others, concerning lost salvation, apostasy, and the unforgivable sin.

John Calvin, a Presbyterian theologian, believed Christians cannot lose their salvation (once saved, always saved doctrine) citing John 5:24; 10:27-30;[128] 17:12; Romans 8:38-39; Eph. 1:13-14; Philippians 1:6; 2 Timothy 1:12; 4:18; Hebrews 10:10-14; 1 Peter 1:5; 3:9-10; and Jude 24- 25. This position would require a qualification to Hebrews 6:4-6 and 10:26-29 as referring to a hypothetical case showing what would happen to a Christian if he/she could apostatize. Calvin concluded that if a Christian seems to have fallen into apostasy, then he/she had never been saved to begin with and should seek the Lord anew, possibly citing 1 John 3:6 that habitual sin indicates an unsaved soul.

Jacobus Arminius, a Dutch theologian, although agreeing with much of Calvinism, believed God calls all persons unto Himself through the pleadings of the Holy Spirit but allows them free wills to accept Jesus as savior by faith or to reject Him. Arminius reasoned that if salvation comes by the grace of God and is conditional on faith, then continued faith is required for continued salvation (conditional preservation doctrine). That is, a Christian could lose salvation by apostasy citing John 5:24; 10:27-28; 15:5-6; Galatians 5:4; 1 Tim. 4:1-2; Hebrews 3:6, 12-14; 6:4-6 (although Calvinists interpret verse 4-6 as showing how impossible it is for a Christian to lose salvation); 10:23, 26-29, 35-39; James 5:19-20; 2 Peter 2:20-22; 3:17; 2 John 8-9; Revelation 2:4-5; 3:5, 16-17. Arminius further believed a Christian could never come back to the fold once he/she had lost salvation citing Hebrews 6:4-6 and 10:26-29. But John Wesley, also agreeing on conditional preservation, believed otherwise, citing James 5:19-20. The next logical question then is, "What constitutes apostasy?" In general terms, we could identify at least most causes: willfully and knowingly giving in to worldly pleasures instead of spiritual things, declining faith in sound doctrine, and neglecting prayer, study, and communion with saints--leading to a loss of conscience (voice of the Holy Spirit) as one distances himself from God (Zech. 7:11-13). We see that both men believed that apostasy was the cause of lost salvation, but they disagreed on its finality.

We also have the question of the *unforgivable sin* that is present in modern day thought. The Bible clearly states that this sin is "blasphemy against the Holy Spirit" as was the popular idea in the early church (Matt. 12:31-32; Mark 3:28-29; Luke 11:14-23; 12:10). Present day thought by some interpret these verses as speaking of one who rejects Christ up to the time of their death, arguing that this act constitutes a blasphemy against the Holy Spirit who witnesses of Christ; in other words, one cannot commit this sin in ones lifetime, only at death—an indication of an habitual and unrepentant heart (1 John 3:6). Furthermore, Jesus had been casting out demons when He directed the quotes in the above verses at the Pharisees. They attributed Jesus' success at casting out demons to demons. This would seem to indicate that rejecting the Holy Spirit's witness of Jesus is equivalent to blasphemy against the Spirit. Those who reject Jesus thus reject the power of the Holy Spirit to effectively draw them to Jesus. But if we consider 1 John 1:7, 9 it states that all Christians' sins past, present, and future are covered by Jesus' shed blood. This verse then assures us that, as Christians, we cannot commit this particular sin or else the "all" in the verse would need to read "most" or "all but one." A further extension of this reasoning leads to the conviction that if a nonbeliever were to commit this sin, there is no future redemption for him/her for it would needs be that it is forgiven if they later become Christian thus contradicting the 1 John 1:7, 9 verse. Similarly, if a supposed Christian were to commit this sin, then we are led to believe that person was never saved to begin with. But 1 John 5:16 seems to speak of Christians who have committed this sin however we may interpret the cause. We also must consider whether this is a spiritual or physical death. If physical, then it does not condemn the soul.

I believe the disciples, all but one, were saved and their sins forgiven the moment they began to follow Jesus, although they did not receive the Holy Spirit until they first met Jesus after the resurrection (John 20:21-23) just as some Christians would later in the early church (Acts 8:14-15; 19:1-2). Judas, not being saved, committed the unforgivable sin of rejecting Christ to the point that he believed Jesus was not the promised Messiah but in some way attributed demonic powers or associations to our Savior's miracles instead of the Holy Spirit, for he regretted his actions but did not receive forgiveness. Another position might be taken giving the disciples' salvation as coming with their receiving the Holy Spirit by citing Peter's amazement at Jesus' resurrection (Matt. 11:3; Luke 24:12, 21) indicating that he did not understand the resurrection up to this point (John 20:6-10). But we know the disciples understood the resurrection before Jesus' ascension (John 21:10-14) and Peter and the other disciples were redeemed before Pentecost, since Peter's preaching brought about 3,000 souls to salvation (Acts 2:1-41). Peter's denial of Jesus and subsequent forgiveness, as Jesus foretold in Luke 22:31-32, points to God's willingness to continue to forgive a Christian's sins after salvation. Peter earnestly repented (Matt. 26:69-75; Mark 14:66-72; Luke 22:54-62; John 18:15-18, 25-27).

The preceding presentation is oversimplified in its analyses of complex subjects which require much study for deeper understandings. For those inclined, this would be a rewarding adventure! Much can and has been said and printed about how we can please God and be sure we are doing His will—we do so if we love Him and our neighbors—the greatest commandment given to us by our Lord (Matt. 22:36-40) is the basis for all the other laws.

From experience, I warn Christians of the dangers of backsliding: the longer we stay away from the communion of believers, prayer, and study, the harder it becomes to hear the Spirit's calling (Psa. 51:11) and make it back to the fold (Heb. 2:1; 3:12-13). It would be better if that person had never heard the good news (2 Peter 2:20-21). I thank and praise our Lord for His patience in calling all backsliding Christians home!

I do not pretend to know for sure, for no one does, the chronology of all God's future plans such as the sequence of the Rapture, Second Coming, Tribulation, and Millennium, only that they will occur, and we must be ready (2 Peter 3:13-14)! We must continually watch for the future signs so we can make the appropriate adjustments to our understanding, as Scripture will continue to be revealed in more detail as we approach the end. We do not need to know all the details of these events, only that they could occur any day. Would it not be wise to ensure that our souls will spend eternity in the Kingdom of God? Because God is eternal (Gen. 21:33; Psa. 90:2; 102:24-27; Isa. 40:28), so shall Christian believers be. Eternity is a very long time!

20

SUMMARY

Let us review all that has been presented of God's plan: past, present, and future. This might be a good spot for the newer Christians to start their studies. Of course, more experienced Christians will have a propensity to research Scripture and reference materials with their studies of this work. My prayer is that my work will find a home in those who have not yet heard the good news or those who have been putting off making the most important decision of their lives: to admit (confess) their sins and seek forgiveness in the blood of the Lamb, Jesus, so they may obtain everlasting peace with our Savior.

We present the following graphic display of God's Plan:

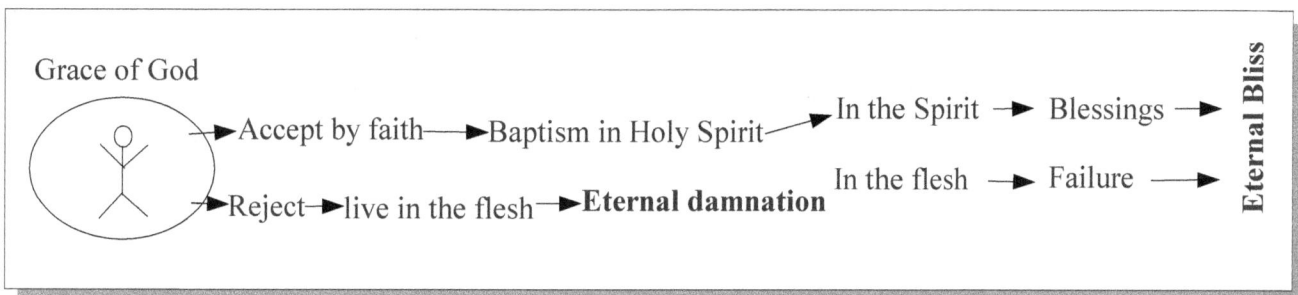

Grace of God

Accept by faith → Baptism in Holy Spirit → In the Spirit → Blessings →

Reject → live in the flesh → **Eternal damnation**   In the flesh → Failure →

Eternal Bliss

Every person must make a choice before their mortal time comes to an end. We can reject God's gift of salvation or accept this free gift by the grace of God. Our destiny for the former choice is eternal separation from God in Hell while our choice of the latter is to achieve redemption and receive the baptism in the Holy Spirit. We are constantly faced, as Christians, to make choices to live in the Spirit or in the flesh. We live in the flesh when we depend on our own free wills to try to live by the Law; i.e., we attempt to do things our way. This thinking always leads to failure and a loss of rewards in Heaven. We live in the Spirit when we put our faith in Christ to lead us in His will for our lives. Our good works will be accepted by our Lord, adding to the rewards we will receive in Heaven.

We now present our summary:

- God created the universe and finally man for fellowship with Him.
- Man disobeyed God and introduced sin into God's perfect creation.
- From creation to the flood, man was made righteous by faith in God.
- From the flood to the giving of the Law, the Ten Commandments were given to God's chosen people, the Israelites, to show them their sins. Rituals and animal sacrifices were demanded by God to cover sins until a better, lasting sacrifice would be made by Jesus.
- The Israelites survived, although often disobediently, until they were punished by God for their apostasy: exiles to Assyria in 721 B.C. and Babylon in 586 B.C. and being temporarily grafted out of the Kingdom.
- Messiah (Jesus) was born in about 5 B.C., was crucified, and was resurrected in about 30

A.D. He willingly gave Himself as the perfect sacrifice to pay for man's sins. His was the final sacrifice to replace the ritualistic daily animal sacrifices that could only cover sins. From this time on, man could find his salvation only through this sacrificial Lamb just by believing and acting on that belief in total commitment to Him. This was the spiritual birth of the church--start of the *Church Age.* Jesus ascended to Heaven forty days later.

- Ten days after Jesus' ascension, at Pentecost, the Holy Spirit was given to the believers to guide, comfort, and teach them. This was the physical birth of the church.
- The temple in Jerusalem was destroyed in 70 A.D. The Jewish nation ceased to exist, the Jews being dispersed worldwide. Judaism and Christianity was forever split.
- The independent nation of Israel was established in 1948 A.D. in the Holy Land.
- Today could be in the very last days.
- The Rapture of the Church will come unannounced but with prophetic signs: Church age saints, both living and dead, will have their bodies raised and united with their souls and taken up to Heaven, the first part of the Second Advent. This event marks the end of the church age.
- The seven year Tribulation period will begin with Antichrist's signing of a peace treaty with Israel.
- Three and a half years later, Antichrist will break the treaty and desecrate the temple.
- Wars to annihilate Israel will be fought, the last one, Armageddon.
- Christ will return to fulfill the promise of the Kingdom of God at His Glorious Appearing to defeat all Israel's enemies, thus saving the earth from complete destruction. Antichrist and his followers will be defeated and cast into Hell, and Satan will be chained for a while. All the nations will be judged by God.
- The Millennium period (Heaven on earth) will begin immediately with the survivors of the Tribulation to fulfill God's Kingdom promises. Jesus will rule from Jerusalem with David as His assistant and His earthly disciples will rule over the twelve tribes of the united Jewish nations of Judah and Israel. The saints will have dominion over the earth.
- One thousand years later the Millennium will end. Satan will be released and will make one last attempt to lead the Millennium people against God. Satan and those unbelievers who follow him will be defeated and cast into Hell. Unbelievers of all time will be judged and cast into Hell; this is the final judgment and the second death.
- A new Heaven and earth with a new Jerusalem will be created for all eternity. God will abide on earth providing eternal bliss for all the believers of all time.

We present a graphic display of God's Plan for His Kingdom through Jesus Christ:

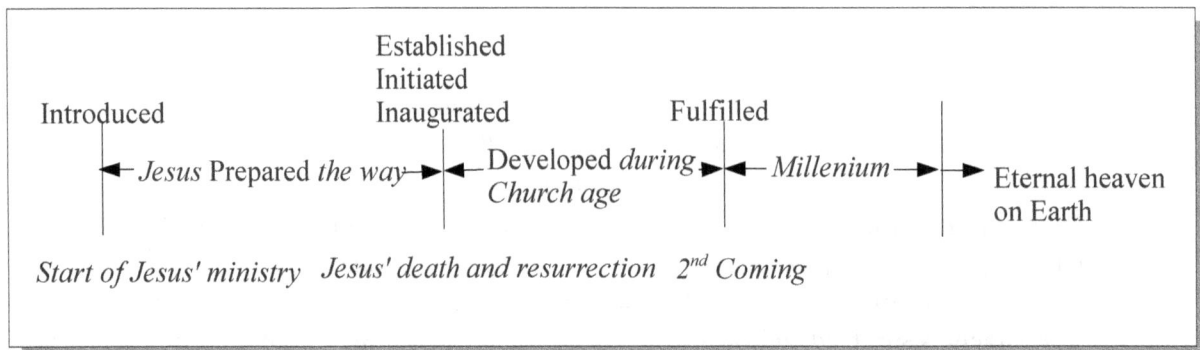

	Established		
	Initiated		
Introduced	Inaugurated	Fulfilled	
←— *Jesus* Prepared *the way* —→	←— Developed *during* —→ *Church age*	←— *Millenium* —→	→← Eternal heaven on Earth
Start of Jesus' ministry	*Jesus' death and resurrection*	*2nd Coming*	

God deserves the glory for creation, for He is the creator. He deserves our praise and thanksgiving because He owns everything including us (Isa. 43:7; Rev. 4:11). Amen!

21

Non-Christian Religions

We offer a final discussion of religions other than Christian, a condensed and very simplified presentation. We do so because of our concern for the salvation of all people who either do not accept God's plan through Jesus or have never had the opportunity to do so. Since Christ has existed from the beginning and paid the penalty for sins past, present, and future (Rom. 3:23-25; Heb. 9:15), all who come to Him confessing their sins and repenting can be saved; this also includes all the Old Testament people (David received salvation, Psa. 116:1-9) and the New Testament people who never get the chance to hear the good news. God's grace is sufficient to forgive their sins because of their faith in Christ even if they never heard His wondrous name or God's plan of redemption (Acts 10:34-35). Our God is omniscient, faithful, and fair in His judgment of each individual; He would never condemn anyone who has not had the opportunity to accept Jesus' offer, for God through the Holy Spirit convicts sinners and their need for a savior. Those who answer the call have in effect, accepted salvation, for Jesus, God the Father, and the Holy Spirit are one who work together. If the above ideas seem suspect and all else fails, we can take comfort in the fact that God does not reveal to us all His redemption plan for whatever reason He sees fit.

We will limit our coverage to some of the major religions who do not recognize the divine Jesus of the Christian faith as Messiah and savior and as one with God. Judaism, Islam, Jehovah's Witnesses, Zoroastrianism, and Mormon religions have already been presented, but they could have been included here if one were of the group that differentiates them from Christian because of either their rejection of Jesus or their offering of a different Jesus than that of the Christian scriptures.

Buddhism

This religion, a sect of Hinduism, was founded by Buddha, later deified about 500 B.C. because of the growing disenchantment with the caste system in India. They disagreed with the Hindu belief in life cycles, deeming them unnecessary; a person abolishes ignorance through proper living and quest of wisdom instead of succumbing to basic pleasures. They believe the highest state of peace and perfection (Nirvana) can be attained through meditation, the total effect of a person's actions as he progresses to higher planes of existence (karma), and no personal God, savior, or divine guidance.

Christian Science

Founded in 1866 A.D. by Mary Eddy Baker who supposedly received revelations on healing. They claim to be the only ones to have the truth on healings. Their beliefs are based on the interpretations of scripture by her. They believe her writings are superior to the Bible. It has been charged that her revelations came not from God but from healer Phineas Quimby. Members have no real teaching on salvation since they believe sin and evil are illusions making Jesus' sacrifice meaningless.

Hare Krishna

This religion was started in the fifteen[th] century as a sect of Hinduism with which it is very compatible with except they have a personal and knowable God, Krishna. Jesus is recognized as the son of Krishna and no more. Members practice meditation, chanting, and self-sacrifice.

Hinduism

We offer a general presentation of this religion since there are many variations and sects due to the complexity of the religion. This religion of unknown origin is hard to describe; it developed in India over a long period of time. Their god is an impersonal and unknowable triune god, Brahman, consisting of Brahma, Vishnu, and Shiva. A collection of wisdom books called Vedas comprise their written record from about 1400-400 B.C. of their oral scriptures. They believe in cycles of birth, death, and reincarnation where the good and bad actions (Karma) of one's life determine the condition of one's soul. Those with negative karma must be reincarnated in another life in the hope of improving their condition. Cycles continue until the individual finally reaches a life of positive karma where he will inherit an eternal state of happiness.

Shinto

This Japanese religion recognizes many gods in inanimate and animated objects, the chief god being the sun-goddess Amaterasu. Its origin is not clearly known but has existed from the earliest histories. They believe they are the divine people of the gods and thus superior. There is no defined doctrine to guide them and no need of a savior since they are the chosen people.

Transcendental Meditation

In India in 1958 A.D., Maharishi Mahesh Yogi started this religion that uses meditation techniques adopted from Hinduism. Although they deny their views as religion-based, the movement is often referred to as The Age of Enlightenment and the Science of Creative Intelligence which has organized teaching centers throughout the world. The Maharishi calls himself a spiritual leader. Some famous, important, and intellectual people seem to be drawn to this group probably because of its glorification of the individual as the master of his destiny. Methods of relaxation and growth are at the core of this religion that recognizes an impersonal creator god who is manifested throughout nature. These techniques are spiritual in that they are supposed to bring the individual closer to God. They do not believe that Christ suffered. This concept is a misunderstanding of Jesus' purpose. They also believe that man is not born in sin and is capable of reaching increasing levels of perfection through his own meditations.

Unification Church

At age 16, Sun Myung Moon supposedly had a vision in 1936 A.D. in Korea in which he claims Jesus appeared to him and asked him to complete His failed and unfinished work. He brought his new religion to America in 1971 A.D. Moon added to the Bible (the Divine Principle) in order to finish it, these writings being superior to the Bible and that Jesus' words will eventually lose their power. He teaches that Jesus' death was not part of God's redemption plan for mankind, and that He failed in redeeming mankind physically although He did succeed in a spiritual salvation. Therefore, Jesus' death had no effect in creating a Kingdom of Heaven on earth. Of course the Christian recognizes that the Kingdom of Heaven on earth was not to be fulfilled at Jesus' death but at His

Second Coming in the last days. Moon claims Jesus was simply an ordinary man but Christians made Him into a god. Moonies (followers) believe Moon has been chosen to complete Jesus ministry. They are taught that they can become equal or greater than Jesus. They also look to Moon as the messiah of the Second Advent to complete the physical redemption--Jesus has been demoted. This religion, where theology is constantly changing due to the added writings, blatantly contradicts the Bible.

Worldwide Church of God

Henry W. Armstrong, self-educated after his conversion in the 1920s, believed that salvation comes from the grace of God through faith in Jesus Christ. He began teaching some unorthodox doctrines in the 1930s, criticizing traditional Christianity. He began a radio ministry (The World Tomorrow), and his followers took the name, "The Radio Church of God." His teachings began to focus more on end time prophecies. The more he developed his doctrines, the further he distanced himself from mainstream Christianity, teaching for example: Jesus is a separate person from God and belongs to the God family, humans have the capability of becoming gods at their resurrections by their good works, the Holy Spirit is not of a triune God (only a spiritual force), strict obedience to laws (often taken from the Old Testament), a second chance at salvation in the end times, observance of some Jehovah's Witnesses teachings, observance of the seventh day (Saturday) sabbath, he alone possessed the truth and all religions were wrong.

In the 1960s, the church name was changed to, "The Worldwide Church of God." His church was viewed by many as a cult, causing some of its members to begin looking more closely at his doctrines. In 1968 at his death, he was succeeded by Joseph Tkach who began changing some doctrines and questioning last day prophecies as non-scriptural. A letter of apology for misleading members was issued. In the 1990s, many doctrines were changed or canceled and the church became more spiritual in worship and more receptive to traditional Christian doctrine, although many Christians questioned its total commitment to traditional Christian doctrine. Some members could not give up their Armstrongism beliefs and started their own churches. In 2009, the church was renamed, "Grace Communion International" and accepts the statement of faith of The National Association of Evangelicals.

Since this church started with many non-scriptural doctrines and few persons are aware of its recent recantings, I have chosen to include them in this section of cults. In time, they may well prove beyond a doubt to hold only traditional Christian doctrines based only on the Word of God.

MAPS

MAP A: THE EXODUS

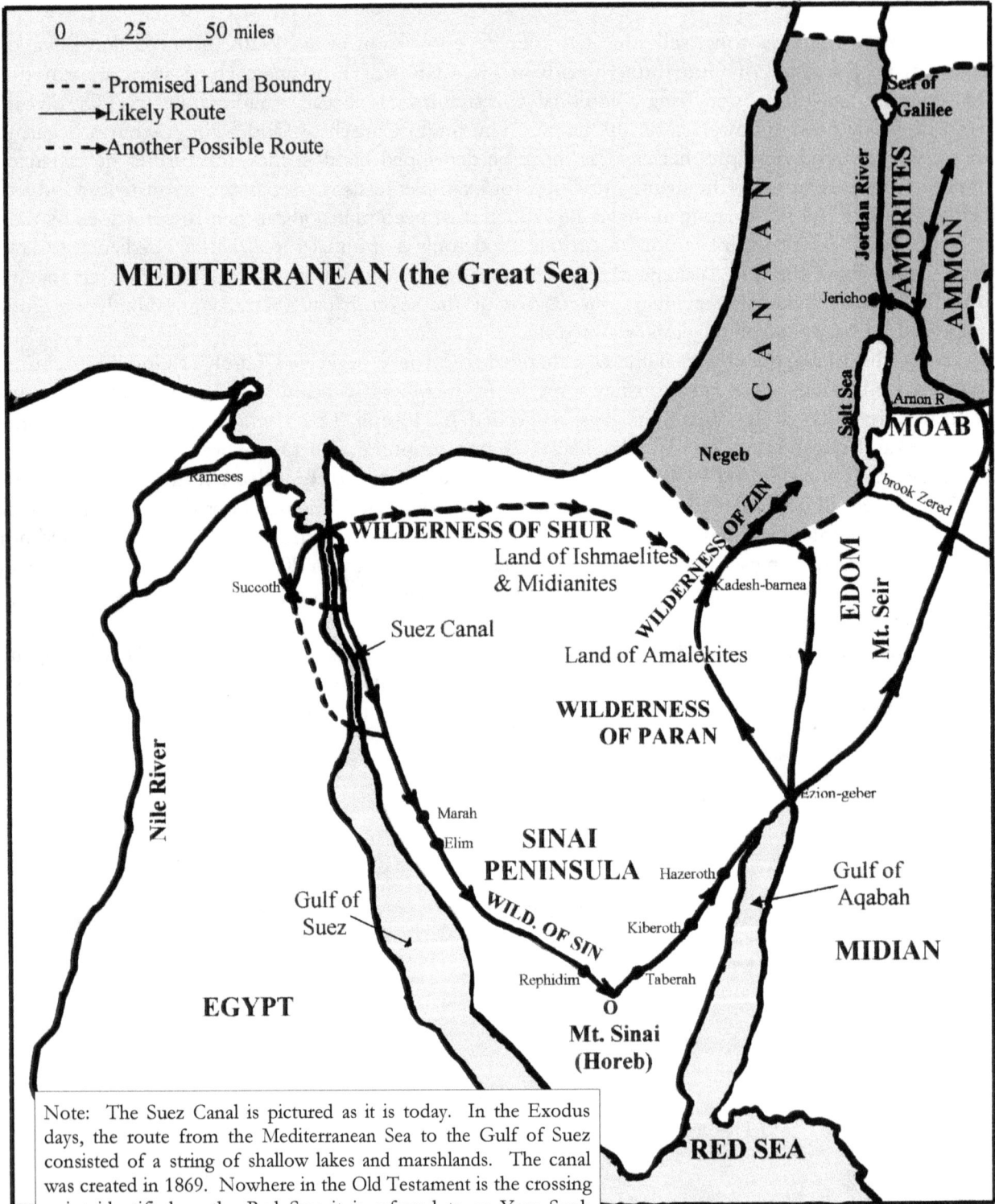

0   25   50 miles

- - - - Promised Land Boundry
———▶ Likely Route
- - - ▶ Another Possible Route

MEDITERRANEAN (the Great Sea)

Sea of Galilee

CANAAN

Jordan River

AMORITES

AMMON

Jericho

Salt Sea

Arnon R

MOAB

Negeb

brook Zered

Rameses

WILDERNESS OF SHUR

Land of Ishmaelites & Midianites

WILDERNESS OF ZIN

Kadesh-barnea

EDOM

Mt. Seir

Succoth

Suez Canal

Land of Amalekites

WILDERNESS OF PARAN

Ezion-geber

Nile River

Marah

Elim

SINAI PENINSULA

Hazeroth

Gulf of Aqabah

WILD. OF SIN

Kiberoth

MIDIAN

Gulf of Suez

Rephidim

Taberah

EGYPT

O

Mt. Sinai (Horeb)

RED SEA

Note: The Suez Canal is pictured as it is today. In the Exodus days, the route from the Mediterranean Sea to the Gulf of Suez consisted of a string of shallow lakes and marshlands. The canal was created in 1869. Nowhere in the Old Testament is the crossing point identified as the Red Sea; it is referred to as Yam Suph meaning Sea of Reeds. The Red Sea became the traditional translation with the Septuagint and Latin Vulgate.

MAP B: THE FORTY YEAR WANDERING

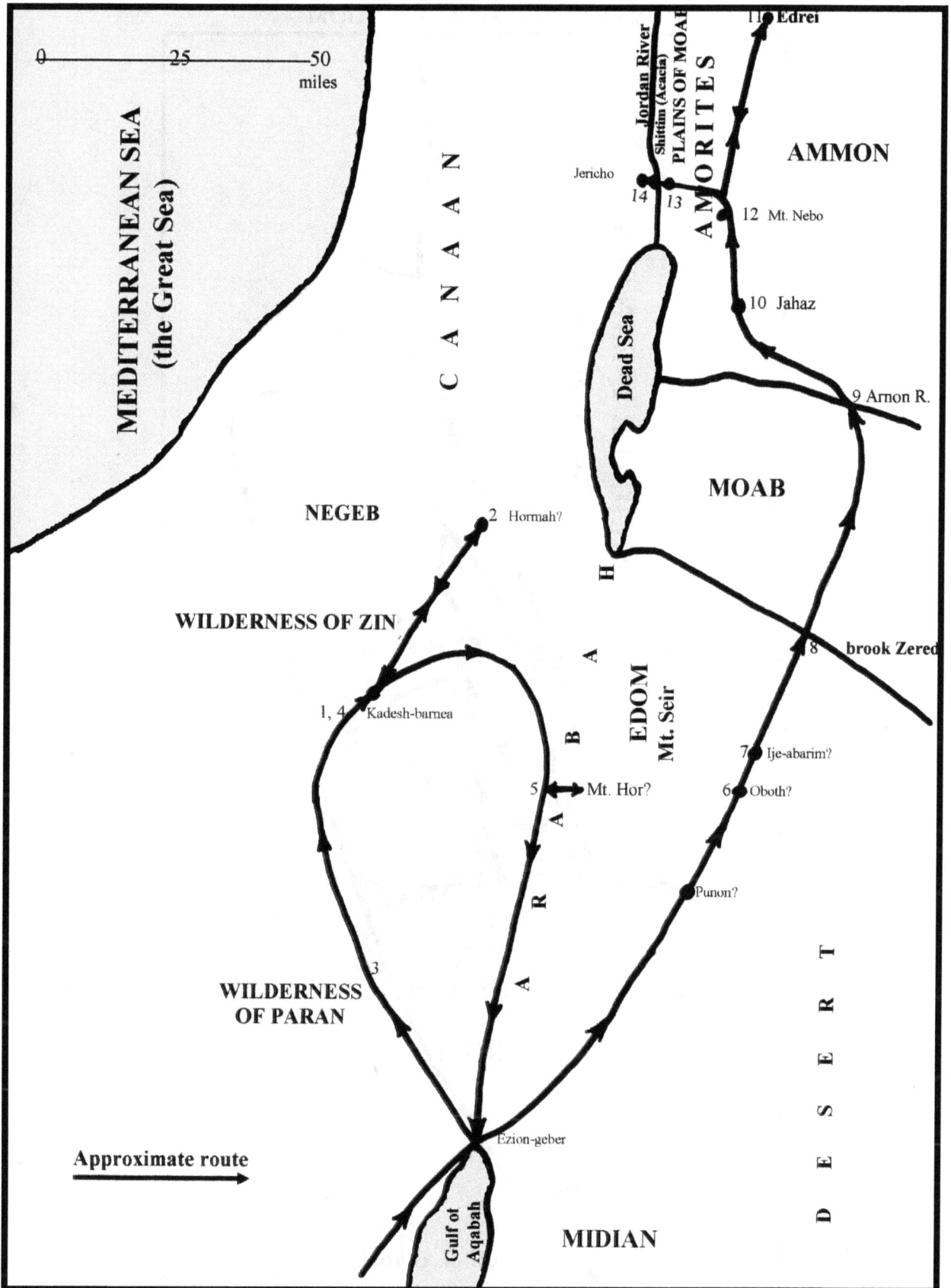

0 — 25 — 50 miles

MEDITERRANEAN SEA (the Great Sea)

C A N A A N

NEGEB

WILDERNESS OF ZIN

WILDERNESS OF PARAN

Approximate route

2 Hormah?

1, 4 Kadesh-barnea

3

Ezion-geber

Gulf of Aqabah

MIDIAN

A R A B A H

EDOM Mt. Seir

MOAB

Dead Sea

Jordan River
Shittim (Acacia)
PLAINS OF MOAB

Jericho

14 13 AMORITES

11 Edrei

AMMON

12 Mt. Nebo

10 Jahaz

9 Arnon R.

8 brook Zered

7 Ije-abarim?

6 Oboth?

5 ← → Mt. Hor?

Punon?

D E S E R T

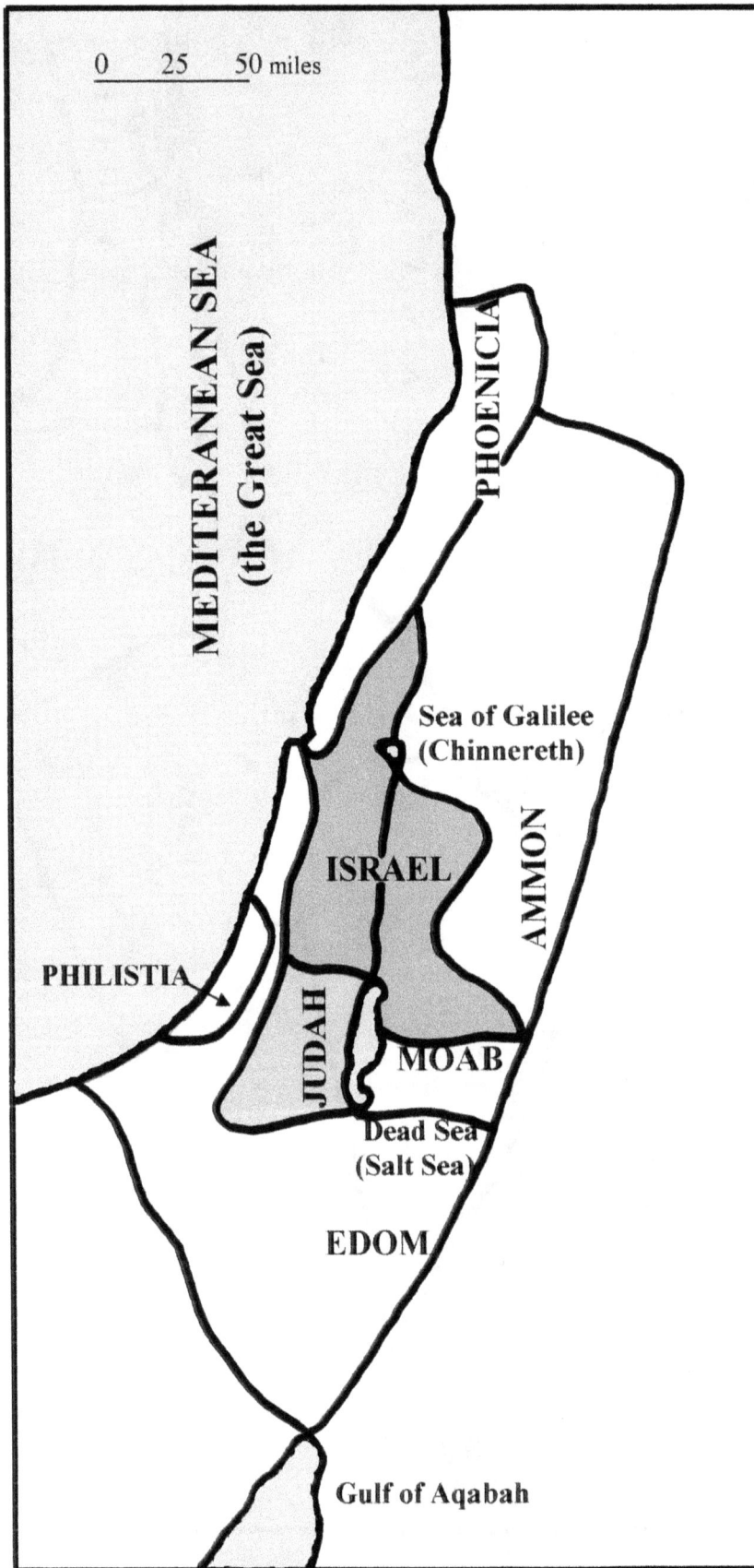

0   25   50 miles

MEDITERANEAN SEA
(the Great Sea)

PHOENICIA

Sea of Galilee
(Chinnereth)

ISRAEL

AMMON

PHILISTIA

JUDAH

MOAB

Dead Sea
(Salt Sea)

EDOM

Gulf of Aqabah

MAP D: ASSYRIAN EMPIRE

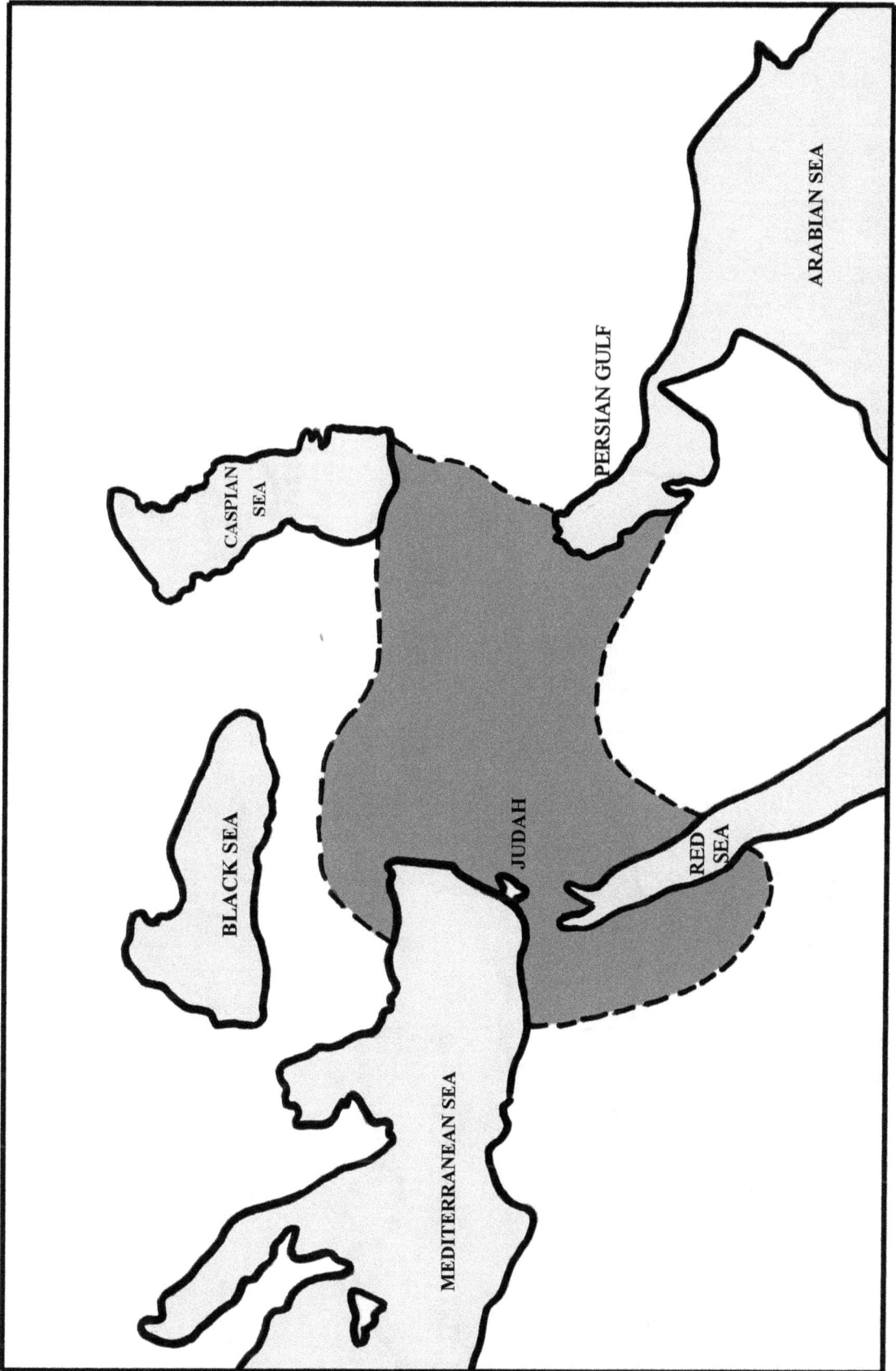

ARABIAN SEA

PERSIAN GULF

CASPIAN SEA

BLACK SEA

JUDAH

RED SEA

MEDITERRANEAN SEA

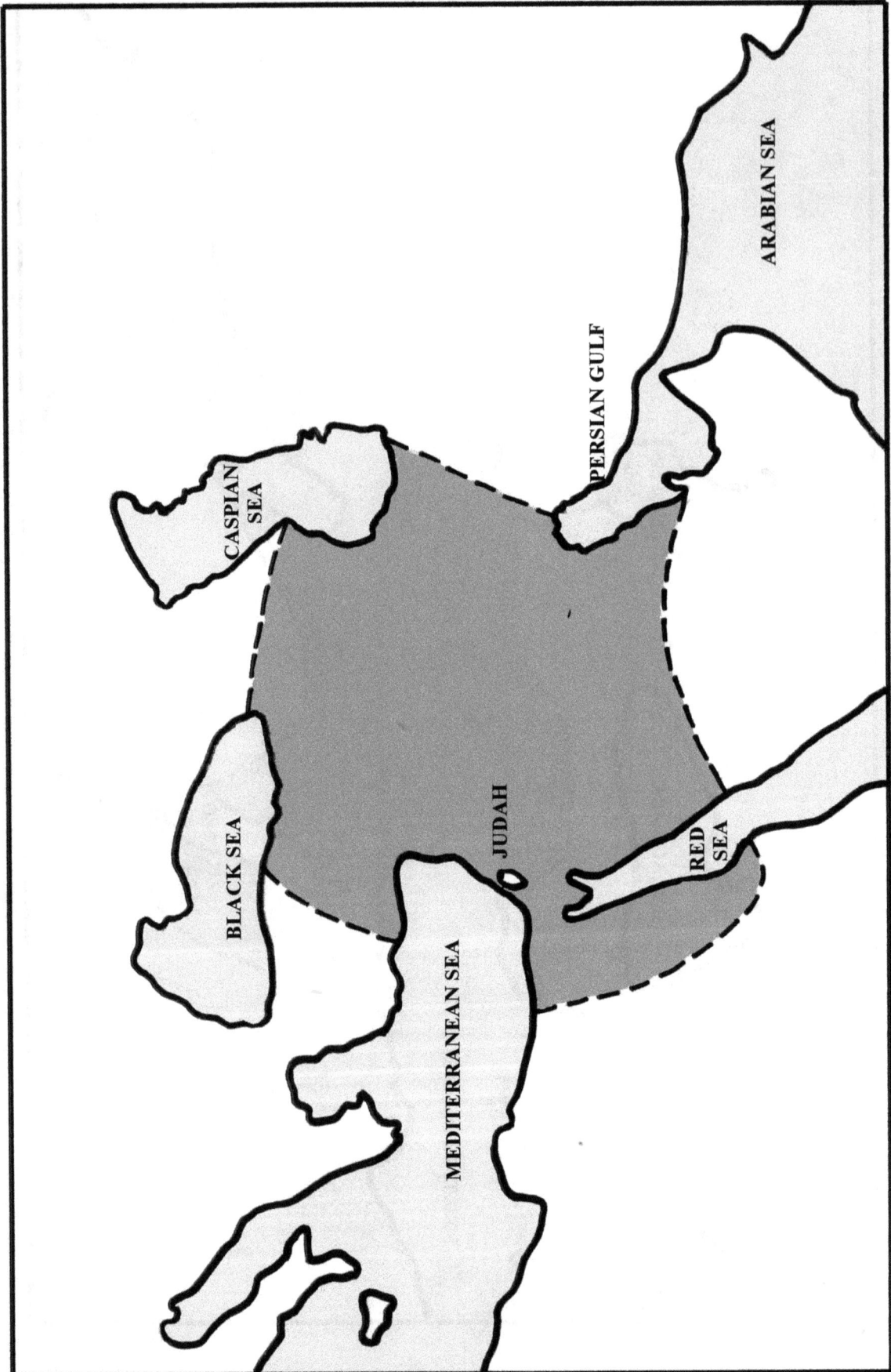

ARABIAN SEA

PERSIAN GULF

CASPIAN SEA

BLACK SEA

JUDAH

RED SEA

MEDITERRANEAN SEA

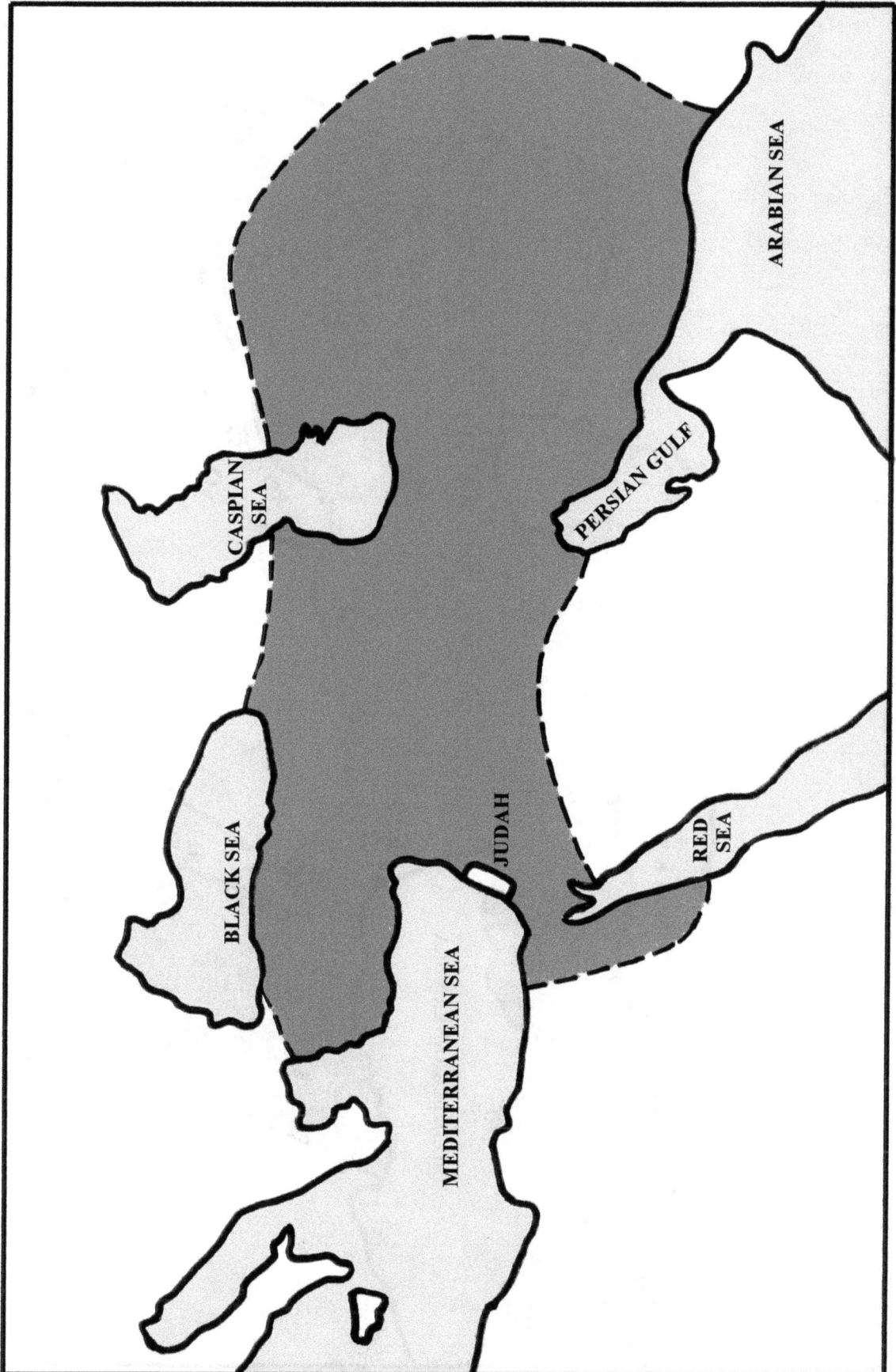

ARABIAN SEA

CASPIAN SEA

PERSIAN GULF

BLACK SEA

JUDAH

RED SEA

MEDITERRANEAN SEA

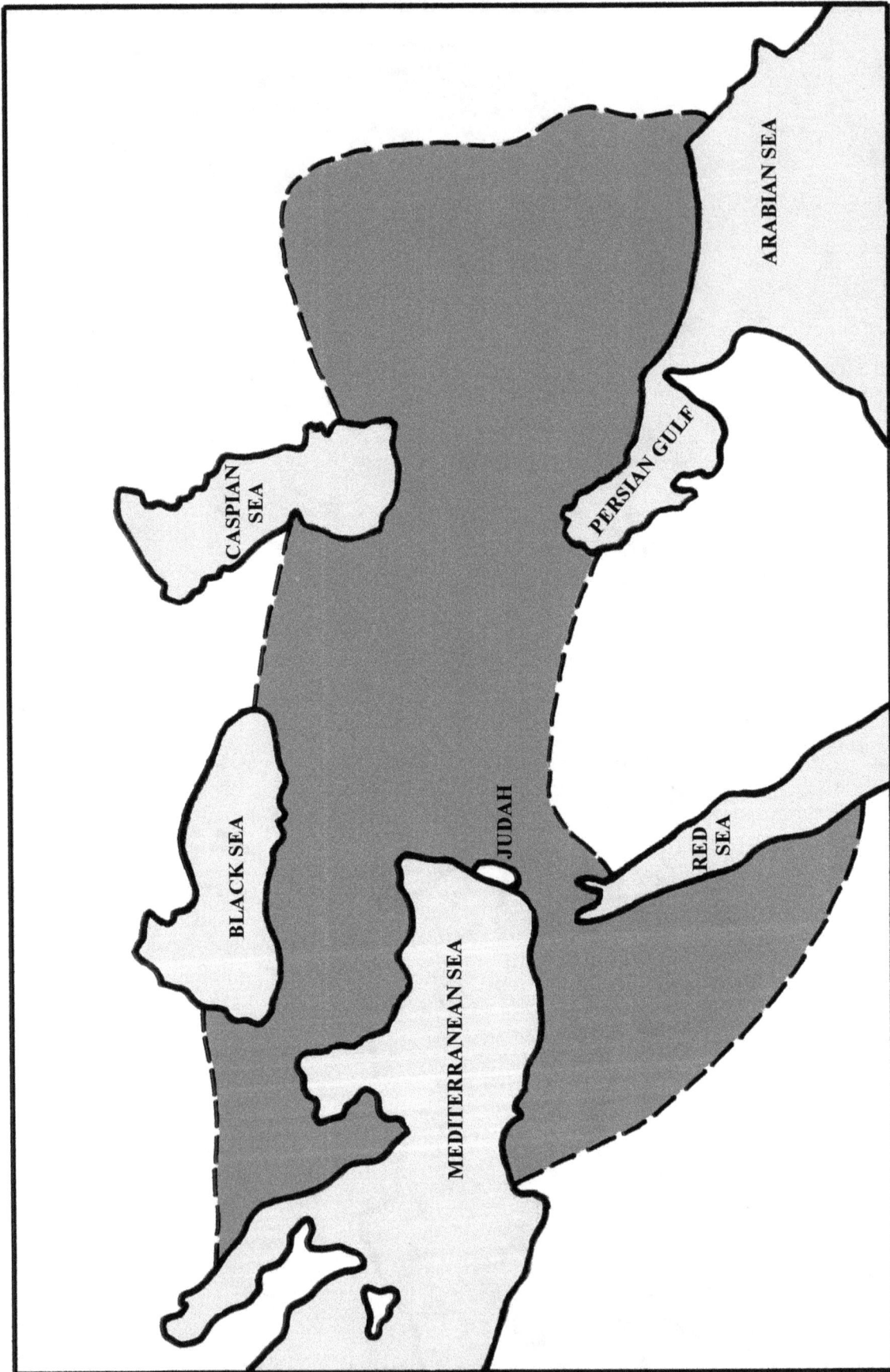

ARABIAN SEA

CASPIAN SEA

PERSIAN GULF

BLACK SEA

JUDAH

RED SEA

MEDITERRANEAN SEA

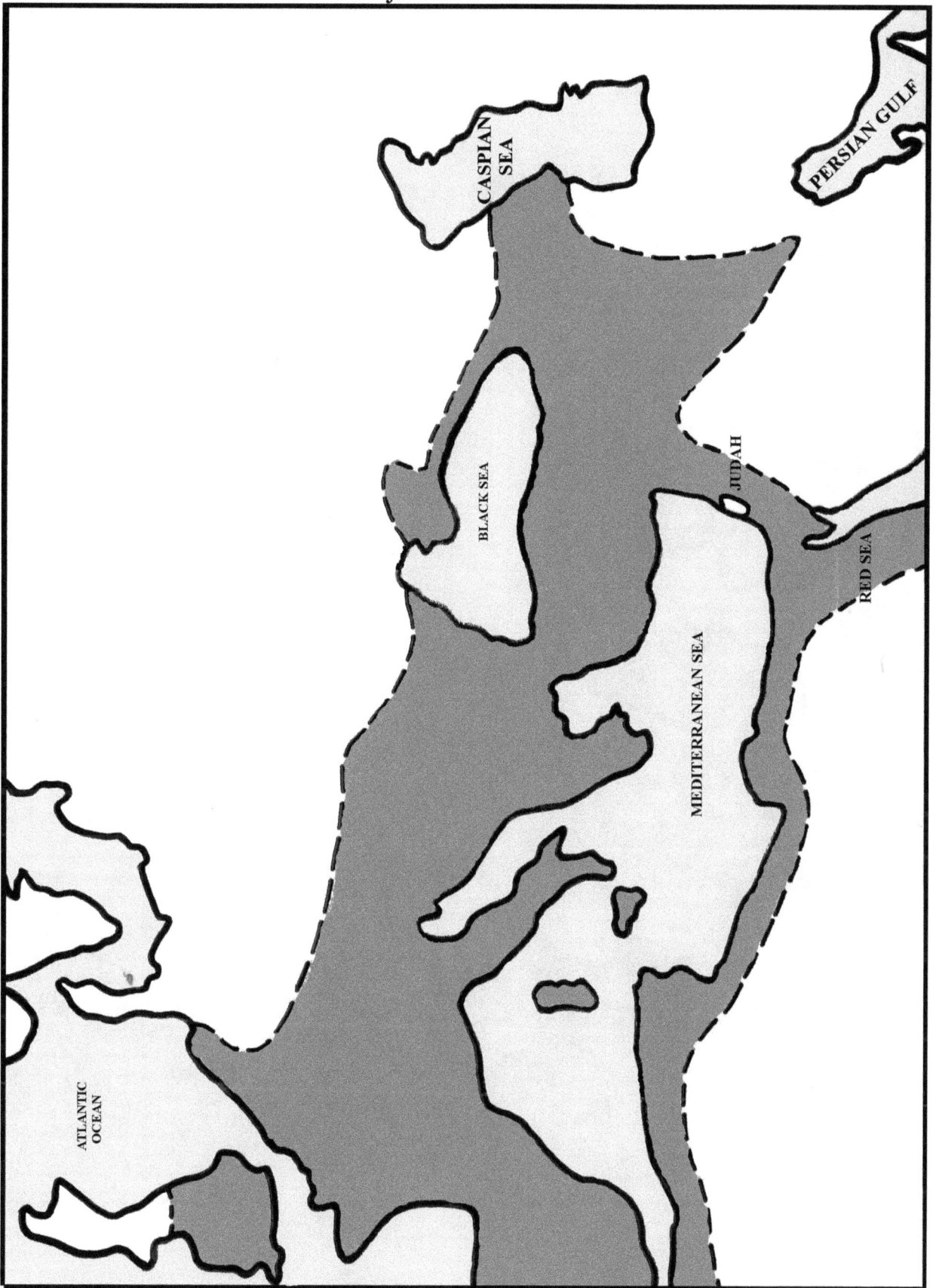

CASPIAN SEA

PERSIAN GULF

BLACK SEA

JUDAH

RED SEA

MEDITERRANEAN SEA

ATLANTIC OCEAN

MAP K: POLITICAL/CHRISTIAN TERRITORIES DURING THE REFORMATION

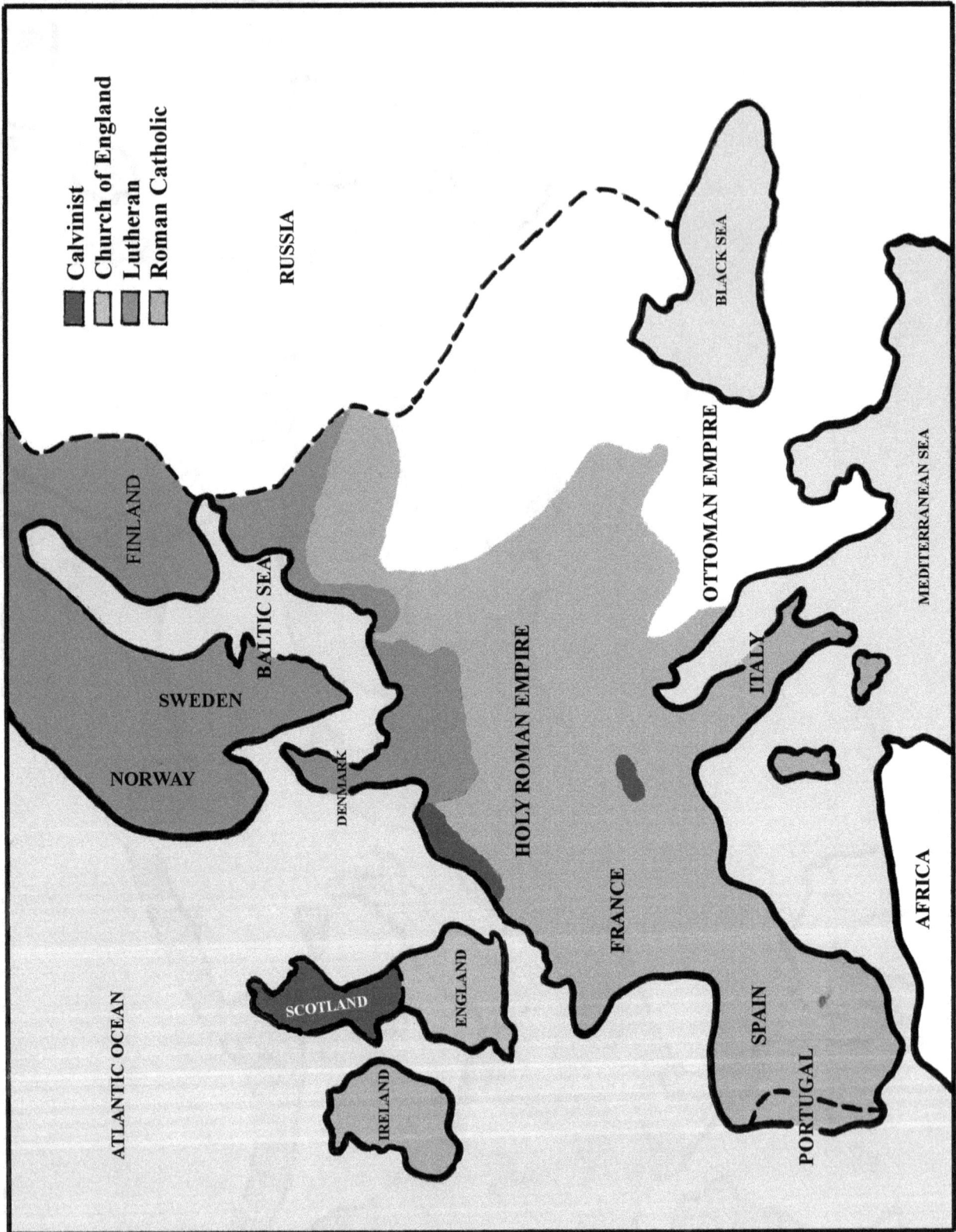

Legend:
- ■ Calvinist
- □ Church of England
- ▨ Lutheran
- ▨ Roman Catholic

RUSSIA

BLACK SEA

FINLAND

BALTIC SEA

OTTOMAN EMPIRE

MEDITERRANEAN SEA

SWEDEN

NORWAY

DENMARK

HOLY ROMAN EMPIRE

ITALY

FRANCE

AFRICA

ATLANTIC OCEAN

SCOTLAND

ENGLAND

SPAIN

IRELAND

PORTUGAL

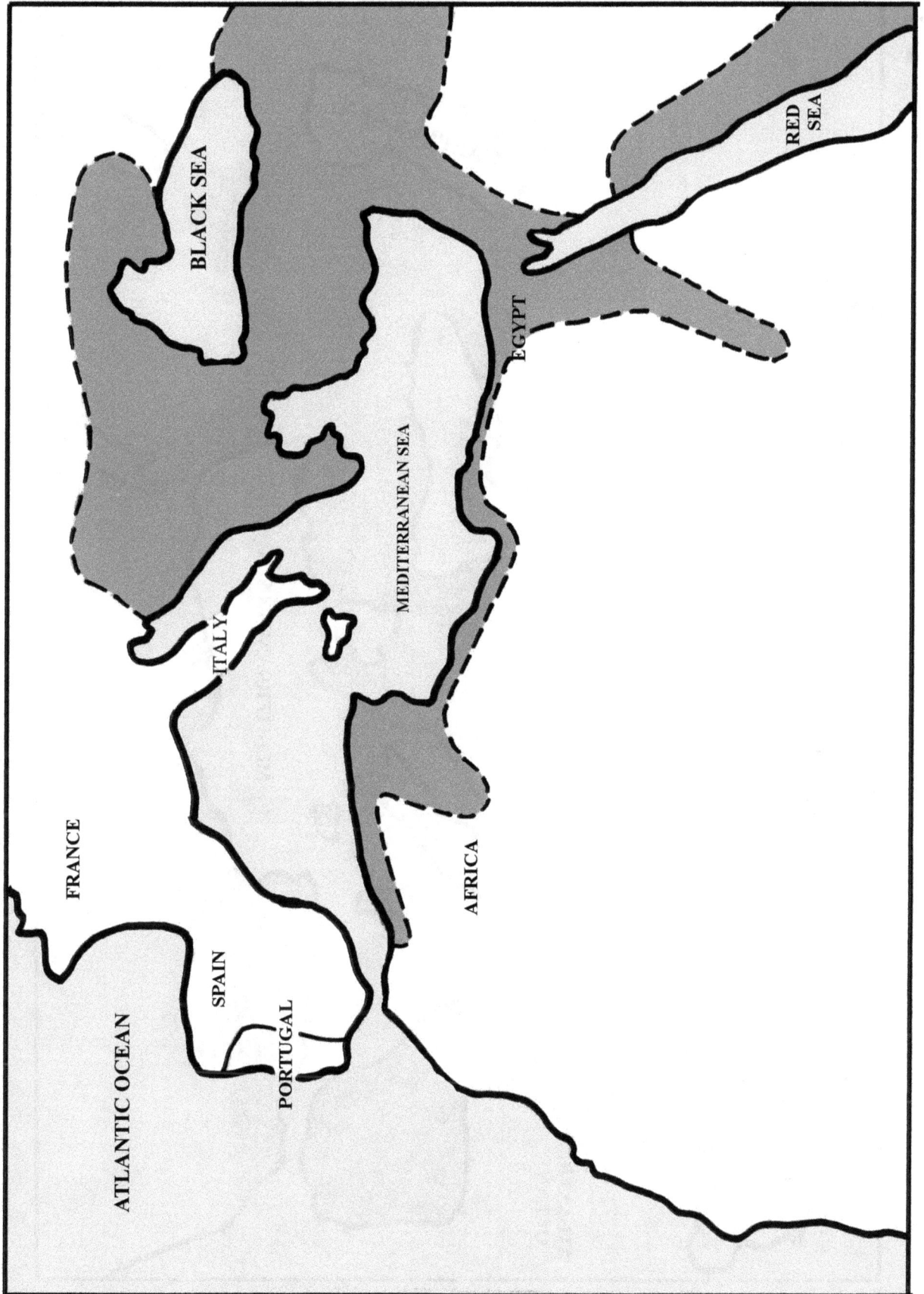

BLACK SEA

RED SEA

EGYPT

MEDITERRANEAN SEA

ITALY

FRANCE

AFRICA

SPAIN

PORTUGAL

ATLANTIC OCEAN

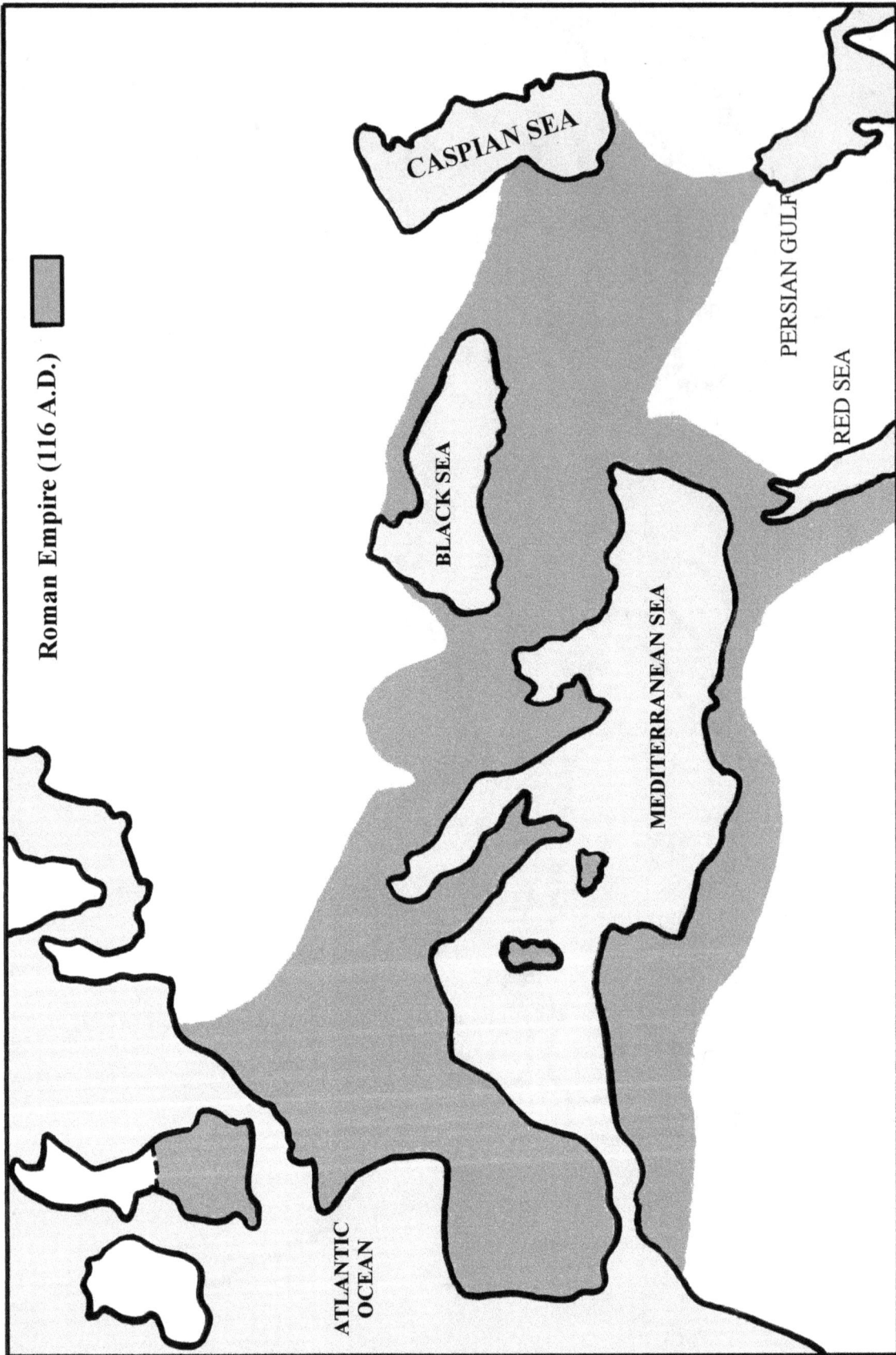

Roman Empire (116 A.D.)

CASPIAN SEA

PERSIAN GULF

RED SEA

BLACK SEA

MEDITERRANEAN SEA

ATLANTIC OCEAN

MAP N: CHRISTIAN EXPANSION IN THE FIRST 4 CENTURIES

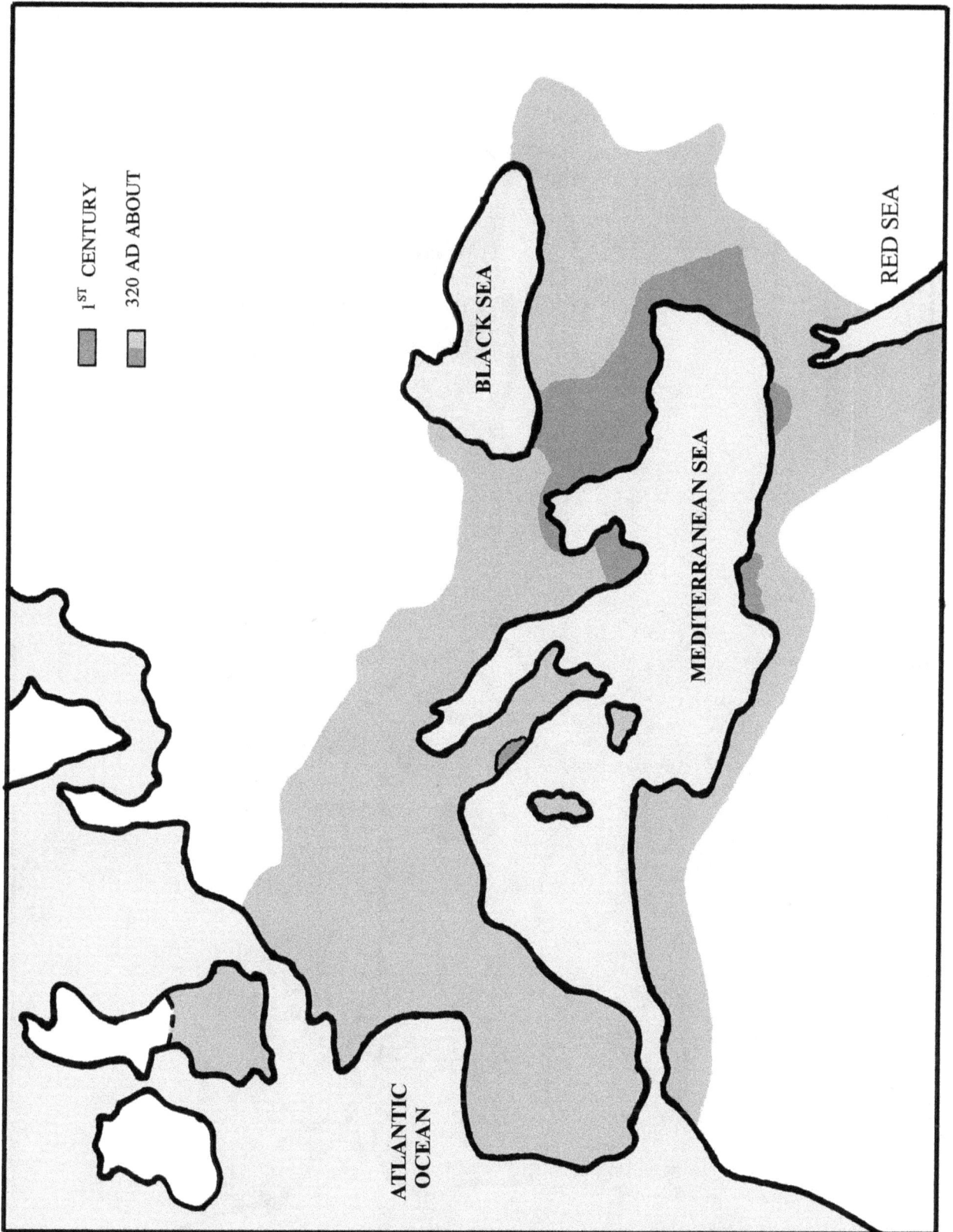

1ST CENTURY

320 AD ABOUT

BLACK SEA

RED SEA

MEDITERRANEAN SEA

ATLANTIC OCEAN

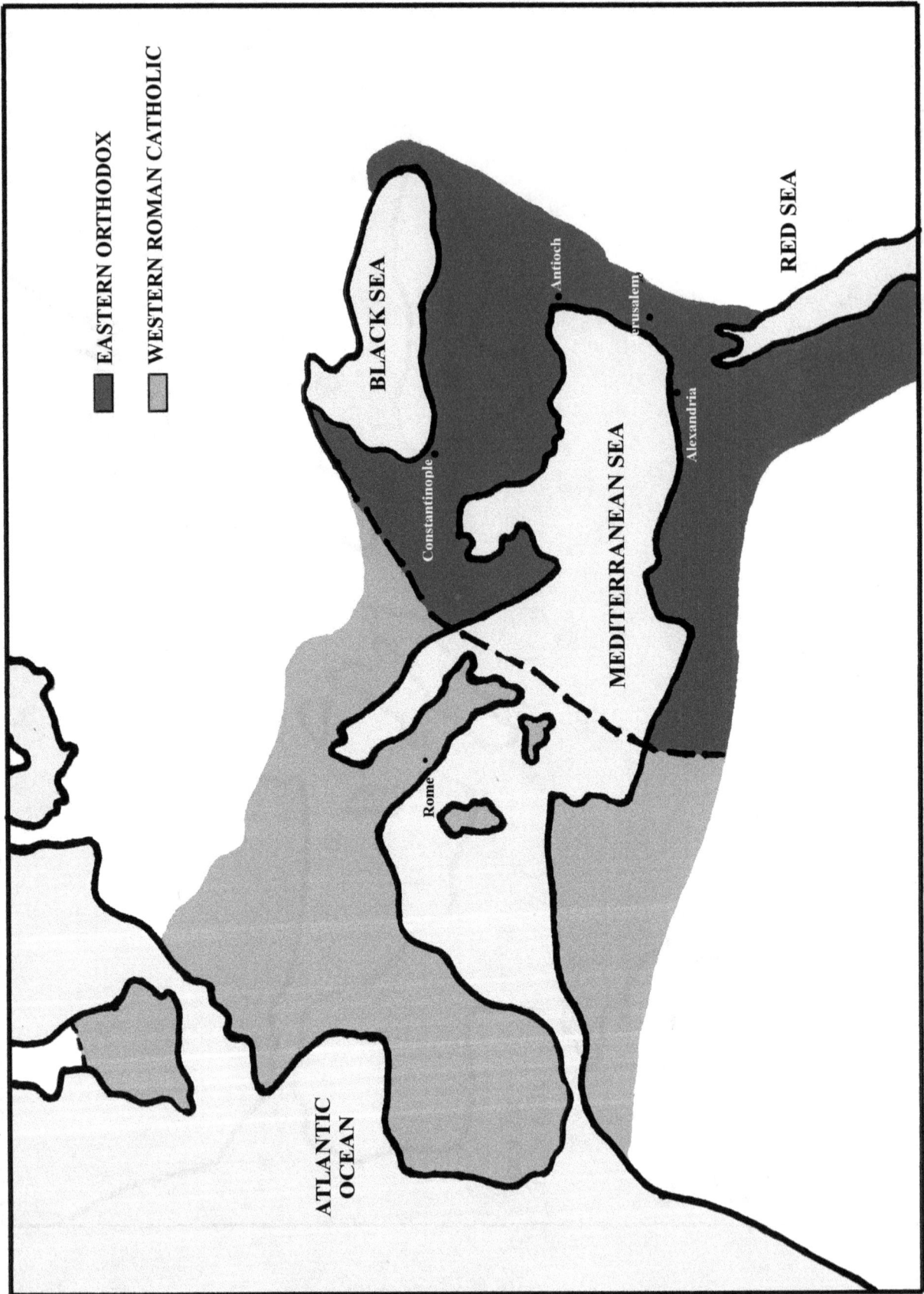

EASTERN ORTHODOX

WESTERN ROMAN CATHOLIC

RED SEA

BLACK SEA

Antioch

Jerusalem

Alexandria

MEDITERRANEAN SEA

Constantinople

Rome

ATLANTIC OCEAN

MAP Q: SPLIT ROMAN EMPIRE, 395 A.D.

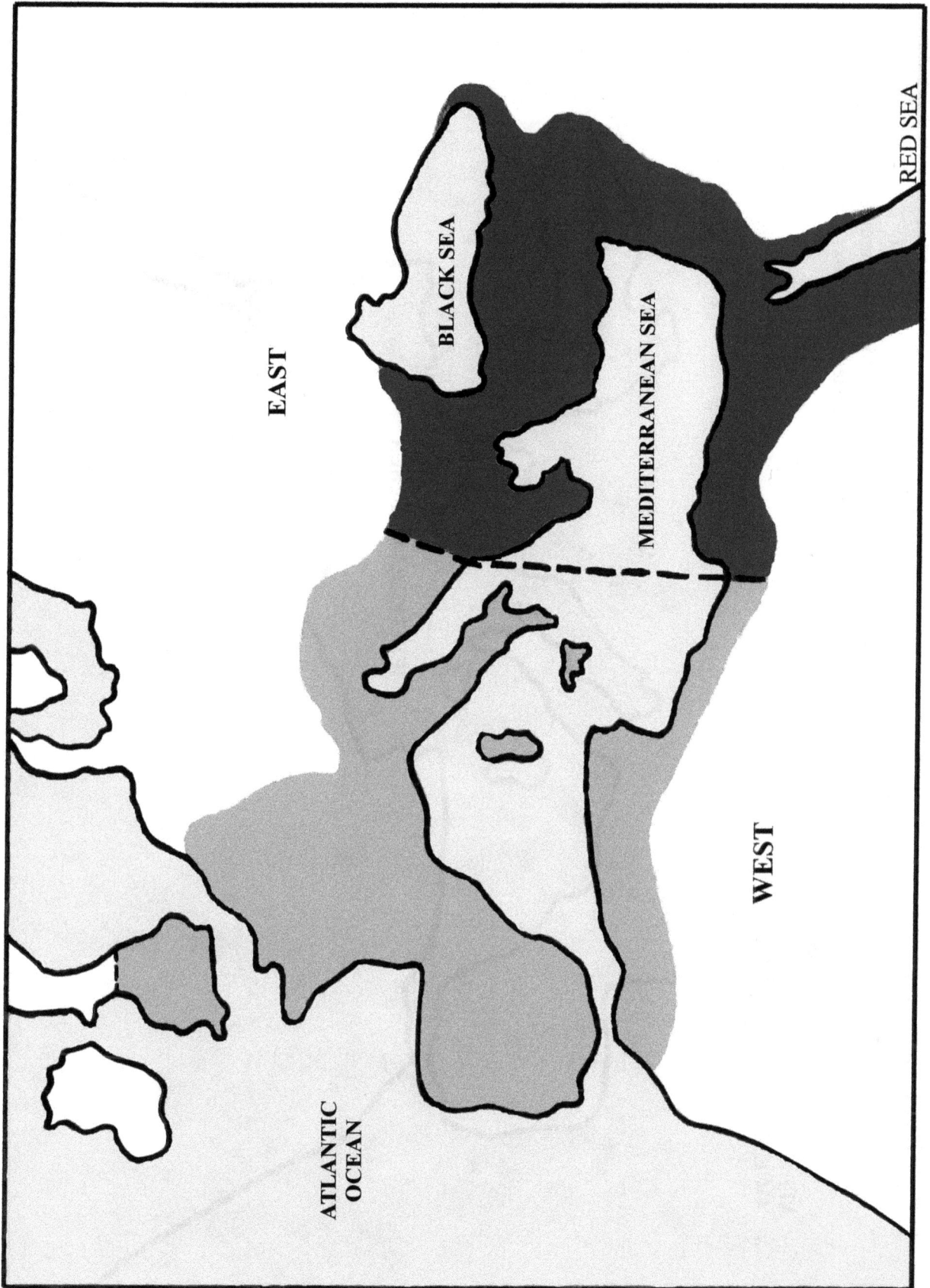

RED SEA

BLACK SEA

MEDITERRANEAN SEA

EAST

WEST

ATLANTIC
OCEAN

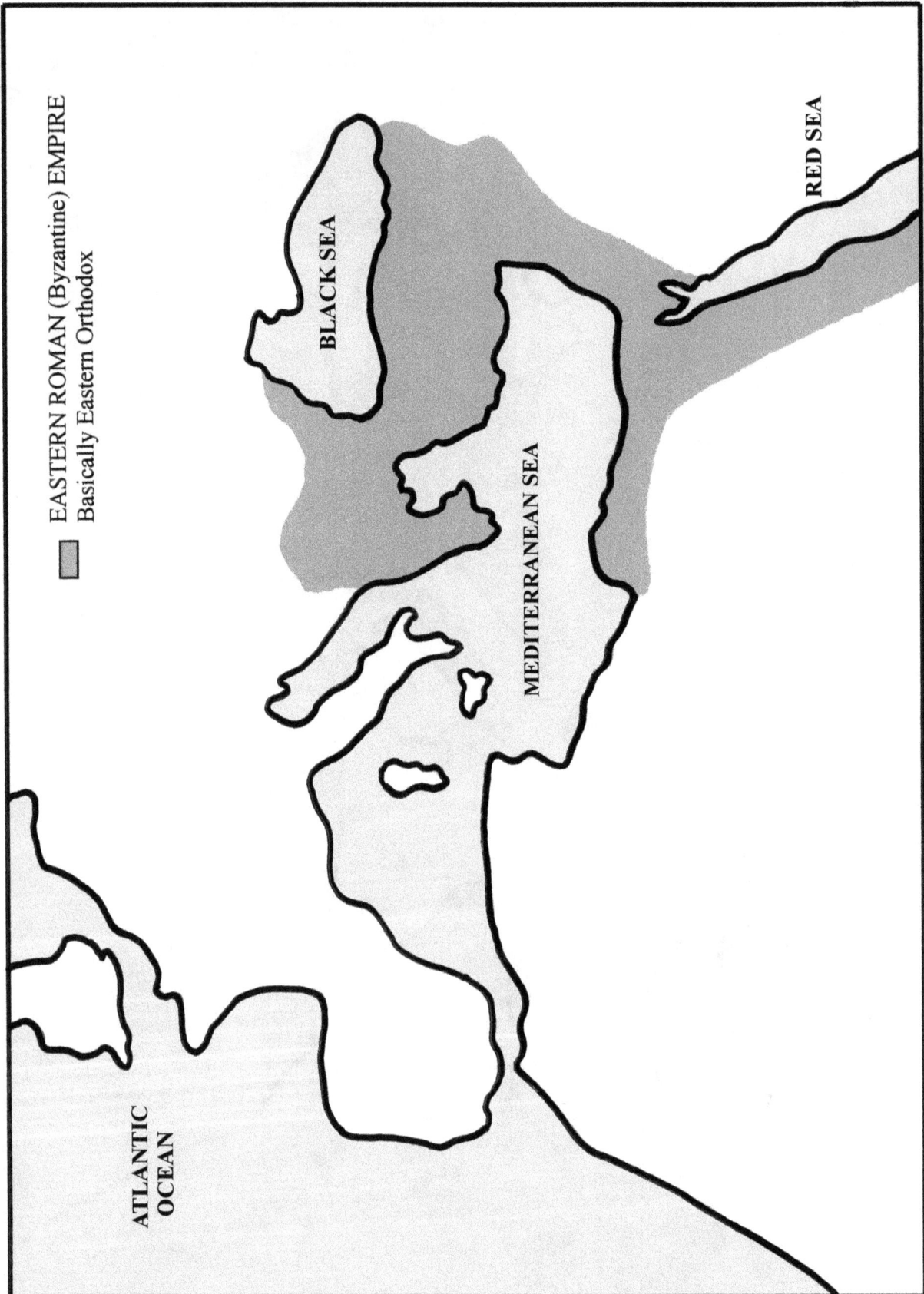

EASTERN ROMAN (Byzantine) EMPIRE
Basically Eastern Orthodox

BLACK SEA

RED SEA

MEDITERRANEAN SEA

ATLANTIC OCEAN

MAP S:
SPLIT WESTERN (ROMAN CATHOLIC) CHRISTIANITY, FRANCE/ROME, 1378 A.D.

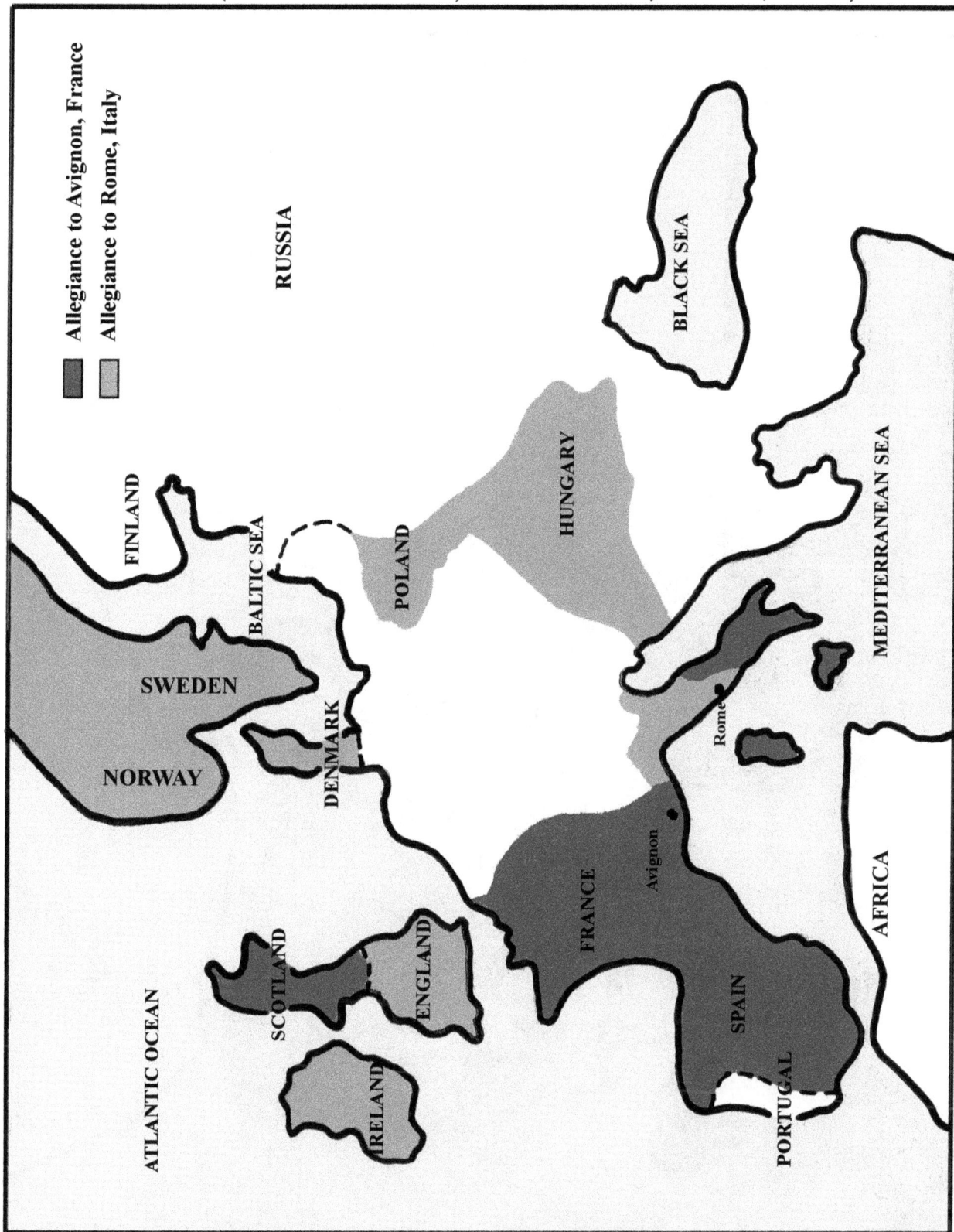

Allegiance to Avignon, France
Allegiance to Rome, Italy

RUSSIA

BLACK SEA

MEDITERRANEAN SEA

FINLAND

BALTIC SEA

POLAND

HUNGARY

SWEDEN

DENMARK

NORWAY

Rome

Avignon

FRANCE

AFRICA

SCOTLAND

ENGLAND

SPAIN

ATLANTIC OCEAN

IRELAND

PORTUGAL

MAP T: RELIGIONS AFTER THE REFORMATION, 1517 A.D.

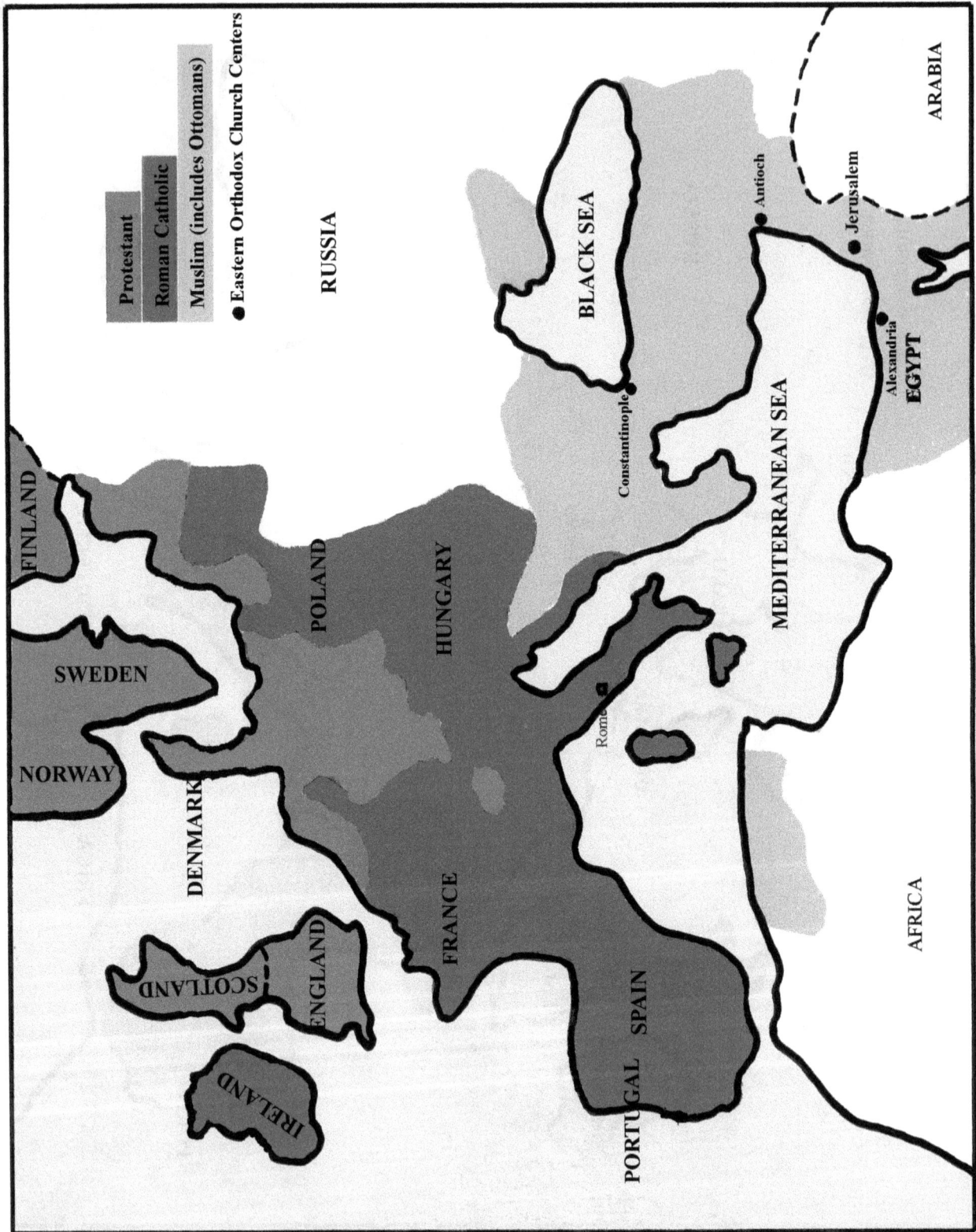

Legend:
- Protestant
- Roman Catholic
- Muslim (includes Ottomans)
- ● Eastern Orthodox Church Centers

RUSSIA

BLACK SEA

Constantinople

Antioch

Jerusalem

ARABIA

Alexandria

EGYPT

MEDITERRANEAN SEA

FINLAND

SWEDEN

NORWAY

DENMARK

POLAND

HUNGARY

FRANCE

Rome

SCOTLAND

ENGLAND

IRELAND

PORTUGAL

SPAIN

AFRICA

MAP U: EARLY ISLAMIC WORLD

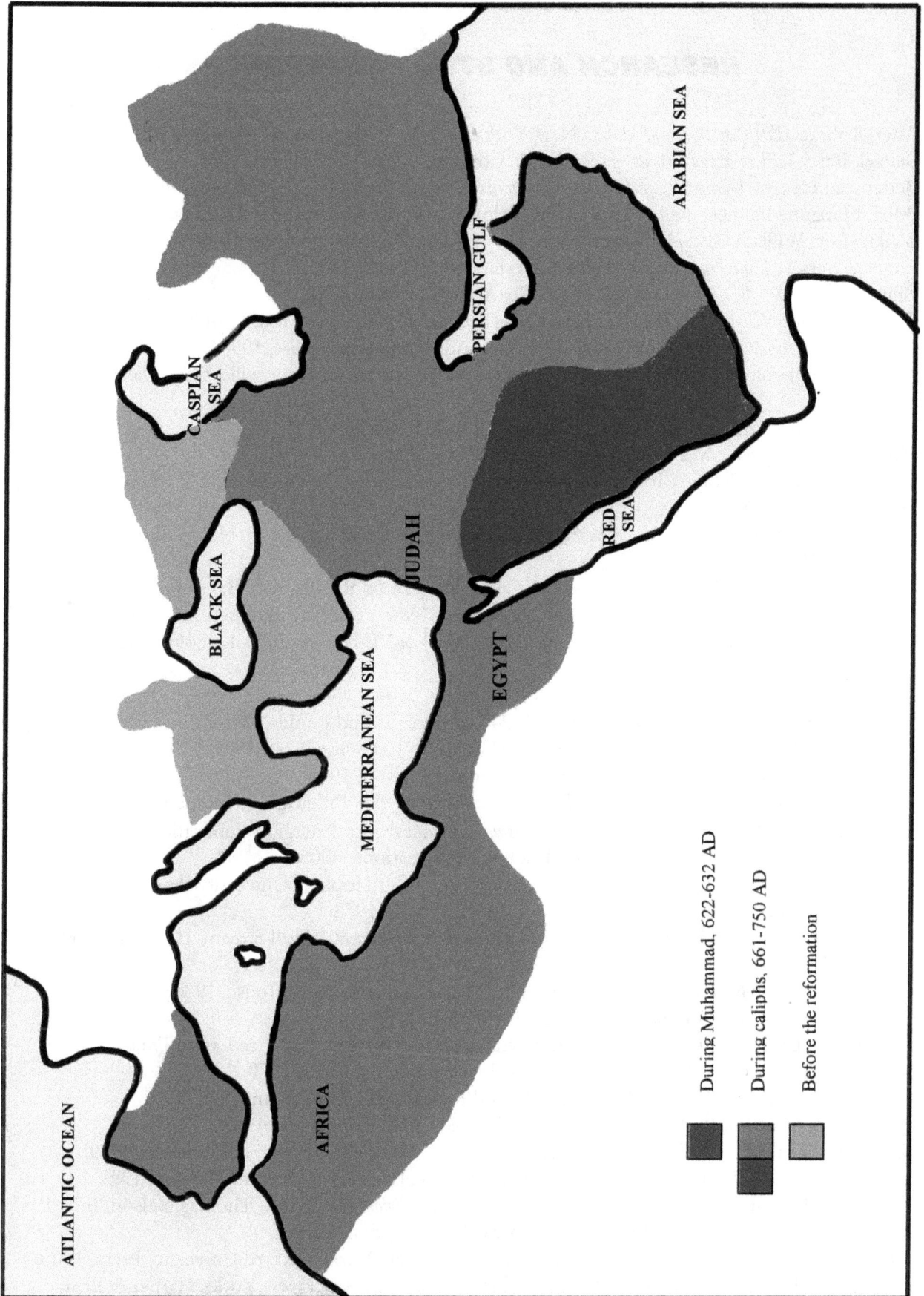

ARABIAN SEA

PERSIAN GULF

CASPIAN SEA

RED SEA

JUDAH

BLACK SEA

EGYPT

MEDITERRANEAN SEA

ATLANTIC OCEAN

AFRICA

During Muhammad, 622-632 AD

During caliphs, 661-750 AD

Before the reformation

RESEARCH AND STUDY REFERENCES

Alter, Robert. *The Five Books of Moses.* New York City: W. W. Norton & Company, 2004.

Beitzel, Barry J. *The Moody Atlas of Bible Lands.* Chicago: Moody Publishers, 1985.

Bettenson, Henry. *Documents of the Christian Church.* New York: Oxford University Press, 1963.

Bonz, Marianne Palmer. *Past as Legacy.* Philadelphia: Augsburg Fortress Publishers, 2000.

Blaikie, Rev. William G. *Bible History.* Nashville: Thomas Nelson and Sons, 1920.

Capps, Charles. *End Time Events.* Tulsa, OK: Harrison House, 1997.

Chilcote, Paul W. *Wesleyan Tradition.* Nashville: Abingdon Press, 2002.

Comfort, Philip Wesley. *Origin of the Bible.* Carol Stream, IL: Tyndale House Publishers, 1992.

Disciples' Study Bible (NIV). New York City: Cambridge University Press, 1990.

Drake, Finis Jennings. *The Rapture and the Second Coming of Christ.* Lawrenceville, GA: Dake Publishing, 1977.

Evans, William. *Personal Soul Winning.* Chicago: Moody Publishers, 1910.

Find it Fast in the Bible. Nashville, Thomas Nelson, Inc., 2000.

Fox, H. Eddie and George Morris. *Let the Redeemed of the Lord Say So.* Franklin, TN: Providence House Publishers, 1999.

Garraty, John A. and Peter Gay. *The Columbia History of the World.* Irvington, NY: Columbia University Press, 1972.

Geisler, Norman and Thomas Howe. *When Critics Ask.* Grand Rapids, MI: Baker Books, 1992.

Gonzalez, Justo L. *The Story of Christianity.* 2 Volumes. New York City: HarperOne, 1984.

Greun, Dietrich, Julia Pferdehirt, and Anna Trimiew. *Who's Who in the Bible.* Lincolnwood, IL: Publications International, 1997

Hagee, John. *Jerusalem Countdown.* Baltimore: Frontline, 2006.

Halley, Dr. Henry H. *Halley's Bible Handbook.* 24th edition. Grand Rapids, MI: Zondervan, 1965.

Hellwig, Monica K. *Understanding Catholicism.* Mahwah, NJ: Paulist Press, 1981.

Hinn, Benny. *Welcome, Holy Spirit.* Nashville: Thomas Nelson, 1995.

Howard, David M. Jr. *Fascinating Bible Facts.* Lincolnwood, IL: Publications International, 1998.

Hushbeck, Elgin L. Jr. *Christianity and Secularism.* Gonzalez, FL: Energion Publications, 2005.

——. *Evidence for the Bible.* Gonzalez, FL: Energion Publications, 2005.

Kraybill, Donald B. *The Riddle of the Amish.* Baltimore: John Hopkins University Press, 2001.

Jensen, Irving L. *The Old Testament.* Chicago: Moody Press, 1978.

LaHaye, Tim and Jerry B Jenkins. *Are We Living in the End Times?.* Carol Stream, IL: Tyndale House Publishers, 1999.

LaHaye, Tim. *The Reese Chronological Bible.* Grand Rapids, MI: Bethany House, 1980.

——. *Revelation Unveiled.* Grand Rapids, MI: Zondervan, 1999.

Larkin, Rev. Clarence. *The Book of Daniel.* Glenside, PA: The Rev. Clarence Larkin Estate, 1929.

Lindsey, Hal. *Late Great Planet Earth.* New York: Inspirational Press, 1970.

——. *Satan is Alive and Well on Planet Earth.* Grand Rapids, MI: Zondervan, 1972.

Lockyer, Herbert. *All the Men of the Bible.* Grand Rapids, MI: Zondervan, 1958

McBrien, Richard P. *The Encyclopedia of Catholicism.* San Francisco: HarperSanFrancisco, 1989.

McDonough, Mary E. *God's Plan of Redemption.* Anaheim, CA: Living Stream Ministry, 1999.

McDowell, Josh and Don Steward. *Handbook of Today's Religion.* Nashville: Thomas Nelson, Inc., 1983.

Mead, Frank S. *Handbook of Denominations.* Nashville: Abingdon, 1975.

Metzger, Bruce M. ed. *The Oxford Annotated Apocrypha.* New York: Oxford University Press, 1965.

Miller, Madeleine S. and J Lane Miller, eds. *Harper's Bible Dictionary.* New York: Harper & Row

Publishers, 1973.

Miller, Steven M. *How to Get into the Bible*. Nashville: Thomas Nelson, Inc., 1998.

Neufeld, Henry. *Identifying Your Gifts and Service*. Gonzalez, FL: Energion Publications, 2006.

——. *Not Ashamed of the Gospel*. Gonzalez, FL: Energion Publications, 2005.

——. *Revelation, a Participatory Study Guide*. CR 2005

——. *To the Hebrews: a Participatory Study Guide*. Gonzalez, FL: Energion Publications, 2005.

——. *When People Speak for God*. Gonzalez, FL: Energion Publications, 2007.

Neufeld, Jody. *Daily Devotions of Ordinary People-Extraordinary God*. Gonzalez, FL: Energion Publications, 2004

New Living Translation. Carol Stream, IL: Tyndale House Publishers, 1996.

Nolt, Steven M. *History of the Amish*. Intercourse, PA: Good Books, 1992.

Noss, John B. *Man's Religions*. New York City: The MacMillan Company, 1969.

Ratzinger, Joseph (Pope Benedict *XVI*). *Catechism of the Catholic Church*. U. S. Conference of Catholic Bishops, 2006.

Reader's Digest Mysteries of the Bible. New York City: Reader's Digest, 1997.

Richardson, V. Riley and Henry Neufeld. *Disciples: Jesus With Us*. Gonzalez, FL: Energion Publications, 2007

Rosen, Ceil and Moishe. *Christ in the Passover*. Chicago: Moody Publishers, 1978.

Smith, William L.L.D. *Nelson's Quick Reference Bible Dictionary*. Nashville: Thomas Nelson, Inc., 1993.

Solle, Dorothee. *Thinking about God*. Philadelphia: Trinity Press International, 1990.

Strong, James. *The Strongest Strong's Exhaustive Concordance to the Bible*. Grand Rapids, MI: Zondervan, 2001.

The Book of Mormon.

The King James Study Bible. Nashville: Thomas Nelson Inc., 1975.

The Living Bible, Carol Stream, IL: Tyndale House Publishers, 1971.

The Samaritan Pentateuch, various translations and sources.

Thompson, Alden L. *Who's Afraid of the Old Testament God?* 4th ed. Gonzalez, FL: Energion Publications, 2004.

Torrey, R. A. *What the Bible Teaches*. Grand Rapids, MI: Fleming H. Revell, 1996.

Trimiew, Anna. *Bible Almanac*. Lincolnwood, IL: Publications International, 1998

Warren, Rick. *The Purpose Driven Life*, Grand Rapids, MI: Zondervan, 2002.

Whiston, William, trans. *Josephus, the Complete Works*. Nashville: Thomas Nelson, Inc., 1998.

Yoder, Joseph W. *Rosanna of the Amish*. Scottsdale, PA: Herald Press, 1995.

Youngblood, Ronald F. *Nelson's Quick Reference Bible Concordance*. Nashville, Thomas Nelson, Inc., 1993.

TOPICAL INDEX

Holy Eucharist: see "Mass"
Holy Ghost: see "Holy Spirit"
Holy Land: see "Palestine"
Holy of Holies (Most Holy Place): 20, 66
Holy Office: see "Inquisition, Roman"
Holy Order: 82
Holy Place: 20, 66
Holy Roman Empire: see "Roman Empire, Holy"
Holy Spirit: 10, 35, 46, 56, 65-67, 69-70, 73, 76, 83, 99, 108, 118, 120-121, 123-125; sending of, 25, 29, 66, 68, 70; as comforter, 66, 74, 124; as helper, 66, 69, 74, 108, 119-120; baptism in, 68, 123-124; as teacher, 68, 124; filling of, 68; fruits of, 69, 83, 119; walking in, 69, 118; sealed in, 67, 118; grieving of, 119
Holy Trinity: 73, 91, 97, 99, 125
Holy War (Jihad): 75
Holy Water: 81
Hor, Mt.: 21
Horeb, Mt.: see "Sinai, Mt."
Hormah: 21
Hosea: 37, 39
Hoshea: 30, his rule, 31-33
Hosius of Cordova: 73
House of Commons: 84
House of Lords: 84
Huguenot: see "Calvanist"
Huldah: 35
Humanism: see "Secularism"
Hundred Years War: 79
Hyrcanus, John: 52
Iconoclasts: 74
Ibzan: his reign, 27
Iddo: 35
Iddo the Seer: see "History of Judah"
Idol Worship: 22, 47; at Mt. Sinai, 20; with Midianites 22; during judges, 26; during kings, 30-33, 35-37; tribe of Dan, 40; of Solomon, 41; of Babylon, 48; end of Jewish practice, 50; of Roman Empire, 72; of Arabia, 75; of Antichrist, 109
Idumean: see "Edomite"
Ije-abarim: 21
Images: 54, 73-74, 77, 81, 91, 100; of Antichrist, 109
Immaculate Conception: 76, 83
Incense: 72
Index of Forbidden Books: 86
Indulgences: 74, 76, 81, 91, 100
Infallibility: of pope, 76, 81, 83, 91; of church, 82-83, 100; of Scripture, 93-97, 99
Infidels: 75, 77
Innocent III, Pope: 77-78, 91-92, 101
Innocent IV, Pope: 92
Inquisition: 77, 79; papal, 78-80, 86; Spanish, 80, 86; Roman, 86-87, 93
Interpretation of Scripture: 51, 53, 58, 62, 64, 71, 77, 82-84, 86, 91, 97-98, 103, 106-107, 111, 114-115
Iran: see "Persia"
Iraq: 12, 48, 75
Isaac: 11-12, 64; his sacrifice, 11, 16, 117; birth, 16; his sons, 17; covenant with-see "Covenant"
Isabella: 80
Isaiah: 36-39, 50, 56
Iscariot, Judas: 65, 121
Ish-bosheth: 29
Ishmael: birth & lineage, 13, 16-17; father of Islam, 74
Ishmaelites: 17, 22
Ishtar: 48
Isis: 64
Islam (Muslim): 16, 70, 74-75, 77, 80, 91, 101, 103, 125; vs Christianity & Judaism, 74-75, 77,

103; expansion, 75, 77-80
Islamic: see "Islam"
Israel (Son of Isaac): see "Jacob"
Israel Street: 42
Israel, Split Nation of (Samaria): northern tribes, 30, 41-42, 67; kings, 30-31; destruction & exile, 32-35, 42, 58, 123; restored, 54, 112, 117, 124;
Israel, Unified Nation of: start, 15-18, 117; move to Egypt, 17-18; sins, 20, 23-24, 26-27; living in Egypt, 19; entering Canaan, 22-23; Syrian servitude, 23-26; ruled by judges, 25-27; pre-split: 29; split kingdom, 30-32, 35, 42; ruled by kings, 29-34; sins in Canaan, 22; at second coming, 32, 49, 54, 64, 112, 117, 124; during tribulation, 106-110; during millennium, 35, 49, 112-113, 124; first stage, 54, 64, 113; final dispensation, 54; God's dealing with, 104-108; cease dealing with, 105; restored in 1948, 124; see "Hebrew"
Israelite: See "Hebrew"
Issachar: tribe of, 40; son of Jacob, 40
Ithamar: 28
J Document: 57-58
Jacob (Grandfather of Jesus): 45-46
Jacob (Israel, Son of Isaac): 11-12, 64, 69; born, 17; move to Egypt, 17-18; Descendants, 17; his sins, 17; covenant with-see "Covenant"
Jacob's Ladder: 17
Jacob's Trouble: see "Tribulation period, Great Tribulation"
Jahaziel: 35
Jair: his reign, 26
James: 119
Japheth: 12
Jared: 13-14
Jaredites: 98
Jason (high priest): 52
Jebusites: 22
Jechoniah: see "Jehoiachin"
Jehoahaz (of Israel): his rule, 31, 33
Jehoahaz (of Judah): see "Ahaziah of Judah"
Jehoahaz (Shallum of Judah): his rule, 32
Jehoash (Joash of Israel): his rule, 31,33
Jehoash (Joash of Judah): his rule, 31
Jehoiachin (Jechoniah, Coniah): his rule, 32, 42-44
Jehoiakim: his rule, 32, 42-44, 111; his sin & punishment, 32, 43; see end notes 22 & 24
Jehoram (Joram of Israel): his rule, 31
Jehoram (of Judah): his rule, 31, 49
Jehoshaphat: his rule, 31, 49
Jehovah: see "God"
Jehovah's Witnesses: 98-99, 125
Jehu (the Prophet): 35
Jehu, King: his rule, 31-32
Jephthah: 19, 26, 49, 64; his reign, 26-27
Jeremiah: 34, 36-37, 39, 56, 58
Jericho: 22-23
Jeroboam I: his rule, 30-31, 35; see end note 23
Jeroboam II: 30; his rule, 31, 33
Jerome: translate Latin Vulgate bible, 61, 86
Jerusalem: capitol, 29-30; during millennium, 32, 103, 112-113, 124; Babylon destruction, 36, 48-49; walls rebuilt by Nehemiah, 51, 104; plundered by Antiochus Epiphanes, 52; destroyed in 63 B.C.: 54; Daniel's 4th world power, 54; Roman occupation in 70 A.D., 54; rebuilt by Herod, 64; one of eastern churches, 72, 74, 83, 101; final control, 103; rebuild in end times, 105; during crusades, 77-78; during the tribulation, 106-107; in eternity, 113, 124; see "Judah, split nation of"
Jesse: father of David, 40, 42, 45-46
Jesus (Christ): 16, 64-49; as second Adam, 11,

65; redeemer, 11, 64, 118; as servant, 11; as apostle, 11; as mediator of new covenant, 11, 37, 66, 105; as Shiloh, 11; as the Star, 11; during end times, 11, 104-117; as high priest, 28, 66-67; as judge, 28, 67, 108, 113; as king, 29-30, 35, 41-42, 45, 65, 67, 69, 111; as the Branch, 38; ancestry, 40-47; crucifixion, 65-66, 105, 113, 123; as the Teacher, 64; birth, 64, 68, 123; baptism, 65; called out of Egypt, 65; early life, 65; start of ministry, 65; as prophet, 66; as the Word, 68, 119-120; from the beginning, 69, 125; stumbling stone, 71, 91; substance controversies, 73-74; cornerstone, 82; created by God (Mormon), 98; Spirit resurrection (Jehovah's Witnesses), 99; first fruit, 107; the bridegroom, 111; between the crucifixion & resurrection, 114; see "Messiah, Yahweh, Y'shua, Jehovah, ascension, Genealogy, Prophecies, Resurrection"
Jew: see "Hebrew"
Jewish Revolt: 52, 54
Jewish Wars: 52, 54
Jezebel: 36
Jihad: see "Holy War"
Joanna: 44-45
Joash: see "Jehoash"
Joel: 36, 68, 111
Johanan: 43
John the Baptist: 65, 106; prophesied, 36, 38
Jonah (The Prophet): 37, 39
Joram: see "Jehoram of Israel"
Jordan River: crossing, 22
Joseph (a Sanhedrin): 65
Joseph (Father of Jesus): 44-47
Joseph (Son of Jacob): 17, 40-41, 64; birth, 17; sold into slavery, 17; rise to power, 17; his sons, 17
Josephus, Flavius: 15-16, 19, 52-54
Joshua: 21-22; his rule, 23-24; his sin, 23; Biblical writer, 57-58
Josiah: 43; his rule, 32, 34, 36; scroll found and revival, 34, 57
Jotham: his rule, 31-33
Judah (Son of Jacob): descendants, 40-41; blood and title lines, 40-42
Judah Avenue: 42
Judah, Split Nation of (Jerusalem): southern kingdom, 30-33, 35-36, 42, 58; kings, 31-32; Babylonian exile & destruction, 34-35, 48-49, 123-124; restored, 49, 50, 54, 112, 117, 124; see "Dispensation of Jews", "Judea", "Palestine", and "Canaan"
Judah the Prince: 61
Judah: Tribe of, 23, 30, 40-41, 67; son of Jacob, 40-41; Jesus' tribe, 67-68
Judaism: 49, 52, 70-71, 77, 91, 125; vs Christianity & Islam, 17, 71, 77, 79-80, 103, 124
Judea: 64; name changed from Judah in 536 B.C., 50; Persian occupation, 50-51; Greek occupation, 51-53; Roman occupation, 54-55; see "Judah, split nation of" and "Palestine"
Judge(s): period of rule, 19, 24-27, 67
Judgment: 114; final, 107, 112-113, 116, 124; church age saints, 108; of nations, 111, 124
Jupiter: 54
Justification: see "Faith"
Kadesh-barnea: 21
Kenan: 14
Kibroth-hattaavah: 20
King James Version Bible: see "Bible"
King of the East: 110
King of the North: see "Russia"
King of the South: 110
King of the West: 110
Kingdom of God/Heaven/on Earth: 22, 37, 56, 64-67, 70-71, 104-129; fulfilled (sealed), 56,

SCRIPTURE INDEX

END NOTES

1   See Luke 3:34-38 for a genealogy from Adam to Jacob.

2   Billy Graham, "Don't Know Why God Lets Bad Things Happen," <u>Pensacola News Journal</u> 26 Nov. 2008:3B

3   Oct. 2008 <http://www.talkorigins.org/faqs/faq-age-of-earth.html>. Oct. 2008 <http://pubs.usgs.gov/gip/geotime/age.html>. The scientific numbers change over time as more data is discovered and the Biblical number does not include gaps.

4   Henry H. Halley, <u>Halley's Bible Handbook</u>, (Zondervan Publishing House, 1965) 77-80. Oct. 2008 <htpp://www.trivia-library.com/b/major-archaeology-discovery-biblical-ur.htm>.

5   Halley, 62, 68-9, 75, 78-9.

6   Attributed to Enoch in Jewish and Arab traditions: Halley, 44.

7   John A. Garraty & Peter Gay,eds. <u>The Columbia History of the World</u>, (Dorset Press, 1981) 87. Other sources identify the Greeks and Phoenicians in about the 11th century: Oct. 2008 <http://www.uh.edu/engines/epi1065.htm>. Oct. 2008 <http://www.helleniccomserve.com/chryssisgrkalphabet.html>.

8   A north to south deep reef along its western border. See Map B.

9   The mentions of Amorites refer to all inhabitants of Canaan.

10   A priest and diviner from Mesopotamia who refused to curse Israel but was self-willed—hoping God would allow him to receive a blessing from Balak after many bribes (Num 12).

11   Some historians identify the Aramaeans.

12   <u>Josephus,</u> trans. William Whiston, A.M. (Thomas Nelson Publishers, 1998) Antiquities VI, 16.

13   Only the priests were permitted to offer sacrifices to God.

14   Some scholars attribute this verse to Zadok, David, or Samuel.

15   Some historians place Ish-bosheth's rule sometime earlier in David's rule.

16   Oct. 2008 <http://iconography/timeliness>. Garraty & Gay, eds., 146, 153.

17   A few translations list Tibni as a king, but most do not recognize him as legitimate.

18   Halley, 209. Oct. 2008 <http://antidisestablishmentarianism/introduction/overview>.

19   Garraty & Gay, eds., 152. Oct. 2008 <http://breathlessness/chronicle/Middle East/ReviveAssyria.html>. Oct. 2008 <http://www.portergaud.edu/academic/faculty/cmcarver/asyr.html>.

20   The most significant name for God in the Old Testament. It identifies God as always existing and a perfect creator and redeemer.

21   See "The Prophets" chapter that follows and Deut. 28:49; 29:24-28; 1 Kings 13:23. Also consider Joel 2:1-11 that could refer to the Assyrian or Babylon invasion and/or to the last days.

22   However, Zedekiah, his brother, would be appointed king for 11 years by Nebuchadnezzar not by God (Jer. 22:30; 36:30) as God had decreed because of his sin when he destroyed the scroll (Jer. 36:11-32). Zedekiah is considered an illegitimate king.

23   Jereboam was the son of Nebat, not from the Davidian line (1 Kings 11:26).

24   Jehoiakim would be the last legitimate king from the Davidian line. Matthew 1:11 lists Josiah as the father of Coniah, bypassing Jehoiakim.

25   Some historians would give Zedekiah as a brother or uncle of Nebuchadnezzar, misinterpreting 2 Chronicles 36:10, and the previously cited verses would need to be ignored. See the end of this chapter.

26   When a man dies childless, it is required under certain conditions, of his brother to marry his widow to provide her with a son to continue his brother's family name.

27   Norman Geisler and Thomas Howe, <u>When Critics Ask,</u> (Baker Books, 1992) 201-2.

28   Geisler and Howe, 385-6. Oct. 2008 <http"//www.ecclesia.org/truth/geneology.html>. Oct. 2008 <http://genealogy.suite101.com/article.cfm/two_genealogies_of_jesus>.

29   Oct. 2008 <http://www.crossroads.ca/unique/un020102.htm>.

30   Oct. 2008 <http://www.mnsu.edu/emuseum/archaeology/sites/middle_east/babylon.html>. Garraty & Gay, eds., 155.

31   Oct. 2008 <http://www.harvardhouse.com/prophetictech/new/temple.htm>. Garraty & Gay, eds., 155 says 587 B.C.

32   This verse could also apply to the Second Coming punishment.

33   Garraty & Gay, eds. 162. Oct. 2008 <http://judaismabout.con/od/abdsofjudaism/f/sacrifices_when.htm>.

34   Possibly could also be speaking of the end times.

35   Garraty & Gay, eds., 166. Oct. 2008 <http://www.religioustolerance.org/zoroastr.htm>.

36 Garraty & Gay, eds., 155, 163. Oct. 2008 <http://www.crystalinks.com/Persia.html>.

37 Garraty & Gay, eds., 166. Some scholars believe he and Cyrus are one and the same.

38 Garraty & Gay, eds., 163-4. Oct. 2008 <http://www.konig.org/page7.htm>.

39 Some scholars recognize this period from 609-539 B.C.: Oct. 2008 <http:/www.konig.org/page7.htm>.

40 Antiquities XIII, 301says 481 years, but this contradicts "Wars" and does not fit our timetable.

41 Justo L. Gonzalez, The Story of Christianity, vol. 1, (Harper Collins Publishers, 1984) 10. Oct. 2008 <http://www.newadvent.org/cathen/11789b.htm>.

42 Gonzalez, 11. Oct. 2008 <http://www.jewishencyclopedia.com/view.jsp?artid=2528letter=p#927>.

43 Gonzalez, 10. Oct. 2008 <http://www.newadvent.org/cathen/13323b.htm>.

44 The title "Herod" was given to his family line of rulers.

45 Gonzalez, 10, Oct. 2008 <http://www.livius.org/ja-jn/jewish_wars/jwar03.html>.

46 These 2 verses could also be eschatological prophecies.

47 Garraty & Gay, eds. 234.

48 Elgin Hushbeck, Jr., Evidence for the Bible, (Energion Publications, 2005) 10

49 Also known as The Law or The Book of the Law or The Law of Moses.

50 Halley, 56.

51 Philip Wesley Comfort, ed. The Origin of the Bible, (Tyndale House Publishers, Inc., 1992) 61.

52 The world language at the time. Many Jews around the Mediterranean Sea spoke Greek.

53 Some historians prefer 72—6 from each of the 12 tribes.

54 Henry Bettenson, ed. Documents of the Christian Church, (Oxford University Press, 1963) 82-4. Comfort, ed. 85.

55 Halley, 747. Gonzalez, 92. Comfort, ed. 89-90.

56 Hushbeck Jr., Evidence for the Bible 12

57 Comfort, ed. 152.

58 Comfort, ed. 153. Oct. 2008 <http://www.jewishvirtuallibrary.org/jsource/reviews/codex.html>.

59 Comfort, 86. Bettenson, ed. 261-2. Oct. 2008 <http://www.newadvent.org/cathen/15030c.htm>.

60 A group of Levites, priests, judges, teachers, students, and leaders; in effect, the supreme court of the Jewish community.

61 See the chapter "The Kingdom to Come."

62 Matthew 16:28; Mark 9:1; Luke 9:27 might be included with these verses, since many people at this time would witness the resurrection and the ascension. More likely, I think, these verses are speaking of the transfiguration if we continue reading the following two verses of each of the above verses cited: Peter, James, and John would witness a partial showing of Christ's ultimate glory when the Kingdom will be established on earth at the Second Coming. The Second Coming is not the subject here because it is evident that more of those persons at that time would be witnesses to this event.

63 Gonzalez, 12. Philip Wesley Comfort, ed. 62.

64 Gonzalez, 36, 39. Oct. 2008 <http://www.eyewitnesstohistory.com/rome.htm>.

65 Gonzalez, 40. Oct. 2008 <http://www.cbn.com/spirituallife/ChurchAndMinistry/ChurchHistory/Second_Century_Persecution_and_Faith.aspx>.

66 Gonzalez, 83-4.

67 Gonzalez, 102, 106. Oct. 2008 <http://www.homecomers.com/mirror/martyrs021.htm>.

68 Gonzalez, 153. Oct. 2008 <http://www. Fsmitha.com/h1/ch25.htm>. Oct. 2008 <http://www.religion-cults.com/heresies/fourth.htm>.

69 Gonzalez, 207, 213. Oct. 2008 <http://www. Fsmitha.com/h1/ch25.htm>.

70 Halley, 769. Garraty & Gay, eds.,243.

71 Bettenson, ed., 15-6. Garraty & Gay, eds., 243. Oct. 2008 <http://www.shoahrose.com/edictofmilan.html>.

72 Elgin L. Hushbeck, Jr., Christianity and Secularism, (Energion Publications, 2005) 98.

73 Gonzalez, 162-5. Henry H. Halley, 765. John A. Garraty & Peter Gay, eds., 232. Elgin L. Hushbeck, Jr., Christianity and Secularism 99.

74 Gonzalez, 179, 253. Henry H. Halley, 765. Oct. 2008 <http://www.newadvent.org/cathen/04308a.htm>.

75 Gonzalez, 179, 252. Oct. 2008 <http://www.newadvent.org/cathen/04308a.htm>.

76 Bettenson, ed., 82. Oct. 2008 <http://www.piar.hu/councils/ecum02.htm>.

77 Halley, 760. Bettenson, ed., 22. Oct. 2008 <http://www.allaboutturkey.com/Theodosius.htm>.

78 Hushbeck, Jr., Christianity and Secularism102. Oct. 2008 <http://www.thirdmill.org/files/English/html/ch/CH.16.html>.

79 Halley, 765. Gonzalez, 256-7. Garraty & Gay, eds., 244.

80 Garraty & Gay, eds., 244. Halley, 765, 770. Bettenson, ed., 51.

81 Hushbeck, Jr. Christianity and Secularism 102. Oct. 2008 <http://www.thirdmill.org/files/English/html/ch/CH.16.html>.

82 Halley, 770-1. Gonzalez, 242. Hushbeck Jr., Christianity and Secularism 99.

83 Gonzalez, 247. Oct. 2008 <http://goodsoldiers.wordpress.com/2008/04/04/Gregory-the-great/>.

84 Oct. 2008 <http://www.newadvent.org/cathen/12575a.htm>. Oct. 2008 <http://www.religioustolerance.org/purgatory1.htm#conp>.

85 Halley, 765. Gonzalez, 258. Oct. 2008 <http://www.newadvent.org/cathen/04308b.htm>.

86 Halley, 765. Gonzalez, 259. Oct. 2008 <http://www.newadvent.org/cathen/04310a.htm>.

87 Gonzalez, 260. Garraty & Gay, eds., 425, 436. Oct. 2008 <http://www.newadvent.org/cathen/11045a.htm>.

88 Charlemagne is recognized by some historians as the first Holy Roman Emperor, but most historians recognize Otto the Great as the first because the name Holy Roman Empire became officially recognized in 962 A.D. upon his crowning.

89 Halley, 765. Gonzalez, 264-5. Garraty & Gay, eds., 438.

90 Halley, 776. Oct. 2008 <http://www.religioustolerance.org/chr_deno.htm>.

91 The Lateran Council II (1139 A.D.) would put the election of popes in the hands of Cardinals—an organization of bishops in Rome.

92 Gonzalez, 265. Oct. 2008 <http://www.christianodyssey.com/history/schism.htm>.

93 The word "Eucharist" used alone can identify the wafer or the communion ceremony (Holy Communion).

94 Halley, 766. Gonzalez, 293-297.

95 Gonzalez, 302, 304-5. Oct. 2008 <http://www.leestoneking.com/1100%20-%201530%20AD.htm>.

96 Oct. 2008 <http://www.newadvent.org/cathen/09017b.htm>.

97 Oct. 2008 <http://www.newadvent.org/cathen/09018a.htm>. Gonzalez, 310.

98 Gonzalez, 347. Oct. 2008 <http://www.websters-online-dictionary.org/definition/transubstantiation>.

99 Halley, 776. Hushbeck, Jr., Christianity and Secularism 105.

100 Hushbeck, Jr., Christianity and Secularism 106. Oct. 2008 <http://www.newadvent.org/cathen/12272b.htm>.

101 Gonzalez, appendix. Oct. 2008 <http://www.newadvent.org/cathen/04288a.htm>.

102 Halley, 779. Oct. 2008 <http://www.christianchronicler.com/history1/renaissance_papacy.html>.

103 Oct. 2008 <http://www.religioustolerance.org/purgatory1.htm#conp>.

104 Oct. 2008 <http://www.htmlbible.com/sacrednamebiblecom/kjvstrongs/STRGRK40.htm>.

105 Oct. 2008 <http://www.Islamtomorrow.com/bible/NicaeaCouncil325.htm>.

106 Oct. 2008 <http://www.cofe.anglican.org?about/history/>

107 Garraty & Gay, eds., 537.

108 Garraty & Gay, eds., 541. Halley, 765.

109 Oct. 2008 <http://www.religioustolerance.org/purgatory1.htm#conp>.

110 Spain and its territory, Portugal, from 1580-1640 A.D.

111 Garraty & Gay, eds., 584, 586. Oct. 2008 <http://www.bartleby.com/67/617.html>.

112 Garraty & Gay, eds., 590, 725-6. Oct. 2008 <http://avalon.law.yale.edu/17th_century/westphal.asp>.

113 Monica. K. Hellwig, Understanding Catholicism,(Paulist Press, 1981), 133. Bettenson, 273, IX. Oct. 2008 <http://www.newadvent.org/cathen/15303a.htm>. Oct. 2008 <http://www.mb-soft.com/believe/txs/firstvc.htm>.

114 Donald B. Kraybill, The Riddle of Amish Culture, (The John Hopkins University Press, 2001) 186.

115 Oct. 2008 <http://www.bible.org/page.php?page_id=177>.

116 Oct. 2008 <http://www.bible.org/page.php?page_id=177>. Hushbeck, Jr., Christianity and Secularism 114.

117 Hushbeck, Jr., Christianity and Secularism 115. Oct. 2008 <http://www.religion-online.org/showchapter.asp?title=27328c=2437>.

118 For protection by the Holy Spirit as with all Christians upon conversion: 2 Corinthians 1:22; Ephesians 1:13; 4:30.

119 Daniel's 1,260 days prophecy.

120 See endnote 103.

121 The previous six likely: Egypt, Assyria, Babylon, Medo-Persia, Greece, and Rome—all who ruled over Israel.

122 The extra 30 days might, instead of allowing time to judge the nations between the Tribulation and Millennium, also allude to the time before the desecration of the temple as a prelude to antichrist's preparation for the Great Tribulation.

123 Henry E. Neufeld, Revelation, (Energion Publications, 2005) 88.

124 Obviously applies to the return from Babylon in 535 B.C. but can also be an eschatological prophecy.

125 One book seems to contain a record of the thoughts and deeds of every person; only the unrighteous will be condemned to the everlasting second death The other book, the Book of Life, contains only the names of the righteous and it was probably compiled before the beginning of time. Both books list the redeemed.

126 God will replace the temple (Rev. 21:22) for there will be no need of it since God will dwell in our presence.

127 God seems to have been enacting the Calvary scene here with Abram (God) offering his son, Isaac (Jesus), as a sacrifice. Isaac also proved his obedience as Christ would, going willingly to the cross, so the unconditional covenant was passed on to him. Later, Jacob would also inherit this covenant because of his faith. See chapter 2 for additional commentary.

128 Chapters 5 and 10 of John are also cited by Calvinists who qualify them as speaking of those who persevere.